W9-CIN-108

Social Capital and
European Democracy

Social capital can be defined as the extent to which citizens are willing to co-operate with each other on the basis of interpersonal trust. This is now seen to greatly facilitate economic and social relationships and thus to play a major role in the efficiency of political institutions and in economic performance. This study examines patterns of social capital in a wide range of European countries and compares the European experience with that of the United States

The authors of this work not only examine the dominant view that voluntary activity promotes social capital and hence good government, but also explore alternative models for the creation of social capital. Theoretical discussion is combined with detailed case studies to provide a new explanation of:

- the origins and nature of social capital
- its effects on political participation and policy making
- the role of the voluntary sector

Contributors go on to examine the possibility that current changes in the voluntary sector may in fact undermine social capital and consider the consequences.

Social Capital and European Democracy is an important step forward in this rapidly growing field of research and adds a unique European perspective to a debate which has been largely US-focused.

Jan W. van Deth is a Professor of Political Science and International Comparative Social Research at the University of Mannheim, Germany, and Director of the Mannheim Centre for European Social Research. **Marco Maraffi** is an Associate Professor of Political Sociology at the University of Milan, Italy. **Kenneth Newton** is Professor of Government at the University of Essex, UK, and **Paul F. Whiteley** is Professor of Politics at the University of Sheffield, UK.

Routledge/ECPR Studies in European Political Science

Edited by Hans Keman, *Vrije University, The Netherlands,* and Jan W. van Deth, *University of Mannheim, Germany on behalf of the European Consortium for Political Research*

The Routledge/ECPR Studies in European Political Science Series is published in association with the European Consortium for Political Research – the leading organisation concerned with the growth and development of political science in Europe. The series presents high-quality edited volumes on topics at the leading edge of current interest in political science and related fields, with contributions from European scholars and others who have presented work at ECPR workshops or research groups.

Also available from Routledge in association with the ECPR

Sex Equality Policy in Western Europe, edited by Frances Gardiner; *Democracy and Green Political Thought,* edited by Brian Doherty and Marius de Geus; *The New Politics of Unemployment,* edited by Hugh Compston; *Citizenship, Democracy and Justice in the New Europe,* edited by Percy B. Lehning and Albert Weale; *Private Groups and Public Life,* edited by Jan W. van Deth; *The Political Context of Collective Action,* edited by Ricca Edmondson; *Theories of Secession,* edited by Percy Lehning; *Regionalism Across the North/South Divide,* edited by Jean Grugel and Wil Hout.

Social Capital and
European Democracy

**Edited by Jan W. van Deth,
Marco Maraffi, Kenneth Newton
and Paul F. Whiteley**

London and New York

First published 1999
by Routledge
11 New Fetter Lane, London EC4P 4EE

Simultaneously published in the USA and Canada
by Routledge
29 West 35th Street, New York, NY 10001

Routledge is an imprint of the Taylor & Francis Group

Editorial material and selection © 1999 Jan W. van Deth,
Marco Maraffi, Kenneth Newton and Paul F. Whiteley

Individual chapters © 1999 the contributors

Typeset in Baskerville by MHL Typesetting Ltd
Printed and bound in Great Britain by
T.J. International Ltd, Padstow, Cornwall.

All rights reserved. No part of this book may be reprinted or
reproduced or utilised in any form or by any electronic,
mechanical, or other means, now known or hereafter
invented, including photocopying and recording, or in any
information storage or retrieval system, without permission
in writing from the publishers.

British Library Cataloguing in Publication Data
A catalogue record for this book is available
from the British Library

Library of Congress Cataloging in Publication Data
Social capital and European democracy/edited by
    Jan W. van Deth . . . [et al.]
        p.   cm.
    Includes bibliographical references and index.
    1. Voluntarism–Europe, Western.   2. Social participation–
Europe, Western.   3. Democracy–Europe, Western.
4. Voluntarism–United States.   5. Social participation–United
States.   6. Democracy– United States.   I. Deth, Jan W. van.

HN380.Z9V647   1999   98-47885

302'.14'094–dc21   CIP

ISBN 0-415-18630-7

Contents

Figures

Tables

Contributors

Jacques B. Billiet is Professor in Social Sciences at the Katholieke Universiteit Leuven, Belgium. He is chair of the committee for Sociology, Political Sciences and Communication Science of the Fund for Scientific Research Flanders, Belgium (FWO), head of the Centre for Datacollection and Analysis at the Department of Sociology (KU Leuven), and project leader of the Inter-university Centre of Political Opinion Research (ISPO) that organizes the general election surveys in Flanders, Belgium. His main research interests in methodology concern validity assessment, interviewer and response effects, and the modelling of measurement error in social surveys. He is also involved in longitudinal and comparative research in the domains of ethnocentrism, and political attitudes and behaviour.

Bart Cambré is a part-time research assistant in the Department of Sociology at the Katholieke Universiteit, Leuven, Belgium where he has been involved in the project 'The political knowledge and the attitude of the Flemings toward the advertising campaign of the Flemish authorities', which is sponsored by the Flemish Government.

Joep de Hart is a researcher at the Social and Cultural Planning Office (SCP), The Netherlands. His publications include books about youth cultures, the sociology of religion, and time-budget research. At the moment he is working on a project about civil society and volunteering in The Netherlands (with Paul Dekker).

Paul Dekker is a Political Scientist and a Research Fellow at the Social and Cultural Planning Office (SCP), The Netherlands. He has published on planning and public administration, social and political attitudes and participation in The Netherlands, often in a cross-national perspective. His present research interests include environmental attitudes, social capital, and the non-profit sector.

Jacint Jordana is Associate Professor in the Department of Political and Social Sciences at the Pompeu Fabra University, Barcelona, Spain. He has published on trade unions and industrial relations, policy networks, and public policy. His current research interests are the collective action theory and the transformation of public policy and governance structures, especially in the field of telecommunications policy.

William A. Maloney is a Senior Lecturer in the Department of Politics and International Relations, University of Aberdeen, UK. His recent publications include: *Managing Policy Change in Britain* (with J.J. Richardson, 1995) and *The Protest Business?: Mobilizing Campaign Groups* (with Grant Jordan, 1997). He has published extensively in political science journals in the areas of public policy, and interest groups. He is currently working on an ESRC-funded project entitled: *Civic Engagement, Social Capital and Cities*.

José Ramón Montero is Professor of Political Science at the Universidad Autónoma of Madrid, Spain and at the Center for Advanced Study in the Social Sciences of the Juan March Institute in Madrid.

Kenneth Newton is Professor of Government at the University of Essex, UK and Executive Director of the European Consortium for Political Research. Recent publications include *Beliefs in Government* (with Max Kaase, 1995), *The Politics of the New Europe* (with Ian Budge, 1997), *The New British Politics* (with Ian Budge, Ivor Crewe, and David McKay, 1988) and articles or chapters on social capital, social and political trust, mass media effects, and mass attitudes in Western Europe towards the scope of modern government.

Thomas R. Rochon is Professor and Director in the School of Politics and Economics at Claremont Graduate University, USA. He is the author of *Mobilizing for Peace: The Antinuclear Movements of Western Europe* (Princeton, 1988); *Culture Moves: Ideas, activism and changing values* (Princeton, 1998); and co-editor of *Coalitions and Political Movements: The Lessons of the Nuclear Freeze* (Lynne Rienner, 1997).

Per Selle is Professor of Comparative Politics at the University of Bergen and Senior Researcher at the Norwegian Research Centre in Organization and Management. His research inerests include voluntary organizations, political parties, political culture, and environmental policy. Selle has published several books and numerous scholarly articles and book chapters. Among his English-language publications are *Government and Voluntary Organizations* (with Stein Kuhle, 1992, second edition 1995) and *Women in Nordic Politics: Closing the Gap?* (with Lauri Karvonen, 1995).

Martti Siisiäinen is Professor of Sociology at the University of Lapland, Finland. He has worked previously at the Universities of Joensuu, Tampere and Jyväskylä. He has investigated social movements and voluntary organizations for the past 25 years. He is at present coordinator of the Finnish part of the international project 'Coping locally and regionally with economic, technological and environmental transformations' (UNESCO) and co-ordinator on the project 'Trust and recession' (The Academy of Finland). He has published widely on political sociology, culture, and voluntary organizations.

Dietlind Stolle is a PhD candidate in the Department of Politics at Princeton University, USA. She is currently completing her dissertation on *Public Life, Community, and Social Capital: A comparative study of Sweden, Germany and the United States*. She has published on social capital in the *American Behavioral Scientist* and in the journal *Political Psychology*.

Mariano Torcal is Associate Professor of Political Science at the Universidad Autónoma of Madrid, Spain, and at the Center for Advanced Study in the Social Sciences of the Juan March Institute in Madrid, Spain.

Eric M. Uslaner is Professor of Government and Politics at the University of Maryland–College Park, USA, where he has taught since 1975. His PhD is from Indiana University. He is the author of six books, most recently *The Decline of Comity in Congress* and *The Movers and the Shirkers*, both from the University of Michigan Press. His current research is on social capital, civic engagement, and the moral roots of trust. He was the co-director (with Paul Dekker) of the European Consortium for Political Research Workshop on Social Capital and Political Science in 1998.

Jan W. van Deth is Professor of Political Science and International Comparative Social Research at the University of Mannheim, Germany and Director of the Mannheim Centre for European Social Research. His main research areas are political culture, social change, and comparative research methods. He is a Corresponding Member of the Royal Netherlands Academy of Arts and Sciences and Book Series Editor of the European Political Science series of the European Consortium for Political Research.

Paul F. Whiteley is Professor of Politics at the University of Sheffield, UK. His previous appointments have been at the University of Bristol, Virginia Technical University, the University of Arizona, and the College of William and Mary in Virginia. He is the author of several books and numerous academic articles on political economy, politial parties, electoral behaviour and public policy-making.

Preface

The term 'social capital' has recently emerged as a potentially powerful concept in modern political science but empirical study of the subject is still relatively rare. The term is mentioned only twice in Goodin and Klingemann's massive *New Handbook of Political Science*, published in 1996, and then under the headings of 'Political Economy' and 'Political Institutions'. This suggests that the present volume, published in collaboration with the European Consortium for Political Research, is both timely and much needed. More than that, the publication of the book shows that academic political scientists are more sensitive to trends and tendencies in the real-world workings of western democracy than their critics sometimes imply. To be more precise, the book shows that contemporary political science is not simply an abstract intellectual exercise conducted in ivory towers, but that its practitioners are engaged with practical questions of how modern societies are organised, how people behave, and how democracy performs in the real world.

In this book social capital is seen as the cement of civil society – the shared norms and values that bind individuals together – and the source of formal and informal organisations that make it possible to co-operate in the collective interest. Many of the problems of collective action cannot be solved by individuals acting alone, but nor can they be readily solved by regulations of the distant state or the formal procedures of indirect democracy. Rather, the solution lies in self-regulation of communities combined with the authority of the democratic state and its institutions. These two themes of autonomous community, on the one hand, and formal authority on the other have been a recurrent part of democratic theory in the nineteenth and twentieth centuries. Most notably they are found in de Tocqueville's account of democracy in America, and in the work of John Stuart Mill on the theoretical foundations of liberty and democracy.

In the 1960s and 1970s the 'political culture' literature analysed mass attitudes and opinions as the foundation of democratic stability. The resulting work was largely in accord with the writings of de Tocqueville and Mill. At the same time, the Marxists and neo-Marxists of western Europe questioned the viability of bourgeois democracy, just as the elitist school of C. Wright Mills in the United States attacked pluralist democracy as a sham.

In the 1970s and 1980s the gap between democratic theory and practice seemed to be widening. During these decades it became clear that mass involvement and participation in politics was limited, and some claimed that it was also declining. There appeared to be a widening gap between the 'politics of the centre' – that is, of the political elites of western nation states – and the social and economic experience of the vast mass of citizens. At one level, the legitimacy of the democracy, and its foundations in civil society, were accepted; at another and more practical level, the performance of the democracies was increasingly viewed as inadequate. The capacity of democracies to solve real-world problems was increasingly questioned.

These questions about the working of parliamentary democracies and their performance on practical matters of social and economic importance has been conducive to the analysis of democratic institutions, on the one hand, and collective action on the other. How can the state best intervene to promote the public good? When, how, and why do individuals get involved in public action to promote the general interest? Unfortunately, however, these questions remained largely unsolved by neo-institutional analysis and political economy alike. To complicate matters, it became clear that there are large cross-national variations in the degree of public involvement in politics, in the degree of self-regulation by means of voluntary co-operation, and in the effectiveness of democratic governance. This underlines the basic puzzles: why are some forms of democracy more viable and sustainable than others, and why are some forms of democracy more responsive and effective than others?

This is precisely the subject matter of the present book, and it is precisely the reason that makes it an important and timely contribution to European political science. All the contributions to the volume try to shed light on the question of how and why social capital (understood as the shared norms of trust that are conducive to co-operation) is indeed the cement of civil society that contributes to political efficacy and democratic performance. In other words, regardless of formal institutions, on the one hand, and the working of rational-choice decisions, on the other, what drives citizens to organise themselves in a manner that is conducive to effective collective action. The answers in the book are by no means definitive, of course, but they do suggest that social capital can developed, and that – in the final instance – it matters for both the quality of daily life and of modern democracy.

Hans Keman
October 1998

Part I

Theoretical perspectives on social capital

1 Social capital and democracy in modern Europe

Kenneth Newton

those, who liked one another so well as to joyn into Society, cannot but be supposed to have some Acquaintance and Friendship together, and some Trust one in another.

(John Locke, *Second Treatise on Government*)

THE NATURE AND ORIGINS OF SOCIAL CAPITAL

The creator and main exponent of social capital theory, Robert Putnam (1993: 167), defines the concept as follows: 'Social capital here refers to features of social organisation, such as trust, norms, and networks, that can improve the efficiency of society by facilitating coordinated actions.' A little later (1995b: 664–5) he uses virtually the same words: 'by "social capital" I mean features of social life – networks, norms, and trust – that enable participants to act together more effectively to pursue shared objectives.' In this way Putnam treats social capital as a mixture or blend of subjective social norms (trust), objective features of society (social networks), and outcomes (effectiveness, efficiency). The advantage of such an approach is that it combines different aspects of the concept in a very interesting way which gives them an explanatory power of enormous potential. Equally, the disadvantage is that it runs together, perhaps even confuses, different things whose relationships are properly the subjects of empirical investigation. Are norms of trust generated by social networks and social organisations? Do these, in their turn, improve the efficiency of society by facilitating coordinated actions? Norms, networks, and collective goods may well be intimately related, but there again, they may not. Whether they are or not is not a matter of definition, but a question for empirical research.

Rather than treating all three as part and parcel of the same thing, and putting them altogether in the same definition, they should be kept apart and the relations between them treated as a matter for investigation. If we do this, then a whole series of further questions arise about the nature, the causes, and the consequences of social capital. The first section of this chapter, therefore, will examine the problem of defining social capital. It will do so not because there is any intrinsic merit in unpacking definitions, splitting conceptual hairs, or bandying words.

Rather the job of defining social capital is seen as a useful exercise which leads directly to building hypotheses about social capital and conducting empirical research into its causes and consequences.

SOCIAL CAPITAL AS NORMS AND VALUES: HABITS OF THE HEART

According to this approach, social capital consists of a set of values and attitudes of citizens relating primarily to trust, reciprocity, and cooperation. Seen in this way, social capital is a subjective phenomenon of social and political culture, which refers to the collective attitudes people have about their fellow citizens, and therefore to the way that citizens relate. Crucial to this treatment are those features of a subjective, world-view which predisposes individuals to cooperate with each other, to trust, to understand, and to empathise. These are the 'habits of the heart' upon which de Tocqueville concentrates in *Democracy in America*, and which are the centre of concern for Robert Bellah and his colleagues (1985) in their analysis of community life in America. High levels of social capital are associated with treating others as fellow citizens, rather than as (potential) strangers, competitors, or enemies. The concepts of reciprocity and trust are central to the concept used in this sense; social capital constitutes the social cement which binds society together by turning individuals from self-seeking and egocentric calculators, with little social conscience and little sense of social obligation, into members of a community with shared interests, shared assumptions about social relations, and a sense of the common good. Trust, wrote Simmel (1950: 326), is 'one of the most important synthetic forces within society'.

Reciprocity, it should be noted, does not entail tit-for-tat calculations, or strict rules about taking turns, in which one action is almost automatically paid for by a compensatory action of equal value. Rather the most important form of reciprocity, so far as social capital is concerned, is a generalised feature of society and its citizens in which good turns go round, and come around. That is, individuals do not do others a good turn because they expect to be rewarded immediately and in kind by those who have benefited. Rather good turns will be repaid, as necessary, at some unspecified time, and by some unspecified person (quite possibly a complete stranger) at some unspecified time in the future (see Sahlins, 1972). Generalised reciprocity, therefore, involves a degree of uncertainty, risk, and vulnerability (Misztal, 1996: 18; Kollock, 1994: 319). It is therefore built upon trust: reciprocity involves risk, and taking risks in society requires trust in others (Luhmann, 1988). It also involves a measure of optimism about both individuals and about future outcomes. Lastly, it may (and often does) have a close connection with religious beliefs about good neighbourliness, doing unto others that which you would have them do unto you, and 'casting one's bread upon the waters for it will be returned unto you after many days'.

Social capital is, thereby, responsible for converting the Hobbesian state of nature in which life (like the British summer) is nasty, brutish, and short, to something that is more pleasant, less dangerous, and longer lived. At a minimum it makes it possible to establish a cooperative and stable social and political order which permits collective behaviour and cooperation without recourse to the ultimate coercive power of the Leviathan. More positively than this, it is associated with the goodwill and understanding which enables citizens to resolve their conflicts peacefully without resorting to violence.

In many ways the concept of trust and social capital fulfils the same function in modern social and political theory as the concept of 'fraternity' in nineteenth-century political discussion. In previous times it was generally believed that a troika of political values – liberty, equality, and fraternity – was a necessary, but not sufficient, condition of democracy. Each was important, but all three were essential. Democracy without fraternity was no more possible than democracy without liberty. A sense of fraternity is what turns an over-weening and self-destructive interest in individual liberty into a sustainable concern for collective liberty. A more or less exclusive interest in individual or atomised liberty – the liberty of each individual irrespective of the liberty of others – is as harmful for democracy as an exclusive attention to equality.

Some of the political polemic of the 1980s and the 1990s has, however, fallen into this precise trap. It has tended to concentrate on the notion of liberty in an atomised form, to the exclusion of both equality and fraternity. Moreover, it has tended to concentrate attention on market freedom, which is only a particular form of atomised liberty. This is excessively narrow. It does not even suffice for an understanding of the impersonal transactions of the market economy, for as Arrow (1972: 357) writes, 'Virtually every commercial transaction has within itself an element of trust, certainly any transaction conducted over a period of time' (see also Fukuyama, 1995; Barber, 1995). Even less does an exclusive concentration on market economic liberty help towards an understanding of the broad foundations of social and political stability and integration. This point is well made in the recent literature on communitarianism, as it is in the parallel work which recognises the crucial importance of civil society, civic virtue, and social and political trust (see, for example, Cohen and Rogers, 1992; Shils, 1991; Duncan, 1995; Burtt, 1993, 1995; Mulhall and Swift, 1992; Etzioni, 1993). The terms civic society, communitarianism, and social capital are certainly not identical – on the contrary, each carries its own theoretical and political baggage – but they all represent a welcome widening of horizons beyond a narrow concern with individualism and individual freedom.

Social capital, defined as subjective norms of trust and reciprocity, is the functional equivalent of fraternity which complements rather than confounds the values of freedom and equality. It is a way of smuggling fraternity back into the modern social science analysis of democracy. At any rate, social capital is an empirical concept which offers us a cutting edge by which we can start to dissect the workings of modern democracy. In other words, it is the social science analogue of the classical view of fraternity as the cement which forms the foundations of economic activity, and which binds society and the political system together. And trust, in turn, is an essential part of social capital – *the* essential part, according to Coleman (1990: 306).

SOCIAL CAPITAL AS NETWORKS: INFORMAL GROUPS AND FORMAL ORGANISATIONS

Some writers focus on social networks of individuals, groups, and organisations, as the crucial component of social capital. The ability to mobilise trustworthy social contacts is seen as a crucial resource, not just in social and political life, but even in supposedly impersonal market relations. In the western world, the importance of social networks is recognised in the process of assembling financial capital in rational-legal market economies. Trust is a necessary link between supply and demand; it puts consumers and producers into contact with each other, it speeds up deals, it turns rational fools into effective cooperators, and it avoids the need to sew up everything by means of expensive and time-consuming contracts which are legally watertight.

Besides being crucial in the market relations of capitalist societies, social networks are also said to be crucial in shortage-ridden Communist societies (Kolankiewcz, 1994: 149–51). They allowed people with different skills or commodities to trade or barter with each other the better to get by in daily life. This placed a premium on families having a wide-ranging network of people with different things to trade.

Viewed in this way, the main features of social capital are to be found in these personal networks which link friends, family, community, work, and both public and private life. Some of these networks are loosely constructed, constantly changing, amorphous, and informal. They take the shape of overlapping and interlocking networks of friends, colleagues, and neighbours. These are the loose-knit and informal networks of people who meet irregularly in their local pub, who participate in the local football supporters club, groups of housewives and neighbours who meet outside schools when collecting their children, or in the supermarket, or at church. At the other extreme, social networks may be highly formalised and tight-knit groups bound together by clubs, associations, and organisations – any form of voluntary association, intermediary organisation, or secondary association which has a formal organisational basis compared with the *ad hoc* and random collection of friends and acquaintances who bump into each other in a local bar on Friday night. In some cases such formal organisations simply institutionalise highly personal and informal networks – the exclusive gentlemen's clubs which are basically old-boy networks – but in other cases they are more inclusive and impersonal – political parties, trade unions, or business organisations.

There is nothing wrong with defining social capital in terms of social networks. At the same time, it may be that the normative and subjective definition is logically prior in the sense that social networks, formal or informal, are necessarily built upon the norms of reciprocity and trust. Without the subjective capacity to empathise, to trust, and to reciprocate in social relations, strong and extensive networks would not be created and formal and informal associations would not proliferate. Or is it, perhaps, the other way round? Do formal and informal networks instil or create citizen capacity to trust and reciprocate?

'Networks of civic engagement', writes Elinor Ostrom, 'foster robust norms of reciprocity' (Ostrom: 1990: 206). There is an obvious chicken-and-egg problem in deciding which comes first: norms of trust and reciprocity without which networks cannot be created; or networks which help to create norms of trust and reciprocity.

The chapter will return to this problem later, but meanwhile, it should be noted that the subjective dimension of social capital – trust and reciprocity – is conceptually different from the objective existence of social networks and formal organisations, even if the two are empirically closely related. However, the connection between the two is properly an empirical question: Under what sorts of social and political circumstances will high levels of interpersonal trust result in close and extensive social networks involving what sorts of people? Attempts to define and conceptualise social capital might do well to take account of the difference between norms and values, on the one hand, and networks, on the other, and keep them distinct so their empirical relations may be studied.

One good reason for following this research strategy lies in the fact that dense and elaborate networks of informal relations and formal organisations may undermine social capital. Under certain circumstances they may generate 'unsocial capital' (Levi, 1996), by fostering conflict, division, and anti-democratic tendencies. Both Putnam and Ostrom have emphasised this 'dark' side of associational life. One of the best examples is the Weimar Republic where a strong, dense, and vibrant associational life was used by the Nazis to infiltrate society and gain control of it (Berman, 1997). In Northern Ireland the rigid separation of Catholic and Protestant clubs, associations, and voluntary organisations succeeds in reinforcing division and conflict, rather than tying society together by its own internal divisions (Simmel, 1955). In other words, different networks and associations have different capacities to produce social capital, just as they have a different capacity to produce unsocial capital, and the relationships remain an empirical question.

SOCIAL CAPITAL AS AN OUTCOME: GETTING THINGS DONE

Social capital may be defined in terms of the collective goods, facilities, and services which are produced in the voluntary sector, as opposed to being produced by families, markets, or governments. 'Social capital', wrote James Coleman (1988: 98), 'is defined by its function ... Like other forms of capital, social capital is productive, making possible the achievement of certain goals that in its absence would not be possible.' In his work on the concept Coleman (1990: 302) emphasises that social capital is a property of social structures and social relations that help to facilitate social action and to get things done. As such, social capital is not defined in terms of normative orders or social networks, but as one of their outcomes. These outcomes may be the capacity to co-operate effectively and efficiently, and they may take the form of tangible and physical products. They may even be literally concrete. For example, a village community may work together to raise money to build a village hall which then becomes a collective facility. In other cases the product may be the continuous supply of fish from a lake which, by common agreement and practice of local inhabitants is not over-fished by any particular individual, because each recognises the interests of the community as a whole. Similarly, social capital may take the form of the village common which is not over-grazed because each local resident recognises the interests of other residents (Ostrom, 1990).

There are many other examples of such shared facilities and resources. When it comes to bringing in crops farming communities often share labour and equipment the better to act quickly and on a large scale. When it comes to raising barns, a task too large for any one family, the community will pitch in together, on the understanding that each family will help the others in a similar way. When it comes to raising capital, each member of a rotating credit association will put money into the kitty, and each, in turn, will take out a lump sum (Ardener, 1964; Geertz, 1962). In modern society, examples of such collective benefits and resources include baby-sitting circles, neighbourhood watch schemes, car pools, and street parties.

This third meaning of social capital brings it closer to financial capital in that it resembles the tangible (sometimes even physical) services, facilities, and resources produced by voluntary cooperation. Once again, there is nothing wrong with defining social capital in this way, except that it is open to question whether any social phenomenon can be defined in terms of either its function or its product. The same phenomenon may have different functions and products, and different phenomena may have the same functions or products. To include the product or function of social capital in its definition is also to confuse matters of definition with matters of empirical investigation. Is it indeed the case that high levels of trust and reciprocity generate extensive and intensive networks which, in turn, generate collective goods and services? And if so, under what circumstances does this occur? There may be many intervening variables between values and attitudes, networks, and their outcome or products which prevents one generating the other. It seems likely that without the individual and subjective attitudes and expectations of trust and reciprocity which make cooperation possible, and without the social networks and organisations which result from these attitudes, there would be no social capital in the third sense of collective facilities and services. At the same time, we should not assume that one is by definition the cause or consequence of another. Rather it seems sensible to treat each of the three different components parts of social capital as discrete phenomena, and to leave the relationships between them as a matter for empirical investigation.

Rather than treating all three as definitionally part of the same thing, they should be carefully separated, and the relations between them made the subject of research. If we do this then a series of important questions emerge about the nature, the causes, and the consequences of social capital.

- Is there an empirical relationship between individual involvement in social networks and voluntary associations, on the one hand, and relatively high levels of trust and reciprocity, on the other? What is the nature and direction of the causal relationship, if any, between the two? Do voluntary organisations engender in their members the social virtues of trust and reciprocity, or is it, on the contrary, those who trust and reciprocate who are most likely to become joiners?
- If there is a relationship between joining and the subjective values which comprise social capital then what sorts of networks and associations are best at generating them? For example, it is not immediately obvious that being involved in racist organisations will produce generalised trust and reciprocity. It is not even evident that it will produce trust between the members of the organisation themselves, since such groups show a propensity to splinter into factions which then fight rancorous political battles among themselves. This is a question tackled by Stolle and Rochon in this book (see also Parry *et al.*, 1992: 103 and Moyser and Parry, 1997: 42).
- There may, indeed, be honour among thieves, but as writers from Madison and Rousseau to Ostrom and Putnam have pointed out, there may be a dark side of social involvement and organisation which can produce the 'mischief of faction', or at worst, irreconcilable conflict and violence. Under what circumstances will networks of informal relations and formal organisations generate social capital, as against unsocial capital?
- Are the norms of social capital such as trust and reciprocity generalised? Whiteley and Seyd (1997) distinguish between social capital and political capital. The former concerns what might be called horizontal or social trust between citizens, and the latter vertical or political trust between citizens and leaders. This useful distinction raises the question of whether those who trust socially also trust politically. And do those who are politically trusting tend to generalise to a wide range of political institutions and actors, or do they trust some institutions or actors more than others?

In short, to start asking questions about the relationship, if any, between the three dimensions of social capital is to ask questions about the relationship between social capital, on the one hand, and voluntary associations on the other. Indeed, the whole question of the number, variety, and penetration of voluntary associations in society is widely held to be a crucial matter for social capital and modern democracy, and therefore the next section of the chapter will turn to this issue.

VOLUNTARY ORGANISATIONS AND SOCIAL CAPITAL

The creation and renewal of social capital in modern society is said to be intimately tied up with the voluntary sector – that huge and diverse range of voluntary organisations, secondary associations, intermediary organisations, and community associations which exist in almost every western society. The voluntary sector is that part of society which is neither family, nor market, nor state. Family, market, and state are collective, but they are not voluntary. As Oscar Wilde said of family, 'God gives us our relatives, thank God we can choose our friends.' The market is not voluntary because (most) people have to earn a living, and work, no less than school, is forced upon us. The state is excluded because its defining features are imperative coordination and ubiquity. We may be able to choose which state we live in, but we can no longer choose not to live in a state. The fact that the voluntary sector is both voluntary and collective makes it different from family, market and state, and gives it a special significance in society.

The exact definition and demarcation of the voluntary sector is problematic, because hard-and-fast lines are difficult to draw and because the voluntary sector shades into other involuntary or non-collective areas of activity. Some 'voluntary' organisations are not, in fact, altogether voluntary. For example, closed-shop trade unions are compulsory, as are professional organisations for lawyers or doctors. Joining some small religious sects may be entirely voluntary, but leaving them is sometimes fraught with difficulties. Examples include the scientologists and the recent case of the Asahari cult in Japan which threatened possible defectors with physical violence or death. Nevertheless, the general principle of voluntary involvement is theoretically fairly straightforward, and in practice it is usually fairly clear, in spite of some grey areas at the margins. The voluntary sector includes business, and trade and commercial organisations, but not individual businesses or firms. It includes parent-teacher associations and school clubs, but not the schools themselves. It covers charitable associations but not compulsory welfare schemes enforced by the state. It includes local authority associations formed by units of local or community government, but not local jurisdictions themselves. It involves voluntary associations of a clan-like nature (for example, the international association of people named McGregor, or McKenzie), but not any given family of McGregors or McKenzies. It includes political parties and pressure groups but neither the organisations nor the quangos of the state. It includes regimental associations for old soldiers, but not the regiments themselves.

The voluntary sector covers a wide variety of forms of organisations from powerful national business organisations with money and full-time paid staff, to small local associations which consist of little more than a man, a dog, and a sporadic and amateur newsletter. The organisations themselves cover almost every conceivable form and type of human interest and activity, and some that are inconceivable in polite society. They cover the daily and mundane activities of everyday life, and the rare and the exotic: the Birmingham Mouse Club, the West Midlands Cold Rolled Copper, Brass, and Steel Association, the West Midlands Association of Private Detectives, and the Birmingham Water Polo Referees Association (Newton, 1976).

From the point of view of empirical research, a more difficult issue than the voluntary–involuntary distinction is that between formal organisations and informal groups. In principle formal organisations are easy to identify. They often have a contact name and address for a president, chair, or secretary. Many have their own offices, elected or appointed officers, officially audited accounts, formal constitutions, and annual reports, and contact information. The more highly organised the group world the easier it is to study because names and addresses appear in handbooks and reference works compiled by umbrella organisations or peak associations, and in the handbooks and guidebooks produced by communities, cities, states, and regions.

At the other end of the continuum there are also loose and amorphous networks of individuals who come together on a casual basis and at irregular times to play darts, talk about football, discuss a novel, raise consciousness, offer mutual support, or play a scratch game of football in the park. They include bible groups, self-help organisations, neighbourhood watch schemes, baby-sitting circles, common-interest communities (Barton and Silverman, 1994), and car pools. These informal groups may be no less important than formal ones for social capital research, and in some respects they may well be a great deal more important. In the first place they are the very substance of society – its basic woven fabric. In the second place, they may take up no less time and involve no less commitment than formally organised groups. At the same time, it is difficult to know how to define them, identify them, measure them or study them. In one sense society consists of them, but, at the same time, they are so all-pervasive, loose-knit, changeable, amorphous, and numerous that it is difficult to study them. Social network analysis offers the starting point for analysis, but it is only a starting point and on its own would reveal little about social capital.

In between the two extremes of highly organised voluntary organisation and *ad hoc*, loose-knit and informal social groups there is, of course a full range of more-or-less organised, and more-or-less formal organisations and associations. But the closer one moves towards the *ad hoc* end of the continuum, the more difficult it is to conduct empirical study. This is why most research concentrates on formally organised organisations, even though there is some evidence to suggest that informal associations and groups are of increasing importance for social capital. This is because different sorts of groups and voluntary associations may have different sorts of implications for the generation of the norms, values, and expectations which lay the foundations for a well-developed social capital.

It is conventional to distinguish between what might be termed the internal effects of voluntary organisations and their external effects. Internally, organisations are believed to have effects on their members in that they socialise them into a democratic culture and teach them the subtleties of trust and cooperation. Externally, organisations link citizens with the political system and its institutions, aggregate and articulate interests, and provide the range and variety of competing and cooperating groups which constitute a pluralist polity. They constitute the veto groups, countervailing powers, interest groups, or pluralist groups so much discussed by writers on modern pluralist democracy. Foley and Edwards (1996: 39) refer to the family of arguments about internal effects of organisations as 'Civil Society I', and the family of arguments about external effects as 'Civil Society II'. As they point out, both are essential to an understanding of democracy. This chapter, however, is mainly concerned with the internal effects of groups, or Civil Society I.

Organisations vary in the strength of their internal and external effects. In recent decades there has been a growth of organisations which have strong external effects and weak internal ones because they involve their members in barely any activity or participation beyond writing out a cheque for the annual membership fee. There seem to be two major types of these low-commitment organisations. In the first, citizens join the organisations simply for the benefits and services they receive in return. Good examples are the motoring associations which exist in all western nations. They usually have a very large but almost totally inactive membership of individuals who pay their annual fee in return for various services for the private motorist. They are characterised by low levels of grass-roots participation and sparse, if any, interpersonal contact. At the same time their membership size, money, and organisational assets make them powerful interest groups in their chosen area of public policy. Putnam (1995a: 71) gives the American Association of Retired Persons (AARP) as another example of this type of voluntary association.

The second main type of cheque-book membership involves people who join some organisations not for the services they provide but for largely symbolic reasons. Some people pay a membership fee to a political party, or an environmental movement, a charity, or an arts society not because they particularly value the service, but because they want to be symbolically allied with the cause. They do not want to be active or involved, go to meetings or join committees, or meet like-minded people at social and political events. They simply want to make a symbolic gesture by paying money to join. Clearly, most or many people who join a party or a social movement are not like this, but some are, and their type of organisational membership has no obvious implications for civic involvement and the formation of norms of social capital.

Cheque-book organisations of these two types provide part of the countervailing power system upon which pluralist democracy rests – they may have powerful external effects. As voluntary associations they contribute little, if anything, to grass-roots democracy – they have minimal internal effects. In this respect they are the opposite of the small, face-to-face groups such as consciousness-raising groups, or groups which meet once a month to discuss a book, which have strong internal effects but very little external impact.

While there is some evidence that cheque-book organisations have grown in number and importance in modern society, there are also indications that loose-knit, more informal, *ad hoc* associations are flourishing. According to Wuthnow (1994), there has been an expansion of such loose-knit, more-or-less organised, weak-obligation, support groups in America in recent times. The literature on the new social movements also characterises them as 'networks of networks' which are more loose-knit, and less bureaucratic and hierarchical than traditional parties and interest groups (Neidhardt, 1985; Neidhardt and Rucht, 1993; Tarrow, 1994: 187–98). Danish research also suggests a growing number of user groups which are made up of decentralised, and informal networks (Gundelach and Torpe, 1997: 51–4).

Putnam (1995a: 72), quoting Wuthnow on 'the weakest of obligations' feature of small support and caring groups, suggests that they 'need to be accounted for in any serious reckoning of social connectedness'. But he continues by saying that 'they do not typically play the same role as traditional civic associations'. The argument here, however, is that these loose-knit and informal groups are an increasing feature of modern society, and that *some* of them in *some circumstances* may well be more important than formally organised voluntary associations in the formation of social capital. For some people, at some times, in some places they are sporadic and with little internal influence on participants; for other people at other times, they may be an intense experience with strong internal effects.

For reasons already mentioned, informal groups are not much studied but there are studies which can be brought to bear on the subject. A Danish study by Gundelach and Torpe (1996) distinguishes between the 'classical' formal organisations of the de Tocqueville model, and what they call network associations. Modern formal organisations are increasingly large, professionalised and businesslike, and remote from their members, a process which appears to have started in some organisations in the United States as early as the 1970s (Gittell, 1980). The socialisation role of creating 'habits of the heart' is now more likely to be played by the network associations which in Denmark, as in the USA, appear to have grown in number and social significance in recent times. According to the evidence of Gundelach and Torpe, they also have a high impact on the attitudes and behaviour of those who participate. The authors of the Danish study conclude that 'we should study other mechanisms of creating democratic values than the voluntary associations and we should develop new theories on democratic values which take the character of the present society into account' (Gundelach and Torpe, 1996: 31). Minkoff (1997) makes much the same sort of argument about national social movement organisations in the USA.

The second study relevant to this discussion of social capital and social organisations is the work on political participation in Britain by Parry *et al.* (1992). Like the Danish research, this distinguishes between 'formal groups such as trade union and interest groups which give an impetus to action [by virtue of] the existence of institutionalised channels of communication', and 'informal or *ad hoc* groups of neighbours concerned over a local development or parents worried at some proposed change in local schooling' (Parry *et al.*, 1992: 86–7). The survey evidence shows that group resources, both formal and informal, are very important for political participation. In addition, although Parry *et al.* do not dwell systematically on the different impact of formal and informal groups, their survey results provide evidence that informal groups are at least as important as formal ones in generating satisfaction with political action (p. 281), in educating their members both cognitively and affectively (pp. 289–90); and in facilitating democratic political action (pp. 423, 427), particularly in local politics (p. 319). Perhaps their most interesting finding is that slightly *more* effort is involved in political participation within informal groups than formal ones (p. 275). This is, at best, only circumstantial evidence of the importance of informal organisations, but it does suggest that they may be no less important than formal ones in the formation of social capital.

Table 1.1 Types of organisation and social capital

	Strong external effects	*Weak external effects*
Strong internal effects	Pluralist organisations	Self-help, support and consciousness-raising groups
Weak internal effects	Cheque-writing organisations	Small, *ad hoc*, informal support and caring groups

Drawing on American evidence, Foley and Edwards (1996: 43) also make the point that some of the amorphous social movements, and some of the apparently cheque-writing organisations have both internal and external (Civil Society I and Civil Society II) effects.

To summarise this section of the chapter; it is suggested that social capital research which focuses on formally organised voluntary associations (albeit for understandable reasons) may be missing part of the story, even a large part of it. While some formal organisations, the cheque-writing ones, have little internal effect on their members so far as the creation of social capital is concerned, some *ad hoc* groups and associations seem to be highly significant in this respect (see Table 1.1). With these possibilities in mind we can now turn to broader issues of social capital and the nature of modern society.

MODELS OF SOCIAL CAPITAL

'Thick' trust and the Durkheimian model

In small face-to-face communities 'thick' trust (Williams, 1988: 8) is the essential ingredient of mechanical solidarity which is generated by intensive and daily contacts between people, often of the same tribe, class, ethnic group, or local community origin. Groups, communities, or tribes of this kind are not only socially homogeneous but they tend to be isolated. As a result, social control is also powerful. Thick trust in communities of this kind is generated and sustained by a tight and intensive network of social interaction, and by the sorts of social sanctions which work best in small isolated communities – 'closure', is Coleman's term (1988: 105–8). The classic analyses of such types of society are offered by Durkheim in his account of mechanical solidarity, and by Toennies in his writing on 'Gemeinschaft'. There are some analogues in the contemporary western world as well. Two kinds may be of some significance. First, the western world still has some small, relatively homogeneous, and isolated communities of the type discussed by Kornhauser (1960) in *The Politics of Mass Society*. They are typically found in rural areas, island societies, or in tightly knit urban communities of a ghetto-like kind: mining villages, working-class dockland areas, and fishing communities are the favourite examples of sociologists and political scientists.

Second, the west may also have pockets of 'thick' trust formed in total institutions such as small sects, churches, ghettos, and minority communities.

It should be remembered that such closed sects, ghettos, and communities are likely to produce trust within them, but distrust of the wider society. To a more limited extent, thick trust may also be generated by the relatively intensive interactions of some groups in modern, western society such as consciousness-raising groups, self-help groups, mutual support groups (single parents, battered wives, the handicapped, for example). Last, voluntary communities of the 'alternative' kind, and some aspects of the new social movements and their communities may also generate thick trust, but probably in a relatively diluted form.

'Thin' trust and the de Tocqueville model of civic virtue

Modern large-scale society in the west is not composed primarily of small, intense and exclusive communities of a face-to-face character, although these are not altogether absent. Rather, it is based upon looser, more amorphous, and more sporadic social contacts formed by work, school, and local community, and by the voluntary associations discussed at length by writers such as de Tocqueville, Durkheim, John Stuart Mill, Toennies, Weber, Simmel, and most recently by Putnam. Modern society does not generate the 'thick' trust of mechanical solidarity, but the 'thin' trust of organic solidarity. Thin trust is the product of weak ties which, according to Granovetter's celebrated article (1973), constitute the strong and enduring basis for social integration in modern large-scale society (see also Evans and Boyte, 1992).

According to this model of thin trust – what might be called the de Tocqueville model – face-to-face interaction in formally organised voluntary organisations is essential for the generation of the norms of social capital. Social contacts outside the nuclear family are not nearly as intense nor as all-embracing as those of primordial society, but secondary associations and voluntary organisations nevertheless have important internal and external effects. Internally, citizens learn the civic virtues of trust, moderation, compromise, reciprocity, and the skills of democratic discussion and organisation. Moreover, trustworthy behaviour is forced on people who know they will meet each other in voluntary organisation circles. Externally, multiple and overlapping groups create overlapping and interlocking social ties which bind society together by its own internal divisions. They also produce the competition between groups and interests which are the basis of pluralist democracy.

The main features of the de Tocqueville model are:

- Formal organisations and secondary relations, compared with the personal and informal relations of mechanical solidarity.
- Multiple organisational membership compared with only one, or a small set of nested relationships in tribal or communal society.
- Overlapping and interlocking organisations which create a set of cross-cutting ties and obligations. A set of isolated and exclusive associations which help to create superimposed cleavages is more likely to bring about conflict

and democratic instability within modern society (Lijphart's consociational democracy apart).

- Impersonal and thin trust.

At the heart of the de Tocqueville model (de Tocqueville, 1968: 355–9) is the idea that membership of formal organisations generates the civic virtues of moderation, cooperation, trust and reciprocity. As Pateman (1970: 105) puts it, 'we learn to participate by participating'. Three important assumptions underlie the de Tocqueville model, however. The first is that voluntary associations are mainly responsible for generating the trust and reciprocity of social capital. Putnam (1995b: 666; see also Putnam, 1993: 171–6) writes that 'people who join are people who trust', and that 'the causation flows mainly from joining to trusting'. Indeed, this quotation distils the thrust of the de Tocqueville/John Stuart Mill/Putnam thesis, and it is built into the basic assumptions of much modern sociology and political science. It is a major plank on which social capital theory is constructed. Nevertheless, it is worth questioning whether voluntary organisations do, in fact, have a major role in this respect. The reason is simple. The great majority of people devote more time, emotional energy, and commitment to school, family, and work than to either voluntary associations, or loose networks of social contacts.

School, work, family, and community also teach the values of reciprocity, trust, compromise, and cooperation, and they account for a far higher proportion of the lives of most citizens. It seems, on the face of it, implausible to ascribe a crucial role to organisational membership and civic engagement which, at the best and then only for a small proportion of the adult population, accounts for a relatively few hours per week or month of modern life. As Margaret Levi (1996: 48) argues 'trust is more likely to emerge in response to experiences and institutions outside the small associations than as a result of membership.' Coleman stresses the import-ance of the family and school in the development of social capital (Coleman, 1988: 109–16). Putnam (1995a: 73) writes that 'the most fundamental form of social capital is the family', and it may also be the most fundamental source for the formation of social capital. Putnam (1995b: 667) also produces cross-sectional data showing that education is by far the strongest correlate of both trust and organisational membership (p. 667. See also Verba *et al.*, 1995: 514; Uslaner, undated: 30). Verba *et al.* (1995: 320) observe that 'Workplaces provide the most opportunities for the practice of civic skills, churches the fewest.' Is it possible that the voluntary sector is just one of many forms of social interaction which generate social capital, and perhaps not even a particularly important one compared with family, work, and education?

There is quite probably an association between being a member of one or more voluntary organisations and having a well-developed sense of trust and reciprocity, but the first is rather less likely to generate the second than to be an expression or symptom of it. Sociable people join clubs; misanthropes do not unless, of course, it is a club for misanthropes. I have not found an example of such a club in the lists I have looked at. (Reader, you may choose to treat this as a challenge.) In short, the argument is that people join voluntary organisations because they trust others, rather than the other way round. This is not to deny the claim that trust feeds and grows fatter upon itself, and that membership of voluntary organisations and associations reinforces trust. At any rate, a central part of social capital research must be to try to untangle the no doubt complex and mutually interdependent causal relations between membership of voluntary associations and social capital (see, for example, the clear and comprehensive account of van Deth, 1997: 11–15).

The second assumption of the de Tocqueville model is that the trust produced by involvement in voluntary associations is generalised, so that it covers both citizen trust in each other and citizen trust in politicians. But to place a high level of trust in ordinary people (horizontal trust) is one thing, to place the same level of trust in politicians (vertical trust), may be another. As Putnam puts it: 'I might well trust my neighbours without trusting city hall, or vice versa' (1995b: 665). The special concern about western democracy is that citizen trust in politicians is declining rapidly (see, for example, Dogan, 1994: 306–7; Listhaug, 1995). It is an empirical question whether trust in fellow citizens and trust in politicians is closely related.

The third assumption is that social capital is a bottom-up phenomenon – that it is generated by grass-roots participation and civic engagement which not only generate democratic values but which also mobilise individuals politically. That there is a close association between membership of voluntary organisations and political activity of various kinds is not in dispute (Verba and Nie, 1972: 184–7; van Deth 1996: 13–16). However, mass values and behaviour, no less than the nature and activities of the world of voluntary organisations, may also be strongly affected by the policy of governments and by the structure of government itself – a top-down process (Tarrow, 1996: 394–5; Levi, 1996: 50; Brehm and Rahn, 1997; Dekker *et al.*, 1997). 'What role organised groups in civil society will play', write Foley and Edwards (1996: 48), 'depends crucially on the larger political setting.' For example, it may be that the move towards a more competitive, market economy in many western states in the 1980s and 1990s has introduced more competition and encouraged the 'entrepreneurial spirit', but perhaps it has also helped to undermine social capital and the sense of trust and cooperation between citizens. When Thatcher insisted that 'there is no such thing as society', she was expressing her personal belief that social capital is of little importance, and by virtue of her own economic and social policies she was making it more difficult for citizens to act as if it was important. An empirical task for social capital research is to explore the connections, if any, between government policies and structures, and the formation of social capital in different political systems.

Abstract trust in modern society

If we can distinguish usefully between the thick trust of a personal kind, and thin trust of a more impersonal kind, then perhaps we can go one step further and talk in terms of 'imaginary' (Anderson, 1983) or 'empathetic' or 'reflexive' (Gundelach and Torpe, 1997) communities which are built on abstract trust. According to Misztal (1996: 72) trust may range along a continuum from personal to abstract. Abstract trust is not built upon the intensive daily interactions of primordial society, nor upon the more limited and sporadic contacts which takes place within the many overlapping formal organisations of industrial society. If thick trust exists between members of the same tribe, and thin trust between members of the same voluntary associations and community organisations, then abstract trust exists between acquaintances.

Some writers argue that modern, mobile, shifting society produces more and more social relations of the acquaintance type, and that, as a result, abstract trust assumes a greater and greater significance. Size, impersonal relations, complexity, fragmentation, differentiation, and speed of change make it progressively difficult to depend upon either personal thick trust or secondary thin trust. As Luhmann (1988) argues, the modern world is full of complexity, uncertainty, and risk. Abstract trust helps to make this manageable.

If thick trust originates in close personal relations, and thin trust in the secondary relations of voluntary associations (at least in the de Tocqueville model), where does abstract trust come from? The answer may be from two main sources. The first and most obvious is education which teaches the young to understand and operate the abstract principles of such things as trust, fairness, equality, and universalism. It teaches the young to imagine themselves in the shoes of others: 'Don't do that Johnny', says the nursery school teacher a hundred times a day, 'How would you like it if little Jimmy did that to you?' Later, as a teenager, Johnny goes off to secondary school – or as Chuck Berry sings – 'Up in the morning and off to school. The teacher is teaching the golden rule' – that is, the fundamental precept of social capital that we should behave in a decent and civilised way to others. Education also provides the disparate citizens of modern society with a common set of cultural references without which daily understandings would be impossible (viz., Bourdieu on cultural capital). It provides us with a common knowledge of a set of dates, places, names, events, concepts, references, quotations, book titles, and factual knowledge which form the basis of daily social interaction. Education, it is said, is what is left after people have forgotten what they have been taught. A willingness to trust and reciprocate may be among the things which stick when all else has been forgotten.

Besides the impersonal trust, empathy, and reciprocity taught both implicitly and explicitly by them, modern schools also set out deliberately to teach the art of cooperation with others. They carefully introduce collective learning tasks, and they devote much time and effort to team games, school plays, school bands, and to joint endeavours of many kinds. Verba *et al.* (1995) document how important participation in school activities is for political and community involvement in adult life. However, the prime effect of education may not be the experience of acting in groups, so much as the ability to understand abstract ideas such as citizenship, universalism, equality, the common good, the benefits of cooperation, and the difficult subtleties of peaceful conflict resolution. For this reason the beneficial effects of education for social capital are particularly strong in the last few years of full-time study: university and college education. Perhaps it is in these last few years of education that people learn most about how to relate not only to those who are known personally, but also to those who one may never meet, but who are, nevertheless, recognised to be members of the same, general community.

In this way education may help to create social solidarity for a community which stretches far beyond the immediate community of known individuals or sporadic contacts, to the much broader world of contemporary international society. There is evidence that levels of interpersonal trust within the European Community is increasing (Niedermayer, 1995: 237). This involves trust between individuals who cannot possibly know each other personally, and who probably know rather little about each other at all, but who are now defined as similar in some important respects. In other words, not only is there such a thing as abstract trust between strangers in the same country, but there seems to be an emergence of abstract trust which stretches across international boundaries as well.

The mass media may also help to create abstract trust and social solidarity of this kind by endlessly repeating a common set of social values. In the early days of public service radio and TV this was a self-conscious policy in some European countries. They deliberately set out to educate and to inform the general public, and to present themselves as the voice of the single and integrated nation. In Britain, Lord Reith regarded the BBC as the voice of the nation with a duty to unite different social groups, interests, and regions. More recently, it is said, the post-modern mass media have become so specialised in their appeal to the small and diverse, that their effect is to divide and fragment into many different consumer groups, each with different values and lifestyles. There is, no doubt, some truth in this, but at the same time it is easy to confuse the effects of packaging and substance. Much of post-modern style is a matter of presentation and appearance. Underneath this there is a certain uniformity of substance which may well be associated with, or convey a common set of values. For example the modern mass media appear to emphasise the importance of success, wealth, physical beauty, race, and gender. In this respect, TV soap operas, one of the most popular forms of media entertainment, might be seen as latter-day morality tales, which present audiences with good and bad role models for behaviour in everyday life. Or, to take another example, if democracy is essentially a method of resolving conflict through peaceful, if heated, discussion, then watching politicians discuss and debate issues on news and current affairs programmes, may help to instil in their audiences the values of argument as against violence. In short, the hypothesis is that an effect of the modern media is to help create social capital by vicarious means rather than by personal and direct involvement in society.

There is, it must also be emphasised, strong disagreement about the effects of the mass media in modern society (Norris, 1996; Newton, 1997). One school emphasises increasing levels of political knowledge, competence, interest, sophistication, and political activity – the cognitive mobilisation school (see, for example, Inglehart, 1990: 335–70; Dalton, 1988: 18–24). Another school emphasises the junk news of the mass media which induces fear, isolation, political ignorance, a sense of political incompetence, and political apathy – the 'videomalaise' school of thought, upon which Putnam (1995b) draws. This chapter can do no more than point out the different interpretations, and suggest that they form a central topic for research on social capital.

Evidence of highly generalised, abstract trust in imaginary communities, is found in the imaginative research of Conover and Searing (1995) who use in-depth focus groups to explore the ideas of ordinary people about citizenship. They write,

> Today, blood and birth, like socialisation and residence, are less important . . . Culture is what counts. Its predominance in the understanding of British respondents was revealed by their reactions to another survey question: nearly two-thirds said they regarded as 'British' people from the Falklands and Gibraltar, people who were not born in Britain and perhaps not born of parents born in Britain, people who were definitely not socialised in Britain and, of course, were not residents of Britain either.

This research seems to point to a very general and abstract notion of what it is to be British, and that as a result, in Conover and Searing's words (1995: 18), 'national communities are imagined communities'.

MODELS OF DEMOCRACY AND SOCIAL CAPITAL

The three models of social capital outlined above seem to correspond to three rather different forms of democracy.

Primary democracy exists in primary, face-to-face communities characterised by intensive and all-embracing primary relations, by thick trust, and by powerful, personal sanctions. In the modern western world this is restricted to a few rather exceptional cases: the 'town meeting democracy' in New England, in small, alternative communities, in a few special organisations, and in a few isolated and homogeneous communities on the periphery of society. By definition it cannot exist at the national political level of large modern states. Primary democracy, based upon thick trust, and strong norms of reciprocity, is likely to depend heavily upon fraternity, but at the expense of liberty and equality. The small, isolated but intensive communities which produce primary democracy are often hierarchical and produce strong social pressures which enforce conformity and consensus rather than individual freedom (Dahl and Tufte, 1974).

Secondary democracy exists in political systems built upon the principle of representation. It involves an advanced form of the division of labour, both economic, and political. It therefore presumes relatively high levels of trust between specialised elites (including the political class) and non-elites. It is associated with the low-intensity relations created by a wide range and a large number of overlapping and interlocking organisational memberships, and by thin and impersonal trust.

Industrial society is characterised mainly by a mixture of primary and secondary democracy based upon both the Durkheimian and de Tocqueville models of social capital. It therefore involves both thick and thin trust of a personal and impersonal nature.

Abstract democracy is built upon abstract notions of reciprocity and universalism which extend beyond personal and impersonal trust, beyond primary associations and secondary organisations, and beyond face-to-face relations and more episodic secondary relations. It covers the members of much broader geographical areas, such as Scandinavians, the Mediterraneans, central Europeans, west Europeans, or north Americans. In abstract democracies abstract trust is of growing importance. We should distinguish between the origin of abstract trust and its domain. It is created by the society and institutions in which citizens of the modern world find themselves – by primary face-to-face relations within the family, community, and workplace, within the secondary associations and informal associations of modern society, and by education and mass media. But it applies to a broader domain – for the British it extends to Gibraltarians and Falkland Islanders, and for citizens of European states it increasingly extends to all other citizens of the European Union.

Post-industrial or post-modern society is characterised by all three types of democracy. Of these, primary democracy is likely to be the least important, and limited to a few areas of peripheral geography and to some small 'alternative' communities. Secondary democracy is important, but of declining significance. Its place being taken by abstract democracy and by the abstract trust of imaginary communities. These forms of democracy are likely to be based on values, attitudes, and expectations created by: (1) primary face-to-face interaction in the home, in the community, and at work; (2) by the formal organisations of the classical Tocquevillean world, and by the more amorphous, and loose-knit associations of modern urban life; and (3) by education and the mass media.

The dilemma of primary democracy, in tribal societies or small village communities, is too little freedom and equality but an abundance of fraternity. In other words, the tight social control of small, self-contained societies tends to produce conservatism, claustrophobia, hierarchy, ascribed status and power, and the suppression rather than the resolution of conflict (see Dahl, 1967: 961). The dilemma of modern, abstract democracy may be too much atomised freedom, tempered by too little trust and sense of fraternity. According to some theorists, post-modern society is increasingly suffering from an extreme form of western individualism. Its population is progressively fragmented, atomised, self-seeking, calculating, and greedy, with weaker and weaker social ties and loyalties, and a diminishing sense of trust and social solidarity (see the discussion in Elshtain, 1995: 5–27). In short, modern society is said to suffer from declining levels of social capital and a consequent erosion of its democratic foundations. Whether this has reached crisis proportions, and whether it is a general western trend has yet to be demonstrated. But it is helpful to separate crisis from change: change from secondary to abstract democracy, from impersonal to abstract trust, and from formal types of voluntary organisation to more informal types of associations and groups.

References

Anderson, B. (1983) *Imagined Communities: Reflections on the Origins and Spread of Nationalism*, London: Verso.

Ardener, Shirley (1964) 'The comparative study of rotating credit associations', *Journal of the Royal Anthropological Institute of Great Britain and Northern Ireland*, 94: 201.

Arrow, K. (1972) 'Gifts and exchanges', *Philosophy and Public Affairs*, 1 (Summer).

Barber, Benjamin (1995) *Jihad vs. McWorld: How the Planet is Both falling Apart and Coming Together – and What this Means for Democracy*. New York: New York Times Books.

Barton, Stephen E. and Carol J. Silverman, eds. (1994), *Common Interest Communities: Private Governments and the Public Interest*. Berkeley, Calif.: Institute of Governmental Studies.

Bellah, Robert N., R. Madsen, W. M. Sullivan, A. Swindler, and S. Tipton (1985) *Habits of the Heart: Individualism and Commitment in American Life*. Berkeley, Calif., University of California Press,

Berman, Sheri (1997) 'Civil society and the collapse of the Weimar Republic', *World Politics*, Vol. 49.

Brehm, John and Wendy Rahn (1997) 'Individual-level evidence for the causes and consequences of social capital', *American Journal of Political Science*, Vol. 41, No. 3: 999–1023.

Burtt, Shelley (1993) 'The politics of virtue today: A critique and a proposal', *American Political Science Review* 87: 360–8.

Burtt, Shelley (1995) 'Response', *American Political Science Review* 89: 148–51.

Cohen, Joshua and Joel Rogers (1992) 'Secondary associations and democratic governance', *Politics and Society*, 20: 393–472.

Coleman, James (1988) 'Social capital in the creation of human capital', *American Journal of Sociology* 94: 95–120.

Coleman, James (1990) *Foundations of Social Theory*. Cambridge, Mass.: Belknap.

Conover, Pamela J. and Donald D. Searing (1995) 'Citizens and members: Foundations for participation', paper delivered to the Annual Meeting of the American Political Science Association, Chicago, Illinois.

Dahl, Robert A. (1967) 'The city in the future of democracy', *American Political Science Review* 61: 953–70.

Dahl, Robert A. and Edward R. Tufte (1974) *Size and Democracy*. Stanford, Calif., Stanford University Press.

Dalton, Russell J. (1988) *Citizen Politics in Western Democracies*. Chatham, NJ: Chatham House.

Dekker, Paul, Ruud Koopmans and Andries van den Broek (1997) 'Voluntary associations, social movements, and individual political behaviour in western Europe', in Jan van Deth, ed., *Private Groups and Public Life*, London: Routledge.

Dogan, Mattei (1994) 'The pendulum between theory and substance: Testing the concepts of legitimacy and trust', in Mattei Dogan and Ali Kazancigil, eds., *Comparing Nations: Concepts, Strategies, Substance*. Oxford: Blackwell.

Duncan, Christopher M. (1995) 'Civic virtue and self-interest', *American Political Science Review* 89: 147–8.

Eltshain, Jean Bethke (1995) *Democracy on Trial*. New York: Basic Books.

Etzioni, Amitai (1993) *The Spirit of Community*. New York: Crown Publishers.

Evans, Sara M. and Harry C. Boyte (1992) *Free Spaces*. Chicago: Chicago University Press.

Foley, Michael W. and Bob Edwards (1996) 'The paradox of civil society', *Journal of Democracy* 7: 38–52.

Fukuyama, Francis (1995) *Trust: The Social Virtues and the Creation of Prosperity.* London: Hamish Hamilton.

Geertz, Clifford (1962). 'The rotating credit association: A "middle rung" in development', *Economic Development and Cultural Change* 10: 241–63.

Gittell, Marilyn (1980) *Limits to Citizen Participation: The Decline of Community Organizations.* Beverly Hills, Calif: Sage.

Granovetter, Mark (1973) 'The strength of weak ties', *American Journal of Sociology* 78: 1360–80.

Gundelach, Peter and Lars Torpe (1997) 'Voluntary associations: New types of involvement and democracy', paper presented to the ECPR Joint Sessions of Workshops, Oslo, 1996.

Inglehart, Ronald (1990) *Culture Shift in Advanced Industrial Society.* Princeton: Princeton University Press.

Kolankiewicz, George (1994) 'Elites in search of a political formula', *Daedalus*, Summer: 143–57.

Kollock, Peter (1994) 'The emergence of exchange structures: An experimental study of uncertainty, commitment, and trust', *American Journal of Sociology* 100: 313–45.

Kornhauser, William (1960) *The Politics of Mass Society,* London: Routledge and Kegan Paul.

Levi, Margaret (1996) 'Social and unsocial capital: a review essay of Robert Putnam's *Making Democracy Work*', *Politics and Society* 24: 45–55.

Listhaug, Ola (1995) 'The dynamics of trust in politicians', in Hans-Dieter Klingemann and Dieter Fuchs, eds., *Citizens and the State.* Oxford: Oxford University Press, 261–97.

Luhmann, Niklas (1988) 'Familiarity, confidence, trust: Problems and alternatives', in Diego Gambetta, ed., *Trust: Making and Breaking Cooperative Relations.* Oxford: Blackwell, 94–107.

Minkoff, Debra C. (1997) 'Producing social capital: National social movements and civil society', *American Behavioral Scientist,* Vol. 40, No. 5 (March/April): 606–19.

Misztal, Barbara A. (1996) *Trust In Modern Societies.* Oxford: Blackwell.

Moyser, George and Geraint Parry (1997) 'Voluntary associations and democracy in Britain', in Jan van Deth, ed., *Private Groups and Public Life,* London: Routledge, 24–46.

Mulhall, Stephen and Adam Swift (1992) *Liberals and Communitarians.* Oxford: Blackwell.

Neidhardt, Friedhelm (1985) 'Einige Ideen zu einer allgemeinen Theorie sozialer Bewegungen', in S. Hradil, ed., *Sozialstruktur im Umbruch.* Opladen: Leske und Budrich.

Neidhardt, Friedhelm and Dieter Rucht (1993) 'Auf dem Weg in die "Bewegungs-gesellschaft"?', *Soziale Welt,* 44: 305–26.

Newton, Kenneth (1976) *Second City Politics: Democratic Processes and Decision-Making in Birmingham.* Oxford: Oxford University Press.

Newton, Kenneth (1997) *The Mass Media and Modern Government,* Wissenschaftszentrum Berlin für Sozialforschung, Discussion Paper FS III, 96–301.

Niedermayer, Oskar (1995) 'Trust and sense of community', in Oskar Niedermayer and Richard Sinnott, eds., *Public Opinion and Internationalized Governance.* Oxford: Oxford University Press, 227–45.

Norris, Pippa (1996). 'Does television erode social capital? A reply to Putnam', *PS*, September, 1–7.

Ostrom, Elinor (1990) *Governing the Commons: The Evolution of Institutions for Collective Action.* New York: Cambridge University Press.

Parry, Geraint, George Moyser, and Neil Day (1992) *Political Participation and Democracy in Britain.* Cambridge: Cambridge University Press.

Pateman, Carol (1970) *Participation and Democratic Theory*. Cambridge: Cambridge University Press.

Putnam, Robert D. (1993) *Making Democracy Work: Civic Traditions in Modern Italy*. Princeton: Princeton University Press.

Putnam, Robert D. (1995a) 'Bowling alone: America's declining social capital', *Journal of Democracy* 6: 65–78.

Putnam, Robert D. (1995b) 'Tuning in, tuning out: The strange disappearance of social capital in America', *PS*, December 1995: 664–83.

Sahlins, Marshall (1972) *Stone Age Economics*. Chicago: Aldine-Atherton.

Shils, Edward (1991) 'The virtue of civil society', *Government and Opposition* 26: 2–20.

Simmel, Georg (1950) *The Sociology of Georg Simmel*. New York: Free Press.

Simmel, Georg (1955) *The Web of Groups Affiliations*, Glencoe, Ill.: The Free Press.

Stolle, Dietlind and Thomas R. Rochon (1996) 'Social capital, but how?: Associations and the creation of social capital', paper prepared for the Conference of Europeanists, Chicago, March, 1996.

Tarrow, Sidney (1994) *Power in Movements, Social Movements, Collective Action and Politics*. Cambridge: Cambridge University Press.

Tarrow, Sidney (1996) 'Making social science work across space and time: A critical reflection on Robert Putnam's *Making Democracy Work*', *American Political Science Review*, 90: 389–97.

Tocqueville, Alexis de (1968) *Democracy in America*. London: Fontana.

Uslaner, Eric M. (undated). 'Faith, hope, and charity: Social capital, trust, and collective action', mimeo.

van Deth, Jan W. (1996) 'Voluntary associations and political participation', in Oscar W. Gabriel and Jurgen W. Falter, eds., *Wahlen und Politische Einstellungen in Westlichen Demokratien*. Frankfurt am Main: Peter Lang.

van Deth, Jan W. (1997) 'Introduction: Social involvement and democratic politics' in Jan van Deth, ed., *Private Groups and Public Life*. London: Routledge, 1–23.

Verba, Sidney and Norman H. Nie (1972) *Participation in America*. New York: Harper and Row.

Verba, Sidney, Kay Lehman Schlozman, and Henry E. Brady (1995) *Voice and Equality: Civic Voluntarism in American Politics*. Cambridge, Mass.: Harvard University Press.

Whiteley, Paul, and Patrick Seyd (1977) 'Political capital formation among British party members', in Jan van Deth, ed., *Private Groups and Public Life*. London: Routledge.

Williams, Bernard (1988) 'Formal structures and social reality', in Diego Gambetta, ed., *Trust: Making and Breaking Cooperative Relations*. Oxford: Blackwell.

Wuthnow, Robert (1994) *Sharing the Journey: Support Groups and America's New Quest for Community*. New York: Free Press.

2   The origins of social capital

Paul F. Whiteley

INTRODUCTION

The dominant model for explaining the origins of social capital suggests that it arises from interactions between individuals within voluntary associations. Such associations are seen as being the key mechanism for promoting co-operation between citizens, and providing a framework in which trust can be fostered (see Putnam, 1993, 1995; Fukuyama, 1995; Coleman, 1988, 1990). This is the basic model developed by Putnam in his analysis of social capital in the Italian regions. He writes:

> Some regions of Italy have many choral societies and soccer teams and bird-watching clubs and Rotary clubs. Most citizens in those regions read eagerly about community affairs in the daily press. They are engaged by public issues, but not by personalistic or patron–client politics. Inhabitants trust one another to act fairly and to obey the law. . . . The community values solidarity, civic engagement, co-operation and honesty.
>
> (Putnam, 1993: 115)

This actually reflects a much older model which can be found in the writings of Alexis de Tocqueville in his celebrated *Democracy in America*. Commenting on the United States of 1832, de Tocqueville wrote:

> In no country in the world has the principle of association been more successfully used or applied to a greater multitude of objects than in America. Besides the permanent associations which are established by law under the names of townships, cities, and counties, a vast number of others are formed and maintained by the agency of private individuals.
>
> (de Tocqueville, 1990: 191)

Having established that American politics is rooted in the principle of free association, de Tocqueville then goes on to conclude that as far as democracy is concerned: 'No political form has hitherto been discovered that is equally favorable to the prosperity and development of all classes into which society is divided' (1990: 239). Thus the notion that free association is the basis of social capital and effective democracy, is a very old idea.

The aim of this chapter is to consider some alternative models of the creation of social capital, which have been relatively neglected in the literature. When evaluated from the perspective of rational choice theory it is apparent that the 'de Tocqueville' model is incomplete, and that other variables need to be examined if the creation of social capital is to be explained. Thus the aim is to examine if other variables can fill this gap and provide a more comprehensive understanding of the processes which create social capital.

These alternative models are based on psychological variables relating to the personality and moral outlook of the citizen, and also the symbolic communities with which he or she identifies. None of these variables can be satisfactorily explained by the interaction of citizens within voluntary associations, although they may be influenced by such processes. Thus these factors which help to create social capital operate independently of the de Tocqueville model.

The chapter is divided into five sections. We begin by defining social capital and examining the dominant de Tocqueville model, relating it to contemporary theories about the emergence of co-operation in collective action games. This shows that the model is incomplete as an explanation of the origins of social capital. This then leads into a discussion of the alternative models of the origins of social capital, and in the third section we specify a multivariate model designed to test these alternatives, using data from the 'world values survey' (Abramson and Inglehart, 1995). Section four discusses the findings from the estimates of the model, and we conclude with some observations about the significance of these findings for further research into social capital.

SOCIAL CAPITAL AND THE DE TOCQUEVILLE MODEL

There is some debate in the literature about the definition and meaning of social capital. Putnam defines it as 'features of social organization, such as trust, norms and networks, that can improve the efficiency of society by facilitating co-ordinated actions' (1993: 167). However, this definition is rather unsatisfactory since it mixes up three distinct features of social capital: citizens' feelings of trust in other members of society, social norms supportive of co-operation, and networks of civic engagement. The first two are psychological phenomena, whereas the last is a behavioural relationship between individuals, moulded by the institutions in which they live.

James Coleman (1988) identifies three distinct forms of social capital: obligations and expectations, information channels, and social norms. He defines the relationship between the first of these, obligations and expectations, and social capital in the following terms: 'If A does something for B and trusts B to reciprocate in the future, this establishes an expectation in A and an obligation on the part of B. This obligation can be conceived of as a credit slip held by A for performance by B' (Coleman, 1988: 102).

Thus social interaction generates 'credit slips' of obligation and norms of reciprocation. He argues that if such obligations are to be translated into social capital, it is necessary for a trustworthy social environment to exist, so that the expectation is that obligations will be repaid. Thus there is, what the computer scientists call, a 'bootstrap' problem: a minimal amount of social capital has to exist already, if it is to be created, since networks of obligations can be constructed and maintained only in a context in which a minimal level of trust between individuals already exists.

Coleman's second type of social capital is based on the idea of trusting other people to provide accurate information as a basis for action. Thus an individual who does not want to spend time learning about the political world can rely on a friend to read the newspapers and follow political events and provide him with such information. Clearly, such a relationship does not create the same obligations or 'credit slips' as the first type of social capital, but again for such communication to be possible a pre-existing level of trust between individuals has to exist.

Coleman's third type of social capital derives from social norms. To illustrate these, he cites the following example: 'Effective norms that inhibit crime make it possible to walk freely outside at night in a city and enable old persons to leave their houses without fear for their safety' (Coleman, 1988: 104).

Clearly norms which abjure self-interest and reinforce the idea that individuals should act in the interests of the collectivity, are particularly important. But again such norms cannot be created in a vacuum and require a minimal level of social capital to exist for them to be produced and sustained in the first place.

Coleman highlights the importance of 'closure' in social networks as a mechanism for generating social capital. In a relatively closed social network participants will interact in more than one arena, which helps to create the conditions for generating social capital; for example, if schoolchildren have parents who are also friends, this will make it easier for the parents to find out about, and sanction, the bad behaviour of their offspring in school; the fact that the parents are in regular communication with and have mutual obligations to one another reinforces their abilities to socialise their children.

From a rational choice perspective, social and political capital are collective goods, and as such are characterised by jointness of supply and the impossibility of exclusion (see Samuelson, 1954). Jointness of supply means that one person's consumption of the good does not reduce the amount available to anyone else, and the impossibility of exclusion means that individuals cannot be prevented from consuming the good once it has been provided, even if they did not contribute to its provision in the first place.[1]

These characteristics mean that there is a collective action problem in creating social capital, since individuals have an incentive to free-ride on the efforts of others. It has been shown that this collective action problem can either be modelled by a prisoner's dilemma game (Hardin, 1971), or alternatively by an assurance game (Chong, 1991). In the prisoner's dilemma game, each actor gains immediate payoffs by taking advantage of the trust of others; the dilemma is that if all actors do this, trust is destroyed and social interaction made very much more difficult. Each would be better off if they trusted the others, but when faced with the prospect of being taken advantage of, they are rational not to trust others in the first place. In this situation, the system will find an equilibrium in which it is difficult or impossible to build trust, and social capital will be minimal.

In the assurance version of the game the dilemma is not so acute since, by assumption, actors are predisposed to co-operate, but a problem still exists of co-ordinating collective action so that an adequate supply of the public good can be provided. Even when people are predisposed to trust others, they are not rational to do so if they cannot be sure that other citizens are actually trustworthy (see also Marwell and Oliver, 1993).

A developing literature suggests that co-operation can be obtained in the prisoner's dilemma, and trust created if a number of conditions are met (Taylor, 1976; Axelrod, 1984; Rasmussen, 1989). First, participants should not discount the future too much, since myopia sharply reduces the payoffs from co-operative action. Second, interactions should be repeated over time, since the dominant strategy in a one-shot game is always non-co-operation; a third and related requirement is that there should be uncertainty about when the game ends, since if this is known with certainty, non-co-operation again becomes the dominant strategy.[2] Finally, co-operators should be in a position to punish defectors, without unduly punishing themselves; if defection cannot be credibly punished then co-operation will tend to break down.

In both the prisoner's dilemma game and the assurance game there are two possible equilibria, one involving mutual defection and the other mutual co-operation. Moreover, both models face the 'bootstrap' problem referred to earlier, namely that if some minimal threshold of social capital does not exist in sociey already, it is very likely that the non-co-operative equilibrium will be reached, even in situations where actors are not predisposed to free-ride (Whiteley and Seyd, 1996).

The de Tocqueville model of social capital is attractive since it shows how voluntary organisations can help to provide social capital and sustain co-operation once it has begun. The value of organisation is that it ensures that individuals interact on a continuing basis, which creates a repeat game, one of the requirements for co-operation to develop. Similarly, the very existence of the organisation implies that its members have to some extent overcome the myopia problem, and are willing to subsume immediate payoffs to longer-term goals. Most importantly, an organisation can sanction non-co-operation by the members using various formal and informal mechanisms, with the threat of expulsion being the ultimate deterrent.

Organisation can solve the bootstrap problem for its members, since the risk of exploitation by fellow members is minimised by creating barriers to entry, and by distrusting outsiders. Potential members can be vetted carefully before they are allowed in, and sanctioned if they attempt to free-ride. Clearly, a widespread network of organisations in a society will solve the collective action problem for those citizens who are members of these organisations. Unfortunately, this does not solve the bootstrap problem, since there is still the issue of spreading social capital beyond the group. A society characterised by a proliferation of mutually suspicious groups, each operating barriers to exclude the others, is likely to face as many difficulties as a 'Hobbesian' society of individualists. Social capital will be equally deficient in both.[3]

It is possible to appeal to the idea that cross-cutting cleavages exist in society (Rae and Taylor, 1970) which solve the problem of spreading social capital beyond the group; if individuals are members of a variety of different groups, none of which have exclusive memberships, then trust acquired from interactions within these different groups might be dispersed throughout society by the existence of overlapping memberships. However, this interesting idea is not so much a solution to the problem, as a description of the kind of society which is possible if social capital is widespread.

The problem is that if social capital is very limited in society, then it is unlikely that such cross-cutting groups will form in the first place. The fact that barriers to entry will be needed in order to protect the group members from exploitation by outsiders, inherently restricts the development of such overlapping groups. This point implies that the de Tocqueville model has only a limited ability to explain the creation of social capital. It might be good at explaining how social capital is created beyond the minimum threshold, but it is not able to explain how social capital might emerge from a primeval state of non-co-operation. It is clear that additional mechanisms are needed to generate the threshold levels of social capital which are required if voluntary organisations are to prosper and mutual trust in society is to be created.

ALTERNATIVE MODELS OF THE CREATION OF SOCIAL CAPITAL

There are three alternative models of the creation of social capital which we will examine in this chapter, and which might explain how societies overcome the bootstrap problem. These models are rooted in psychological variables associated with the personalities and moral codes of individuals, variables which lie outside conventional rational choice accounts of collective action.

The three explanations to be examined are, first, that social capital is generated by the personality characteristics of individuals, which are formed principally by processes of socialisation within the family, although they may be influenced by interactions between individuals within voluntary organisations. Second, that social capital is generated by an individual's normative beliefs and moral codes, which again may be influenced by voluntary activities, but which are ultimately an internalised set of values acquired in early life. Finally, social capital is created by membership of 'imaginary' communities, that is communities which individuals identify with, but which they never actually interact with on a face-to-face basis. We discuss each of these in turn.

The idea that willingness to trust other people depends on the personality of the individual is a commonplace observation, and it is surprising that it has been ignored in accounts of the formation of social capital. This is discussed mainly in the psychology literature and is concerned with individual personalities and values (Bagley and Verma, 1986; Wrightsman, 1994; Allen, 1994). The present analysis focuses on one aspect of this issue, the relationship between life satisfaction and trust in other people. The hypothesis is that individuals who are generally happy and satisfied with their lives are more likely to trust other people than individuals who are unhappy or dissatisfied. The influence of life satisfaction on politics has been discussed mainly by Inglehart (1977, 1990; see also Abramson and Inglehart, 1995) in relation to post-materialist values and political culture. Inglehart suggests that life satisfaction is a durable component of basic values arguing that:

> Overall life satisfaction is part of a broad syndrome of attitudes reflecting whether one has a relatively positive or negative attitude towards the world in which one lives. Life satisfaction, happiness, interpersonal trust, and whether one supports radical social change or defends one's existing society all tend to go together in a cultural cluster.
>
> (1990: 43)

Thus if most individuals in a society are happy and satisfied with their lives, that should generate high levels of trust and social capital in that society.

The second model of the creation of social capital suggests that social trust is rooted in individual morality. A major criticism of the de Tocqueville model is that it has little to say about the role of morality in the creation of social capital (see Uslaner in this volume). Ever since the publication of John Rawls's *Theory of Justice* (1971) debates about morality have been at the forefront of political theory. Recently James Q. Wilson (1993) has suggested that the empirical evidence from anthropology and psychology supports the proposition that human beings have a universal 'moral sense', which pervades their thinking and conditions their attitudes to other people. In an echo of an argument developed by the biologist Richard Dawkins (1989), Wilson suggests that this moral sense has an adaptive value in the evolution of the species. He writes: 'If it did not, natural selection would have worked against people who had such useless traits as sympathy, self-control, or a desire for fairness and in favor of those with the opposite tendencies' (Wilson, 1993: 23).

The present hypothesis is that individuals with a strong moral sense which promotes empathy with others and a desire for fairness, are likely to be predisposed to trust other people in comparison with individuals who lack such a moral sense. Thus a society in which most people believe in strong moral principles should also have high levels of social capital. Again, relationships between individuals within voluntary organisations may enhance such a moral sense, but it is not the source of such morality, which in Wilson's view derives originally from altruistic behaviour towards kinship groups.

Finally, the role of 'imaginary' communities in politics arises out of the social-psychological literature on social identity (Tajfel, 1981; Johnston and Hewston,

1990) which demonstrates that individuals have a strong tendency to identify with one group rather than another, even when the perceptual cues which establish such identities are extremely tenuous. The experimental evidence shows that individuals do not need to interact directly with other members of the preferred group in order to identify with it.

Some of the most powerful political emotions involve identification with imaginary communities such as the nation state, or an ethnic group. These are imaginary communities because they are generally so large and geographically dispersed that individuals have no chance of interacting with anything other than a small minority of the other members. Of course it could be argued that members of such communities, such as citizens of a nation state, interact with each other on a daily basis. But these other citizens are usually highly unrepresentative of the community as a whole, making it hard to argue that identification with that community originates from interacting with a representative sample of its members.

To illustrate this point, most Americans are very patriotic and identify strongly with the symbols of the United States as a nation.[4] Yet they do not interact on a face-to-face basis with a representative sample of fellow Americans in the manner of the de Tocqueville model. This is because, like all industrial societies, the United States is very stratified by ethnic, class, and geographical cleavages which make neighbourhoods and friendship groups highly segmented. Patriotism is clearly not based on face-to-face interaction with fellow citizens, but largely derives from socialisation processes in early life, and the strong desire for human beings to identify with larger symbols which give meaning to their lives (Edelman, 1985; Taylor, 1992).

This suggest the hypothesis that individuals who most strongly identify with the imaginary community of the nation are likely to trust other people more than individuals who do not identify in this way. In other words, strong patriots are more trusting towards their fellow citizens than weak patriots, which implies that a strongly patriotic society should have more social capital than a society which lacks such patriotism.

In the light of this discussion we go on to specify a model of the origins of social capital, as a means of testing these alternative ideas in the next section.

MODELLING THE ORIGINS OF SOCIAL CAPITAL

In the light of the above discussion we can specify the alternative models of the origins of social capital in the following equation:

$$S_i = a_i + b_1 L_i + b_2 M_i + b_3 V_i + b_4 I_i + b_5 SES_i + b_6 AGE_i + b_7 SEX_i$$
$$+ b_8 IDEOL_i + b_9 RELIG_i + u_i \tag{1}$$

where:
S_i = Individual i's level of social capital (social trust)
L_i = Individual i's level of life satisfaction

M_i = The strength of individual i's moral code
V_i = Individual i's level of voluntary activity
I_i = Individual i's level of patriotism, or committment to the nation state
SES_i = Individual i's Socio-Economic Status
AGE_i = Individual i's Age
SEX_i = 1 if the respondent is male, 0 otherwise
$IDEOL_i$ = Individual i's ideological score on a left-right scale
$RELIG_i$ = Individual i's religiosity
u_i = is an error term, where $E(u_i) = \sigma_u^2$

The model contains indicators of the four different models of the origins of social capital, and the effects are estimated in the presence of controls for various confounding factors. The model is estimated using all 45 countries in the 1990–3 World Values Survey, which provides a sample of more than 92,000 cases (see ICPSR, 1994).

The dependent variable in the model measures the willingness of an individual to trust their fellow citizens, and so it focuses on one key aspect of Coleman's notion of social capital. It can be seen from Table 2.1 that in response to a general question about trusting other people almost two-thirds of the respondents felt that you 'Can't be too careful'. Thus the global level of social capital is not that high.

Table 2.1 The indicators of social capital in the World Values Survey ($N = 92,141$)

Question: Generally speaking, would you say that most people can be trusted or that you can't be too careful in dealing with people?

	Percentage
Most people can be trusted	35.5
Can't be too careful	64.5

Question: How much do you trust various groups of people?

a) Your family

Trust them completely	79.8
Trust them a little	14.2
Neither trust nor distrust them	2.6
Do not trust them very much	1.4
Do not trust them at all	1.9

b) Your own nationals

Trust them completely	19.7
Trust them a little	44.4
Neither trust nor distrust them	22.7
Do not trust them very much	10.2
Do not trust them at all	3.1

Table 2.2 The indicators of voluntary activism in the World Values Survey

Question: Please look carefully at the following list of voluntary organisations and activities and say which, if any, you are currently doing unpaid voluntary work for.

Type of organisation	*Percentage of respondents doing voluntary work*
Social welfare services for elderly, handicapped or deprived people	4.8
Religious or church organisation	7.5
Education, arts, music or cultural activities	3.9
Trade union	3.0
Political parties or groups	3.1
Local community action on issues like poverty, employment, housing, racial equality	1.5
Third world development or human rights	1.0
Conservation, the environment, ecology	1.6
Professional association	2.6
Youth work (e.g. scouts, guides, youth clubs, etc.)	3.6

However, respondents were very likely to trust members of their own family, and to a lesser extent their own nationals, and so willingness to trust others depends, not surprisingly, on their perceived closeness. These three measures of social capital can be combined into a scale, and this is used as the dependent variable S_i in the model.[5]

The indicators used to construct the voluntary activism scale V_i which is used to test the de Tocqueville model appear in Table 2.2. In the survey, respondents were asked if they are members of different voluntary organisations, and this is followed up by a question eliciting if they do unpaid work for this organisation. It is possible that simply being a member of an organisation will bring them into frequent contact with other members, allowing the processes of interaction which underpin the de Tocqueville model to take place. However, it is more likely that many members of such organisations never interact with each other in a significant way, because they are not active. Many of them will simply be 'credit card' members, who pay their dues and do little else. Accordingly, we use the question which asks if they do unpaid voluntary work for the organisation to provide the best indicator of the de Tocqueville model. Voluntary work will bring them into frequent contact with other people, and such interactions should build trust and social capital. Again these indicators can be combined into an overall scale.[6]

The indicators of life satisfaction appear in Table 2.3, and it is evident that most people are happy and satisfied with their lives, jobs and homes. The last three indicators used a ten-point scale along which respondents assigned themselves, depending on how satisfied or disatissfied they are with their life or job. Not surprisingly, they are happier with their home lives than with their work lives, but there is not much difference between the two. The mean score in the second

Table 2.3 Personality variables in the World Values Survey

Question: Taking all things together, would you say you are . . .

	Percentages
Very happy	22.1
Quite happy	58.7
Not very happy	16.8
Not at all happy	2.4

Question: All things considered, how satisfied are you with your life as a whole these days?

Dissatisfied								*Satisfied*	
1	2	3	4	5	6	7	8	9	10
Per cent 2.7	1.6	3.9	4.8	12.1	11.0	15.4	22.4	12.4	13.6

Mean = 6.9

Question: Overall, how satisfied or dissatisfied are you with your job?

Dissatisfied								*Satisfied*	
1	2	3	4	5	6	7	8	9	10
Per cent 2.4	1.5	3.6	4.4	10.5	10.2	14.1	21.2	13.5	18.5

Mean = 7.2

Question: Overall, how satisfied or dissatisfied are you with your home life?

Dissatisfied								*Satisfied*	
1	2	3	4	5	6	7	8	9	10
Per cent 2.2	1.2	2.4	3.2	8.5	8.0	12.9	22.4	16.4	22.7

Mean = 7.6

indicator shows that most people are reasonably satisfied with life, but that a minority are rather dissatisfied. These four items can be combined into an overall personal satisfaction/dissatisfaction scale.[7]

The indicators of personal morality are a series of ten-point scales in which the respondent is asked if various courses of action are justifiable or not. The indicators in the table are a selection from a battery of 24 items in the World Values Survey, chosen because they all correlate significantly with one of the factors extracted from a principal components analysis of all items.[8] This particular factor was chosen because it relates to everyday aspects of morality, as can be seen in Table 2.4, and concerns the sort of moral choices that individuals face on a day-to-day basis. The other three factors loaded significantly on items which were essentially wider political issues like attitudes to abortion and euthanasia, or were remote from everyday experience such as attitudes to political assassinations and killing in self-defence.

Table 2.4 The indicators of morality in the World Values Survey

Question: Please tell me for each of the following statements whether you think it can always be justified, never be justified, or something in between?

Claiming government benefits which you are not entitled to

Never									*Always*
1	2	3	4	5	6	7	8	9	10
Per cent 64.9	9.3	6.8	3.6	5.2	2.7	1.7	1.6	0.9	3.3

Mean = 2.26

Avoiding a fare on public transport

Never									*Always*
1	2	3	4	5	6	7	8	9	10
Per cent 63.4	9.8	7.5	4.2	5.8	2.9	1.7	1.5	0.8	2.3

Mean = 2.23

Cheating on tax if you have the chance

Never									*Always*
1	2	3	4	5	6	7	8	9	10
Per cent 59.7	9.6	8.0	4.6	6.7	3.0	2.2	2.1	1.1	3.2

Mean = 2.46

Buying something you knew was stolen

Never									*Always*
1	2	3	4	5	6	7	8	9	10
Per cent 76.1	8.1	4.9	2.6	3.4	1.5	0.9	0.8	0.4	1.2

Mean = 1.72

Keeping money that you have found

Never									*Always*
1	2	3	4	5	6	7	8	9	10
Per cent 48.4	9.3	8.8	5.1	10.1	4.7	3.1	3.1	1.7	5.7

Mean = 3.10

Lying in your own interest

Never									*Always*
1	2	3	4	5	6	7	8	9	10
Per cent 48.2	11.9	10.9	6.0	9.8	4.7	2.9	2.4	1.0	2.3

Mean = 2.77

Interestingly enough, most people are rather moralistic, as can be seen in Table 2.4, since on average they score well towards the low end of the ten-point scale, which implies that they feel that the activities cannot be justified. Even so, there are some interesting differences in responses; people are much more relaxed about keeping money that they have found than they are about buying stolen goods, and feel easier about telling lies in their own interest than about avoiding paying the fare on public transport.

Table 2.5 measures the strength of the respondents' identification with the 'imaginary' community of the nation state. This is measured in two different ways: first, by asking individuals which geographical area they identify with most strongly from a list of such areas, which includes their town, their region, their nation, their continent, and the world as a whole. Some 29.4 per cent of respondents selected the nation as the primary region with which they identified.[9] The nation is the best example of an imaginary community because, as mentioned earlier, individuals will never interact on a face-to-face basis with the overwhelming majority of their fellow citizens, and the cleavages in a society make it unlikely that they will even interact with a representatitve sample of them either. Thus nationalism cannot be explained by the same processes which can generate social capital in small groups.[10]

In addition to the predictors associated with the different models, equation (1) contains a number of social background variables designed to be controls in this model. The first control for the socio-economic status of the respondent, consists of the factor scores from a principal components analysis of three different variables: age completing education, income and social class.[11] The research on political participation shows that high socio-economic status individuals are more likely to participate in politics than individuals with low status (Verba and Nie, 1972; Barnes and Kaase, 1979; Parry, Moyser and Day, 1992). By implication, an individual with high socio-economic status may also have more political capital, making it necessary to control for their social status

Table 2.5 The indicators of strength of attachment to the imaginary community of the nation in the World Values Survey

Question: Which of these geographical groups would you say you belong to first of all? (A list of groups follows)	
	Percentages
Respondents who choose the nation as the first group	29.4
Respondents who did not choose the nation	70.6
Question: How proud are you to be (name of nation)?	
Very proud	45.6
Quite proud	37.3
Not very proud	12.6
Not at all proud	4.5

in order to get an accurate picture of the relationship between social capital and the predictor variables.

Age is also an important social background variable in the context of the study of basic values like trust. Inglehart's (1990) analysis of post-materialist values is rooted in the idea that basic values are inculcated into individuals during their pre-adult years (1990: 68–71). Applying this idea to the present context, it seems likely that different age cohorts will have different levels of social trust because of differences in the political and economic environments which existed in society during their formative years. The precise relationship between social trust and pre-adult experiences is unclear; it may be that economic insecurity in early life promotes solidarity and a willingness to trust other people, or it may be that the reverse is true. Whatever these relationships are, it is clearly important to control for age in the model.

The control for gender derives from the hypothesis that men and women have markedly different experiences during their early socialisation (Randall, 1987), and this might influence their willingness to trust other people, and therefore their levels of social capital. The control for ideology reflects the fact that basic ideological beliefs may well influence the individual's willingness to trust other people. It is debatable, but nonetheless plausible, that ideologies of the left which emphasise co-operation, solidarity, and fraternity are more likely to develop an ethos of trust in other people, than ideologies of the right which emphasise individualism, competition, and a social-Darwinist struggle for survival. Thus a control for ideology is essential.

Finally, there is a control for religiosity in the model, since like leftist ideology, strong religious beliefs should generally create an ethos which is trusting, altruistic, and favourably inclined towards co-operation with other people. De Tocqueville (1990: 300–3) regarded religion as one of the key factors which sustained American democracy by promoting republican and democratic values. More recent research shows that religiosity promotes volunteering (Wuthnow, 1991), which is, of course, the mechanism for creating social capital in the de Tocqueville model.

Table 2.6 contains information about the social background variables which are controls in the model. It can be seen that just over 40 per cent of the respondents in the World Values Survey left full-time education at age 16 or under, and a surprisingly large 23 per cent continued full-time education from the age of 21 and beyond. Some 47 per cent of respondents are middle class, with only 20 per cent being unskilled working class. The average age of respondents in the survey was 42 years old, although the median age is 40 indicating that age profiles are skewed slightly by the presence of older respondents. It is also noteworthy that there were rather more females in the survey than males.

Religiosity is measured using a ten-point scale of attitudes to the importance of God. Respondents showed a marked tendency to think that God is important in their lives, with the mean score being just over 6.0. Similarly, the mean score on the left–right ideology self-placement scale was 5.5, indicating a slight tendency for respondents to place themselves on the right, rather than the left of the scale.

In the light of this discussion, we consider estimates of the model next.

Table 2.6 Social background control variables in the model

Socio-economic status	Percentages
Age finished education:	
Less than 12 years	9.8
13 to 16 years	31.9
17 to 20 years	34.5
21 or more	22.7
Income scale:	
Lowest two deciles	20.3
Next two deciles	26.0
Next two deciles	24.6
Next two deciles	18.7
Top two deciles	10.2
Socio-economic scale:	
Upper, upper middle class	14.2
Middle-class non-manual workers	32.9
Skilled and semi-skilled manual workers	32.3
Unskilled manual workers	20.2
Age:	
21 or under	9.5
22 to 30	20.8
31 to 40	21.1
41 to 50	16.8
51 to 60	14.4
61 to 70	11.6
70 plus	5.8
Sex:	
Male	47.6
Female	52.4

Religiosity:

Attitudes to God

	God not at all important								God very important	
	1	2	3	4	5	6	7	8	9	10
Per cent	15.4	5.7	6.2	4.7	10.6	7.5	7.6	9.5	6.6	26.3

Mean = 6.13

Ideology

Left-right self-placement

	Left									Right
	1	2	3	4	5	6	7	8	9	10
Per cent	4.2	3.6	9.0	10.3	29.6	15.1	10.6	9.2	3.3	5.2

Mean = 5.47

ESTIMATING THE MODEL

The first model estimates in Table 2.7, relate to the four determinants of social capital, and the second model includes the same variables with the additional control variables. It is noteworthy that all the standardised coefficients are highly significant in both models, except for the ideology variable in model two.[12]

The strongest effect relates to the influence of life satisfaction, or the personality index, on the social capital scale. Thus respondents who are very satisfied with their lives are more trusting than respondents who are dissatisfied with life. The second strongest effect is that of the imaginary community scale, which implies that very patriotic respondents are more trusting of their fellow citizens than respondents who do not share their strong identification with the nation. The third strongest effect is associated with the moral index, which implies that individuals with strong moral values are more trusting than individuals without such values.[13] Of the four determinants of social capital, the voluntary activity scale, which is the direct operationalisation of the de Tocqueville model, has the weakest effect.

The standardised coefficients suggest that satisfaction with life is more than three times stronger in influencing social capital than voluntary activity. Similarly, identification with the imaginary community of the nation is also nearly three times more influential than voluntary activity in promoting social

Table 2.7 Social capital regression models (standardised coefficients, *t* ratios in parentheses)

Predictor variables		
Personality index	0.19***	0.17***
(Satisfaction with life)	(30.8)	(19.0)
Moral index	−0.12***	−0.13***
	(19.0)	(14.2)
Voluntary activity scale	0.04***	0.05***
	(5.7)	(5.0)
Imaginary community scale	0.13***	0.14***
	(21.2)	(14.9)
Socio-economic status scale	–	0.07***
		(7.2)
Age	–	0.05***
		(5.1)
Sex	–	0.05***
		(5.4)
Ideology	–	0.00
		(0.4)
Religiosity	–	−0.03***
		(2.9)
R^2	0.09	0.10
F ratio	601.2***	142.1***

Note
$p < 0.01 =$***$; p < 0.05 =$** .

capital. A similar point can be made about the moral index. Thus up to this point the results suggest that the de Tocqueville model is the weakest of the four models of social capital creation. Interactions between individuals in voluntary organisations may play a role in creating social capital, but it is not as important as the psychological variables, whose origins might be attributed chiefly to socialisation processes within the family and to pre-adulthood experiences.

The control variables, though significant, have very little influence on the magnitude of the effects of the social capital variables. They suggest, however, that high-status individuals are more trusting than low-status individuals; the elderly are more trusting than the young; males are more trusting than females; and the religious more trusting than the atheists.[14]

One striking feature of the social capital models in Table 2.7 is that the goodness of fit of the models is very low. In fact, recent methodological work casts doubt on the importance of a goodness of fit statistic like R^2 in judging the effectiveness of regression models in general (Charezma and Deadman, 1992: 15–20). However, the poor fit does raise questions about the ability of these models to capture the determinants of social capital.

One possible explanation of the poor fit relates to the nature of the world values data, since as the principal investigators point out, the quality of the data varies considerably across nations, particularly since both random and quota samples were used in the data collection (ICPSR, 1994).[15] Thus one possible explanation for the low goodness of fit is that the data has a lot of measurement error and 'noise' in comparison with most other surveys of this type.

One way of dealing with this problem is to look at country-specific regression, for nations in which the quality of the data collection might be expected to be high. For this reason, and because it is interesting to examine country-specific regressions anyway, the social capital model is estimated for five separate countries in Table 2.8. The results in Table 2.8 indicate that the low goodness of fit in the model cannot really be attributed to methodological problems in specific country surveys, since the goodness of fit for each of these countries is also relatively low.

Despite this point, common patterns emerge in the models. The strongest effect is always due to the life satisfaction scale, and the imaginary community scale is always the second most important estimate, with the exception of Germany. The moral index is also stronger than the voluntary activity scale in every model, except for Britain. However, the voluntary activity scale is significant in every model except, again, for Germany. In this case the largest effect is found in Italy and the weakest, apart from Germany, is in Britain. Overall the findings seem to indicate that the de Tocqueville model, while significant, has the least impact of the four alternative models on social capital.

Apart from these findings the control variables have a mixed effect in these country-specific models. Age is significant in four of the countries, but it switches signs in Italy, so in that country the young are more trusting than the elderly. Socio-economic status is significant in three of the countries, as are ideology and religion. In general the estimates suggest that the four variables play a significant

Table 2.8 Social capital regression models by country (standardised coefficients, *t* ratios in parentheses)

Predictor variables	United States	France	Britain	Italy	Germany
	(1,948)	(2,629)	(2,713)	(2,182)	(2,526)
Personality index (satisfaction with life)	0.22*** (6.4)	0.16*** (4.5)	0.15*** (5.0)	0.18*** (4.8)	0.26*** (7.3)
Moral index	−0.10*** (3.0)	−0.14*** (3.8)	0.05 (1.5)	−0.17*** (4.5)	−0.13*** (3.5)
Voluntary activity scale	0.07** (2.0)	0.07* (1.9)	0.06** (2.1)	0.10*** (2.6)	0.03 (0.8)
Imaginary community scale	0.10*** (3.0)	0.16*** (4.5)	0.10*** (3.2)	0.19*** (5.0)	0.11*** (3.3)
Socio-economic status scale	0.13*** (3.7)	0.09*** (2.7)	0.06* (1.9)	0.04 (1.2)	0.00 (0.2)
Age	0.08** (2.3)	0.02 (0.5)	0.07** (2.1)	−0.09** (2.4)	0.06* (1.9)
Sex	0.02 (0.5)	0.03 (1.0)	0.08** (2.5)	0.06* (1.8)	0.06* (1.7)
Ideology	−0.09*** (2.7)	−0.16*** (4.7)	0.03 (1.0)	−0.17*** (4.6)	0.01 (0.2)
Religiosity	0.07* (1.9)	0.10*** (2.7)	0.04 (1.3)	0.08** (2.0)	0.04 (1.0)
R^2	0.17	0.12	0.07	0.15	0.15
F ratio	17.70***	12.32***	9.68***	13.30***	15.62***

Note
$p < 0.01$ = ***; $p < 0.05$ = **; $p < 0.10$ = *.

role in the creation of social capital, but there is much about variations in social capital across individuals and countries which is not captured by the model.

DISCUSSION AND CONCLUSIONS

Research into social capital suggests that face-to-face interactions within voluntary organisations is the best way to create trust, although as we have seen, there is a bootstrap problem which cannot be theorised away in standard rational choice accounts of this process. It appears, however, that individual values and psychological variables which can only be explained effectively by socialisation processes within the family and in early adulthood experiences, play a more important role in creating social capital than does face-to-face interaction within organisations. Not only is the de Tocqueville model theoretically incomplete, it appears to be rather weak empirically in comparison with other plausible accounts of the creation of social capital.

Overall, while rival models appear to be more persuasive than the de Tocqueville model, it is clear that none of the models is capable of explaining more than a modest amount of variance in social trust, either within specific nations or cross-nationally. Thus it appears we are still some way away from providing a comprehensive explanation of the formation of social capital in the modern world.

Further research should aim to clarify the concept so that the distinct components of social capital relating to trusting other individuals, organisations and the state can be identified. Similarly, further research into the personality correlates of trust may clarify the mechanisms by which trust is created and sustained. It appears from Table 2.1 that personal knowledge of others, particularly family members, enhances trust so that interpersonal relationships are clearly very important to the formation of social capital. But it is possible that such relationships enhance some forms of trust while inhibiting others. After all, some people are untrustworthy, and getting to know them will reveal this fact rather than encourage people to trust them more. A detailed analysis of the micro-level processes which create and sustain trust is clearly the way forward towards a greater understanding of the genesis of social capital.

Notes

1 The textbook example of a collective good is national defence. Once government has provided defence its 'consumption' by an individual does not reduce the supply available to others, and the individual benefits from national defence, even if he or she has not contributed to its provision in the first place.

2 If both actors know for example that the game will be repeated 100 times, then it is rational for them not to co-operate on the last play of the game. If this is true, then it is also true of the 99th, 98th, etc. plays of the game. Certainty about when the game ends re-establishes defection as the dominant strategy, by this process of backwards induction.

3 Fukuyama, for example, argues that there is a widespread lack of trust outside the family in Chinese society, and for that reason most commerce in that society is based on the extended family (1995: 74–5). Thus family relationships, which are 'closed' in Coleman's terminology, sanction untrustworthy behaviour. However, in Fukuyama's view this severely limits the ability of Chinese societies to develop large-scale corporations.

4 In the 45 countries included in the World Values Survey Americans were the second highest ranked in patriotism in response to the question: 'How proud are you to be ...?' Some 76.8 per cent of Americans were very proud to be that nationality, in contrast with only 27.9 per cent of Russian respondents who were proud to be Russians.

5 A principal components analysis of the three variables produced one significant factor (eigenvalue = 1.37), which explained 45.7 per cent of the variance, and the

factor score from this analysis were used to create the scale.

6 A principal components analysis of these variables produced three significant components (eigenvalues > 1.0). The first principal component had an eigenvalue of 2.06 and explained 20.6 per cent of the variance; all ten variables are correlated with this component with loadings greater than 0.35. So the factor score from this first component is used as the voluntary activism scale.

7 A principal components analysis of the four variables produced one significant component (eigenvalue = 2.27), which explained 56.8 per cent of the variance; each variable was correlated with this component with a loading of at least 0.67 or greater, thus the factor score from this component is used as the personality scale.

8 One signficant factor (eigenvalue = 2.89) is extracted from a principal components analysis of the six items, and it explains 48.1 per cent of the variance in the data.

9 This was the second most popular geographical region with which people identified. Some 40.7 per cent of respondents identified first with their town or locality, but this is much less of an imaginary community for people living in rural areas, since they are likely to know many of their fellow villagers.

10 Given that most people have rather tenuous links to fellow citizens, dying for one's country is a highly irrational act.

11 The eigenvalue from the principal components analysis of these three variables was 1.68 and it explained 56 per cent of the variance in these indicators.

12 With this very large sample the t ratios are unusually large in any case.

13 The negative coefficient on the moral scale is purely an artefact of the coding.

14 The coefficient of the religiosity variable is negative, but again this is an artefact of the coding.

15 In the preamble to the codebook they write: 'This study was carried out with limited funds, with fieldwork supported by sources within the given country in most cases. Almost inevitably, the quality of the sample varies from one society to another, since both available funding and survey research infrastructure are limited in many of the societies included here' (ICPSR, 1994: 7).

References

Abramson, Paul R. and Ronald Inglehart (1995) *Value Change in Global Perspective*, Ann Arbor: The University of Michigan Press.

Allen, Bem. P. (1994) *Personality Theories*, Boston: Allyn and Bacon.

Axelrod, Robert (1984) *The Evolution of Co-operation*, New York: Basic Books.

Bagley, Christopher and Gajendra K. Verma (1986) *Personality, Cognition and Values*, London: Macmillan.

Barnes, Samual and Max Kaase (1979) *Political Action: Mass Participation in Five Western Democracies*, Beverly Hills: Sage.

Charemza, Wojciech W. and Derek F. Deadman (1992) *New Directions in Econometric Practice*, Aldershot: Edward Elgar.

Chong, Dennis (1991) *Collective Action and the Civil Rights Movement*, Chicago: The University of Chicago Press.

Coleman, James S. (1988) 'Social Capital in the Creation of Human Capital', *American Journal of Sociology*, vol 94 Supplement, s95–s119.

Coleman, James S. (1990) *Foundations of Social Theory*, Cambridge, MA: Belknap Press.

Dawkins, Richard (1989) *The Selfish Gene*, Oxford: Oxford University Press.

Edelman, Murray (1985) *The Symbolic Uses of Politics*, Urbana and Chicago: University of Illinois Press.

Fukuyama, Francis (1995) *Trust: The Social Virtues and the Creation of Prosperity*, London: Hamish Hamilton.

Hardin, Russell (1971) 'Collective Action as An Agreeable N-Prisoner's Dilemma'. *Behavioral Science*, 16: 472–81.

ICPSR, (1994) *World Values Survey Codebook, 1981–1984 and 1990–1993*. Ann Arbor: Inter-University Consortium for Political and Social Research.

Inglehart, Ronald (1977) *The Silent Revolution; Changing Values and Political Styles Among Western Publics*, Princeton, NJ: Princeton University Press.

Inglehart, Ronald (1990) *Culture Shift in Advanced Industrial Society*, Princeton, NJ: Princeton University Press.

Johnston, L. and M. Hewstone (1990) 'Intergroup Contact: Social Identity and Social Cognition' in (eds) D. Abrams and M.A. Hogg, *Social Identity Theory: Constructive and Critical Advances*, Hemel Hempstead: Harvester Wheatsheaf.

Marwell, Gerald and Pamela Oliver (1993) *The Critical Mass in Collective Action*, Cambridge: Cambridge University Press.

Parry, Geraint, George Moyser and Neil Day (1992) *Political Participation and Democracy in Britain*, Cambridge: Cambridge University Press.

Putnam, Robert (1993) *Making Democracy Work: Civic Traditions in Modern Italy*, Princeton, NJ: Princeton University Press.

Putnam, Robert (1995) 'Tuning In, Tuning Out: The Strange Disappearance of Social Capital in America', *Political Science and Politics*, vol 28, no 4: 664–83.

Rae, Douglas and Michael Taylor (1970) *The Analysis of Political Cleavages*, New Haven: Yale University Press.

Randall, Vicky (1987) *Women and Politics*, London: Macmillan.

Rasmussen, Eric (1989) *Games and Information*, Oxford: Basil Blackwell.

Rawls, John (1971) *A Theory of Justice*, Cambridge, MA: Harvard University Press.

Samuelson, Paul (1954) 'The Pure Theory of Public Expenditure', *Review of Economics and Statistics*, 36: 387–9.

Tajfel, H. (1981) *Human Groups and Social Categories: Studies in Social Psychology*, Cambridge: Cambridge University Press.

Taylor, Charles (1992) *Sources of the Self: The Making of the Modern Identity*, Cambridge: Cambridge University Press.

Taylor, Michael (1976) *Anarchy and Cooperation*, London: John Wiley.

Tocqueville, Alexis de (1990) *Democracy in America, Volume 1*, New York: Vintage Books.

Verba, Sidney and Norman Nie (1972) *Participation in America: Political Democracy and Social Equality*, New York: Harper and Row.

Whiteley, Paul F., and Patrick Seyd (1996) 'Political Capital Formation, Party Activism and Participation in Voluntary Organizations in Britain', paper presented at the Workshop on Social Involvement, Voluntary Associations, and Democratic Politics, ECPR Joint Sessions, 28 March to 3 April, Oslo, Norway.

Wilson, James Q. (1993) *The Moral Sense*, New York: Free Press.

Wrightsman, Lawrence S. (1994) *Adult Personality Development. Volume 1 Theories and Concepts*, London: Sage.

Wuthnow, Robert (1991) *Acts of Compassion*, Princeton, NJ: Princeton University Press.

3 Collective action theory and the analysis of social capital

Jacint Jordana

INTRODUCTION

The notion of social capital, defined by the rational choice sociologist James Coleman (1988, 1990) and developed by Robert Putnam in his *Making Democracy Work* (1993), has achieved broad acceptance among social scientists working in various disciplines. Social capital, identified narrowly with the presence of trust in societies, has been understood as a key factor in explaining economic growth and political stability, among other phenomena. An important element in explaining the success enjoyed by Robert Putnam's book over recent years, is that it manages to provide a certain connection, albeit somewhat strained, between the comparative politics perspective and the rational choice approach, while indicating their possible interrelationships. Perhaps for this reason, and despite the problems unresolved by Putnam and picked up by numerous critics, discussion and controversy have not stopped.[1] In this respect, this chapter aims to review some rational choice models of collective action, in order to discuss the possibilities of reinforcing the theoretical basis of the concept of social capital.

The concept of social capital in *Making Democracy Work* represents an attempt to establish a clear link between the rational choice theoretical approaches to the analysis of society and the tradition of comparative analysis in political science. The latter has provided significant understanding of cultural, social, and institutional differences among countries with regard to politics, however, this contribution has been through one-off works or through an occasional masterpiece of analysis and interpretation. In any case, the combination of detailed historical information and robust empirical research methods have been the hallmark of the modern comparative approach to political science. These works, usually backed up by sophisticated methods of statistical investigation and an imaginative and direct approach to the subject, have produced high-quality empirical research.[2] The rational choice approach, with its characteristic attempt to develop deductive structures for the analysis of political and social phenomena akin to the analytical approach employed in economics (expected utility, theory of public goods, game theory, etc.), has promoted formal reasoning and methodological individualism in political science. Nevertheless, as we will see later, this approach has often suffered from a weak link to empirical evidence which proponents attempt to explain in terms of analytical modelling and empirical proof. Otherwise, very attractive and often counter-intuitive propositions have been developed with these more deductive approaches, as the study of the dynamics of co-operation shows.

In Putnam's case, his synthesis at the beginning of the 1990s is based on the empirical sophistication of many decades of behavioural studies, formal arguments derived from the economic analysis of politics and recent revisions reinterpreting the role of institutions in social and political processes. This type of work basically represents a point of arrival in that it provides an interpretation of the whole and identifies black boxes whose internal workings are not explained by our current theories and interpretations. *Making Democracy Work* provides a link between these two main approaches through the notion of social capital. However, it employs the notion in an ambiguous way and the arguments are not developed very tightly as in most work in rational choice, which is the focus the author explicitly adopts (Putnam, 1993: 167). As we will later analyse, this has produced some theoretical confusions. Nevertheless, it is precisely this ambiguity which allows a reconstruction of the concept and which yields a definition which differs from the prosaic notion developed previously by Coleman.[3] While it is unclear whether this step is sufficient in itself to offer something conceptually new, the whole debate allows us to explore the theoretical grey area between the two camps. The intention is to facilitate the development of new theoretical structures without casting off those which have proved fruitful in analysing social and political problems in the past.

NOTES ON THE BASIS OF THE RATIONAL CHOICE APPROACH

Rational choice approaches in political science expanded during the 1980s and became well established and recognised in the 1990s. However, the method and models developed by political analysts are now to some extent quite different from the dominant art of model building in economics. The spell of economic reasoning that characterised much rational choice theorising in previous decades is wearing off, and more and more political scientists and sociologists working within this field are developing models from the ground up, instead of deriving them from the postulates of neo-classical economics. In doing so, a re-examination of classical problems of political science, such as the dynamics of group identity or the limits of government action, among many other questions, are now much more important in current rational choice theory. In this respect, the attention given to the concept of social capital by different rational choice analysts is another example of this shift.

Some basic aspects or core assumptions unify and identify the tasks of rational choice theorising in sociology and political science. One rather narrow approach developed by Buchanan (1986), and the public choice school sees rational choice as the science of self-interested individuals involved in a complex exchange of public goods in the context of political institutions. Self-interest is the core trait of *Homo Oeconomicus*, but for a more general approach to rational choice theory building we need only the assumption of rationality to act as a common hypothesis controlling human action. Although self-interest usually prevails as an assumption, altruism, or several other non-egoistic motivations or orientations of interest can also be utilised in these models (Scharpf, 1989; Margolis, 1982).

Linked to the hypothesis of rationality, a second core assumption of the rational choice approach is the principle of methodological individualism. This is the consideration that 'in the social sciences, the elementary events are individual human actions, including mental acts such as belief formation' (Elster, 1989a: 3), and it includes the attempt to construct social and political theory on the basis of individuals' intentions, looking for the micro-foundations in each theoretical explanation. Finally, a third core element is the analysis of interaction. Several families of models exists: collective action, market equilibrium, bargaining, social institutions, etc., but they always employ a theoretical procedure that connects a model of man (which includes the rational choice assumptions) with the aggregate results and propositions about the global effects of the interactions in a concrete model.

These elements are broadly shared by the new generations of rational choice scholars. However, the focus among authors varies significantly, and many specific new areas of work have developed recently. In comparison to the economic approach to society, in these new areas some distinguished research interests are more present than others, such as the dominance of non-market based explanations, a careful attention to how actors construct their preferences, or the frequent integration in models of public and private organisations which aggregate and intermediate interests. Also, in political science the need for the empirical plausibility of rational choice models has been more broadly considered. This involves formulating hypotheses in terms which are approachable from an empirical standpoint, bearing in mind alternative and competing explanations and the possible appearance of anomalies. Thus, the sensitivity towards knowledge of political reality tends to prevail when the demands made by the rational choice method (axiomatic-deductive) for generalisation prove too onerous. Also, the discrepancies between various notions of rationality have been sufficiently clarified (see for example Anand, 1993), and it is now more usual to find consistent applications and the adoption of more specific definitions of rationality, related to aspects such as the evaluation of information, maximising behaviour, learning, or the theory of utility, among many others.

It is also worth noting that a new field has appeared (currently attracting considerable attention), focusing the analysis of many hypotheses regarding the role of tastes, frames, and preferences in rational choice (Quartone and Tversky, 1988). The experimental study of behaviour, usually linked to the validation of the formal properties of rational behaviour, has furnished many intriguing results, and it represents a very significant challenge for the present development of the standard theory of rationality (Sen, 1987, 1993).

Making models and experimenting with simulations, it is important to consider the choice of a strategy to provide explanations. Even though there may be preferences one way or the other, some authors adopt a more down-to-earth approach (looking for regularities or laws which can be observed), while others go for a more theoretical line of attack (developing theories capable of providing predictions, regardless of how realistic their premises are). There is a long-term methodological debate in the whole social sciences field, related to realism. On the one side there are those who defend realistic assumptions as a necessary point of departure for a theory's fundamental statements (Nagel, 1963), and on the other those more concerned with the predictive capabilities of a theory, regardless of the assumptions (Friedman, 1953). This debate remains unresolved, and also from the rational choice approach the different positions only reflect a much broader discussion about the basis of scientific knowledge. However, it is interesting to recall the position of Jon Elster, who indicated bounds to the debate, arguing that many explanations in the social sciences can only 'isolate tendencies, propensities and mechanisms and show that they have implications for behaviour [but] what they are more rarely able to do is to state necessary and sufficient conditions under which the various mechanisms are switched on' (1989a: 9).

Employing the rational choice approach to explore the micro-foundations that could support the concept of social capital is a task that fits in well with the direction signalled by Elster. As we better understand the mechanisms that lead to or have influenced the emergence and stability of social capital, the better equipped we are to explain how social capital works (though it does not automatically mean that a complete theory of social capital could be built from these foundations).

A CLOSER LOOK AT THE CONCEPT: SOCIAL CAPITAL AND INSTITUTIONS

What type of relation exists between social capital and institutions? As we will show, this relationship is not sufficiently clear in Putnam's book. However, this is not a specific problem of the concept of social capital, but of the narrow sense of the concept of institutions as it is employed by Putnam. If a conceptually richer idea of institutions were articulated it would be easier to grasp the theory behind the link between institutions and social capital. In this respect, it is not surprising that authors, like Eleanor Ostrom, employ a much more refined concept of institutions and go into this relationship in greater depth.

Radically stated, *Making Democracy Work* presents a quite anti-institutional perspective. In its argument, the book does not strongly define institutions beyond viewing them as political and administrative bodies. Thus, we could deduce from the book that institutions simply mean the rules operating on decision-making processes and resource allocation, as well as public-sector management bodies. Adopting this interpretation, institutions merely play a passive role as intermediate variables and are devoid of explicative value. Much of this reasoning is based on the argument that one can compare northern and southern Italy because the 'institutional change' variable is constant and the same for the whole of the country. Hence from his point of view, Putnam argues that the performance difference he finds cannot be attributed to differences in institutional 'formulae'.

Against this quite naive 'anti-institutional' standpoint, one has to say that recent political science has produced important advances in the analysis of institutions, both in terms of systematisation and conceptualisation, and in the development of specific models. Different reviewers coincide in signalling the existence of three different types of neo-institutionalism, the rational choice approach constituting one of them.[4] From this approach, the idea of institution is broadly understood as a mechanism to enforce rules and formal norms, by means of socially open and explicitly formulated incentives. This type of neo-institutionalism based on rational choice thus focuses on issues like where the analysis of rules, routines and norms embedded in institutions is connected with the postulate of individual reasoning in the explanation on policy outcomes (Kato, 1996), or how the transmission of information on political and social contexts limits the scope for independent individual decisions to certain forms of behaviour (Ostrom, 1991).

Generally speaking, the task of institutions is to allocate resources and information more efficiently (or just differently), as a global alternative to the market (or more widely, to non-guided allocation mechanisms) in a given society, or even as a way to reduce the effects of market failure or market absence in specific cases.[5] However, the concrete mechanisms that institutions employ to do this are very diverse, ranging from isolated norms to the establishment of formal organisations. The outcomes produced are also quite different, signalling the most appropriate response, giving selective incentives, or also offering public goods (that are defined by the characteristics of non-rivalness and non-excludability), among other socially oriented interventions.

In his work, Putnam does not elaborate on his own concept of institution. Probably, the discussion of a more theoretical concept of institutions would have led on to an exploration of differences between organisations acting as political institutions (throughout Italy and thus not important in the analysis) and informal rules acting as institutions to promote co-operation (that produce key differences between northern and southern Italy). However, this would have done much to complicate the clear-cut conclusions reached in *Making Democracy Work*. Why is there not much more clarification related to the use of the concept of institutions? Presumably, this was not actually possible in the logic of Putnam's work, because his attractive theoretical framework was extremely strained. Putnam's concept of social capital shares several important elements in common: (a) an updated transposition of classical concepts or intuitions, present in the work of one or more of the great social thinkers; (b) conceptual positioning at a crossroad which is sufficiently ambiguous from the standpoint of various theoretical perspectives and traditions to provide apparently attractive issues or subjects for further study; (c) this ambiguity extends to the core of the theory and its conceptual proposition: there is no extensive theory, rather we have to build it up from the outside in order to make it workable; and (d) its appeal lies in a re-hash of those ideas which seem important and which we realise are lacking in the models or usual interpretations of more than one school of thought. Put simply, it boils down to finding and naming a large 'black box' in the current political science debate.

Despite its relative ambiguity, the formulation of Putnam's central propositions suggest a line of theoretical development with certain roots in the rational choice approach and its methodological individualist view, but with a strong interest in linking the individual micro-level theorising with macro-level socio-political explanations (looking for indicators explaining economic-institutional performance). Because of the very limited exploration of this rational choice neo-institutionalist path (basically only in some sections of Chapter 6 of *Making Democracy Work*), it might also appear that Putnam is merely scouting the area, and concentrating his efforts on the identification of explanatory factors which determine the extent to which social capital is present in different situations. At the same time he is keeping the lid firmly on the 'black box' this concept represents and abstaining from analytical methods which would allow development of his micro-foundations.[6]

The key variable *Making Democracy Work* employs to demonstrate the existence of social capital is trust, which makes co-operation easier (i.e., it reduces information costs and misperceptions). This means outlining a theoretical framework about the type of collective action necessary to sustain social capital, in other words, a theory of collective action that explains social capital. However, in the book there are no clear theoretical statements that link the existence of tertiary associations (like soccer clubs or choral groups) with the emergence of trust, and generalised trust with the existence of civic communities whose members always co-operate, even when they do not know one another personally. Maybe the problem is, as Margaret Levi (1996: 46–7) points out, that 'Putnam never offers a precise definition of trust . . . Sometimes he uses the term trust to suggest confident expectations due to knowledge, institutional arrangements, or incentive systems that enable an individual to predict behaviour and thus count on someone else. In other cases, trust seems to imply a general morality within the community itself'.

Nevertheless, it is possible to find more concrete theoretical rational choice developments on social capital and institutions in other authors who do not attempt to establish the interpretation that Putnam does. Usually, these authors focus on social capital at the micro level based on three analytical pillars: processes of social interaction and the management of externalities; the logic and dynamics of associative forms (taking place in groups and networks); and finally, the extent of citizens' participation in collective action. This takes us on to various aspects of basic social theory, in particular micro social theory.

First, it is worth recalling Coleman's conception of social capital. He pointed out that social capital refers to something present in the relations among persons, and that it 'is not a single entity, but a variety of different entities having two characteristics in common: They all consist of some aspect of social structure, and they facilitate certain actions of individuals who are within the structure' (1990: 302).

Thus, for Coleman the definition of social capital owes its cohesion to the relational effects present in the social structure that benefit the actors, but not to their causes, because these could be quite different. As an example of these effects, generalised trust is one of the most recognised. So, from a macro-level point of view one could analyse the level of trustworthiness in a given society, or also the actual extent of obligations held (Coleman, 1990: 306). Other effects were also pointed out by Coleman, such as the information potential that relationships could provide (saving the time to get the source) or the relational benefits (market opportunities, job offers, etc.) that organisations could produce for their members as a by-product of their activities.

An example that introduces institutional analysis is exemplified by the work of Eleanor Ostrom (1994, 1995), who argues that crafting institutions is one form of investing in social capital, because this represents an activity which focuses on 'the arrangement of human resources to improve flows of future income' (1995: 131). In her articles, Ostrom understands an institution as a set of rules to allocate benefits and assign payments, because she is considering how to manage self-governing complex systems, like water or other common resources. However, the idea of creating social capital by bargaining among individuals for whom rules will be adopted to create self-government might be broadly generalised. The interaction to negotiate rules is an investment beyond bargaining: it also implies more personal relationships, and more secure institutions could easily appear in return. However, this example is probably not applicable to all types of institutions, because the effects of social capital could be very different depending on the specific incentives that institutions provide to individuals for involvement in their supervision. Human inequality, input heterogeneity and attention to different human needs are some variables, among others, that institutions have to take into account when they are created and adapted to changing environments. However, following this line of thought is not easy, because, as Ostrom says: 'the lack of theories of institutional change and development based on firm micro-foundations has limited the capacity of . . . understanding how individuals develop their own social capital in the form of rules by self-governing communities' (1995: 133).

An entirely different conception of social capital was developed by Ronald Burt is his book *Structural Holes* (1992). Although it is not a proper rational choice argument, but one based on the network analysis approach, close links could be established in some aspects with institutions and rational choice. For Burt, social capital 'is a quality created between people [it] predicts that returns to intelligence, education, and seniority depend in some part on a person's location in the social structure of a market or hierarchy' (1997: 339).

For example, he predicts that in a firm, managers with more social capital get higher returns because they are able to benefit, thanks to their relationships, from the existing disconnections between individuals in specific social or market structures. Linked with the formulation of these structural settings, it seems clear that Burt also assumes maximising behaviour by individuals, in order to obtain the maximum return on their assets.

Thus, from this point of view institutions play a key role in how social capital is accumulated, maintained or consumed by individuals. Norms embedded in formal institutions, or also institutionalised informal rules, could create a particular behaviour by individuals as to how they manage their social capital. As Burt says 'the structural holes argument defines social capital in terms of the information and control advantages of being the broker in relations between people otherwise disconnected in social structure' (1997: 340).

It is no secret that there are many institutions in our society designed to control the danger of excessive inequality in terms of social capital, or also the reverse, to promote and reward the continuous appearance of brokers to connect structural holes. For example, with regard to the first point there are regulations in all countries which cover the use of privileged information by public officials; also, in many labour markets the tendency to give broad publicity to job creation increases the prestige of the employer. An example of the latter effect is when incentives are given by government to create new professions, like entrepreneurial promoter or community assistant, in order to improve economic activity.

From these arguments, it is easy to deduce that there are many different ways to produce or control social capital, ranging from the unexpected by-product of spontaneous co-operation to the intentional intervention by government. After all, as Coleman cautioned, the causes of social capital are much more diverse than the effects. Nevertheless, this does not necessarily hinder the attempt to interpret the logic of some of the most important mechanisms present in the production of social capital in our contemporary societies. A parallel can be drawn with the variety of social capital effects insofar as there are also different routes to the creation of social capital. Many analysts, however, tend to focus their research into social capital at the macro level and only address the effects of generalised trust.

Thus, considering the research on social capital (both causes and effects) as a wide field, it might be possible to develop concrete interpretations about some causes or variables that intervene in the production of social capital. The analysis of how concrete institutions matter for social capital represents then one of these collections of possible interpretations. Other groups of mechanisms to be analysed could be, for example, the appearance of social capital when co-operation takes place in non-formal settings, for obtaining specific public goods. From the rational choice approach, these questions are strongly linked to the theory of collective action, as we will see when reviewing the links existing between institutions and co-operation.

In Putnam's case, he does not discuss the models in greater depth, and concentrates on concepts like trust and community, as basic ingredients of his notion of social capital, although these are more effects than causes. Putnam's institutionalist argument related to the interpretation of social capital is consistent, in the sense that some formal institutions (like the public administration or other bodies) do not matter for explaining social capital differences. However, the argument is rather circumscribed, because other institutionalist mechanisms are not considered explicitly in the comparative analysis of the causes of social capital. Instead the explanation of the origins of co-operation from a rational choice point of view, is brought out as is the notion that co-operation will develop if there is sufficient social capital in a given society. Nevertheless, if we look for an analysis of what causes social capital, only two concrete mechanisms are suggested; one relates to the formation of trust, linked to the enforcing role of norms of reciprocity and mutual help, and the other relates to the existence of civic networks which dominate horizontal co-ordination (Putnam *et al.*, 1993: 171–7). The latter mechanism seems close to social network analysis as it is empirically approached in the book, but the former mechanism is clearly a common element of neo-institutionalist analysis, but is not discussed empirically in the study. The question is then, whether any complete interpretation about how social capital works could be based simply on analysing one single mechanism. In my opinion, it is necessary to introduce more complexity for global interpretations. However, it is also necessary to discover how other specific mechanisms for creating social capital operate. Reproducing explanations such as the mechanism of horizontal networks of civic engagement for other cases, would improve interpretations, and allow one to consider the basic mechanisms that produce social capital in a given society as a whole.

In other words, as Levi points out *Making Democracy Work* has no 'theory that identifies the mechanism of production, maintenance and growth of social capital' (1996: 46), and from this point of view, we have no theoretical basis to argue that some type of voluntary associations produce networks of horizontal interactions that reinforce co-operative attitudes. It would be necessary to look for such arguments. Neo-institutionalist approaches are the common field for these attempts to re-conceptualise and improve the theoretical basis of co-operation and collective action. This line of theoretical research presents some interesting ways of constructing relatively complex models of collective action. These models introduce new variables, besides the size of the group, such as the combination of different types of behaviour, or the possibility of misperceptions relative to the nature of the public good in dispute, as endogenous factors in the type of interaction taking place among the actors. Next, we need to specify how the rational choice models of collective action and institutional analysis could help to explain the production of some forms of social capital. It is not the aim to re-construct Putnam's propositions in more formal terms, but to some extent, trying to maintain the attractive macro-causal links signalled by Putnam in a context where more consistent micro foundations could be established.[7]

MODELS OF COLLECTIVE ACTION AND SOCIAL CAPITAL

One of the spin-offs from the study of basic human co-operation and conflict in the rational choice tradition, has been that it has facilitated further development of the theory of collective action. This theory, or to be more precise, groups of models and theories, which are somewhat general and ambiguous as to the limits of their application, take basic co-operation models as their starting point. However, it develops applications in the area of phenomena which involve a relatively large number of participants, and it always involves some type of public or semi-public good.[8] Explaining why co-operation in large groups succeeded was a recurrent empirical problem, but it was not a theoretical problem until Olson (1965) proposed his interpretation about the tendency towards co-operative failure in large groups, because of the contradiction between individual rationality and collective optimisation. The identification of free-rider behaviour, and the argument that only second-order solutions (such as selective incentives) could resolve the problem of co-operation were two of the most significant hypotheses that Mancur Olson introduced in his *The Logic of Collective Action*. However, from a present-day perspective the cases of Olson's free-rider hypothesis, or the second-order solution can both basically be interpreted as black boxes for highly complex phenomena – the dynamics and problems of collective action, which we are only just beginning to understand (i.e., Lichbach, 1996; Heckathorn, 1996).

During the 1970s and the 1980s, the theory of collective action came of age and it became clear that there were many different problems concerning the analysis of collective action and there was no unique dilemma. Instead of the prisoner's dilemma game representing the essence of collective action, as many of Olson's interpreters supposed, new developments indicated many different problems of collective action existed and that each problem could be isolated and examined using the appropriate variables and games. Chong (1991), for example, examining the civil rights movement, suggested that the assurance game provided a better representation of the dilemmas of such a movement than does the prisoner's dilemma. This situation is also summarised by Lichbach: 'there is no one characteristic collective action situation, no one model of all collective action problems. Different situations embody different assumptions which lead to different models that hold different conclusions' (Lichbach, 1996: 50).

This was a typical confusion, because of many different game theoretical models that were always based on the prisoner's dilemma game, as the basic logic shaping the structure of interaction. They attempted, with different approaches, to find out the basic 'logic of collective action', instead of considering that all the models focused on different questions, without stumbling on the possibility of searching and applying other games for the problems of collective action (Udehn, 1996: 210–24). To some extent the same thing happened with Olson's thesis concerning the tendency to failure in large groups and the importance of selective incentives in avoiding free-rider behaviour. It was only towards the end of the 1980s that the problem was made conceptually clearer, and analysts understood that this tendency was completely dependent on the nature of the public good in dispute. When the number of collective action participants increases, but public good production costs are stable or falling and benefits do not diminish, then the possibility of co-operation paradoxically increases with the size of the group (Kerr, 1989; Kimura, 1989).

In this section I would like to indicate some possible lines for further development and extension of the ideas on social capital in the context of current theories and models of collective action. First, I will briefly review recent developments in collective action theory. Second, I will focus on the social capital mechanism introduced by Putnam, the role of voluntary associations and the networks of civic engagement, with a view to improving the linkages between micro and macro analysis. Then, I will develop some ideas which explore the analytical opportunities of collective action theory for a better understanding of some social capital mechanisms. Implicitly it is assumed that the collective action models which take the rational choice principle as their starting point may be sufficiently flexible for this purpose.

Historically, there have been many discussions of the dominance of hierarchical and coercive solutions as a traditional way of resolving the dilemmas of collective action (e.g. Hobbes' solution). These solutions usually transform the collective action problems, but they are not always feasible or reasonable, given a concrete public good in dispute. On the contrary, in contexts where no hierarchy exists (or the adequate centralised institutions), co-operative behaviour has to appear from above, without central co-ordination. We have then three other types of solution. First, there is the communitarian solution, that means resolving the collective action problem in a decentralised way, with the help of communal institutions (promoting aspects such as common values, reputation, low time discount, etc.) that externally impose co-operative behaviour on the actors (Taylor, 1987). Second, there is a contractual solution when individuals directly negotiate on how to produce a specific public good or collectively bargain and agree over the type of institution they need to overcome their co-operation dilemmas. Third, there is a market solution when the provision of a public good appears without bargaining among actors, from a spontaneous order, in which unco-ordinated expectations lead to co-operation, producing an equilibrium that sustains contributions to collective action by individuals (Lichbach, 1996).

With regard to the market solution, the question is how to explain the appearance of co-operation given a situation in which an individual rationally decides not to co-operate. The standard model of the prisoner's dilemma in game theory predicts a non-co-operative equilibrium when there is no threat of a coercive sanction, and stresses the predominance of individual desertion strategies from a rational maximiser point of view. The paradox appears when empirical findings show that voluntary co-operation often occurs, contradicting the predictions of game theory. However, the paradox produced by these predictions depends on the specific assumptions on which the model is based, because some small variations in the standard assumptions of the prisoner's dilemma could increase the likelihood of co-operation (i.e., there is a folk theorem signalling that co-operation appears in a prisoner's dilemma when the game is played infinitely). The less restrictive the assumptions the broader the model's application and the better the fit to a wide range of empirical problems, which weakens the apparent paradox.[9] From this point of view, the basic problem is to find which assumptions of the model could be relaxed, without a loss of internal consistency or a diminishing of its explanatory capability.

However, from within the rational choice approach, there appear to be two other ways to elucidate the mentioned paradox. First, again focusing on a market solution to the dilemma, it is possible that the game the actors actually play is not the same as the one assumed, and the non-co-operative equilibrium does not apply so strongly to the actual game.[10] The other way consists of adopting a non-market solution, which means looking for the existence of norms or other mechanisms that increase the likelihood of co-operation for individuals, changing the actors' behaviour or his evaluation of risks in making choices.

The three procedures mentioned for studying collective action problems within the rational choice approach, have been broadly developed over the last few years, and have tried to resolve the co-operation paradoxes mentioned above. In this sense, the use of game theory analysis as a common language is a basic aspect that all strategies share. We conclude that game theory, as a basic and general mathematical theory applied to explain the factors conditioning human co-operation, does not resolve the problems, thus co-operation occurs much more often than predicted by the models. It seems clear that game theory has a contribution to make to social theory but cannot supplant it. Among these different procedures, the first conceptualises collective action as a prisoner's dilemma game, in which the basic question is how to find co-operative solutions, to make individual and collective rationality coincide. Thus, the discussion about the possibility of co-operation concentrates on the conditions of the game and the variables that intervene in the model.

There are dozens of proposals in which researchers try to improve their understanding of how basic prisoner's dilemma co-operation problems work, and affect collective action mechanisms, where a large number of participants are involved. Many formal ways of theorising have been explored: from one-shot games to finite repeated games, from simultaneous choices to sequential ones, from complete to incomplete information assumptions, from time discounting to reduced time discounting, etc., and the combination of some of these modifications in new models has also been frequently attempted (Kreps, 1991; Binmore, 1990). More specifically, the number of active co-operators with respect to all the participants in the game is also an important variable for different models of collective action (Shelling, 1973; Hardin, 1982).

Another way of exploring prisoner's dilemma co-operation problems consists in developing computer simulations of the evolution of repeated games, where models with different characteristics of individuals (choice mechanism, preferences about risk, time discount rate, information costs, etc.) are checked, with tournaments of individual players. There is an important distinction in these types of collective action models between forward-looking decision making, where the expectations of rational or limited rational individuals about future pay-offs guide present choices, and backward-looking decision-making models, where actors continuously learn from the past by adjusting their present choices, in the light of their past successes and failures (Macy, 1993; Heckathorn, 1996).

Instead of analysing the character of individuals in collective action settings, another way to investigate the problems of co-operation in computer simulations of repeated prisoner's dilemma games is to compare sequential strategies available to players. This is the case of evolutionary models in which actors are competing with different sequential strategies, where the most successful individual winning strategies tend to proliferate, while the less successful tend to disappear. It is supposed that actors perceive the best sequential strategies from observational learning, and imitate them. Axelrod's model (1984) of a prisoner's dilemma competition is well-known and is one where prudent co-operative attitudes, the tit-for-tat strategy, wins out against much more aggressive strategies.

Second, there is another strategy that focuses on the analysis of collective action problems. It is based on the identification of different social dilemmas as the representations of different collective action frameworks. The underlying idea is that depending on the nature of the public good that created a collective action problem, the structure of the setting for its provision (in which collective action occurs) will be different, because the structural incentives and the way actors need to organise for the production of its imputs could differ. Thus, there could be a collection of different collective action problems, based on the nature of the public good involved. Here structures of interaction are understood as different social dilemmas that underlie collective action. There are some inventories of the dilemmas arising in collective action systems, usually presented in basic form as pure game theoretical models which could be complicated by introducing new variables in the model.

In a recent proposal, Heckathorn (1996) tried to prove that: 'exactly five games characterise the structure of opposed and complementary interests within which collective action occurs' (1996: 252–3). The dilemmas or games are the chicken game, the assurance game, the altruist's dilemma, the privileged game and the prisoner's dilemma. It depends on the relative value of the public good (the proportion between the benefits of its consumption and the aggregated costs of contributing to its production) and the shape of the production function (the relation between the proportion of public good produced and the proportion of possible contributors implied in this production) that determine which game is played by the actors. Within the different structures of interaction, we have also the possibility of analysing the effects of different attitudes derived from culture, forms of participation, etc. (e.g. absolute gains vs. relative or egalitarian gains) for the individuals involved in the dilemma. In this case, what is important to note is that different decision criteria could modify the results of the dilemma itself (see Scharpf, 1989).

Finally, a third way in which collective action theories are refined consists of expanding their explanatory focus. Looking for other approaches that could explain the actual tendency to co-operate could throw up institutionally based approaches which explain co-operation as a result of a combination of rules, attitudes, and other factors. Many institutions, when effective, easily promote co-operation among individuals, solving the problems of collective action. As it was commented earlier, hierarchical, contractual and communal institutions could resolve collective action problems in a different way. Probably, the most interesting institutions here are communal institutions, because of their decentralised and non-intentional nature (hierarchical are centralised, and contractual are intentional). From the rational choice point of view, in analysing an institutional setting, the aim is to understand the impact of institutions in combination with the models previously indicated. Considering the models, with their actors' beliefs, intentions and strategies, the basic task is finding which equilibria are possible and which ones are actually achieved.

Voluntary participation in associations, and the number of associations itself, seem to be good indicators of the existence of civic communities and networks of civic engagement which are very important in the production of social capital (Putnam *et al.*, 1993: 91–5). In addition to the excellent performance of this variable in many empirical tests (Putnam, 1995b; Deth, 1996), the theoretical reason argued by Putnam is based on the classical Tocquevillian perception about the effect that participation in associations produces on individuals' public-spiritedness. In this sense, Putnam points out that: 'Participation in civic organisations inculcates skills of co-operation as well as a sense of shared responsibility for collective endeavours' (Putnam *et al.*, 1993: 90), but he does not develop this theoretical link more strongly. In Chapter 6, by presenting the dilemmas of collective action, he highlights the point that game theory has studied lack of co-operation in a variety of situations which bear on this basic problem, but despite indicating that game theory makes this integration possible, Putnam parades this range of models without any analysis of what sets them apart and what they have in common. He does not place each model in context or take on board the idea that such a discussion might be necessary to locate his hypothesis about how social capital is produced within these analytical frameworks, for dealing with the dilemmas of collective action in associations and networks. It would be very worth while pursuing this strand to gain a deeper understanding of how social capital effectively works. To go deeper in this analysis of how social capital is effectively produced from these mechanisms would mean prising open the 'black box' of social capital a little. If we want to define and use finer indicators at the macro level we need to go back to the micro level in order to discriminate between the components which are used to build social capital and provide indicators which have a sound theoretical grounding.

Examining collective action, we could find different types of collective actors, depending which frame of reference of action for the participants dominates (it refers to where there are separate purposes or a collective purpose in the action) and how the control over the resources for the action is organised (it could be separate or collective). Typical collective action in associations combines a collective purpose, so that there exists a preference as a collective actor, and also collective control over resources and leadership, in the sense that the preferences of individuals prevail over the hierarchical organisation (Scharpf, 1997: 55–7). However, we can examine when effectively members' preferences prevail, and which conditions make the centralised control of the resources of the association easier or more difficult. This question is important because it strongly affects how collective action develops and is solved in an association. When hierarchical institutions are not relevant in an association, other types of solution to collective action problems have to emerge.

Associations constituted as formal organisations usually establish democratic voting procedures, as a sort of institutionalising of a contractual solution to their problems of collective action. Thus, many problems of collective action are resolved by mechanisms of these types, but they are not specially adequate for improving interaction. Nevertheless, what is more interesting in analysing how associations produce social capital is when communitarian institutions are used to solve collective action problems, or when self-co-ordinating collective action appears, despite the presence of structural problems in the associations' logic of collective action, given the specific public good to be produced. From Olson onwards, we knew that small groups, where face-to-face interactions are habitual, overcome the difficulties posed by spontaneous collective action more easily; also, we knew that local and neighbourhood communities usually share mutual knowledge (facts, persons, actions, etc.) which makes the adoption of social norms for the production of public goods less difficult. In addition, enjoying interaction in small groups seems to be a non-intentional result from interaction, that could reward many individuals for the direct cost of collective action. And finally, many collective action processes in small groups do not present any distinct problem, because the public good or the joint good in production consists in enjoying oneself (i.e., many sport, cultural or leisure groups).[11]

What is the mechanism that is present in all these processes of collective action? We find that in small groups, or in associations based on groups where personal interaction takes place, there are many opportunities to overcome collective action problems through individual involvement; thus, the opportunities and institutional incentives to look into, think about and learn about co-operation are bigger than the existing ones in associations which solve their collective action problems within hierarchical or voting institutional procedures.[12]

To understand how learning to co-operate in specific settings could help to improve the existing levels of social capital in a given society, we need to adapt the explanation to another mechanism, also formulated by Tocqueville, and re-examined by Elster (1997). It is the 'indirect effect', which refers to when a person learns concrete behaviour in a specific aspect of life, he or she will probably transfer this behaviour to other fields.[13] In *Democracy in America*, Tocqueville discovered that Americans transferred their attitudes from commerce to politics and vice versa, transporting the learning from associative life in one field to the other. The transfer of mental habits by each individual who experienced co-operative practice, moving from different spheres of life, could be the basic factor that contributes to the growth of social capital. This occurs as a consequence of the increasing probability that many holes in the networks of social structure could be filled, generating more interactions at lower costs, because of the individual's adoption of co-operative attitudes learned in specific settings, to many other life circumstances, including outside their original networks.

The third part of this section presents some general observations about the analytical capabilities of collective action theory for understanding specific social capital mechanisms. In his book, Putnam indicates that all societies have networks, both formal and informal of 'communication and personal exchange' and he classifies these in two large groups: horizontal networks (fabric type) and vertical networks (tape type). He qualifies the latter as a place where the agents present asymmetrical relationships which involve hierarchy and dependency, while the former group of social networks leads him to the following conclusion: 'If horizontal networks of civic engagement help participants solve dilemmas of collective action, then the more horizontally structured an organisation, the more it should foster institutional success in the broader community' (Putnam *et al.*, 1993: 175).

From a social network perspective, and taking the above distinction as a point of departure, we could summarise this by saying that social capital basically exists across social networks, being produced, used and enjoyed in interactions by individuals. However, bear in mind this suggestive argument about two different types of networks of communication and exchange and its consequences for the emergence of social capital. It is necessary to go forward from this line of reasoning to focus on the extent to which collective action models help in developing ideas, in order to establish better micro-foundations for the social capital concept. The basic theoretical question of how can social capital be created and sustained in a rational choice world is examined in this context.

We have previously seen how collective action theory could help our understanding concerning the link between the dynamics of voluntary participation in associations and the emergence of social capital. Now, trying to generalise, the aim is to establish a similar study approach, improving our understanding of the existing connection between social networks and social capital through collective action models. There is some analytical work linking social networks analysis and exchange theory with collective action theory (Macy and Flache, 1995; Marwell and Oliver, 1993; Gould, 1993), and from this perspective, it is necessary to make a clear distinction between the dynamics of collective action within specific groups and associations, and collective action in a broader community or network, or also in a whole society.[14] In this respect, it is only the latter that will be examined now.

A basic distinction between groups and networks is identified by Yamagishi and Cook, who argued that 'group-generalized exchange involves the incentive structure of an n-person prisoner's dilemma (nPD) whereas the network generalised exchange (more closely) resembles the incentive structure of an n-person assurance game (nAG)' (1993: 239, cited in Macy and Flache, 1995: 78).

However, it is not always clear if this distinction could serve for all types of situations, it refers clearly to the idea that the basic problem in both settings is not the same. In fact, while the prisoner's dilemma has only a non-co-operative equilibrium, the assurance game presents two possible equilibria: whether the players are willing to co-operate or not willing to co-operate (Sen, 1967). Thus, explaining the equilibrium reached is a matter of the dynamics of the game, and the existing signals, incentives and opportunities available to the players.

Here we need to introduce another distinction related to the level of trustworthiness that could exist in a given network. One type of trust refers to transmission of true information between individuals belonging to the network during their interactions (about actor's preferences, about commitments, etc.). This type is called 'weak trust' by Scharpf (1994), quoting from Granovetter's notion of 'weak ties' in collective action (1973). Probably this 'weak trust' represents the maximum level of trustworthiness that could be created within a network by a co-operative equilibrium in an n-person assurance game, in which all the members of the network are able to participate. Another type of trust is 'strong trust', referring to situations where actors do not pursue strategies beneficial to themselves in case these strategies negatively affect their correspondents in the interaction. It is clear that it is not possible simultaneously to maintain many interactions of this type, because of their high costs in terms of self-restraining high-value strategies. However, given the important degree of security that this type of trust involves, selected interactions in which 'strong trust' will be sustained could be very helpful for individuals' actions in a specific network. Thus, this type of interaction could not consist of n-person games, but has to be established in terms of small group games, usually dyadic or triadic games. Here it is interesting to note that Axelrod's model of a tournament in his *The Evolution of Cooperation* (1984) is based on dyadic interactions, always representing a prisoner's dilemma game, in a network of 'individuals' that move on employing diverse sequential strategies (that are imitated when they become successful).

Among the several aspects we could study in a given society, there is the network perspective, which has been explored by many scholars for decades (Cook and Whitmeyer, 1992; Scott, 1991). So, we could find networks in social and political settings, or in the economic and philanthropic aspects of life, and so on; multiple networks exist, composed of individuals or organisations that interact within their network as well as members of other networks. Probably, individuals belong to diverse networks but not always with the same level of intensity in all of them. Many relationships in existing networks require usually lower transaction costs than similar interactions taking place in anonymous settings, except when open-market conditions are really effective (then, the necessity of detailed information is greatly reduced, because price is a good indicator of quality). This is caused by the need to negotiate detailed agreements when there is no previous connection, which often become complicated to establish and are also accompanied by associated risks that are difficult to evaluate. For example, there are usually lower transaction costs using the social networks, as is the case when one is on holiday and needs to visit friends of friends, or when one meets someone recommended for a specific job. These are not always the optimal practices, but they are often sufficiently effective to choose, when one needs some type of information, help or support in contexts which the market does not supply adequately.

These procedures are possible because acting inside social networks means that the risk of opportunism is lower. And this risk is reduced thanks to two mechanisms, the small time discount manifested by the individuals that belong to the network, and the higher visibility of transactions to other members. These operating mechanisms could be recognised as a premium for the participants in the network, as Scharpf does, arguing that 'there is a premium, therefore, on relationships that allow actors to accept higher degrees of vulnerability because they are able to trust each other' (1997: 137).

The first mechanism is based on how the 'members' of the network interact. When the possibility of casual encounters among 'members' increases heavily with respect to 'non-members', it is reasonable for individuals to use different time discount measures in each type of interaction. Why does the possibility of casual encounters increase? There is not just one reason, but many. However, from an actor's point of view, it is reasonable to think that people previously known are those whom one will most probably meet in the future; from the whole network's perspective, it is possible that many signs will be present in order to identify who is in and who is not in the network, in order to promote the continuous reinvestment of the social capital generated within the network. Besides, it is clear that these practices carry significant rewards: 'membership in a network allows access to a larger number of potential partners of trustworthy interactions and thus increases the value of social capital' (Scharpf, 1997: 138).

The second mechanism is related to how reliable information circulates within the network. It is supposed that results from specific interactions among members of the network are quickly transmitted across the network using the web of relationships each individual has or, thanks to more formal procedures, to all the members forming part of it. Thus, opportunistic behaviour of any member tends to be highly visible, and this challenges the structure of rewards related to opportunistic behaviour for each actor, when we consider sequential processes of interaction, instead of one-shot games. Also, the structure of rewards for non-opportunistic behaviour transforms itself, because it increases the expected value of being confident.

After these considerations about conceptual typologies, one could return to the opposition pointed out by Putnam between the vertical (tape type) and the horizontal (fabric type) networks in a more theoretically grounded form, to produce a better understanding of how social capital is created and sustained. In this case, the theory of collective action and public goods provision is adopted as a way of explaining the different structures of interaction that appear between individuals forming part of social networks. Between anonymous market and strict hierarchy, networks represent contexts where 'weak trust' interactions are often present, because all their members simultaneously play an n-person assurance game, where co-operative equilibrium is maintained thanks to the two mechanisms mentioned above. However, in parallel to the global equlibria, people in organisations and informal social networks also present many different forms of internal interactions, and when dyadic or triadic relationships appear, it depends on different aspects of the equilibria produced (often 'strong trust' relationships). Probably the nature of the good or activity that defines the aim of the interaction would have a strong influence on the form of that interaction which takes place, although many other variables are also important to explain each concrete interaction that appears within the network.

At this point, the question is then answering to what extent it is possible to establish a theoretical link between the n-person assurance game played by all participants in the network and the small group games (in a dyadic or more complex form) that the individuals continuously play among themselves. This is an issue which lies beyond the scope of this chapter for reasons of space and subject matter. Nevertheless, I would like to point out some possible lines for its development.

The first question concerns which type of small group game predominates among the interactions of individuals who belong to a specific network. Probably, the prisoner's dilemma game has an important role, as one of the most frequent games played, but other games could be present, and we are not able to establish any hypothesis on this. However, we could try to find out which conditions would make the appearance of one or other game more probable (and also the appearance of a co-operative equilibrium in each game). A possible condition is the type of good or activity to be produced usually by the interaction (Heckathorn, 1996). Other possible conditions to introduce in the analysis are the level of inequality among the players, measured in terms of resources or information available to each player, also the type of choice function individuals employ in their shots for the game: learning from the past, forward rationality, applying hazard, coping from the others' success, etc. (Macy and Flache, 1995). Finally, we have also institutionally induced elements, like selective incentives, the use of social norms, or some type of governmental intervention, among many others.[15]

Since these different conditions are extremely complex in their interactions it is difficult to establish a comprehensive theoretical interpretation, but more modestly, it might be possible to discuss which of the conditions could best explain the appearance and existence of social capital in networks – understanding it in terms of stability and robustness of an n-person assurance game in a co-operative equilibrium. In this respect, we can keep the point that Putnam made about horizontal and vertical networks and translate it to an analysis of the degree of hierarchical dependencies existing in the network. These could be represented by strict organisational or administrative logic and by differences in the availability of information, or by an unequal distribution of resources between the individuals who are members of the network.

Then, one could plot the concrete dyadic game that individuals play on a horizontal axis, ranging the possibilities from those where it is extremely difficult to avoid the conflictive equilibria to those that strongly enforce co-operative equilibrium. As an indicator, we could use a measure like the relative value of the good produced by the interaction (the relative proportion between contribution and reward, when co-operation operates), or more complex ones related to the organisation and nature of the good's provision. On a vertical axis, we plot the inequalities among actors. Thus, we could map a basic typology of different forms taken by human interaction and then derive and interpret the different mechanisms of social capital creation and maintenance involved in promoting generalised trust and even the possibility of specifying the fitness of some 'collaborative' institutions in each case for the promotion and the stability of social capital.

From this point of view, it is possible to understand why some structures of interaction maintain or enforce the value of trust contained in the social capital of a given community, and others destroy it. As was mentioned before, generalised trust is a frame, the result of many factors that contribute to changing perceptions and decision criteria in relation to social dilemmas in which rational maximising behaviour often would mean non-co-operation. But we still need to establish a connection between the logic of co-operation in networks and the emergence of generalised trust. In this sense, Margaret Levi points out that trust is an individual belief in lowering subjective risks with slight information costs, and wonders what the mechanism that produces its emergence is (1996: 47). She suggests the existence of cognitive processes: 'Projection . . . is the psychological mechanism by which a trustworthy person projects her trustworthiness onto another; thus, the more trustworthy one is, the more likely one is to trust. In both of these cases, membership in society or team teaches one the heuristic or allows one to project safely' (Levi, 1996: 47–8).

We can observe that some type of linkage appears to exist between this 'projection' mechanism and the 'indirect' effect we spoke of in Tocqueville and Elster. This is because both consist of cognitive processes that explain different forms of diffusion of social capital. Then, within the theory of collective action, it would be possible to ask which type of interactions more intensively facilitate these cognitive processes, projecting individual propensities in many dyadic-type games, to the establishment and continuance of a co-operative equilibrium in n-person games such as the assurance game, that will represent the existence of a high level of social capital in the network. Given that so many networks exist, the more interconnected they are, the more extended the social capital in a given society will be.

CONCLUDING REMARKS

As we have seen, at the micro level it is essential to distinguish the various forms of social capital production and discuss how to identify and measure them. Avoiding cross-referencing errors, and clarifying what really makes up groups of phenomena, in turn, permits one to find and clearly define what makes up the concept at the macro level. For example, Brehm and Rahn (1997) in their empirical findings reach the conclusion that in the field of political participation it is possible to establish that the macro-causal relationship flows strongly from political participation to trust, being much lower in the opposite direction, from trust to participation. Why is it in this direction? Only by looking for concrete mechanisms at the micro level, and developing hypotheses for each case, will it be possible to understand why the relationship operates in this way.

We find another example in an interesting article by Mancur Olson (1987), who highlights an idea about the causes of failure of aid to underdeveloped countries. He refers to the lack of organisational experience in these countries as the key variable explaining why their public administration bodies and also the international organisations in the field experience extremely low success rates in the policies they carry out. Thus, promoting organisational learning seems a basic ingredient to improving the politico-economic performance levels of under-developed countries, because it would help these societies to cast off their dominant tribal, clientele or clan relationships. In fact, Olson's concept of organisational experience runs parallel to Putnam's concept of social capital, but Olson also introduces a normative dimension. He argues that it is necessary to adopt institutions that respond to the level of organisational experience existing in a country. In other words, we could say that institutions work differently depending on the organisational settings each country presents, and we have to choose the best institutional design given a social capital level. With this hypothesis in mind, a micro-analysis of how social capital is produced in networks and organisations would provide lessons for designing institutions that will help to increase the actual level of trustworthiness.

Introducing more theoretical background in the analysis of social capital formation at the micro level, as we noted briefly in this chapter, could help to improve our understanding of how social capital is present in our societies, and to what extent it could be enforced. Therefore, it would be also possible to discuss Putnam's hypothesis that in general all societies tend towards two types of equilibrium: the co-operative, and the untrusting and opportunistic, each possessing pathways which reinforce their respective equilibrium states, as he concludes: 'Once in either of these two settings, rational actors have an incentive to act consistently with its rules. History determines which of these two stable outcomes characterises any given society' (Putnam *et al.*, 1993: 178).

Meanwhile, in the absence of multiple equilibria theories of social capital, this is not much help in seeking explanations and merely suggests some 'path-dependent' dynamics (Levi, 1996: 46), that in many other countries may not apply.

Recently, there has been a debate about the need to seek micro foundations in explanations and to employ formal methods in building explicative theories for political science. Then, several authors examined the results produced by the rational choice model as applied to politics, understanding the latter as a conventional scientific activity, and tried to establish some methodological leanings (Green and Shapiro, 1994). As we have seen, the analysis of social capital represents an applied field in which rational choice approaches could help us to understand basic aspects of its logic, improving our capacity to deal with this intriguing concept. However, some methodological points about rational choice represent issues of a controversial nature and make these applications difficult, and for this reason it is worth bearing in mind for further discussion the possible usefulness of these models in lending support for the social capital concept.

We deal with just three aspects related to this type of problem, aiming to make clear that they do not impede rational choice theorising, but introduce many caveats to the appearance of simplicity that traditionally has characterised this approach. One methodological point consists in the attempts to make explicative formulations less oriented by the method. Instead of adducing a universal principle (rationality) as the inspiration for constructing a single body of deductive laws, one should employ a somewhat more inductive concept; the development of medium level theoretical generalisations as a step towards building higher level, wide-embracing theories. For this reason, the possible failure to build a universal theory covering the social sciences should not hinder the task of theorising. On the contrary, it should facilitate theorising as an intermediate task in reconciling empirical knowledge with the grand schemes we employ to order our interpretation of social phenomena. Another important point refers to the instrumental adoption of the hypothesis of rationality in explaining individual behaviour. Even conceding a certain pre-eminence to the explicative value of rationality, one must avoid 'rationalisation' of theories and models and the introduction of further behavioural and theoretical principles (Barry, 1982). If this means reducing the internal consistency of models and making them excessively indeterminate, the way to discriminate among them is by intensifying and improving their empirical comparisons. This is the key to developing theoretical generalisations if they are to answer the question of understanding politics (Green and Shapiro, 1995: 119). The problem is that there is no common set of rules for building models based on rationality assumptions as applied to political and social fields.

A third point to mention refers to the so-called bootstrap paradox, or how to explain the origins of co-operation, the 'effective' first initial step, when rationality dictates non-co-operation. In my opinion, this is more a methodological problem than a theoretical one for the rational choice approach. Many scholars pointed out this paradox as the big question, the Achilles' heel of this approach, because any explanation of how co-operation appears, including the role of incentives, institutions or coercion, requires a previous upper-order explanation of how external factors conditioning co-operation have been created and sustained by rational individuals. It is supposed that (simulating a backward induction) these individuals always confront the same problem concerning the contradiction between individual rationality dictating non-co-operation and the beneficial collective purposes that co-operation could provide.

It is clear that in philosophical terms, the paradox exists, and could provoke worthwhile insights to the limits of rationality in the social sciences. However, for the current tasks of model building in rational choice, it is not a very central problem to solve. The first reason is that the global perspective is not affected: we have seen that different games can be played in the co-operation processes, and the paradox only applies to the standard prisoner's dilemma game. Thus, the paradox is limited to a specific, albeit quite important, range of empirical phenomena. The second reason refers to the consistency of rational choice models. When we introduce second- or third-order variables in the model to explain co-operation (like specific institutional arrangements), the basic problem is not the endogenous explanation of these new variables (generating an infinite causal chain), but the maintenance of a genuine constraint on the role of external variables, avoiding 'ad hoc' explanations and limiting the basic hypotheses to the strictly necessary ones, in order to provide coherent and attractive explanations.

There is also a third reason why one should not consider the paradox as a persistent theoretical problem. This is because many arguments are provided to solve this question quite well, and usually they consist in investigating 'combinations of solutions' (Lichbach, 1996: chapter 7). Understanding social order as an eminently complex reality, where multiple factors interact constantly, many authors have adopted ways of modelling in which actors present mixed motivations. Elster (1989b: 49) thus suggests that they are essential for co-operation: 'certain motivations act as catalysts for others, while the latter act as multiplicators for the former'. Collectively, different authors combine other types of solutions, making dozens of distinct proposals, ranging from the more basic atomistic collective action to sophisticated induced processes of co-operation, in specific social settings.

Finally, one should recall the argument that social capital is an explicative variable in economic performance and democratic quality and not the other way round. This idea is extremely important if we want to think of society in global terms, although analytically we ought to separate society into different spheres. In this sense, thinking of more integrated social sciences, it is worthwhile ending with one of Coleman's thoughts on the concept, which puts our problems into sharp relief: 'whether social capital will come to be as useful a quantitative concept in social science as are the concepts of financial capital, physical capital, and human capital remains to be seen; its current value lies primarily in its usefulness for qualitative analyses of social systems and for those quantitative analyses that employ qualitative indicators' (Coleman, 1990: 305–6).

Notes

1   The concept has attracted heavy criticisms such as those made by Sidney Tarrow (1996) in his article for the *American Political Science Review*, or in the contributions for the special issue of *Politics and Society* (1996) devoted to Putnam's book. Setting aside the notion's intrinsic theoretical merits, the reasons for the social capital wide dissemination are intriguing. Perhaps part of the explanation lies in the problems the social sciences are currently experiencing in putting forward new and interesting interpretative models of political and social reality following the resounding failure of the great unifying models of the 1980s. However this is more a sociological than a scientific issue and I do not intend to explore it here.

2   For discussions of the profiles and the limits to the traditional kind of comparative analysis in political science, see among others, the reading of Dogan and Kazancigil (1994) or Schmitter's (1991) essay.

3   See chapter 12 of Coleman's work, *Foundations of Social Theory* (1990: 300–21). Among others, Coleman also mentions an article by the French sociologist Pierre Bourdieu (1980), as one of the first to employ the concept of social capital in a similar way.

4   Fresh reviews of the different approaches to institutions in contemporary political science can be found in Hall and Taylor (1996) and Kato (1996).

5   A type of institution, for example public organisations that assign resources. From Coase's theorem, it is possible to argue that these organisations could be socially

more efficient than market mechanisms in the sense that they internalise more externalities (Papandreou, 1994: 64). Another example is the argument of North (1990: 43) that some formal institutions may lower the costs of expressing preferences (like the tenure for judges).

6   Some of Putnam's later articles take this direction more strongly, looking for other long-term macro variables such as time spent watching TV or variations in membership in associations, in order to explain how societies retain, increase or lose their social capital (Putnam, 1995a, 1995b).

7   To explain differences in social capital Putnam *et al.* indicate that 'collaborative institutions elsewhere seem to work more effectively' (1993: 166–7) referring to the problems of lack of trust in southern Italy. It is precisely here that Putnam makes a couple of conceptual leaps just after explicitly introducing the notion of social capital. First, he stops worrying about how to explain institutional change, and second, without recalling the relationship developed by Ostrom and others between institutional concepts and rational choice, he then centres his interest on understanding why 'collaborative institutions' work with varying degrees of success in different areas. However, what is quite unclear is the relationship between the much more specific content of formal political and administrative institutions (which are identical in northern and southern Italy) and the generic concept of 'collaborative institutions', that possibly includes informal norms – like reciprocity – and sanctions as well as several types of formal associations and social networks, among many other things.

8   See for example the reviews of Pamela Oliver (1993) or Todd Sandler (1992).

9   As examples of different proposals, see among others Brewer and Kramer (1986), Fleishman (1988), McDaniel and Sistrunk (1991), Kondo (1990), Marwell and Oliver (1993) or Macy (1989, 1993).

10 In game theory, it is necessary to make the hypothesis that the actors really have the beliefs that the analysts consider in their models (Scharpf, 1997: 6.)

11 However, this activity does not represent any private good, because it maintains the rivalry quality. Non-excludability, the other property of public goods, is not completely present in these cases (nor can you always exclude anyone from enjoying an activity as a participant). For this reason, type of activities implies more properly a joint good than a pure public good.

12 In this sense, Putnam identifies 'civic commitment networks' as an example of horizontal networks and considers neighbourhood associations, choirs, co-ops, sports clubs or political parties as organisations of this nature. But here he makes a conceptual leap in the theory and daringly jumps from discussing social networks in the abstract to specific types of association, without providing many supporting arguments (1993: 174–6).

13 As Elster insists, it is necessary that a mechanism is not deterministic, because it could often appear in an individual simultaneously with other mechanisms, acting in the opposite way, which could block the expected effect (Elster, 1997).

14. This is the type of distinction that Putnam does not establish in his analysis of social capital, conducing him to a conceptual leap in examining the logic of civic engagement.

15. Remain the logic of second-order solutions to collective action (Heckathorn, 1996).

References

Anand, Paul (1993): *Foundations of Rational Choice under Risk. An Essay on the Philosophy of Mathematical Economics*, Oxford: Oxford University Press.

Axelrod, Robert (1984): *The Evolution of Cooperation*, New York: Basic Books.

Barry, Brian (1982): 'Methodology versus Ideology. The "Economic Approach" Revisited', in E. Ostrom (Ed.), *Strategies of Political Inquiry*, Beverly Hills: Sage.

Binmore, Ken (1990): *Essays on the Foundations of Game Theory*, Oxford: Basil Blackwell.

Bourdieu, Pierre (1980): 'Le capital social. Notes provisoires', *Actes de la recherche en Sciences Sociales*, 3.

Brehm, John and Wendy Rahn (1997): 'Individual-Level Evidence for the Causes and Consequences of Social Capital', *American Journal of Political Science*, 41 (3).

Brewer, B. and R. Kramer (1986): 'Choice Behaviour in Social Dilemmas: Effects of Social Identity, Group Size, and Decision Framing', *Journal of Personality and Social Psychology*, 50.

Buchanan, James (1986): *Liberty, Market and the State*, Brighton: Wheatsheaf Books.

Burt, Ronald S. (1992): *Structural Holes. The Social Structure of Competition*, Cambridge: Harvard University Press.

Burt, Ronald S. (1997): 'The Contingent Value of Social Capital', *Administrative Science Quarterly*, 42.

Carling, A. H. (1987): 'The Shelling Diagram: On Binary Choice with Externalities', *Behavioural Sciences*, 32.

Chong, Dennis (1991): *Collective Action and the Civil Rights Movement*, Chicago: University of Chicago Press.

Coleman, James S. (1988): 'Social Capital in the Creation of Human Capital', *American Journal of Sociology*, 94.

Coleman, James S. (1990): *Foundations of Social Theory*, Cambridge: Harvard University Press.

Cook, Karen S. and J.M. Whitmeyer (1992): 'Two Approaches to Social Structure: Exchange Theory and Network Analysis', *Annual Review of Sociology*, 18.

Crawford, Sue, and Eleanor Ostrom (1995): 'A Grammar on Institutions', *American Political Science Review*, 90.

Dogan, Mattei and Ali Kazancigil (eds.) (1994): *Comparing Nations. Concepts, Strategies, Substances*, Oxford: Basil Blackwell.

Elster, Jon (1989a): *Nuts and Bolts for Social Sciences*, Cambridge: Cambridge University Press.

Elster, Jon (1989b): *The Cement of Society*, Cambridge: Cambridge University Press.

Elster, Jon (1997): *Egonomics*, Barcelona: Gedisa.

Fleishman, J. (1988): 'The Effects of Decision Framing and Others' Behaviour on Co-operation in a Social Dilemma', *Journal of Conflict Resolution*, 32.

Friedman, Milton (1953): *Essays in Positive Economics*, Chicago: Chicago University Press.

Goldberg, Ellis (1996): 'Thinking About How Democracy Works', *Politics & Society*, 24 (1).

Gould, R.V. (1993): 'Collective Action and Network Structure', *American Sociological Review*, 58.

Granovetter, Mark (1973): 'The Strength of Weak Ties', *American Journal of Sociology*, 78.

Green, Donald and Ian Shapiro (1994): *Pathologies of Rational Choice Theory. A Critique of Applications in Political Science*, New Haven: Yale University Press.

Green, Donald and Ian Shapiro (1995): '¿Por qué han sindo tan poco esclarecedoras las explicaciones de lo político en términos de elección racional?', *Revista Internacional de Filosofía Política*, 5.

Hall, Peter and Rosemary Taylor (1996): 'Political Science and the Three New Institutionalisms', *Political Studies*, 44.

Hardin, Russell (1982): *Collective Action*, Baltimore: Johns Hopkins University Press.

Heckathorn, Douglas (1996): 'The Dynamics and Dilemmas of Collective Action', *American Sociological Review*, 61.

Kato, Junko (1996): 'Review Article: Institutions and Rationality in Politics – Three Varieties of Neo-Institutionalists', *British Journal of Political Science*, 26.

Kerr, N.L. (1989): 'Illusions of Efficacy: The Effects of Group Size on Perceived Efficacy in Social Dilemmas', *Journal of Experimental Social Psychology*, 25.

Kimura, K. (1989): 'Large Groups and the Tendency towards Failure: A Critique of M. Olson's Model of Collective Action', *Journal of Mathematical Sociology*, 40.

Kondo, T. (1990): 'Some Notes on Rational Behaviour, Normative Behaviour, Moral Behaviour, and Co-operation', *Journal of Conflict Resolution*, 34.

Kreps, David M. (1991): *Game Theory and Economic Modelling*, Cambridge: Cambridge University Press.

Levi, Margaret (1996): 'Social and Unsocial Capital: A Review of Robert Putnam's *Making Democracy Work*', *Politics & Society*, 24 (1).

Lichbach, Mark I. (1996): *The Cooperator's Dilemma*, Ann Arbor: University of Michigan Press.

McDaniel, W. and F. Sistrunk (1991): 'Management Dilemmas and Decisions', *Journal of Conflict Resolution*, 35.

Macy, Michael W. (1989): 'Walking Out of Social Traps', *Rationality and Society*, 1.

Macy, Michael W. (1993): 'Backward Looking Social Control', *American Sociological Review*, 58.

Macy, Michael W. and Andreas Flache (1995): 'Beyond Rationality in Models of Choice', *Annual review of Sociology*, 21.

Margolis, H. (1982): *Selfishness, Altruism and Rationality. A Theory of Social Choice*, Cambridge: Cambridge University Press.

Marwell, Gerald and Pamela Oliver (1993): *The Critical Mass in Collective Action. A Micro-Social Theory*, Cambridge: Cambridge University Press.

Nagel, E. (1963): 'Assumptions in Economic Theory', *American Economic Review*, 53.

North, Douglas C. (1990): *Institutions, Institutional Change and Economic Performance*, Cambridge: Cambridge University Press.

Oliver, Pamela (1993): 'Formal Models of Collective Action', *Annual Review of Sociology*, 20.

Olson, Mancur (1965): *The Logic of Collective Action. Public Goods and the Theory of Groups*, Cambridge. MA: Harvard University Press.

Olson, Mancur (1987): 'Diseconomies of Scale and Development', *Cato Journal*, 7 (1).

Ostrom, Eleanor (1991): 'Rational Choice and Institutional Analysis: Toward Complementary', *American Political Science Review*, 85.

Ostrom, Eleanor (1992): *Crafting Institutions for Self-governing Irrigation Systems*, San Francisco: Institute for Contemporary Studies Press.

Ostrom, Eleanor (1994): 'Constituting Social Capital and Collective Action', *Journal of Theoretical Politics*, 6 (4).

Ostrom, Eleanor (1995): 'Self Organisation and Social Capital', *Industrial and Corporate Change*, 4.

Papandreou, Andreas (1994): *Externality and Institutions*, Oxford: Clarendon Press.

Putnam, Robert (1995a): 'Tuning In, Tuning Out: The Strange Disappearance of Social Capital in America', *PS*, 28 (4).

Putnam, Robert (1995b): 'Bowling Alone: America's Declining Social Capital', *Journal of Democracy*, 6 (1).

Putnam, Robert, with Robert Leonardi and Raffaela Nanetti (1993): *Making Democracy Work. Civic Traditions in Modern Italy*, Princeton: Princeton University Press.

Quartone, G., and A. Tversky (1988): 'Contrasting Rational and Psychological Analyses of Political Choice', *American Political Science Review*, 82.

Sandler, Todd (1992): *Collective Action. Theory and Applications*, Ann Arbor: University of Michigan Press.

Scharpf, Fritz W. (1989): 'Decision Rules, Decision Stiles and Policy Choices', *Journal of Theoretical Politics*, 1.

Scharpf, Fritz W. (1994): 'Games Real Actors Could Play: Positive and Negative Coordination in Embedded Negotiations', *Journal of Theoretical Politics*, 6.

Scharpf, Fritz W. (1997): *Games Real Actors Play. Actor-Centered Institutionalism in Policy Research*, Boulder: Westview Press.

Schmitter, Philippe (1991): *Comparative Politics at the Cross-roads*, Working Paper Series #27, Madrid: Instituto Juan March de Estudios e Investigaciones.

Scott, J. (1991): *Social Network Analysis*, London: Sage.

Sen, Amartya (1967): 'Isolation, Assurance and the Social Rate of Discount', *Quarterly Journal of Economics*, 81.

Sen, Amartya (1987): 'Rational Behaviour', *The New Palgrave. A Dictionary of Economics*, 4.

Sen, Amartya (1993): 'Internal Consistency of Choice', *Econometrica*, 61 (3).

Shelling, Thomas (1973): 'Hockey Helmets, Concealed Weapons, and Daylight Saving: A Study of Binary Choices with Externalities', *Journal of Conflict Resolution*, 17.

Tarrow, Sidney (1996): 'Making Social Science Work Across Space and Time: A Critical Reflection on Robert Putnam's *Making Democracy Work*', *American Political Science Review*, 90 (2).

Taylor, M. (1987): *The Possibility of Cooperation*, Cambridge: Cambridge University Press.

Udehn, Lars (1996): *The Limits of Public Choice*, London: Routledge.

van Deth, Jan W. (1996): 'Social and Political Involvement: An Overview and Reassessment of Empirical Findings', paper delivered at the ECPR Joint Sessions, 'Social Involvement, Voluntary Associations, and Democratic Politics', Oslo.

Yamagishi, T. and Karen S. Cook (1993): 'Generalized Exchange and Social Dilemmas', *Social Psychology Quarterly*, 56 (4).

Part II

Voluntary activity, participation and social capital – case studies of different countries

4 Civic engagement and volunteering in the Netherlands

A 'Putnamian' analysis

Joep de Hart and Paul Dekker

INTRODUCTION

'Social capital', 'civil society', 'civic community' and also 'citizenship' have in a brief space of time become popular as overarching concepts for studying developments in social and political participation. More than the alternative concepts, civil society focuses on voluntary associations. These are organizations which do not form part of the state machinery, whose core does not lie in the individual sphere or the formal economy, and which are open to voluntary membership. The term civil society is used to indicate the importance of such associations for a broad range of social trends.

Its rediscovery in Western political thinking is linked to its emergence as a concept used by dissidents in Eastern Europe during the 1970s and 1980s. Although the term derives a good deal of its glamour from this, its positive reception in the West must nevertheless be seen primarily in the light of the need for an alternative to the state, the market and the small community, which until recently were the three main concepts defining the politics of the Netherlands and Europe. With the disappearance of 'real existing' socialism, belief in the state as a controlling centre of society appears to have been subjugated once and for all. In addition, enthusiasm for the market as a panacea has also subsided significantly as a result of the persistent economic recession and high unemployment in both the East and the West.

Among the recurring themes in contemporary discussions are the decreasing voluntary engagement of citizens in matters related to the public interest, the bureaucratization and commercialization of social life, and the rejection of politics in favour of social democracy and self-regulation. Finally, the multidimensional process of individualization undermines the importance of traditional attachments such as family, neighbourhood and church. In the international discussion 'civil society' is pushed forward as a supplement to and partly an alternative for social regulation through these three spheres. Strengthening the civil society could contribute to a deepening and revitalization of political democracy, a recovery or preservation of social cohesion, and possibly also to an increase in the efficacy of government policy.

Voluntary organizations, especially those with idealistic and altruistic objectives, are virtually always placed at the core of the civil society. In this chapter we will primarily deal with the active involvement of individuals in voluntary organizations, indicated by questions in population surveys about voluntary work. Although question wordings differ, these questions all focus on activities that are not carried out just for the benefit of the respondent and his or her family, and that are carried out on an unpaid voluntary basis, and in some form of organized context. Although voluntary work can be found in statutory bodies and market organizations as well as in community networks without much formal organization, the bulk of volunteering in Dutch society is carried out in voluntary organizations. Voluntary work may be regarded as the cement of civil society.

An influential participant in the present debates about civil society in the Western world is the American political scientist Robert Putnam. After he had demonstrated, on the basis of large-scale and long-term research in Italy, that the effectiveness of political and social institutions is in large measure determined by the level of citizen engagement in community affairs (Putnam 1993a), he notes in a series of articles a steady decline in civic engagement on the part of Americans in recent decades (Putnam 1993b, 1995a/b). Putnam's American questions and findings form the guideline for the exploration of developments and individual correlates of voluntary work in the Netherlands. In this regard we have drawn particularly on his article 'Tuning in, tuning out: the strange disappearance of social capital in America' (Putnam 1995b).

In Robert Putnam's recent publications on the erosion of the civic community in the US, volunteering is one of the indicators for social capital in addition to other forms of social connectedness – ranging from contact with neighbours to membership of organizations – and of trust, especially confidence in other people, but also trust in institutions. This chapter does not go further into the question of trust. The participation aspect is central and, as noted, not primarily in the passive sense of group membership but in the active sense of voluntary work.

Before turning to the individual-level analyses of volunteering, a brief survey is provided on pages 77–82 of the present situation of Dutch civil society in a longitudinal and cross-national perspective. This is done with the aid of both institutional data and data from various opinion polls. On pages 82–5 we further introduce the 'Putnamian' perspective on volunteering. On pages 85–8 the reporting of time-budget data starts with an analysis of shifts in participation in voluntary work since 1980. On pages 88–92 the research focuses on the effects of time-pressure. In view of the marked sexual differences in participation in paid and unpaid employment and in the development of labour force participation in the Netherlands in recent decades, this has been done separately for women and men. It is not just the pressures of paid employment and household activities, however, which are important for voluntary work; competition from other leisure activities and the growing restlessness evident in leisure behaviour are also examined. The leisure sphere includes television viewing. On account of the importance assigned to this aspect by Putnam, the impact of media usage is separately discussed on pages 92–9. The concluding section returns to the effects of volunteering for political attitudes and behaviour and for political democracy.

DUTCH CIVIL SOCIETY IN A CROSS-NATIONAL AND TIME PERSPECTIVE

Using material from various sources as well as cross-national and longitudinal data, this section outlines the present state of Dutch civil society. In this way the reader can obtain an idea of the Netherlands as a case study for research into civil society in Europe. Apart from volunteering this section also examines other indicators of civic engagement. Moreover, the longitudinal data make it possible to establish the extent to which the trends identified by Putnam in the US also apply to the Netherlands.

Table 4.1 provides an overview of data on membership and voluntary work. The figures reveal the Netherlands to be a country with a strong voluntary sector. The degree of organization is high and the proportion of volunteers substantial. With respect to the latter it may be noted that North America outscores all West European countries.

Closer analysis of the relationship between passive membership and active membership (i.e. volunteering) in individual sectors suggests a classification of the countries shown in Table 4.1 into three types of civil society (Dekker and van den Broek 1995): active civil societies in North America (many members and a high proportion of active members), broad civil societies in Scandinavia and the Netherlands (more, but less active members), elitist civil societies in Southern Europe (small numbers of relatively active members); the other European countries have average scores between the North and the South.

Table 4.1 Membership and volunteering in 12 nations, 1981 and 1990; population aged 18 and over (rankings and percentages)[a]

	Membership			Volunteering		
	1981	1990		1981	1990	
The Netherlands	3	1	[85]	4	5	[36]
Belgium	10	8	[57]	7	7	[28]
Germany (West)	9	6	[67]	7	6	[30]
France	11	11	[39]	12	11	[23]
Italy	12	12	[35]	10	10	[24]
Great Britain	8	9	[53]	9	12	[22]
Ireland	7	10	[49]	6	8	[26]
Denmark	3	3	[81]	11	8	[26]
Norway	3	3	[81]	4	4	[37]
Sweden	2	1	[85]	3	3	[39]
Canada	6	7	[65]	1	2	[43]
USA	1	5	[72]	2	1	[46]

Sources: European Values 1981 and 1990 (see Dekker and van den Broek (1995) for sampling and question wording).

Note
a   The percentages in brackets are for 1990 only because different categories were used in 1981.

Analyses of the 1994 Volunteers in Europe survey (cf. Gaskin and Davis Smith 1995) confirm the high level of Dutch volunteering. A comparatively high proportion of voluntary work in the Netherlands takes place in the fields of cultural affairs, recreation and education; religion and ideological areas by contrast are not particularly popular (SCP 1996: 540). Data on environmental action from 1992 and 1995 Eurobarometer surveys and from the International Social Survey Project 1993 module show for the Netherlands a high degree of organization (i.e. numerous members and donors) with a comparatively low proportion of protest participation (Nas *et al.* 1996: 127–8). The strong emergence and institutionalization of environmental concerns as a new social movement has been combined by a marked decline of involvement in 'traditional organizations' such as churches, trade unions and political parties (SCP 1995: 554–67). These and similar trends portray the Netherlands as a country with a rapidly modernized civil society (Dekker *et al.* 1997). In comparative terms the country certainly provides an interesting critical case for those seeking to defend the proposition that civic engagement is held back by the development of the welfare state.[1]

So much for the Netherlands in an international perspective. We may now turn to trends in the Netherlands. Table 4.2 presents an overview of the number of members of and donators to large social organizations in 1980 and 1993/94.

The number of members of or donors to large organizations has increased by 58 per cent since 1980 to 22 million, though in many cases this will be only a weak form of involvement and participation. In return for a financial contribution, donors receive a membership or donor's newsletter (see Maloney and Selle in this

Table 4.2 Members of and/or donators to large social organizations by subject or type, 1980–93/94 (in absolute numbers × 1,000 and changes as a percentage of the number in 1980)

	1980	1993/94	Change
Broadcasting organizations (full members and supporting members)	3,944	5,060	+28
Consumer organizations (including tourism, traffic, housing and education)	3,356	4,513	+34
Health care (including half the Red Cross)	2,137	4,142	+94
International solidarity (including half the Red Cross)	1,178	3,217	+173
Nature and the environment	484	2,181	+351
Employees	1,616	1,654	+2
The elderly	387	500	+29
Political parties	342	234	−32
Women's organizations	271	226	−17
Abortion/euthanasia	29	160	+452
Employers and the self-employed	137	144	+5
Total	13,881	22,031	+58

Source: Information from the organizations (see SCP 1995: 547–8).

Note

Organizations with a minimum of 50,000 members/donators in 1980 or 1993/94.

volume). The main growth, however, is not in consumer organizations that primarily serve their own material interests. Table 4.4 shows that the strongest growth has taken place in organizations which are concerned with moral issues (abortion and euthanasia), nature and the environment, and international solidarity (the Third World, human rights and refugees). In absolute terms, health and international solidarity are the sectors showing the greatest growth (both gaining two million). Political parties and women's organizations show a decline.

The only group of organizations which has suffered a substantial loss according to Table 4.2 is the political parties (a drop of 32 per cent for the three major parties). This decline is not limited to the three major parties and was also under way before 1980. Voerman (1996: 199) presents the following numbers of members of all parties represented in parliament as a percentage of the electorate: 15% in 1946, 12.5% in 1956, 6.7% in 1967, 4.4% in 1977, 3.5% in 1986, and 2.9% in 1994. Compared with other West European countries, Katz and Mair (1992) found the Netherlands to have the lowest level of party membership of all countries, and, after Denmark, the second highest decline in membership.

Population surveys of the organizational propensity among the Dutch population over a somewhat longer period record strong increases in the fields of sport and leisure since the 1960s. These data confirm the institutional figures of shrinking membership of women's organizations and political organizations between 1980 and the mid-1990s (SCP 1996: 371).[2] Taking all sorts of voluntary organizations together, surveys demonstrate a rising trend in membership: since 1980 both membership of at least one organization and membership of two or more associations has increased and these increases are not attributable to sharp rises in specific segments but are reflected in various age and education categories (SCP 1996: 541).

Before we focus on volunteering, some details of political participation are shown in Tables 4.3–5. Table 4.3 shows the electoral turnout since 1970, when

Table 4.3 Turnout at general elections, 1970–95 (percentages of electorate)

	70	71	72	73	74	75	76	77	78	79	80	81	82
European parliament										58			
National parliament		79	84					88				87	81
Provincial councils	69				75				80				68
Municipal councils	67				69				74				68

	83	84	85	86	87	88	89	90	91	92	93	94	95
European parliament		51					47					36	
National parliament				86			80					79	
Provincial councils					66				52				50
Municipal councils					73			62				65	

Source: Central Bureau of Statistics (statistics of general elections).

Table 4.4 Political participation, population aged 18–74, 1975–95 (in per cent)

	75	80	85	91	93	95
Has in recent years attented a meeting						
of a political party	13	14	13	7	8	10
Has put forward an opinion during a meeting	12	16		18	22	27
Has written a paper to put forward an opinion	5	7		7	8	11
Has in the last two years taken part in a government						
inquiry procedure/public hearing		16	14	13	16	17
Has in the last two years taken part in a collective						
action for an (inter)national issue		12	20	13	14	14
Has in the last two years taken part in a collective						
action for a (sub)local issue		26	25	22	29	32

Sources: Cultural Changes in the Netherlands, 1975–95.

compulsory voting was abolished in the Netherlands. In the case of the European elections there are signs of a secular fall and a similar trend may also apply to the provincial government elections. Contrary to these 'secondary elections', the parliamentary elections and those for the municipal councils display no evidence of any secular shift.

Tables 4.4 and 4.5 show the extent to which, according to population surveys, the Dutch have participated in politics. In both tables stable and rising trends predominate. Although the survey data call for some qualification,[3] the doubling between 1977 and 1994 in the percentage of Dutch people who were active in at least two of the ways named in Table 4.4 convincingly reject the idea of declining political involvement. Increases in some activities suggest a relative strengthening of individual and in all probability often rather fleeting forms of participation

Table 4.5 Political activities[a], electorate, 1977–94 (in per cent)

	1977	1981	1986	1994
Has contacted a cabinet minister or member of parliament	6	6	8	6
Has contacted a mayor, alderman or municipal councillor	18	14	14	16
Has tried to activate a political party	4	7	8	7
Has activated an interest group	8	11	10	10
Has activated radio, tv or newspaper	5	7	6	9
Has signed a petition	41	45	47	56
Has joined an action group	8	12	12	13
Has joined a demonstration	6	12	19	25
Has lodged a complaint	8	10	9	15
Has taken part in at least two of these activities	22	28	31	40

Sources: National Election Studies 1977–94; respondents who participated in two or more waves of interviews.

Note

a Presented as possibilities to do something against an unjust bill; has the respondent ever used one of these?

(writing letters and notices of objection, signing petitions, taking part in demonstrations). This could correspond with Putnam's suggestion for America of an increase in 'paper-and-pencil' participation at the expense of participation involving face-to-face contacts. There are however also contra-indications (speaking at a meeting) and – with some doubt given the possible biases in the material – it appears more plausible to speak of a widening of the activism repertoire rather than of the replacement of collective, personally committed forms of participation by individualistic and arm's length activities.

To what extent are the trends in formal membership in voluntary associations also reflected in the active, voluntary and unpaid participation in those organizations? Table 4.6 shows the changes in participation in voluntary work between 1977 and 1995 according to the surveys of living conditions. As the table shows, most of the fields of activity have a comparatively stable number of volunteers, with slight fluctuations. This also applies to the informal assistance provided to neighbours, the elderly and the disabled. Compared with the second half of the 1970s the number of volunteers within the recreational sector and in

Table 4.6 Volunteering, informal help and social contacts, population aged 18 and over, 1977–95 (in per cent)

	1977	1980[a]	1983	1986	1989	1992	1995
Volunteering for:							
political and charitable causes	4	5	5	5	5	5	7
employees' and employers' organizations	4	6	4	4	4	4	4
religious and philosophical causes	7	11	9	9	10	9	11
culture, sport, hobby	17	29	25	25	25	23	27
child care, schools, youth work	10	13	15	15	14	13	18
women's groups (% of female population only)	4	6	5	5	4	4	3
organized care-provision, information, etc.	4	7	3	2	2	2	4
Number of above mentioned sectors of volunteering:							
none	67	55	59	59	59	61	5
one	23	28	26	25	26	26	28
more than one	10	17	15	16	15	13	18
Informal care, help-your-neighbour, etc.	11	9	13	11	13	12	14
Has contacts with neighbours at least once a week					59	63	63
Ditto: friends and acquaintances		56			61	65	65
Ditto: relatives		63			65	64	62

Sources: Survey of Living Conditions 1977–86; Continuous Living Conditions survey 1989–92; Time-Budget Survey 1995 (weighted results).

Note
a Different question wording in 1980.

education, child care and youth work has clearly risen. The aforementioned increase in membership in recreational organizations therefore has its counterpart in a growing willingness to undertake volunteering. Taken as a whole the percentage of volunteers in 1995 is larger than in 1977. Even if one makes generous allowance for the possibility that a shift has taken place from 'heavy' voluntary work (e.g. executive member of a party or trade union) to 'light' voluntary work (making sure that the football is put away again after a training session), there is little reason to assume a decline in civic engagement in the Netherlands. Included in Table 4.6 are time-series on informal help and figures on social contacts. Like the membership and voluntary work figures, these in no way suggest a decline in the social capital in the Netherlands.

To sum up, the Netherlands may be regarded as a country with a substantial and highly modernized civil society. Moreover, there are no signs of stagnation in this area. Membership of and donations to large organizations are growing, voluntary work is stable or rising, political activism has increased and electoral turnout has fallen only in the case of unimportant elections. A shift towards less intensive, less committed forms of civic engagement – and ones that therefore build up less social capital – is however probable. This applies not just to the figures for political participation just examined but also to the shift in membership in Table 4.2. In the rapidly growing sectors of international solidarity, environment and moral issues, the main accent is probably on 'cheque-book activism' and other support for tertiary organizations of sympathizers. For the time being, however, there would appear to be more evidence of a supplementation of social engagement by means of more individual and occasional forms of participation than of an undermining of the social capital stored in secondary associations.

PUTNAM AND VOLUNTEERING

Putnam has examined the effect of a number of divergent factors for developments in the social capital. One of the most important of these, according to Putnam, is the level of education. Among Americans this turns out to be closely correlated with civic engagement in all its forms. Highly educated Americans participate significantly more often, not just because of their greater financial flexibility but, more particularly, on account of the skills and interests they acquired at home and at school.

In view of the rising level of education among the population in recent decades one would therefore expect the social capital to have increased during this period. The opposite, however, turns out to be the case and other factors must therefore also be at work. Another factor that plays a role – if only a subordinate one – in relation to social participation is the family situation. Married and cohabiting people – especially those living together with their family – are more engaged civically than single people. Much more important, however, according to Putnam is the effect of age; older Americans participate more frequently than do young Americans in virtually all forms of civic engagement.

Upon closer consideration this turns out to concern intergenerational differences rather than life-cycle stage effects. The intergenerational differences, Putnam argues, are closely related to the advent of television and its integration into the daily pattern of activity. In contrast to other leisure pursuits, watching television provides a distinct obstacle towards participation in virtually all forms of social activity outside the home. Other factors according to Putnam play no or only a marginal role in changes in civic engagement among the population. This includes greater time-pressure: people with a heavy workload may feel more pressured but in their desire for more leisure they do not cut back on social participation. Nor can shifts in the social capital be ascribed to the changing position of women and the advent of two-career families. Although participation in the United States has fallen more among women than among men, working women (increasingly) display more social engagement than do housewives.

These then are a number of conclusions reached by Putnam in relation to the US situation. Have comparable developments taken place in the Netherlands? And what effect have the factors cited by Putnam had in addition to other factors on voluntary work in the Dutch context? These are the questions on which we focus in this and the next sections. In the remainder of this section we give a general description of changing time conditions of volunteering in the Netherlands, and we introduce the time-budget surveys conducted by the SCP on which the next sections are based.

Voluntary work is predominately performed in people's free time. Volunteering demands not just the availability of a certain amount of leisure time but (among other things) also certain cognitive skills. The degree to which these matters are available and distributed within the population, among individuals and in households is to a large extent determined by the labour system, the way in which production is organized in society and the nature of the education system.

Post-war Dutch society has been characterized by a rapid growth in the service (tertiary) sector, the replacement of physical by mental labour, a continuing rise in the level of education and the major importance of means of communication. Within the labour sector the number of part-time jobs rose sharply and the participation of women in the labour force has grown rapidly over the past two decades. On the other hand elderly people and the less well educated have left the labour process in large numbers and young people consistently deferred their entry into the labour market by extending the time they spent in education. In consequence, paid employment and the establishment of a professional career have become increasingly concentrated in a period of life (20–50 years) that also involves many other pressures, such as the fact that small children generally form part of the household during this life-cycle stage.

When it comes to the availability of free time, a distinction needs to be drawn between the time left once paid employment has been performed and the time remaining when all other commitments have been discharged (education and courses, household tasks and the care of other members of the household, and physical requirements such as eating and sleeping). In the former case one may speak of 'gross' free time and in the latter of the 'net' free hours. Although the average number of hours worked per year has fallen over recent decades the Dutch have certainly not found themselves less busy, for their net free time or leisure has also fallen. The post-war generations of Dutch people on average spend four to five hours a week more on their weekly package of tasks than did their elders (SCP 1993, 1995).

Major shifts took place in the social position of women in the Netherlands between 1980 and 1995. In 1980 a third of the female element of the potential working population (aged 15–64) participated in the labour market, whereas in 1994 the figure had risen to nearly 50 per cent. In the process the Netherlands has made up a considerable amount of lost ground over the past two decades, moving from the rearguard of Western nations as regards the labour force participation of women into the middle of the pack. The participation rate of (in particular) married women has risen very sharply since the 1960s. Although over 50 per cent of working women have a part-time job the number of women in the 18–64-years age group citing their principal occupation as housewife fell between 1980 and 1995 from 63 to 32 per cent, while the amount of time that women in this age group devoted a week to paid employment rose on average during the same period from 7.2 to 14.6 hours. The increased amount of time taken up by paid employment has been coupled not so much with a smaller time-investment in household activities as with a reduction in the amount of leisure. Various surveys have indicated that among men, paid employment is associated with more voluntary activities but in the case of women with fewer (SCP 1996).

A number of other important developments have taken place in the leisure sphere. The post-war rise in prosperity has had a major impact on the consumption and recreation patterns of Dutch people. There has, for example, been a sharp increase in the degree of individual variation, as well as in the ability to make use of technical aids. An increasingly sharp dividing line has arisen between (a) the highly educated and that element of the population aged under 50, who have found themselves ever busier, and (b) the less well-educated and older part of the population with a growing number of net free hours.

The group of highly educated people in their middle life-cycle stage has traditionally supplied many volunteers and, in terms of its social position and skills, should also do so today. This group finds itself, however, with an ever more crowded diary and a daily schedule of increasingly changing commitments. Beneath them there is an ever growing number of people (both men and women) who have to combine a paid job with household and caring tasks or supplementary educational commitments (e.g. further or refresher training). On the other hand there are also groups who have found themselves with a greater number of free hours during the same period and who, in principle, therefore now have more time for voluntary work, such as the elderly and the poorly educated.

In particular the group aged 50–65 has seen a substantial increase in its leisure time compared with the 1970s. Early retirement has meant that people have been able to leave the labour process earlier than ever before and, within the family cycle, a high proportion at this life-cycle stage have reached the 'empty nest stage' at which children leave home. At the same time the present category of pensioners forms a comparatively well-educated and prosperous population category in comparison with earlier cohorts of pensioners, and have moreover become accustomed through the post-war growth in prosperity and the welfare state to an alternating pattern of leisure activities and an active role within society.

In the next sections we further analyse trends and diversity in volunteering with data drawn from the periodic time-budget surveys conducted by the SCP. The surveys are based on national samples and have been conducted every five years since 1975. On account of limitations in the 1975 data the longitudinal analyses relate primarily to the period 1980–95. For the sake of manageability we will confine ourselves to a comparison of two years: 1980 and 1995.[4]

Most of the data in these surveys are collected by means of diaries, in which a representative sample of the population notes down all its activities every quarter of an hour during seven consecutive days in a week in October. In addition to the diary, the respondents complete a questionnaire. The report below is based on the results obtained with the diary method. In comparison with the usual questionnaire survey, the diaries allow for a much better, more detailed and, above all, more reliable insight in this way into actual voluntary work and the way that this is fitted into other activities and commitments in people's daily lives.[5] Although the time-budget surveys can provide an important supplement to the amended public opinion polls, on which political science participation studies generally draw, they have also substantial limitations. The SCP time-budget surveys do not contain any opinion questions at all and few attitudinal measurements, while politics is only explored as an area of leisure activity in addition to watching television, playing sport, helping neighbours and gardening. There is a question about party affiliation and one about the respondent's self-assessment of his or her level of political interest. This is not sufficient to devote serious attention to the political implications of voluntary work, for which reason this paper makes no attempt to say anything about the relationships between social capital and political democracy. For the moment we are concerned with the social bases of social capital, and we are taking a sociological rather than a political-science approach towards civic engagement.[6]

On the basis of the results of the time-budget surveys, the relevance of various socio-structural characteristics for volunteering is first examined. This is followed by a discussion of the relevance of various aspects of the utilization of time, including leisure activities.

TRENDS IN VOLUNTEERING AMONG SUBPOPULATIONS

Table 4.7 shows how the developments, which were mentioned in the introduction, have been reflected at individual level between 1980 and 1995 in the participation in voluntary activities. Apart from sex, age, education and church involvement,

Table 4.7 Participation in voluntary work according to time-budget diary: number of volunteers in the population, time spent by volunteers on voluntary work, and proportion of leisure time spent by volunteers on voluntary work, population aged 18 and over, in 1980 and 1995 (in per cent and hours per week)

	Number of volunteers		Hours by volunteers		Proportion of leisure time of volunteers	
	1980	1995	1980	1995	1980	1995
Entire sample	33	32	4.3	4.9	8.4	8.9
Men	36	31	4.6	6.0	8.9	11.2
Women	29	33	4.0	4.0	7.9	8.0
18–34 years	30	22	4.3	4.5	9.1	9.4
35–54 years	37	39	3.8	5.0	7.9	10.4
55–74 years	33	36	5.2	5.3	8.5	8.5
Primary education	28	27	4.0	4.7	7.8	8.8
Secondary	38	34	4.3	5.3	8.3	10.0
Tertiary, university	47	36	4.9	4.4	10.0	9.0
Students	34	25	–	–	–	–
Employed	34	28	3.8	4.2	8.4	9.7
Unemployed, disabled, retired	33	36	6.5	7.1	9.6	10.5
Housewives	30	41	3.7	4.2	7.4	8.1
Living with parents	28	20	–	–	–	–
Single	35	33	6.0	4.6	9.7	7.8
Living with partner, no children	28	28	5.1	5.1	9.5	8.9
Living with partner, youngest child is < 14	36	39	3.6	4.8	8.0	10.5
Lving with partner, youngest child is > 14	33	31	4.3	5.2	7.8	9.8
No church affiliation	25	23	3.9	4.7	7.3	8.7
Church members	27	34	4.4	4.7	8.7	9.1
Regular churchgoers (ditto: except voluntary work for church or religious organization)	51	57	4.6	5.5	9.1	10.8
	(38)	(40)	(4.1)	(4.4)	(8.0)	(8.0)
N	2,354	2,918	768	933	768	933

Sources: Time-Budget Surveys 1980 and 1995 (– = N < 100).

respondents' employment position and family-cycle stage have been included in Table 4.7. The latter two characteristics may be regarded as indicative of the degree to which people are socially tied.

The total percentage of participants in voluntary work remains constant: measured in terms of the time-budget diary, voluntary activities were and are carried out by roughly a third of the adults. Overall the differences in participation between the various population categories have widened. Whereas the population aged 35 and over held up its degree of voluntary work, the youngest group (and students or those living with parents) shows a clear drop in participation between 1980 and 1995. Maybe because of a shift among the young (higher educated), educational differences have declined. In 1980, the highly educated were the most active population group, but 15 years later this was no longer the case. In the intervening period the participation rate fell by 11 percentage points, while among the other education categories it remained much the same. The churchgoing population contains a very high proportion of volunteers, even when activities on behalf of a church or ideological organization are left out of account. It is, however, evident that the regular churchgoers have concentrated to a greater extent than before on activities with some form of church connection.

In comparison with 1980 men have been participating less and women more in voluntary activities. The higher level of participation among women is attributable to the group of women without a paid job. In comparison with 1980 the participation rate among housewives has increased the most of all the groups: in 1995, 41 per cent of the women who stated housewife as their profession participated in voluntary work during the research week, while in 1980 the figure was 30 per cent. This makes housewives a population category with one of the highest participation rates. Within the group for whom paid employment is the main daily activity there was a sharp sex-difference in 1980. At that time 36 per cent of working males were active in voluntary work, compared with 23 per cent of working females. In 1995 the two groups had converged and the number of volunteers was 29 and 21 per cent respectively.

On a weekly basis, volunteers have on average devoted 36 minutes more to voluntary work (from 4.3 to 4.9 hours). The increase applied to virtually all groups in Table 4.7, with the exception of single households (among whom volunteers on average spend 1.5 hours a week less on participation) and again the best educated element of the population, which reduced the time set aside per week for voluntary work by an average of half an hour. The greatest amount of time is invested in voluntary activities by participants from groups with a relatively large amount of leisure: the unemployed, those incapacitated for work and pensioners. The greatest increase in the time set aside for voluntary activities is displayed by men, the 35–54 years age group and parents with young children. The latter two groups devoted the least time to such activities in 1980.

With respect to the differences between the age groups and the sexes as regards the amount of time invested in voluntary work, the number of hours taken up by activities outside the fields of education, employment or household tasks is clearly a factor. Individuals aged 55 and over have substantially more hours at their disposal than the younger age groups (in 1995 some 15 to 17 hours per week); the same applies to the unemployed or those incapacitated for work in comparison with those in full-time employment or in education. For this reason the amount of time devoted to voluntary activities has also been shown as a percentage of the total net number of free hours at people's disposal.

In 1995, the oldest age group devoted the most time to voluntary work in an absolute sense, but in terms of the proportionate share of leisure activities, not just the elderly but also the middle life-cycle category (35–54 years, generally with children of primary school age) attach high priority to such activities. The middle-aged group devoted a greater proportion of its free time to voluntary work in 1995 than it did 15 years before. This also applies to the male element of the population. This observation becomes even more significant when it is considered that both groups had less free time at their disposal in the latter research year than they did in 1980 (respectively 0.8 and 1.0 hours less).

WORK, FAMILY, LEISURE ACTIVITIES, AND TIME-PRESSURE

So far volunteering has been related to a number of socio-structural characteristics, social position and religious background. This section is devoted to the way in which people organize and allocate their time. As in other countries, clear shifts have taken place in the Netherlands in recent decades in both the time-budget set aside for daily obligations and in the utilization of leisure time. The ever shrinking time-investment in informal social contacts noted for example by Putnam in the United States is also evident in the Netherlands. The time-budget surveys conducted by the SCP indicate that during an average week the time invested by the population in informal social contacts (i.e. conversations with other members of the household, receiving visits and calling on other people) fell by over 14 per cent between 1975 and 1995.[7]

Since the 1970s the proportion of Dutch people who have been able to concentrate solely on either employment, education or household chores and family care has consistently fallen. The share of the population combining a number of these tasks on a day-to-day basis grew between 1975 and 1995 from 37 per cent to nearly 50 per cent. In particular the highly educated, those in employment and people in the middle life-cycle stage have found themselves increasingly obliged to strike a balance between a paid job, the pursuit of education and/or carrying out household activities or caring for children. The total number of hours taken up each week by such commitments is designated here as the *time-pressure* that people are under. Compared with the position 10 or 20 years ago, the time remaining when all these tasks have been completed and physical care such as eating and sleeping has taken place, designated here as *free time* or *leisure*, has declined. This applies particularly to those population groups with the largest number of task-combiners (SCP 1996: 357–68).

In itself a busy job or family life need not form an obstacle towards performing voluntary work in one's leisure time. The question then arises as to how much one is able to concentrate on such activities in one's free time. Concentrating on a single task (for which the evenings and the weekend can be released) has become increasingly difficult for well-educated Dutch people aged under 50. Particularly in this element of the population a growing number of partners have a job and both perform household and caring tasks, distributed over various stages of the day.

Under the pressure of circumstances Dutch people have begun to organize their free hours differently. Particularly among the busiest element of the population, time-intensive activities have increasingly given way to capital-intensive activities. Furthermore, the time-budget surveys indicate an increase in the diversity of the leisure repertoire in the Netherlands. In other words, the number of activities they undertake in their leisure hours per unit of time has widened in comparison with the situation in, say, the mid-1970s. One might also say that leisure behaviour has become more 'restless' and that modern people are more demanding of the activity in which they invest their time. This could be more related to the generally perceived feeling of being busier than ever than to a decline in the actual amount of leisure.

It may be assumed that the room which people have (or consider they have) for social participation and their participation in volunteering are affected by the package of obligations they are required to undertake in other areas of life and the number of hours more or less at their free disposal once these have been fulfilled. Table 4.8 shows the time-investment in a number of more or less daily recurring commitments in terms of their effect on participation in voluntary work: the number of hours involved in performing paid employment, the time taken up by managing a household and care of any other members of the household, the total number of hours taken up by all commitments (job, family care tasks, education) together and the necessity in certain cases of combining a number of these tasks (employment, household activities and education). On account of the sharply differing effects that such variables have on the pattern of activities for the two sexes (De Hart 1995), the position for men and women has been shown separately.

On the basis of the data above and in so far as voluntary work is concerned, Putnam's conclusion that the time-pressure of commitments does not constitute an obstacle towards the intensity with which people take part in various forms of social participation must be qualified. Major time-pressure and the piling up of commitments is associated for both sexes – as it is when individuals are required to combine various task – with less intensive participation in voluntary work. Particularly among men these factors have become more important since 1980 for the amount of time people devote to voluntary work.[8]

Generally speaking the factors analysed are more closely correlated with the time that people set aside for voluntary work than with the decision whether or not to take part. In some cases they work out differently in the lives of men and women. Among men, for example, participation falls if a great deal of time is taken up by household and family care tasks, while among women the frequency of participation in voluntary activities rises in such circumstances.

The participation and time-investment in voluntary work is related to the amount of leisure people have after they have discharged all their commitments. In 1995, 21 per cent of the respondents who had fewer than 40 hours per week at their free disposal were actively involved in volunteering, compared with 37 per

Table 4.8 Number of volunteers and time spent by volunteers on voluntary work, related to some other aspects of the time-budget[a], men and women aged 18 and over, in 1980 and 1995 (in per cent and hours per week)

	Men				Women			
	Number of volunteers		Hours by volunteers		Number of volunteers		Hours by volunteers	
	1980	1995	1980	1995	1980	1995	1980	1995
Entire sample	36	31	4.6	6.0	29	33	4.0	4.0
Paid work								
none	36	35	5.7	8.7	30	37	4.0	4.1
1–30 hours	39	29	4.4	5.6	28	34	4.3	3.7
>30 hours	36	29	4.0	4.5	25	18	2.6	3.4
Household/ family duties								
<10 hours	37	31	4.5	7.0	26	24	5.9	4.5
10–20 hours	38	29	5.2	5.0	22	23	4.3	4.4
20–30 hours	35	39	3.9	4.9	29	39	4.9	4.1
>30 hours	19	21	2.1	5.9	31	37	3.4	3.6
Combination of tasks[b]								
none or one	38	33	4.7	6.8	31	36	4.0	4.2
two or more	32	27	4.2	4.2	24	27	3.8	3.4
Time-pressure[c]								
<35 hours	40	35	5.8	8.8	29	37	5.5	4.4
35–50 hours	33	35	3.8	5.5	32	37	3.4	4.1
>50 hours	36	26	4.0	4.0	25	24	3.1	2.9

Sources: Time-Budget Surveys 1980 and 1995.

Notes

a   All activities in hours per week.

b   The tasks are: paid work, household care, and education. By combination of tasks is meant a time-investment of at least 5 hours per week in each of two or three of these.

c   Total amount of time per week spent on paid work, household care, and education.

cent with a greater amount of leisure time. As in Table 4.8, figures for the male and female population are presented in Table 4.9.

People who spend a lot of their leisure outside the home, intensive television-viewers and people who read little account for a comparatively low proportion of volunteers. The correlation with television viewing and reading has increased since 1980 and is stronger among women than men. The time devoted to social contacts inside and outside the home is only relevant for the time that people make available for voluntary activities: those who maintain intensive social contacts set aside less time for voluntary work. Among men this relationship was reversed 15 years ago.

The various aspects of individual circumstances and leisure activities have been examined separately above, but it needs to be borne in mind that the

Table 4.9 Number of volunteers and time spent by volunteers on voluntary work, related to leisure activities[a], men and women aged 18 and over, in 1980 and 1995 (in per cent and hours per week)

| | Men | | | | Women | | | |
| | Number of volunteers | | Hours by volunteers | | Number of volunteers | | Hours by volunteers | |
	1980	1995	1980	1995	1980	1995	1980	1995
Entire sample	36	31	4.6	6.0	29	33	4.0	4.0
Amount of free time[b]								
<40 hours	29	19	3.1	3.3	22	23	2.5	2.7
40–60 hours	38	35	4.1	4.7	31	37	3.9	4.1
>60 hours	42	38	6.6	10.5	37	39	6.3	4.9
Informal socializing[c]								
<8 hours	35	32	4.8	6.1	28	32	3.7	4.3
8–15 hours	39	30	4.1	6.4	30	36	4.3	3.9
>15 hours	33	27	5.5	4.8	29	30	3.8	3.6
Leisure time out of home[d]								
<5 hours	25	26	4.5	5.7	26	26	4.3	4.4
5–12 hours	44	31	4.2	7.0	31	36	3.4	4.1
>12 hours	36	33	5.3	5.4	30	34	4.7	3.6
Television viewing								
<5 hours	41	35	5.6	5.5	32	43	5.4	4.1
5–15 hours	39	33	4.3	6.4	32	35	3.4	3.8
>15 hours	28	25	4.6	5.6	13	24	3.1	4.1
Newspaper reading								
none	28	19	7.3	5.8	18	28	4.5	3.8
<4 hours	37	35	4.5	6.2	33	35	3.9	3.8
4 hours or more	39	35	4.0	5.8	30	36	3.8	4.6
Reading total[e]								
<3 hours	33	22	5.1	5.6	22	25	4.2	3.3
3–7 hours	35	44	4.2	6.6	34	38	4.1	4.1
>7 hours	40	34	4.6	5.8	29	40	3.5	4.5

Sources: Time-Budget Surveys 1980 and 1995.

Notes

a   All activities in hours per week.

b   The part of the week remaining after deducting all commitments for work, education or household care, and also after deduction of time for sleeping, meals and other personal care.

c   Conversations with other members of the household, receiving guests, paying visits to others.

d   The amount of leisure time spent outside the home (voluntary work and church going excluded).

e   Newspapers, magazines, books.

effect of such factors on participation in volunteering is only properly understood when considered in concert. Self-evidently, a leisure pattern characterized by a high degree of diversity in combination with comparatively little free time will be associated with a lower time-investment in volunteering. Other analyses (not shown in Tables 4.8 and 4.9) indicate that the youngest age group, which participates in voluntary work on only a limited scale, is characterized by a combination of little leisure, high time-pressure of commitments and a wide variation in leisure pursuits. The unemployed, those incapacitated for work and pensioners by contrast have a relatively large amount of leisure, little time-pressure of tasks and a below-average variation in their leisure repertoire.

In addition participation in social organizations and involvement in volunteering is of course not just affected by the life-cycle stage, education level or work position, in combination or otherwise. Personal factors of this kind play their role in interaction with other, external factors, such as the availability of facilities where people live. This section has been primarily concerned with the package of commitments facing people in other areas of life and the way in which they organize their daily lives, the number of hours more or less freely at their disposal once those commitments have been discharged and the way in which they decide to organize their leisure activities. One further aspect of modern leisure activity is examined below, namely media use, especially television viewing. Since this factor plays much the same role for Putnam as the butler in a classical detective play and is regarded by him as the chief culprit for the perceived erosion of America's social capital, this topic is taken up at somewhat greater length in this chapter.

MEDIA USAGE

The diffusion of television in Dutch society took place rapidly. In 1956 there were 99,000 licensed holders of a television set in the Netherlands; in 1959 the figure had already reached 585,000 while in the mid-1960s it had reached 2.1 million. The number of licensed television holders per 100 inhabitants rose further between 1965 and 1993 from 17 to 37.

That the advent of television had a radical impact on the use of leisure time is common knowledge. In 1960 a quarter of Dutch households owned a television set; currently 97 per cent of households have a colour television set. The use of television rose spectacularly in the course of the 1960s and accounted for roughly ten hours of the weekly time-budget. Since then the number of transmission hours and the number of channels have grown rapidly, but the viewing time has grown much more gradually. As the Netherlands entered the 1990s the average person spent 12 hours a week watching television (including videos, teletext and cable newspaper), a figure that had risen in 1995 to 12.4 hours.

The same average Dutch person has been devoting steadily less time to reading. In 1975, he or she still spent 2.5 hours (on a weekly basis) on newspapers, 2 hours on magazines and 1.6 hours on books, whereas 20 years later the time-investment had shrunk to 2, 1.4 and 1.2 hours respectively. By way of illustration Figure 4.1 shows various results from time-budget studies conducted since the 1950s. This compares the proportion of leisure time devoted to the use of television with the amount of time taken up by informal socializing (conversations, visiting), participation, reading, and other leisure pursuits.

The use of television in the Netherlands forms part of large-scale changes in the use and provision of media. These include the connection of the larger part of the country to the cable network, the trebling in the number of available channels between 1975 and 1990 (an increase that took place particularly rapidly between 1985 and 1990), the marked increase in the number of transmission hours (for the Dutch channels this doubled between 1980 and 1990) and the extension of broadcasting throughout the day, the advent of teletext, the distribution of video recorders (2 per cent of households in 1980, rising to 20 per cent in 1985 and 60 per cent in 1993), etc.

The arrival of television in the living room appears to be coupled with a lower investment of time in other activities, although the relationship is seldom direct and clear-cut. How much time now devoted by people to viewing television would be reserved by them for such other activities is unclear, as many activities can simply be combined with watching a television programme. That does not of course apply in the case of activities outside the home, such as voluntary work.

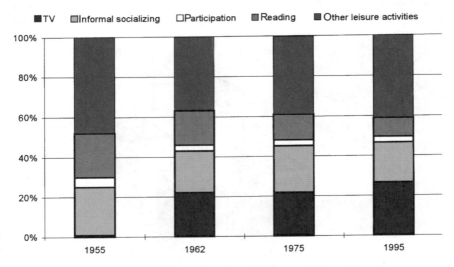

Figure 4.1 Time spent on television, informal socializing, social participation, and reading; population aged 12 and over, 1955–95[a] (in per cent of the total leisure time). *Sources*: CBS (1957, 1965); Time-Budget Surveys 1975 and 1995.

Note:
a   Registered in 1955/56 and 1962 on weekday evenings (17.30–24h.) and at the weekend, in 1975 and 1995 for all days of the week.

The figures from the time-budget surveys suggest that the more time Dutch people devote to watching television, the less time they invest in varying social contacts.[9] People who watch a lot of TV set aside comparatively little time for visiting friends and acquaintances, receiving visitors at home, conversations with other members of the household, conducting correspondence or telephone calls. This relationship remains present when the effects of education level or sex of the respondent, age or income level are controlled.

To his negative rating of television in terms of civic engagement, Putnam adds that the relationship with reading newspapers is inverse; passionate newspaper readers are inclined to invest much more energy in social forms of participation and organization such as voluntary work (Putnam 1995b).

On the basis of the figures in the most recent SCP time-budget survey, an analysis has been conducted to establish in the case of 1995 whether Putnam's conclusion also applies to our country. A two-fold distinction has been drawn; in the first place between people who watch little and much television, and secondly between people who spend little or alternatively a great deal of time in reading the newspaper.[10] This provides a typology of four categories of Dutch people. Figure 4.2 provides a comparison of time-investments in voluntary work in the four categories. Similar to Putnam's analyses of civic engagement in the US, possible educational effects (education measured with three levels mentioned in Table 4.7) have been eliminated.

Figure 4.2 provides a confirmation of Putnam's observations for the US. People who watch a lot of television and set aside little time for reading

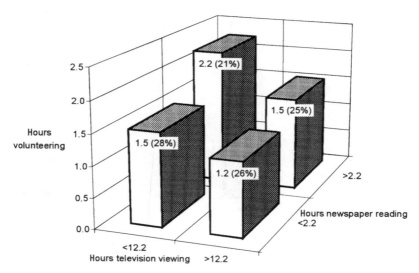

Figure 4.2 Time spent on volunteering by hours of media usage during the week, population aged 18 and over (in hours per week; adjusted for effects of education. Media usage categories as percentage of population in brackets). *Source*: Time-Budget Survey 1995.

newspapers display the lowest level of voluntary activities. A comparatively small time-investment in watching television in combination with the intensive reading of newspapers is indeed coupled with a high investment of time in voluntary work. The high average of volunteering results from a higher proportion of voluntary workers as well as a larger time-investment of those volunteers (SCP 1996: 550).

Of course, the differences shown in Figure 4.2 do not reveal the use of media as a cause of volunteering. A statistical adjustment for educational effects is certainly not enough to get a pure correlation between media usage and civic engagement.[11] Preferences for different media might just be a consequence of the different media coverage of different interests people have anyway. A study of media effects cannot be restricted to an analysis of time-investment, but has to include the contents of what is read and watched. Recently, Norris (1996) has advocated a more differentiated interpretation of television experience, which takes into account the multiplicity of TV channels and programs, and the diversity of TV viewers. Norris's American findings suggest a positive impact of watching national news and public affairs programmes on civic engagement. With the data at hand we cannot explore these issues, but we can give a global impression of differences between newspapers and TV as sources of information. Table 4.10 shows for a number of fields whether people are interested and how they cover their information needs. This is done for the population as a whole as well as for the two extreme categories in Figure 4.2.

For the population as a whole, TV turns out to be the more important source of information for most fields, also for the more 'serious' ones like national and international politics. As far as the extreme categories of media users are concerned, specialized newspaper readers show interest in more subjects than people who concentrate on television. Marked television viewers are especially less interested in politics, social and economic issues, science, culture and art, than marked newspaper readers. Differences are nearly absent for spectacular news events, crime, sport news, or consumers' information. However, concentration on TV or on newspapers is apparently not just a consequence of being interested in different topics. For each of the 17 fields one-sided television viewers rely mainly on television programmes, and one-sided newspaper readers on newspapers as the primary source of information. Thus, our very preliminary content analysis of media usage suggests overall media preferences, which cannot be explained by different fields of interest and which might be part of different lifestyles.

In terms of the advent and diffusion of television as outlined before, the factor of age merits special attention. For Putnam (and other authors who have compared the correlates of television viewing and reading), media use acts as an indicator of generational differences. A distinction may be drawn between those who by and large grew up without television and the generations from the television era. The two groups roughly coincide with Dutch persons aged 45 and over, whose formative years almost all preceded the 1960s, and the more recent birth cohorts. The assumption is that the former category was predominantly socialized in a word culture and the second by contrast in an image culture. The difference

Table 4.10 Use of television and newspapers as source of information[a], population aged 18 and over: all and specialized television viewers and newspaper readers (in per cent)

	Total population			Marked television viewers[b]			Marked newspaper readers[c]		
	None[d]	Television	Newspaper	None[d]	Television	Newspaper	None[d]	Television	Newspaper
Foreign politics	25	88 (61)	66 (31)	34	92 (75)	51 (19)	13	79 (38)	84 (55)
National politics	16	87 (56)	72 (36)	23	91 (76)	53 (19)	7	80 (32)	90 (59)
Local politics	27	12 (6)	58 (49)	35	16 (11)	49 (42)	19	7 (2)	66 (57)
Spectacular international news (hijackings, disasters, etc.)	6	91 (59)	73 (32)	10	94 (76)	56 (17)	2	85 (36)	93 (57)
Spectacular domestic news (disasters, accidents, etc.)	2	89 (50)	77 (38)	3	92 (64)	59 (20)	1	84 (24)	94 (66)
News about events in own residence	7	10 (6)	56 (46)	8	13 (9)	47 (40)	6	7 (3)	65 (56)
Information about the environment	12	74 (50)	66 (36)	17	83 (67)	51 (23)	7	61 (28)	85 (54)
Information about the position of women, emancipation, etc.	55	52 (36)	55 (36)	62	61 (50)	38 (22)	43	35 (16)	70 (55)
Education	39	54 (31)	71 (51)	49	65 (47)	56 (35)	26	41 (14)	87 (66)
Social economic news	36	63 (41)	71 (51)	49	76 (62)	54 (33)	23	56 (24)	84 (70)
Financial news	58	46 (30)	74 (60)	69	57 (46)	59 (45)	45	39 (19)	85 (73)
Information about art and culture	43	53 (33)	67 (48)	56	63 (50)	51 (35)	28	43 (19)	83 (62)
Science and technology	43	56 (41)	53 (34)	5	69 (57)	38 (21)	29	41 (23)	68 (47)
Information about crime and lawsuits	20	69 (48)	71 (48)	22	80 (67)	56 (29)	19	53 (26)	87 (70)
Sport news	32	87 (69)	69 (26)	32	92 (80)	58 (18)	34	80 (54)	79 (40)
Consumers' information	20	59 (44)	43 (24)	19	69 (59)	32 (14)	22	43 (22)	57 (36)
Information about traffic problems, public transport	27	48 (29)	58 (38)	30	58 (44)	43 (24)	23	38 (16)	71 (53)

Source: Time-Budget Survey 1995.

Notes

a Respondents could choose one or more of the following possibilities: television, newspapers, periodicals, magazines, radio, cable newspaper, teletext (between brackets: mentioned as most important source of information).

b People who spend more than 12.2 hours a week on viewing television and less than 2.2 hours on reading newspapers (see Figure 4.2).

c People who spend less than 12.2 hours a week on viewing television and more than 2.2 hours on reading newspapers (see Figure 4.2).

d Not interested in this topic, and for that reason not using any source of information.

between these two cultural types has been the subject of considerable discussion (see for example Lash 1990, Dahlgren 1995). The broadly based speculations and theories that have emerged as a result cannot be readily operationalized in terms of their repercussions for voluntary work. The analysis is confined to comparison between Dutch persons who grew up in the television age and the older element of the population.

Figure 4.3 provides an impression of the correlation between the amount of time devoted to watching television and reading newspapers and participation in voluntary activities. The position is shown separately for individuals aged 18–45 (i.e. born after 1950) and individuals aged 45 and over (born before the advent of television in the 1950s). Since the amount of leisure available varies considerably for the two groups, the analysis has been based not on the number of hours spent watching television and reading newspapers in an absolute sense but on the percentage of free time devoted to those activities. Once again the effects of sex, education and degree of urbanization of the place of residence have been controlled.[12]

As far as television viewing is concerned, the pattern is consistent with the formulated expectation among both young and old: intensive use of television is coupled with a limited willingness to participate in voluntary work. The situation differs when it comes to the reading of newspapers. In the younger age category the association is along the predicted lines: reading newspapers is linked with a

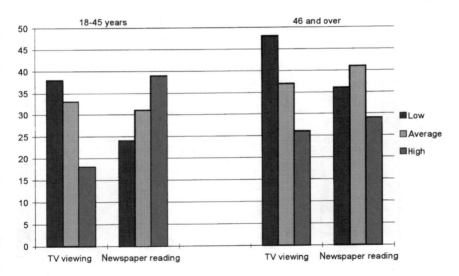

Figure 4.3 Number of volunteers by time spent on media usage[a], for two age categories in 1995, population aged 18 and over (in per cent; adjusted for effects of education). *Source*: Time-Budget Survey 1995.

Note:
a   Categories of television viewing: low =< 14% and high > 36% of leisure time; categories of newspaper reading: low = none, high > 7% of leisure time.

distinctly greater willingness to perform voluntary work. In the older category, however, this is not the case. Here, setting aside a large amount of free time for reading newspapers is coupled with a comparatively low participation rate.

In interpreting the observed correlations, it needs to be borne in mind that the relationship between watching television and reading newspapers differs for the two age groups. In the case of the younger group, the intensive use of television is associated with a relatively low time-investment in reading the newspaper.[13] This population group has considerably less free time than the older, and the intensive use of television is, consequently, more likely to be at the expense of consulting other sources of information and entertainment. In the population group aged 45 and over, individuals who watch little television also devote less time to reading the newspaper. This is in contrast to those who watch a lot of television – a group that combines intensive viewing behaviour with relatively intensive reading of newspapers.

The ambiguity of many of the assumed effects of television has already been noted. In particular, care must be taken not to make overhasty causal relationships. Nor must the productive effect of television (and other media) be overestimated. Or to stand matters on their head: television viewing may also form a kind of 'time out' from interaction, activities and commitments and it is perfectly conceivable that television viewing forms a kind of residual activity for people who barely participate in society: a buffer to fill the empty hours.[14]

According to Putnam, education and growing up with television are the most decisive factors for civic engagement. Therefore we want to take the analysis of the relationship between these two aspects and volunteering one step further. So far

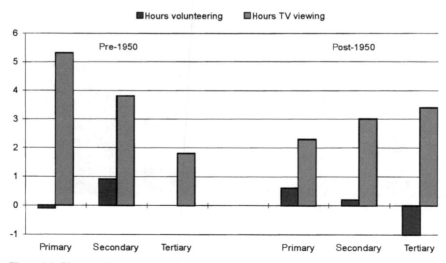

Figure 4.4 Changes in time spent on television viewing and volunteering between 1980 and 1995 by education and cohort, population aged 18–75 (in hours per week; adjusted for amount of leisure time). *Sources*: Time-Budget Surveys 1980, 1995.

the correlation between television viewing and participation in voluntary work only has been discussed, controlling for level of education. Young and old are less prepared to devote time to voluntary activities the more time they spend on television. What however have been the changes over time? Figure 4.4 provides an impression. This shows the relationships between year of birth, level of education and shifts among the Dutch population since 1980 in television viewing and the time devoted to voluntary work respectively.

The hypothesis is that Dutch people who grew up before the television era were more dependent on newspapers as a source of information and entertainment than the generations who grew up with television from childhood. Furthermore, the former category grew up with more of an ethic of civic engagement and involvement in the social environment. It is also assumed that people are less dependent on visual resources and more oriented towards reading if they have been more trained in the textual transfer of information by a longer education. The cognitive skills which the better educated are deemed to have in greater measure also lower the threshold for taking part in various forms of social participation.

In combination these two hypotheses (i.e. media socialization and cognitive skills) lead to the expectation that the least well-educated members of the television generation will be the most inclined to exchange voluntary work against television as a leisure and information medium. On the basis of the same argument the best educated Dutch persons who grew up before the television era would have given up their participation the least in favour of watching television. The number of unencumbered leisure hours that people have at their disposal each week varies considerably between the two categories. This factor (which, as noted, affects participation in voluntary work) has been controlled. Participation in voluntary work can decline because people run into physical limitations as the years go by. In order to reduce this effect as much as possible as well, people aged over 75 have been left outside the analysis.

The time devoted to watching television rose between 1980 and 1995 in all the categories distinguished, but most of all among the group born before 1950. In the oldest group viewing time rose less markedly the higher the level of education, while among the youngest group the relationship is the opposite.

In all cases the change in viewing time has been greater than the changes in the time devoted to voluntary work. Among the oldest group with secondary education and those with primary or secondary education in the youngest group there has been no shift whatever within the time-budget from voluntary work to television use since both viewing time and the time devoted to voluntary work have risen.

Returning to the hypothesis formulated above, the following may be established. Over the 15-year period under review, both the best educated who underwent their formative years in the pre-television age and the least well educated born during the television age made more time available for watching television.[15] Contrary to the expectation, however, the time devoted to voluntary work also increased (by 0.6 hours) among the latter group during this period, while among the former group it remained unchanged.

SUMMARY AND DISCUSSION

Inspired by Putnam's analyses into the decline in civic engagement, this chapter has examined trends and correlates in volunteering in the Netherlands. On the basis of highly diverse material, it was concluded in Section 2 that civic engagement in the Netherlands was at a high level by European standards and that there was no suggestion of stagnation. According to the available survey material, political participation and involvement in voluntary associations are rising. While there were reasons for placing question marks against the longitudinal reliability of the data, a decline in civic engagement is highly improbable. This conclusion was confirmed in Section 3 and later by data on volunteering as generated by the stricter method of diary keeping for time-budget studies. The percentage of volunteers has remained stable and their input is rising despite the falling amount of leisure time. In terms of the broad trends there appear to be fewer grounds for concern in the Netherlands than Putnam has for America.

Apart from this, these concerns have also been contested in the US with contraindications of growing engagement (cf. *The Economist*, 18 February 1995; Schudson 1996). As far as the differences in participation in volunteering are concerned, however, the Dutch findings often correspond with Putnam's expectations and findings (as well as those of other earlier authors who have not been named here).

Between 1980 and 1995 the youngest group of adults, like the best educated element of the nation, exhibited a decline in participation in voluntary work, while the level of participation held up among the population aged 35 and over, and housewives, in particular, became much more active. The most time is devoted to voluntary activities by participants in groups with a comparatively large amount of free time at their disposal: the unemployed, persons incapacitated for work and pensioners. Generally speaking major time-pressure and an accumulation of commitments are associated – as are task-combinations – with less intensive participation in voluntary work among both men and women. This certainly applies if a wide daily variation of activities is sustained into people's spare time and a wide range of leisure activities are then developed. It is therefore striking that a decline in free time in the 35–54-year-old category and among parents of children of primary-school age in recent decades has been coupled with the greatest increase in the time set aside for voluntary activities. The more time Dutch people devote to viewing television, the more that the time invested in social interactions in the leisure sphere falls. Intensive-television viewers do less voluntary work: they generate fewer volunteers and devote less time to volunteering.

Unmistakably there is a negative correlation between television viewing and volunteering; to that extent our findings correspond with those of Putnam for the United States. But as to whether the advent and dissemination of television provides the predominant explanatory factor for tendencies that could point to an erosion of the social capital (as Putnam claims) remains an open question as far as Dutch volunteering is concerned. What is clear is that the rapid diffusion in the use of television in the Netherlands from the second half of the 1950s onwards brought about major changes in the leisure pattern. According to time-budget surveys in the 1950s and 1960s, television viewing was initially (and also in the course of the 1960s) associated among young and old alike with a growing popularity for passive and household forms of leisure activities (with the exception of reading) and a decline in social interaction and activities outside the home. The new 'cult of domesticity' did not leave association life unspared: the population began to set aside less time for this purpose. Since the introduction of TV, however, there have been a number of other developments in the leisure field. These include the sharp increase and democratization of leisure, the marked increase in real income and wider scope for expenditure and the decline in physically taxing activities at work and in the household with the continuing spread of mechanization.

After thorough consideration and weighing various possibilities, Putnam explains age differences in civic engagement in America in terms of the impact of television. Our data are not derived from panel studies and it is therefore not possible to say anything with any certainty about individual shifts in the time-budget. The patterns of shifts in population groups over the past 15 years render it implausible, however, that a simple exchange has taken place between TV and volunteering. In so far as the age differences identified by Putnam also come to the fore in the Netherlands, an explanation in terms of life-cycle stage characteristics is often more plausible than the notion of the television generation. The fact that Dutch people aged under 50 have such busy schedules at present (both men and women, particularly the better educated and those in employment) appears largely due to the cumulation of life-cycle stage commitments in education, employment and households with children and working partners. Whether the current generation will settle down somewhat at a higher age is unclear at this stage. Whatever the case may be, lack of time means that the post-war baby-boomers find themselves increasingly obliged to use their time as efficiently as possible and to place more exacting demands on their leisure activities. By increasing the efficiency of their activities (with the use of household appliances), mobility (vehicles) and flexibility (e.g. video recorders) the heavily pressed youthful element of the population seeks to carry out as many activities as possible in its free time. Particularly among this group, a time-intensive leisure pattern is increasingly giving way to capital-intensive forms of leisure activities. This is possible because purchasing power has risen proportionately more over the years than the number of freely disposable hours.

The hectic consumer has also left his traces in the public sphere. In all sorts of areas of leisure activity (e.g. museums, events, the performing arts) it has been noted that the present-day visitor has a less committed attitude, that clients, visitors and participants attend increasingly casually and concentrate on special events, that people are also less prepared to concentrate on a single activity or to tie themselves to a single product and that the desire has arisen to make one's own selection from the range on offer and then to determine oneself how and when these are used. The modern consumer and visitor want instant gratification. It is increasingly difficult to capture their attention and it is not easy to motivate them to act on a group and sustained basis.

Seen in this light, a decline in participation in voluntary work and other forms of civic engagement would not have been surprising, but this does not turn out to have occurred. There is no question of any overall trend towards a retreat into the private domain. The slight increase in the amount of time devoted on average to volunteering does not, as such, point to a more fleeting kind of engagement.

So much for the empirical moderation of concerns about the decline of social capital in the Netherlands. However, one must keep aware of the limits of the data we have presented. Our indicators of organizational affiliation, participation in activities and time involved in volunteering may disguise important changes in the commitment, goals and side effects of involvement. As far as our organizational data (Table 4.2) are concerned, a move from 'secondary' face-to-face organizations to 'tertiary' advocacy organizations is quite plausible (cf. Maloney and Selle in this volume). The political participation figures (Tables 4.4 and 4.5) suggest a (relative) shift from organizational involvement to less binding activities. There is no reason to idealize traditional party membership as real participation against its modern degenerated versions of 'cheque-book activism'. However, it is a reasonable assumption that the capacity of civic engagement to build up social capital has probably declined because of this kind of shift. In the case of the time-budget figures about volunteering, we have fewer doubts about the longitudinal reliability of the data, although one is inclined to assume some inflation in the meaning of the concept. However, the possibilities of differentiation for goals and fields of volunteering (see shifts in Table 4.6), kinds of work done and social relations implied are limited with these data. Those who 'employ' volunteers see major shifts, not in the general willingness to do something for others or the society as a whole, but in the willingness to do regular work during longer periods (van Daal *et al.* 1992: 61–90). Not only consumers, but volunteers too want thrilling experiences and have fashions (political parties are out, environment and refugees are still OK, being a buddy for a terminal AIDS patient past its peak).

Of course, more data and further analyses are always asked for at the end of a chapter like this. For time budget studies two directions of further data gathering and analyses appear to be particularly fruitful to us. First, an interesting field for further research is the issue of individualization. Is it possible to measure trends in flexibility and fragmentation of civic engagement in longitudinal time-budget studies? How do differences in the time-structure of civic engagement between subpopulations fit into other differences of their diaries? Fleeting involvement may manifest a fragmentation of political identities and loyalties, but also an overall flexible, time-pressured modern lifestyle.

Second, the idea of a trade-off between time and money may be a fruitful perspective on civic engagement. Like running the home, political participation is a question of time and money (and civic skills; Verba *et al.* 1995). Are the same people saving time by spending money in both spheres? How do these new developments fit in with the rise of modern electronic media? What does this mean for the notions of civil society, civic community, and social capital?

Other proposals for further research depend upon the specification of central aspects of civic engagement one is interested in. Sweeping concepts of social capital and civil society are too broad to direct empirical research. 'Social trust', 'political participation' and 'political competence' appear to be the individualized (or individually measurable) benefits of social capital and civil society that get most interest from political scientists in present research. However, apart from the issue of the direction of causality, until now there is only mixed evidence for a very special treatment of active involvement in voluntary organizations. In cross-national analyses of the correlates of social trust and political participation and competence with *European values data* we found that passive membership is by and large as important an activity as being a member of voluntary associations, and we found that education was often more important than membership (Dekker and Van den Broek 1996, Dekker *et al.* 1997; cf. Almond and Verba 1989, van Deth 1996). Moreover, the ideas of trust and political competence definitely need differentiation and we should not simply suggest that both are always positively linked (with a reference to well-known findings of Almond and Verba 1989). To specify our concepts, we can distinguish between a micro-perspective on involvement of individuals in social networks and a macro-perspective on involvement of voluntary associations in policy making, between interpersonal trust and generalized trust, two concepts of civil society (Misztal 1996, Foley and Edwards 1996).[16] As far as the micro-world of political socialization is concerned, we finally want to stress the importance of comparing (involvement in) voluntary associations with other social settings like family and neighbourhood, schools, workplaces and other involuntary institutions. There is no reason to restrict questions about the production of trust, civic skills and abilities to co-operate, to the involvement in voluntary associations (cf. Newton and Whiteley in this volume).

Notes

1   Given the high scores of Sweden and the US in Table 4.1, however, there is little reason to postulate a simple connection between civic engagement and the welfare state. Comparative research of cross-national differences in scope and structure of the non-profit sector appears to reject all ideas of simple relationships between market, state and non-profit sector (Salamon and Anheier 1996; cf. Putnam 1995b: 671).

2   For a matter of fact, the membership figures for political parties in population surveys are well above the institutional counts just reported. Apart from the expansion of 'political parties' by 'political associations', this is probably attributable to the idea of a 'family membership' among respondents, the provision of socially desirable responses and selective non-response.

3   The surveys in both tables are subject to an increasing level of non-response that is probably biased in terms of social involvement (SCP 1996: 535–7). In the case of the election surveys shown in Table 4.4 there is a demonstrable over-

representation of politically involved persons; and in all those cases where the respondent was asked whether they had 'ever' done anything, the percentages almost automatically rise in an ageing population.

4   The 1975 sample is too small ($N = 1,309$) to permit certain further subdivisions to be made. For the sake of comparability it has therefore been decided to use the larger sample of 1980 ($N = 3,263$).

5   The percentage of participants in voluntary activities according to the diary method is lower than when the figures are collected on the basis of the questionnaire method. The diary method is less likely to encourage socially desirable replies than is a questionnaire. However, the results of the two data-collection techniques are not comparable as they stand. The activities as recorded in the diary that fall within the customary definition of volunteering are: activities in social and political organizations (as a member of a political party, trade union, action group or neighbourhood council – provided not as an additional paid job), activities to promote special interests and of a political nature (ditto), activities on behalf of other voluntary associations (nursing associations, sporting clubs, etc.), voluntary work and unpaid care for non-family members, activities on behalf of a religious or ideological organization (as an elder, deacon, member of a church or parochial council, etc. – but excluding church-going) and participation in activities associated with works councils and other business organizations (such as a staff council). Activity qualifies as participation if at least a quarter of an hour was spent during the research week on voluntary activities (excluding travel time). In accordance with the customary definition of volunteering and care, help provided to neighbours, the elderly and the handicapped has been left out of account. In the customary Dutch definition of volunteering, it is essential that this be conducted in an organized context. A time-budget survey diary does not, however, provide any clue about the organized nature of respondents' activities. In view of the nature of the selected activities it may however be assumed that these are generally conducted in an organized context.

6   With the aid of other material we have in the past devoted attention to the political aspects of voluntary work as part of the SCP survey 'Civil society and voluntary work' (SCP 1995, Dekker and Van den Broek 1995/1996). At the present time, research is carried out for this project among a representative sample of Dutch people and additionally also in four localities in which an attempt is made to strike a balance between traditional political-science attitudinal and behavioural questions, questions about the actual use of time and also questions into social relationships and community awareness. We hope to be able to report on these findings from 1998 onwards.

7   In 1975 the Dutch population aged 12 and over still devoted 23 per cent of their free time on average to such contacts; in 1985 this was 21 per cent and in 1995 20 per cent (SCP 1996: 373).

8   Further analyses not reported here indicate that this applies to all three of the previously distinguished age groups among the male population but most of all to the youngest group (18–34 years).

9   Cross-cultural time-budget surveys in which owners and non-owners of a television set have been compared in a period when television ownership was not yet commonplace arrive at the same conclusion (Szalai 1972).

10   Both television viewing and reading the newspapers have been dichotomized at the average score for 1995.

11   Cf. Uslaner (1996), who includes a number of behavioural and attitudinal variables in his analysis of membership in voluntary associations, trust in other people and other social capital indicators. His conclusion: 'Watching a lot of television doesn't make you mean. Television viewing has no direct effect on trust – or on membership in voluntary organizations' (p. 4). Uslaner suggests 'an optimistic world view' as the real thing: 'Heavy television viewers are unlikely sources of civic activism. They are frequently bored, are unlikely to say that things are going their way, believe in hell, and don't want friends around when they are relaxing. If they had extra free time, they wouln't spend it helping others or improving their own intellects. They would probably devote it to more television. If we took away their television sets, they still would be bored and pessimistic' (p.17).

12   Reading newspapers cannot simply be regarded as an indicator of political involvement. The correlations noted remain intact when political interest is also controlled for.

13   This is in fact almost entirely attributable to the 35–54 age group; in the group aged under 35 there is virtually no correlation between viewing television and reading newspapers.

14   According to Bryce (1987) the 'time-orientation' of households is decisive for the extent to which television regulates the activity pattern (instead of the other way round). In households where there is a relatively tight timetable of activities, in which much is planned and in which activities are for preference completed individually and chronologically, television viewing fills the empty spaces between the various activities. In households where the members seek wherever possible to carry out tasks simultaneously and in which there is little planning, television has replaced the clock: the pattern of activities is arranged around television.

15   The number of hours of television viewing per week was as follows for the older age groups in 1980. Primary education: 10.2 hours, secondary education: 10.1 hours, higher education: 9.3 hours. Among the younger age groups the figures were 10.5, 8.8 and 6.0 hours respectively.

16   As remarked in the introduction to this chapter, we only deal with the private background and not with the public consequences of civic engagement. However, as we started with the civil society notion ourselves and focused on Putnam in this article, a longer quotation from a critical review of Putnam's civil society conception is justified:

> We maintain that the civil society argument as it is commonly presented is partial at best and seriously misleading at worst. In many respects, it presupposes precisely the sort of political peace that it imagines civil society providing. Where emphasis is placed on the ability of civil society to oppose a tyrannical state, its ability to oppose a democratic one is either ignored outright or countered with qualifications that themselves undermine the power of the civil society argument generally. When emphasis is placed on the formation of 'habits of the heart' conducive to cooperation and collective action, as it is in Robert Putnam's argument, the mechanisms by which such 'microsocial' effects translate into 'macropolitical' outcomes are weakly specified or contradictory or both. (Foley and Edwards 1996: 47).

References

Almond, G. A. and Verba, S. (1989 [1963]). *The Civic Culture*. Newbury Park: Sage.

Bryce, J. (1987). 'Family Time and Television Use' in *Natural Audiences*, ed. T. Lindlof. Norwood, NJ: Ablex.

CBS (Centraal Bureau voor de Statistiek) (1957). *Vrije-tijdsbesteding in Nederland 1955–56; deel 2: avond- en weekendbesteding*. Zeist: W. De Haan.

—— (1965). *Vrijetijdsbesteding in Nederland 1962/1963, deel 3: avond- en weekendbesteding/deel 7: verenigingsleven*. Zeist: W. De Haan.

Curtis, J. E., Grabb, E. G. and Baer, D.E. (1992). 'Voluntary Association Membership in Fifteen Countries', *American Sociological Review* 57: 139–52.

Dahlgren, P. (1995). *Television and the Public Sphere*. London: Sage.

De Hart, J. (1995). *Tijdopnamen*. The Hague: Vuga.

Dekker, P. (ed.) (1994). *Civil Society*. The Hague: Vuga.

Dekker, P. and van den Broek, A. (1995). 'Citizen Participation in Civil Societies', paper presented at the eighteenth Annual Scientific Meeting of the International Society of Political Psychology, Washington DC, 5–9 July.

—— (1996). 'Volunteering and Politics' in *Political Value Change in Western Democracies: Integration, Values, Identification and Participation*, ed. L. Halman and N. Nevitte. Tilburg: Tilburg University Press.

Dekker, P., Koopmans, R. and van den Broek, A. (1997). 'Voluntary Associations, Social Movements and Individual Political Behaviour in Western Europe' in *Social Involvement and Democratic Politics*, ed. J.W. van Deth. London: Routledge.

Foley, M.W. and Edwards, B. (1996). 'The Paradox of Civil Society'. *Journal of Democracy* 7/2: 38–52.

Gaskin, K. and Davis Smith, J. (1995). *A New Civic Europe?* London: The Volunteer Centre UK.

Katz, R. S., Mair, P. *et al.* (1992). 'The Membership of Political Parties in European Democracies, 1960–1990'. *European Journal of Political Research* 22: 329–45.

Lash, S. (1990). *The Sociology of Postmodernism*. London: Routledge.

Misztal, B.A. (1996). *Trust in Modern Societies*. Cambridge: Polity Press.

Nas, M., Dekker, P. and Hemmers, C. (1996). *Maatschappelijke organisaties, publieke opinie en milieu*. Rijswijk (NL): SCP.

Norris, P. (1996). 'Does Television erode Social Capital? A Reply to Putnam', *Political Science and Politics* 29: 474–80.

Putnam, R. D. (with R. Leonardi and R.Y. Nanetti) (1993a). *Making Democracy Work*. Princeton: Princeton University Press.

—— (1993b). 'The Prosperous Community', *The American Prospect* 13: 35–42.

—— (1995a). 'Bowling Alone', *Journal of Democracy* 6/1: 65–78.

—— (1995b). 'Tuning in, Tuning out', *PS: Political Science & Politics* 28: 664–83.

Robinson, J. P. (1972). 'Television's Impact on Everyday Life' in *Television and Social Behavior* (Vol. 4), E. A. Rubinstein *et al.* Washington, DC: US Government Printing Office.

Salamon. L. M. and H. K. Anheier (1996). 'Social Origins of Civil Society', paper presented at the second Annual Conference of the International Society for Third Sector Research, Mexico City, 18–21 July.

Schudson, M. (1996). 'What if Civic Life Didn't Die?'. *The American Prospect* 25: 17–20.

SCP (Social and Cultural Planning office) (1993). *Social and Cultural Report 1992*. Rijswijk (NL): SCP.

—— (1995). *Social and Cultural Report 1994*. Rijswijk (NL): SCP.

——— (1996). *Social Cultural Report 1996.* The Hague: Vuga.

Szalai, A. (ed.) (1972). *The Use of Time.* The Hague: Mouton.

Uslaner, E.M. (1996). 'Social Capital, Television and the "Mean World" ', paper presented at the 1996 Annual Meetings of the American Political Science Association, San Francisco, 28 August–1 September.

van Daal, H. J., Plemper, E. and Willems, L. (1992). *Vrijwilligersorganisaties in de thuiszorg.* The Hague: Nimawo.

van Deth, J.W. (1996). 'Voluntary Associations and Political Participation' in *Wahlen und politische Einstellungen in westlichen Demokratien*, eds. O.W. Gabriel and J.W. Falter. Frankfurt am Main: Peter Lang.

van Deth, J. W. and Leijenaar. M. (1994). *Maatschappelijke participatie in een middelgrote stad.* The Hague: Vuga.

Verba, S., Schlozman, K. L. and Brady, H. E. (1995). *Voice and Equality.* Cambridge, Mass.: Harvard University Press.

Voerman, G. (1996). 'De ledentallen van politieke partijen, 1945–1995' in *Jaarboek Documentatiecentrum Nederlandse politieke partijen 1995.* Groningen: Rijksuniversiteit.

Williams, T. M. and Handford, A.G. (1986). 'Television and Other Leisure Activities' in *The Impact of Television*, ed. T.M. Williams. New York: Academic Press.

5   Contracting out the participation function

Social capital and cheque-book participation

William A. Maloney

Putnam (1995a; 1995b) has famously argued that there have been decreases in the levels of social capital[1] in the United States over the last 30 years or so, and that this 'Bowling alone' phenomena has led to an erosion of the 'civil community'.[2] Accordingly all of the facets which undergird the 'civil community' such as social trust, tolerance, generalized reciprocity are in decline. As Foley and Edwards (1996: 41) point out, for Putnam civil associations are critical to the successful functioning of democracies: 'Civil associations provide the "networks of civic engagement" within which reciprocity is learned and enforced, trust is generated, and communication and patterns of collective action are facilitated.' High levels of trust are seen to be important, because the greater the levels of trust the less likely that citizens will behave 'opportunistically' (i.e. they are less likely to defect from cooperative collective action).

The most significant changes in civil society in recent years have been the decline of 'classic secondary associations' and the growth of what Putnam terms 'tertiary associations' (e.g. Greenpeace; the American Association of Retired Persons – which grew from 400,000 members in 1960 to 33 million in 1993).[3] Putnam argues that these new mass membership organizations are of great political importance in terms of policy making, but from the point of view of 'social connectedness' they are sufficiently different.

> For the vast majority of their members, the only act of membership consists in writing a cheque for dues or perhaps occasionally reading a newsletter. Few ever attend any meetings of such organizations, and most are unlikely ever (knowingly) to encounter any other member. (1995a: 71)

Such cheque-book participation *may* be adding to the depletion of social capital resources because cheque-book organizations tend towards hierarchy and create vertical links between members and the group. The membership ties which exist are to 'common symbols, common leaders, and perhaps common ideals, but not to one another' (Putnam, 1995a: 71). These organizations are seen as further fragmenting an already dangerously fragmented party system (Bell, 1975; cited in Godwin, 1988) and as: 'a symptom of a sick society in which individual citizens choose to abandon true democratic participation where persons meet and debate face-to-face. Instead, they select ersatz political participation in which the electorate responds only to a national elite that communicates through direct mail' (Topolsky, 1974; cited in Godwin, 1988: 4–5). These trends may be taking advanced democracies closer to *mass societies* (Hayes, 1986). The relationship in tertiary groups is more client–patron, than interaction among equals.

This chapter examines the *substance* of cheque-book participation which is becoming an increasingly popular *specialized participatory activity.* For example, Selle (in this volume) notes how social movements in Norway have gradually changed their character and to an increasing degree have become 'professionalized negotiating institutions'

> closely linked to the public sector. . . . *The voluntary organizations are no longer to the same extent proper intermediate democratic structures between the individuals and government.* Of course they still influence government policy, but it has become more and more difficult to clarify just who they represent. (Selle, 1998: original emphasis).

Verba *et al*.'s (1995: 67) survey (of 15,000 individuals) found that just over two-thirds of the respondents limited their participation in politics to cheque writing. In fact, even publics which one may expect to have mobilized via more social network means, have in fact grown in size and stature via direct mail, and television and radio contacting. For example, in 1982 the 'leader' of the Moral Majority organization, the Rev. Jerry Falwell, had a base of over 600 television and radio outlets that broadcast his weekly 'Old Time Gospel Hour'. The electronic church is an important part of the New Right. While Guth *et al*.'s survey of five prominent religions found that:

> Religious TV and radio, along with direct mail, mobilize conservatives directly for Christian Right causes, and recruit them into specific organizations groups . . . . The role of the clergy as a source of information and mobilization is not altogether obvious . . . ministers and priests are not cited as a source of information by a major in any group . . . interest groups provide a political vehicle not matched by local churches, no matter how successfully they fulfil activists' spiritual needs. (1995: 72)

The growth of cheque-book participation is also prevalent in the United Kingdom.

PARTICIPATING IN CHEQUE-BOOK GROUPS[4]

Here we examine: some of the reasons supporters gave for joining Amnesty International British Section (AIBS) and Friends of the Earth (FoE); which strategies supporters believed to be most effective in achieving organizational objectives; whether the route to membership (i.e. direct mail or social network)

Table 5.1 Reasons why people might join AIBS/FoE (in per cent)

	Very important		Not very important		Played no role whatsoever	
	AIBS	FoE	AIBS	FoE	AIBS	FoE
I liked the nonparty political approach of AIBS/FoE	70	64	16	17	13	17
AIBS provided the best opportunity to defend human rights/FoE acts as a counter-balance to big business	97	71	2	17	0	9
As a member I felt I could join like-minded people in fighting for human rights/the environment	64	65	25	24	8	9
To keep me informed about human rights/environmental issues	75	85	18	12	6	2
I was attracted by AIBS/FoE's responsible campaigning style	64	69	21	19	12	9
I felt that joining allows me to be active in political issues	24	27	33	30	40	40

is the result of, or leads to, different attitudes/behavioural patterns, or mobilizes different sets of *participants*. Supporters were asked how important a role each person played in their decision to join (see Table 5.1).

Our data showed that the overwhelming majority of members did not see membership of AIBS and FoE as a means of being 'active in political issues' (73 per cent of AIBS and 70 per cent of FoE members said that it was 'not very important'/'played no role whatsoever' in their decision to join). In addition to this, over 70 per cent of FoE members and almost all the AIBS members believed that the groups offered the best means to 'defend human rights'/'counterbalance big business'; 64 per cent of AIBS members and 65 per cent of FoE members stated that 'joining like-minded people in fighting for human rights/the environment' was an very important/important in their decision to join. It is worth noting that AIBS and FoE members exhibited high-level political efficacy: 70 per cent of AIBS members and 74 per cent of FoE members stated that their support has a 'significant/noticeable effect' on the organization's ability to protect human rights/the environment.

The cumulative effect of these responses may lead one to conclude that cheque writing is a purposive act of funding the protest work carried out by the groups; it is the group goal which is sought, not active political participation. Thus it is *participation by proxy*. However, participation by proxy should not be immediately discounted as lacking any substance or meaning. Groups which represent opinion on certain public issues may be important because they are visible in the public arena, and this is not an insignificant point.

Another interesting finding was that many AIBS and FoE members were attracted to these organizations because of their responsible campaigning style.

Table 5.2 Some of the ways in which AIBS/FoE campaigns for human rights/the environment were considered the most effective by members (in per cent)

	Most effective		Second most effective	
	AIBS	FoE	AIBS	FoE
Grass-roots campaigning on key human rights/ environmental issues	19	13	14	14
Taking more non-violent direct action to campaign on human rights/green issues	9	7	15	5
Working closely with politicians and government to influence legislation	21	40	22	22
Attempting to persuade companies to improve their environmental policies	n/a	9	n/a	27
Trying to change British public opinion through information	17	21	26	17
Acting as a 'world/green policeman' by exposing human rights violators/polluters	31	8	21	13

This seems somewhat at odds with accounts such as Dalton (1996) which see supporters of these groups as being attracted to more unconventional *elite-challenging* participation. Members were asked which activities they thought were most effective and as Table 5.2 indicates they tend not to see conventional-type participation as being particularly effective in pursuit of organizational goals: 21 per cent of AIBS members and 40 per cent of FoE members felt that 'Working closely with politicians and government to influence legislation' was *the most effective* way for AIBS and FoE to campaign, and 17 per cent of AIBS members and 21 per cent of FoE members thought that 'Trying to change British public opinion through information' was *the most effective* means.

From a social capital perspective two complementary points emerge for discussion. First, data of this sort does not indicate an alienated and excluded groups of citizens which many of the participants in the 'new social movement' sphere are so often labelled. These figures are suggestive of relatively high levels of trust in the political system. Second, it could simply be a recognition of the *realpolitik* with members (particularly FoE members) accepting that more influence over outcomes is achieved by sticking to the *rules of the game*.

SOCIAL CONNECTEDNESS AND PARTICIPATION

Godwin (1988) has argued that the *mode of recruitment* is significant. He distinguishes between two basic types of recruits – social network (who joined as a result of social interactions, e.g. discussions with a colleague or friend) and direct marketing (individuals who responded to a direct mail solicitation or other advertisement). Godwin's research addressed certain questions including: Do direct marketing techniques lead to different types of political participant? If yes, how do they differ from those who have traditionally participated in interest group and party politics? In short, is it important whether an individual joins a group via social network ties or direct mail solicitations? He hypothesized that direct-marketing recruits (direct mail) would be less committed to their political groups than members recruited via social ties, would stay in membership for a shorter period, and would possibly have lower levels of generalized tolerance and trust.

As Godwin (1988: 315) points out, critics of direct marketing politics argue that it encourages alienation, intolerance, extremism and aggressive attitudes and behaviour. Thus from a Putnamian perspective it would diminish a society's levels of social capital. It encourages overlapping memberships of similar types of group, (through the targetting of similar individuals and the trading of membership lists between groups) rather than cross-cutting memberships. Consequently, through the bombardment of partial information direct marketing recruits become less tolerant of opposing ideas and become more alienated from the political system. Individuals are not exposed to opposing views, and much of the literature stresses the non-negotiable nature of the work. Thus direct mail recruits are not educated in the language of trust, reciprocity, accommodation and tolerance. In short, they are not engaged in a process of deliberation and debate in search of the common good. As Verba *et al.* put it: 'In a fuller participatory democracy, political activity becomes a mechanism whereby citizens engage in enlightened discourse, some to understand the views of others, and become sensitized to the needs of the community and nation. Thus educated, they transcend their own interests to seek the public good' (1995: 529).

Thus when Godwin compared direct marketing recruits with social network recruits in environmental organizations he found a complex pattern:

> direct-marketing joiners tend either to participate less in politics and be less politically interested, knowledgeable, and active or they participate at very high levels and are highly interested and knowledgeable. In contrast social-network recruits tended to have moderate levels of participation, interest, and knowledge (1992: 315).

In short, Godwin (1988, 1992) found that direct marketing recruits were either highly committed to the cause and easily mobilized, or they had very low levels of interest but were persuaded to join by the direct mail solicitations they received. Social network recruits fell between these polar points. They cared more about the issues of interest than the weakly committed direct marketing recruits, but did not possess the intensely held belief of the strongly committed direct marketing recruits. The differences between direct marketing and social network joiners are not, however, particularly large.

However, with regard to political extremism, intolerance and alienation, the results were more straightforward. Direct marketing recruits scored high on all of these, while social network recruits scored lower. However, the fears of the direct marketing critics that this type of participation is the cause of these negative views are not confirmed. Godwin (1988: 64) found that the longer individuals remained members of a direct marketing organization the less alienated and aggressive they became. Godwin (1992: 317–18) concluded that: 'It would appear that even cheque-book participation reduces political alienation, as contributors believe their contributions make a difference. This, in turn, reduces the support for aggressive political participation.'

Our data showed that AIBS (and FoE) members tend to join as a result of group stimulation: 28 per cent of AIBS and 24 per cent of FoE members joined their respective groups in response to a press advertisement/media campaign, whereas only 4 per cent of AIBS and 5 per cent of FoE became involved at a local group meeting.[5] Following Godwin's distinction we divided our AIBS sample into direct marketing recruits and social network recruits. This revealed that 13 per cent of Amnesty members were recruited through a social network, while 65 per cent were recruited through direct marketing techniques. That these sorts of organizations are largely constituted by direct marketing recruits is hardly surprising, but it is not unimportant.

We found very minor differences between direct marketing recruits and social network recruits in terms of commitment to Amnesty (91 per cent of social network recruits and 86 per cent of direct marketing recruits stated that they were committed members of the group), or the intention to renew their subscription (98 per cent and 96 per cent of social network recruits and direct marketing recruits respectively said that they intended to renew subscription), and somewhat unsurprisingly 44 per cent of social network recruits and 9 per cent of direct marketing recruits said that talking to a member of the groups was important in their initial decision to join. Both sets of recruits differed little in their perceived political efficacy with 64 per cent of social network recruits and 70 per cent of direct marketing recruits believing that their support had a 'significant or noticeable effect'. With regard to the most effective type of activities, gender, education level, class and income, there is very little difference between the two sets of respondents. The major difference between the sets appears to be in the level of their 'active' participation in group activities: 27 per cent of social network recruits were members of a local Amnesty Group and had taken part in an *Urgent Action Scheme*, while only 13 per cent and 9 per cent of direct marketing recruits respectively were members of a local group or had taken part in such a scheme.

CHEQUE-BOOKS AND PARTICIPATION

Elsewhere we (Jordan and Maloney 1997; Maloney, 1996) have questioned whether cheque writing can be construed as meaningful participation and as enhancing democracy. While we raised this caveat we did not wish to overstate the case. As Richardson argues: 'We should, perhaps, not be too cynical about "credit card membership". Having made a contribution one is reassured that someone else is taking action on one's behalf to seek policy changes beneficial to the favoured cause' (1995: 135).

Stated bluntly, *one contracts out the function* leaving the job of influencing policy to the professionals. People may choose to pay others to do the job for them, either because they don't have the time or inclination to be more active, or because they don't have the expertise. Is this that different from companies employing lobbyists, or joining peak associations where they pay the subscription and do little or no more? In fact, does participation need to mean active participation? Is vicarious participation enough to be both beneficial and functional? It could merely be an extension to representative democracy. Individuals choose which groups to fund, and these groups represent their interest. If an individual is dissatisfied with the service offered by the group, they can choose to support another group. The public interest group market is awash with competitor groups all engaged in a fierce struggle for market share.

With increasing complexity in the policy process and the process of *issue niche specialization* (see Browne, 1991) individuals motivated to participate in politics may in fact develop a portfolio of *interest shares*. The party/electoral channel of representation has been increasingly seen as deficient. The breadth of support on which successful parties rely is seen, in one sense at least, as a democratic weakness: the party often cannot afford to reflect the narrow, and intensely held, concerns of individuals (see Cigler and Loomis, 1995 edn: 19). These it is argued, can be better expressed through single-issue groups. Berry (1984: 55) suggests that if one is politically active and willing to spend £100 to pursue one's political goals in a year then the interest group can be seen as a better 'investment' in that one can better target the cash on one's personal priorities – be they protecting the wilderness or whatever.

In addition to this, voting is a relatively 'minimalistic' participatory activity, yet it is still seen as an important legitimating exercise for democracies. Cheque writing does not seem to be much less minimal in terms of legitimation: '(cheque-book) groups' can represent individual interests. In fact, one could argue that it requires more 'effort' than simply voting. Individuals have to decide which group to patronize, decide whether they should renew their subscription at the end of each membership year, and if they think that their money would be better spent elsewhere, they need to find an alternative group. Many public interest group supporters also support several other groups, vote regularly, sign petitions, etc. and can arguably be presented as being very politically active[6] – certainly in contrast to the large bulk of the population who do no more than vote on a regular/irregular basis.

Parry *et al.* (1992: 428) argue that citizens exhibit higher levels of involvement on local issues than national issues. Thus, it may well be that researchers have been looking in the wrong place; like the drunk who searched for his keys under the lamppost, just because the light was better there! In the UK issues such as unemployment stimulate particularly low levels of actions, in spite of the highest levels of unemployment since 1945; individuals tend to see national 'problems' as issues of 'high politics'. Parry *et al.* argued that: 'One may vote and support a political party [or join a cheque-book group] and thereby seek to influence policy. For most people, however, action beyond that is best taken nearer home. It is about the local environment, housing or transport' (1992: 428).[7]

Similarly, Foley and Edwards (1996: 44) concluded that while large-scale tertiary groups were the most visible manifestations of concern for the environment or peace, Washington-based associations, given their high-profile media orientation, camouflaged the extent of grass-roots action. They (1996: 44) cite a recent national directory of environmental organizations which listed 645 groups, while the Citizen's Clearinghouse for Hazardous Wastes ('a national clearinghouse for grassroots environmental organizations') claimed that it was in contact with some 7–9 thousand groups nationwide. They also cited the 1987 *Grassroots Peace Directory* which listed 7,700 organizations, of which only 300 claimed to be national in scope.

Foley and Edwards also highlight the fact that many tertiary groups have important grass-roots bases. While it is correct that for the vast bulk of supporters participation is limited simply to cheque writing, there is more going on at the local level than Putnam concedes. They highlight the Sierra Club which has state and local chapters that: 'routinely sponsor community-service projects like urban clean-ups and "environmentally aware" outdoor activities broadly similar to those sponsored by the boy scouts, a group close to the heart of Putnam's "civic community"' (1996: 43–44).

We too have evidence of more local level involvement of cheque-book associations' members. FoE has a network of local groups, as does AIBS. A 1989 internal Amnesty survey showed significant levels of local participation, 21 per cent of members were active in local groups,[8] and out of a total membership of over 100,000 some 9,500 wrote letters on behalf of Amnesty more than 12 times per year. Our 1993 data recorded that 16 per cent of national group members belonged to local groups, 14 per cent had taken part in the urgent action scheme, and 51 per cent had taken part in letter-writing campaigns. There is a great deal more activity within groups such as AIBS than initially appears. However, as Foley and Edwards (1996: 43) highlight, Putnam ignores the importance of political associations, and focuses on groups which he believes produce the desired outcome of the civil community he envisages. He discounts tertiary groups because the main (and possibly the only) link between supporters (*not* members) and groups, is financial. In fact, cheque-book groups may be making a greater contribution to the civil community than Putnam is prepared to concede. Possibly even far more than his beloved choral societies, birdwatching clubs and bowling leagues.

CONCLUSIONS: CONTRACTING OUT AND THE DEMOCRATIC PROCESS

New forms of minimalistic cheque-book participation have been criticized as having added little value to the democratic structure. In fact, in some instances the situation is seen as being inimical to democracy. However, many of the critics of this type of participation tend to overlook the fact that it reduces entry barriers to *participation*. It has encouraged far greater numbers of citizens to take an interest in politics – even though cheque-book participators conform to the standard (SES) model.

As Godwin (1988: 47) points out, without direct mail solicitations from groups an individual would have to spend time and effort identifying which groups they may wish to patronize, then choose from the available pool, find out how they can join the organization and then pay the annual subscription. Once they have crossed the membership threshold they may then be asked to undertake additional obligations: attend meetings; take part in letter-writing campaigns to politicians; join a rally, etc. Members may after one year's *experiential search* (Rothenberg, 1992), decide to leave one group to join another because their expectations of membership were not fulfilled. As Godwin (1988: 47) concludes: 'In short, membership in citizen action groups may require more than a simple contribution; it can entail substantial time and effort as well.' Even critics such as Hayes (1986: 143) concede that while most of the new citizen groups do not conform to the traditional membership-based model: 'The continuing susceptibility of such large and diffuse constituencies to the free-rider problem suggests, however, that if alternative organizational forms had not emerged, most of these interests would remain unorganized today.'

Some commentators have criticized direct mail membership for encouraging political intolerance because individuals motivated to participate via this method are likely to hold multiple cheque-book memberships all within the same ideological perspective. Within this ideological cocoon there is little room for debate and an exchange of views with those from competing ideological perspectives. In addition to this, some charge many groups with supplying members with propaganda rather than technically sound information, after all the information provided is both a (weak) selective incentive, but also the primary means through which groups inform their members that their continued support is crucial to the organization's (and their) objectives. In spite of these arguments, Godwin (1988: 50) maintains that if political mail motivates the public to pay attention to important issues and the actions of their representatives, then it could be perceived as strengthening democracy.

In addition to this, Whiteley (in this volume) has hypothesized that social capital can or may be generated 'by membership of "imaginary [or abstract] communities", that is communities which individuals identify with, but which they never actually interact with on a face-to-face basis'. The supporters of AIBS and FoE fall firmly into this grouping. Imaginary communities are large and geographically dispersed and individuals within them can only socially interact with a very small fraction of the group. In spite of this 'social barrier' individuals within these groups can develop very strong levels of group identification: 'joining like-minded people' (see Table 5.1) in pursuit of a cause may develop a sense of 'community' or belonging. Membership of these groups may not be as detrimental to the generation of social capital as the Putnam/ Tocqueville model suggests.

In conclusion, John Stuart Mill argued that: '*any participation, even in the smallest public function, is useful*' (1972 edn.: 217; quoted in Parry *et al.*: 433

emphasis added). While cheque-writers' contribution may in fact be small, it is certainly better than not participating at all. There is little or no strong evidence to suggest that cheque-book participation is detrimental in the way that Putnam implies or envisages. It may be a supplementary/complementary participatory activity to more active political involvement, or at least of a similar level of commitment as voting in liberal democracies. Could it be that citizens are becoming *participatory dualists* seeing local political matters as being best addressed by individual action, and national matters of concern such as human rights and the global environment as best addressed by 'group' action? Many question over the impact of direct mail on the levels of social capital remain to be answered. The two most important are: Does cheque-book participation erode social capital? Or, is it a useful supplement to more active participation? This chapter has drawn some tentative conclusions, but in the time honoured tradition we need *light, more light!*

Notes

1   Putnam (1995b: 664) defines social capital as 'the features of social life networks, norms, and trust that enable participants to act more effectively to pursue shared objectives'.

2   Putnam (1995a: 68 and 72) argued that the US has witnessed a new paradox of participation, namely falling engagement in politics and government, despite rising levels of educational attainment.

3   Tertiary associations are similar to staff groups (Hayes, 1986), mail order groups (Mundo, 1992); and protest businesses (Jordan and Maloney, 1997).

4   We carried out a postal survey of 500 Amnesty International (British Section) members, and 1,000 supporters of Friends of the Earth (FoE) Limited based in London. The surveys were carried out between March and July 1993. The sample names and addresses were provided by the organizations, and the response rates were: Amnesty = 72.4 per cent (*n* = 362); and FoE = 68.1 per cent (*n* = 681). Amnesty is a human rights organization which works 'impartially for the release of those imprisoned for their opinions, to seek for them a fair (and public) trial, to enlarge the right to asylum, to help political refugees find work, and to urge the creation of effective international machinery to guarantee freedom of opinion' (Power, 1981: 10; Ennals, 1982: 65). Amnesty was formed in 1961 and by 1992 it had approximately 1.1 million members, subscribers and regular donors in 150 countries, over 8,000 local Amnesty groups in 70 countries, and a budget of £12.75 million (Amnesty International, 1993). The discussion of Amnesty in this chapter relates solely to the British Section. FoE is an environmental organization which was formed in 1971 by a disaffected executive director of the Sierra Club (David Brower) with the specific task of 'waging political battles to protect the environment'. In 1994 it had 96 staff, an annual income of £5.3 million, 112,000 supporters, and there were over 300 local groups (in England and Wales) which are autonomous from the London-based organization and which campaign on issues of their own choosing.

5   This is in contrast to the membership of the Green and Conservative parties which have many members who joined via social network ties. For example, 23

per cent and 22 per cent of Conservative party members respectively joined as a result of social contacts, and family contacts (Whiteley *et al.*, 1994: 78). Similarly, 37 per cent of Green party members said that 'Talking to a Green Party member was a decisive/very important/important factor in their decision to join' (Rüdig *et al.*, 1992: 58).

6   For example, 74 per cent of AIBS and 66 per cent of FoE members stated that they were members of other 'campaigning or environmental organizations', and 90 per cent of AIBS and 77 per cent of FoE members say that they 'vote at every General Election'.

7   Parry *et al.* (1992: 429–30) point out that this is not unproblematic: 'the relative lack of citizen participation in national-level issues means that there is a significant arena where the ordinary person makes little direct impact'. Thus the allocation of resources still remains in the hands of the political elite, with the citizenry influencing policy outputs through voting for political packages at election time.

8   In 1992 AIBS had 331 local campaign and adoption groups.

References

Berry, J (1984), *The Interest Group Society*, (Boston: Little Brown and Company).

Browne, W P (1991), 'Organized Interests and Their Issue Niches: A Search for Pluralism in a Policy Domain', *Journal of Politics*, 52: 477–509.

Cigler, A J and Loomis, – A (1995), 'Contemporary Interest Group Politics: More Than "More of the Same" ', in A J Cigler and – A Loomis (eds) *Interest Group Politics*, 4th edn (Washington, DC: Congressional Quarterly Press): 393–406.

Dalton, R J (1996), *Citizen Politics*, 2nd edn (New Jersey: Chatham House).

Ennals, M (1982), 'Amnesty International and Human Rights', in P Willetts (ed.) *Pressure Groups in the Global System: The Transnational Relations of Issue-Orientated Non-Governmental Organizations* (London: Frances Pinter).

Foley, M W and Edwards, B (1996), 'The Paradox of Civil Society', *Journal of Democracy*, 7 (3): 38–52.

Godwin, R K (1988), *One Billion Dollars of Influence* (Chatham House, NJ: Chatham House).

Guth, J L, Green, J C, Lyman, A K and Smidt, C E (1995), 'Onward Christian Soldiers: Religious Activist Groups in American Politics' in A J Cigler and B A Loomis (eds) *Interest Group Politics*, 4th edn (Washington, DC: Congressional Quarterly Press): 55–76.

Hayes, M T (1986), 'The New Group Universe', in A J Cigler and B. A. Loomis (eds) *Interest Group Politics*, 2nd edn (Washington, DC: Congressional Quarterly Press): 133–45.

Jordan, G and Maloney, W A (1997), *The Protest Business: Mobilizing Campaign Groups* (Manchester: Manchester University Press).

Maloney, W A (1996), 'Mobilization and Participation in Large-Scale Campaigning Groups in the UK: The Rise of the Protest Business', paper presented at the Workshop on Social Involvement and Participation in Voluntary Associations, and Democratic Politics, ECPR Joint Sessions, 28 March to 3 April, Oslo, Norway.

Mundo, P A (1992), *Interest Groups: Cases and Characteristics* (Chicago: Nelson Hall).

Parry, G, Moyser, G and Day, N (1992), *Political Participation and Democracy in Britain* (Cambridge: Cambridge University Press).

Power, J (1981), *Amnesty International: The Human Rights Story* (Oxford: Pergamon Press).

Putnam, R D (1993), *Making Democracy Work* (Princeton: Princeton University Press).

Putnam, R D (1995a), 'Bowling Alone: America's Declining Social Capital', *Journal of Democracy*, vol. 6, no. 1: 65–78.

Putnam, R D (1995b), 'Tuning In, Turning Out: The Strange Disappearance of Social Capital in America', *PS: Political Science and Politics*, vol. XXVIII, no. 4 (December): 664–83.

Richardson, J J (1995), 'The Market for Political Activism: Interest Groups as a Challenge to Political Parties', *West European Politics*, vol. 18, no. 1: 116–39.

Rothenberg, L S (1992), *Linking Citizens To Government* (New York: Cambridge University Press).

Rüdig, W, Franklin, M N and Bennie, L G (1993), 'Green Blues: The Rise and Decline of the British Green Party', *Strathclyde Papers on Government and Politics no. 95*, Department of Government, University of Strathclyde, (Glasgow: Department of Government, University of Strathclyde).

Tocqueville, A de (1956), *Democracy in America*, R D Heffner (ed.) (New York: Mentor).

Verba, S, Schlozman, K L and Brady, H E (1995), *Voice and Equality: Civil Voluntarism in Americam Politics* (Cambridge, MA.: Harvard University Press).

Whiteley, P, Seyd, P and Richardson, J (1994), *True Blues: The Politics of Conservative Party Membership* (Oxford: Clarendon Press).

6   Voluntary associations and social capital in Finland

Martti Siisiäinen

INTRODUCTION

The purpose of this chapter is to examine the present state of Finnish voluntary associations from a social capital perspective – social capital in association with cultural and, to a certain extent, economic capital that is accumulated in voluntary associations is here called organizational capital. Organizational capital is primarily social capital, but it also has its cultural and economic aspects. According to Putnam social capital refers to such features of social organization as 'networks, norms, and social trust that facilitate co-ordination and co-operation for mutual benefits' (1995: 67). In this chapter I deal only with organizational networks (voluntary associations) and trust or confidence in institutions. As to the latter problem, I am especially interested in the relationship between the numbers of members in associations and trust in institutions.

Social capital has both an individual and political component. Its individual component is mediated through memberships. Association is an accumulation of individual resources. It can transform the quantity of its individual members into a new quality of organization (see Siisiäinen 1988). But organizational capital is also capital on the system level, functioning as a democratic (or antidemocratic) resource.

This chapter deals with three interrelated subproblems: First, how much social capital is invested in present voluntary associations in Finland as measured by association memberships and participation? Second, is Finnish social capital invested in voluntary associations declining in the 1990s (the question of the crisis of the system of voluntary associations). This has two aspects: first, it is important to examine the development of membership figures in different association types since the beginning of 1980s, and second, to look at the formation of new associations in the 1990s. The third issue examines the relationship between association memberships and trust in social institutions. Finnish membership figures are also compared internationally, especially with Norwegian, Swedish, Estonian, Latvian and Lithuanian data.

Finland – the promised land of voluntary associations?

To set the scene it is important to review a short history of voluntary associations in Finland. The first modern voluntary associations were founded at the end of the eighteenth century (see Stenius 1987; Siisiäinen 1991). Such organizations at this time were invariably upper-class societies but from 1809 onwards they slowly began to reach the common people as well and the years from 1861 to 1880 were characterized by principles of liberal equality. The period from 1896 to 1905 laid a network of mass movements based on class interests and the networks of voluntary associations began to divide into socialist and right-wing camps. Both sides had their own organizations in all fields of civil society (temperance, sports, education and art, co-operatives, etc.), with a network of local branches all over the country.

Even though Finland has witnessed exceptional political periods – both rightist (during the 1920s and 1930s) and leftist (during the second half of the 1940s) – the number of voluntary associations has increased more or less steadily from the beginning of the 1920s to the present.

From 1920 to the mid-1990s, 140,000 new associations were registered in Finland (see Table 6.1). It is typical of Finland that all large movements have used the organizational weapon of registered association. Therefore the register of associations show in a unique way the formation of new (organized) collective interest from 1919 to the present. Table 6.4 shows the cumulative curve of the development and differentiation of the Finnish system of voluntary associations. Economic and professional associations have been the most popular type of association (27 per cent), with political organizations taking second place (22 per cent). However, this cumulative or systemic presentation of the development of the system of voluntary associations does not tell us much about the ideology behind the political dynamics of their organization. If we identify the most dynamic periods (see Figure 6.1), we can easily see that they coincide with the peaks of cycles of protest in Finland (see Siisiäinen 1992a).

Finland has witnessed five cycles of protest during the twentieth century. The first, headed by the socialist workers' movement, lasted 13 years, from the General Strike of 1905 to the Civil War in 1918. The next (1928–32) was dominated by semifascist political forces. During this period more than 3,000 left-wing associations were banned. During the years following the end of World War II (1944–8) the underground period of the Communist Party (CP) ended. Together with its ally, the People's Democratic League (SKDL), the Communists won a quarter of the seats in Parliament in the first elections. It was the aim of the Communist Party to create a people's front with the help of hundreds of new voluntary associations and the trade union movement. However, the right-wing forces recovered from their defeat in the war and were able to re-establish their leading position at the end of the 1940s. The years from the end of the 1940s to the mid-1960s were a time of gradual right-wing development.

The fourth cycle of protest, 1966–76, started among young academics. This movement was transformed at the end of the 1960s into a political movement and

Table 6.1 Registration of different types of voluntary associations in Finland 1920–1994

Type of associations	1920–44 N	%	1945–64 N	%	1965–79 N	%	1980–9 N	%	1990–4 N	%	1919–94 N	%
Political	5965	21	11535	26	9120	27	2920	13	550	5	30090	22
Economic and professional	8955	31	13575	31	9465	28	4860	22	1395	14	38250	27
Social welfare	1475	5	2060	5	2140	6	1567	7	870	9	8112	6
Culture and education	1865	7	4235	10	3275	10	4070	18	2225	22	15670	11
Sports	2395	8	3580	8	2685	8	3686	16	2170	21	14516	10
Other hobbies	2830	10	4360	10	4255	12	3233	14	1970	19	16648	12
Religion	1055	4	845	2	660	2	499	2	185	2	3244	2
War and peace	2695	9	1060	2	1330	4	344	2	65	1	5494	3
International	30	0.1	900	2	360	1	454	2	190	2	1934	1
Other	1415	5	1670	4	1045	3	799	3	565	6	5494	3
Total	28680	100	43820	100	34335	100	22432	100	10185	100	139452	100
Associations/year	1147		2200		2300		2243		2037		1859	

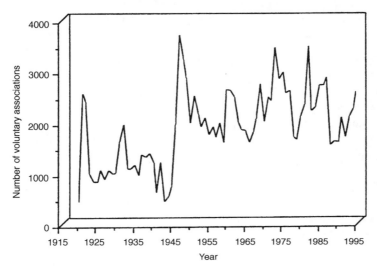

Figure 6.1 The registration of new associations in Finland, 1919–94.

soon after that became totally party political. The last cycle of protest characterized by the growth of new social movements started in Finland in the second half of the 1970s, a few years later than in other advanced European countries. During this period many associations started to turn green. The spirit of this era of 'silent revolution' can be seen in the increase of the number of nature conservation associations and associations promoting other kinds of 'soft' values (camping, sailing, pets and other animals, physical culture) and culture.

After this last, ecological, cycle fewer associations were founded at the end of the 1980s, but the number of new associations started to rise again in the 1990s (see Table 6.1).

VOLUNTARY ASSOCIATIONS AND TRADITIONS OF COLLECTIVE ACTION IN FINLAND

At a general level it has been argued that all political and ideological collective action can only be understood against the background of a 'collective consciousness' of a people. This holds true both for those tendencies that maintain the values and discourses that have been prevalent in a community, as well as for those that oppose dominant value systems and political institutions. This is because to gain support challenges must be formulated in a way that can be understood on the basis of earlier 'collective memories' and ideological tensions that dynamicize the ideological formation or discourse in question (cf. Connerton 1989). It is also true that repertoires of collective action, at least in part, have shown historical continuity in different countries (see Tilly 1988; cf. Tarrow 1989;

Siisiäinen 1992b). New organizations arise on the basis of old organizational cultures and are interpreted with the help of older organizational frames.

The adoption of the formal organization, i.e. the *registered association,* as the mode of functioning in social movements has been a dominant tendency in Finnish collective action. The adaptation of the activities of movements to the requirements of formal association has had important consequences for the prevailing repertoire of collective action in these movements. This is to say that as a rule the transformation of social movements into registered voluntary associations implicitly means a choice is made in favour of a non-action-orientated, non-violent, non-anarchist and non-disruptive repertoire of action. In its ideal form this kind of voluntary association turns into a 'bürgerliche Idealverein'. According to Negt and Kluge, it is not likely to be dominated by the will of its members which arises on an *ad hoc* basis, but rather it is codified formally into a statute, which is a general formulation of intention. It is only by operating through the Registry of Associations that the will of the members becomes binding at all. The life interests of the members are related matters ('Begleitsumstände'), not the goals of the association (1976: 422).

Voluntary associations can be approached from the perspective of their subjects or from the perspective of the political system. For the subjects who create associations their mutual interactions are a way to reduce 'a double contingency inherent in interaction. On the one hand, ego's gratifications are contingent on ego's selection among available alternatives. But, in turn, alter's reaction will be contingent on ego's selection and will result from a complementary selection on alter's part' (Parsons 1968, cited in Luhmann 1986: 148).

Voluntary organizing can be attained through trust: association members have to trust that the organization purports to reach the goals that they share and are the reason for their contribution to the association. Richter puts it in the following terms:

> Confidence is a way of reducing the complexity of modern society. Individuals cannot control all the actions necessary to achieve their goals. Therefore, they delegate powers to regulating systems, and by making their own contribution to these systems they also make it possible for others to attain their goals. However, individuals must have confidence in the regulating systems, in our case, the voluntary associations, in order to achieve their aims. (Richter 1985: 244 – translated by the editors)

In Luhmann's view, history and organization are two principal ways to reduce contingency and complexity: in history there are no alternatives; in organizations alternatives are reduced by communicative rules (Luhmann 1978).

Associations as 'action systems' are means of communication between civil society/citizens and the political subsystem. All subsystems have their specific way of communicating. In order to be taken into consideration by the political or economic subsystem, social movements or voluntary organizations have to use a form of communication that the subsystem in question can cope with. If ecological movements want to get their message heard they have to cast it in a language that the subsystems can understand by their own logic. For example, the logic of economy is based on cost/price–benefit/profit calculations.

> The key to ecological problems, as far as the economy is concerned, resides in the language of prices. This language filters in advance everything that occurs in the economy when prices change or do not change. The economy cannot react to disturbances that are not expressed in this language – any event, not with the intact structure of a differentiated function-system of society. The alternative is the destruction of the money-economy . . .
> (Luhmann 1991: 62)

The same principle holds true for other subsystems, too. Ecological and other problems developed in the environment of the system can be understood from the system perspective as disturbances. The registration of a voluntary association means that its action becomes standardized, its repertoires of action and its relation to the political system legally patterned. Registered associations are 'filters' which convert the communication of movements into such form that the political, legal and economic subsystems can process it or, in practice some part of it. The paradox for protest movements 'seems to be that one has to recognize the dominant social structure . . . to assume a position against it' (Luhmann 1991: 126).

The importance of registered associations in Finnish protests and protest movements goes in two directions. First, registered associations have in most cases been (among) the originators of protest movements. They have often organized a social movement which has extended the protest into new areas. In many cases registered associations have provided the activists of protest movements with organizational capital, that is, with the skills needed in organizing and leading an effective movement. Second, protest movements have generally produced a large number of new registered associations. The highest peaks in the numbers of new registered associations in Finland overlap with the culmination of cycles of protest. This has been the case with all earlier cycles of protest (see Siisiäinen 1992a).

The importance of the state (including local government) as a force directing the actions of protest movements is connected with the central role of the national elite and intelligentsia in organizing protests. During the rise of Finnish capitalism, the national elite and main professional groups were dependent on the state. The roots of the tradition of legalism in Finland date back to the turn of the nineteenth century and are connected with the national elite's special close relationship to the state (see Konttinen 1991). The rise of the so-called people's movements during the second half of the nineteenth century was organized by the national elite and intelligentsia with the aim of building a Finnish nation.

Even though Finland was a part of the Russian Empire up to 1917, it already was a state. Therefore 'the national movement there did not have to fight to bring about a separate political status; its task lay in reinforcing existing institutions *vis-à-vis* Russia and in the creation of a nation and ideology corresponding to a state' (Alapuro 1989: 148). Nationalist intellectuals in Finland endeavoured to promote the nation's affairs by appropriating the existing state. Almost the whole upper class in Finland lacked a strong basis outside the state and thus was dependent on the civil service of the grand duchy. In contrast to many other small nations under Russian rule (e.g. the Baltic countries), the power vacuum in 1905 did not lead to violent outbursts in Finland. Finnish nationalists

> tried to serve the good of the nation by organizing mass movements in order to educate and elevate the peasantry to become useful members of society. . . These nationalist-inspired movements opened the way to the politicization of the common people, but they also had a moderating influence on the process of organization. (Alapuro 1989: 151)

Since then the demands of social movements have very often been addressed by the state, and the political system has been fairly open to issues raised by social movements. In the openness of the political system, formal voluntary associations have a central role in transforming inputs from civil society to meet the requirements of the system.

VOLUNTARY ASSOCIATIONS AND THE NEW SOCIAL MOVEMENTS

Ecological movements and squatters' groups have been selected for a closer examination as being representative of the most radical types of new social movements.[1] The reason for this is that their features and repertoires of action display the greatest differences *vis-à-vis* those of traditional movements. Thus, the appearance of traditional forms of collective action, even within these two types of new movement, is the most convincing proof of their power in the Finnish movement/organization sector.

New types of struggles on behalf of the cultural and natural environment started in Finland at the end of the 1970s. This activity attained two high points during the 1980s; the first of these occurred during the early years of the 1980s and the second in the late 1980s (see Litmanen 1990; Järvikoski 1991). The cases examined here are the movements of 1988 against the felling of trees in a national park ('Talaskangas'), of 1989 against the same threat in another park ('Sopenmäki') and of 1991 against the building of a road through a national park ('Jerisjärvi') to a commercial holiday centre.

The role of registered associations and formal organizational structures in these movements is an interesting complex of intertwined phenomena. Formal, hierarchical structures are almost totally absent in these movements. On the other hand, registered associations (*Luonto-liitto*/The League of Nature and *Luonnonsuojeluliitto*/The Finnish Association for Nature Conservation) have played a very essential role in organizing the struggles for national parks. Once such struggles have started they have rapidly found support among established organizations (e.g. the YWCA, a local church, party organizations, etc). As a rule the struggles have generally resulted in the establishment of new registered associations to continue the fight in a more effective and systematic way (see Siisiäinen 1992a).

State orientation has preserved its central importance also in the new ecological struggles. First of all this is because the state has been the main adversary in these three struggles; it has both declared the forests in question national parks and then given permission for work to be carried out in the parks. It is also in conformity with Finnish political traditions that the demands of protestors have found support within (mostly opposition) political parties and that arenas of negotiations have quite often been open within the state apparatus. The Finnish state has developed very effective strategies of integration and co-option which were originally developed in response to the movements of the 1960s and are still utilized in the case of the new social movements.[2]

In many central European countries the squatters' movement is one of the organizational forms that differ most from traditional voluntary associations. Squatting, as with other new movements, started later in Finland than in central Europe, and squatters have been relatively few in number. According to a study by Anne Eronen (1991), no more than 33 proper squatting cases were reported in *Helsingin Sanomat* in 1979–90.

The case of squatting is the clearest demonstration of the importance of registered associations in promoting all kinds of movements in Finland. Robert Michels remarked in his research on oligarchic tendencies (1966) that if they flourish in the most democratic political movements of their time, that means they are universal. In an analogous way, we could say that if voluntary associations and the tendencies that coalesce with them (importance of state orientation, avoidance of actionist forms, obeying the law), dominate even in the most unconventional movement in Finland, it is strong evidence for the hegemonic role of formal associations in Finnish political culture.

During the second half of the 1970s, associations for live music were founded in all big cities, in many smaller towns and also in certain rural municipalities. These associations can be regarded as the forerunners of the new movements proper. They were later connected in a concrete way to squatting: many early squats were started during or immediately after concerts organized by associations for live music or were directly planned by them. Other occupations were planned by leftist youth organizations. Many squatting activists had gained experiences from other movements and associations. They were thus not isolated outcasts but active young people with effective social and organizational networks (see Eronen and Ristimäki 1991; Eronen 1991; Siisiäinen 1992a).

Almost as a rule, squats resulted in the foundation of registered (or sometimes non-registered) voluntary associations to continue their activities. This is one manifestation of the strength of organizational traditions in Finnish collective action. The owners of occupied buildings often made the establishment of an association officially representing the occupants a condition for future negotiations. The occupants usually agreed and founded an association. These associations in turn acted as the organizers of new occupations (see Eronen 1991).

As a conclusion we can say that even among the most radical new movements and struggles, i.e. ecological struggles/movements and squatters' groups the form of registered association still appears to be a major means of advancing interests. The development of the Finnish welfare state has historically been given impetus by protest movements. In practice this influence was generally spread out by registered associations founded by movement members to negotiate with the state. This is also true of the new social movements examined in this chapter. Municipalities and state authorities in general require the establishment of a registered association as a precondition for negotiations, and movements usually comply.

SOCIAL CAPITAL IN VOLUNTARY ASSOCIATIONS IN THE MID-1990s

In this section the development of social capital in the 1990s is examined, first by studying the formation of new voluntary associations in comparison with the earlier periods and second, on the basis of membership figures of different types of voluntary associations.

Formation of new voluntary associations in the 1990s

Figure 6.1 indicates that there was a rapid increase in new associations in the 1990s, suggesting that there was no such phenomenon as a general crisis of associations in Finland. However, many associations are in crisis because they are losing members (see next section) and especially have trouble in building bridges to potential younger members.

A sign of a well-functioning sector of voluntary organizations is their capacity to renew themselves, as indicated by the formation of new associations. On the other hand, stagnating or retrograding sectors are characterized by slow, or lack of, renewal. Table 6.1 presents the formation of new associations in the 1990s in comparison with earlier periods.

There is no reason to speak about the general crisis of voluntary associations in the 1990s on the basis of registration figures. Judgements about the condition of the system of associations must be more specific and analytic. Upon closer examination different tendencies can be found regarding different types of associations. In both progressing and regressing sectors there are developing and stagnating associations. Even though the number of sports clubs has grown rapidly in the 1990s, some traditional sports associations are not doing too well. And although political organizations face more problems than, perhaps, any other type of association, in politics, too, a couple of important newcomers have appeared in Parliament (the Green party(ies) and The Young Finnish Party).

This interpretation is accentuated if we compare the proportion of different types of associations created in 1920–89 with those established in the 1990s. Political organizations have lost more ground than the others (from 23 to 5 per cent). Also proto-modern associations based on economic and/or labour interests (including trade unions, employers organizations, farmers societies, etc.) have lost their share from 30 to 14 per cent. But, on the other hand, there are those associations that have been able to advance and occupy new footing: the proportion of different kinds of sports clubs and groups has risen from 10 to 21 per cent, the share of cultural and/or educational associations from 10 to 22 per cent. Also other leisure time and hobby associations have increased their share from 11 to 19 per cent. Changes in the share of other types of association have been smaller. At the same time there have been changes in the contents of activities in these sectors. The subjective interpretations of students of sociology playing indoor bandy against a registered team (association) of philosophy students are quite different in comparison with those athletes that 'were running Finland onto the world map' earlier this century. Many of the new sports associations are less competitive, more playful and all this often occurs outside large national central organizations.

Part of the changes have been very rapid and can be seen even in comparing the situation in the 1980s and 1990s. The share of political associations of all new associations has decreased from 13 to 5 per cent, the share of economic and/or professional organizations from 22 to 14 per cent. On the other side, the increases, too, have been fast: from 16 to 21 (sports), 14 to 19 (other hobbies), 18 to 22 per cent (culture and/or education).

If we analyse more specific categories in Table 6.1, many of those associations which have increased their share in the period 1990–4 in comparison with 1920–89 are associated with the values of Inglehart's silent revolution and post-materialism. Thus health groups increased by 3.0 per cent, new kinds of sport and physical exercise groups by 12 per cent, animals and pet groups by 2.0 per cent, and environmental groups by 0.9 per cent. There was also an increase in groups associated with 'Gemeinschaftliche' values: support of culture (+2.9 per cent), learning (+2.0 per cent), art (+1.9 per cent), old people (+1.7 per cent), tradition (+1.4 per cent) and kinship/family groups (+1.0 per cent). A large proportion of the new hobby clubs that have been increasing rapidly in the 1990s, for example motor clubs (+2.0 per cent) can also be seen as a part of the process of community development in urban Finland.

From the above figures and other studies on the 1990s in Finland we can conclude that some kind of transformation is going on among Finnish voluntary associations. This is connected with the transformation/dissolution of the Finnish welfare state. It is not the whole system of voluntary associations or social capital that is invested in them which is in crisis. The crisis of associations is selective.

At the moment the future prospects for Finnish voluntary associations can be categorized as follows (see Siisiäinen 1995):

1 Defunct associations that are tied to vanishing (or vanished) collective identities. Many ideological associations that were founded between the two world wars belong to this category.
2 Associations that are in crisis but are still partly able to function. Many political associations and parties belong to this group (cf. Sundberg 1996).

Their ideological frame and mode of action is inherited from previous decades. Their future depends on their ability to build bridges to the personal frames of young people born in the 1980s.

3   Big semi-state associations ('halbstaatliche Vereine'), which compensate for the deficiencies of the welfare state and take responsibility for those tasks that the decline of the structures of the welfare state produces. Many of these associations combine a bureaucratic ethos with one of genuine solidarity. For example, most associations for handicapped people belong to this category.

4   Associations which transform voluntary action towards competing with commercial profit organizations, a common phenomenon in the case of certain kinds of sports clubs.

5   Interest organizations, for example trade unions, acting according to cost-benefit calculations. In Finland there are no grounds for saying that this kind of activity would be in crisis either. On the contrary there are new activist groups in unions that have appeared during the 1980s and 1990s. For example, young engineers stress the importance of unions and are more union-oriented than most of the traditional working-class cadres (see Jokivuori *et al.* 1996).

6   Associations built on strong close ties and 'Gemeinschaft'-type solidarity. This includes neighbourhood or block associations, village committees and company sports teams whose importance has been growing since the 1970s.

7   Idealist–philanthropic associations based on common value rationality in the Weberian sense and solidarity, including many associations for the Third World countries or associations which arrange adoptions from the Third World.

8   'Traditional' associations acting for global values that have been changing under the influence of the new social movements and during the silent revolution. For example, for the first time in its history the well-established Finnish Association for Nature Conservation adopted a position on the use of illegal methods in action against real or imagined destruction of (planned) national parks at the end of the 1980s.

9   Anti-association activity, i.e. alternative movements proper. There are actually only a few examples of this kind of association in Finland. Perhaps the best examples can be found in the movements fighting for animal liberation that have attacked fox farms and some buildings.

10   Religious movements following a non-rational (and non-negotiable) logic.

Some successful associations still follow the logic of interest politics (for example the trade unions of new middle classes) whereas others could be characterized as 'new tribes' (see Maffesoli 1996). These associations are based more on *gemeinschaftliche* values and function outside the *bürgerliche Öffentlichkeit*. So it can be concluded that voluntary associations as such are not in crisis but that the system of associations is witnessing inner differentiation.

Association memberships

It is very difficult to compare membership figures between different countries because quite different things are often meant by the conception of association. For instance, in certain countries belonging to a church is an association membership, whereas in other countries such memberships are defined outside the concept of association (e.g. the Nordic countries). With some reservations it is possible to make crude comparisons between countries with similar (e.g. the Nordic countries) or almost similar modes of civic engagement (the Western European countries).

In the 1960s the proportion of those who were reported belonging to various associations varied in the US between 60 and 80 per cent. In the Federal Republic of Germany about half of the adult population belonged to some association (including political parties and trade unions) in the 1970s. In the early 1980s, 56–8 per cent of 16 to 65 year olds were members of one association or other. Of the 15 to 65 year olds in Austria 50 to 60 per cent belonged to some association in the 1970s and early 1980s (see Richter 1985; Siisiäinen 1991). In the World Values Surveys (1981 to 1983) analysed by Curtis *et al.* (1992) 15 nations were compared.[3] The highest proportion of respondents reporting voluntary association membership was in the US (73 per cent), in Northern Ireland (67 per cent), Sweden (68 per cent) and Norway (62 per cent). When church membership was excluded Swedes (65 per cent) and Norwegians (60 per cent) ranked highest. The picture again changes if union membership is also excluded (see Curtis *et al.* 1992: 143).

It is clear that the membership figures for the Nordic countries were from the 1960s to 1980s at least on the same level, perhaps even somewhat higher than in other Western democracies. In an earlier Nordic comparison, Finns have been shown to be a little more passive than Swedes, Norwegian and Danes. The differences have, however, been diminishing. In a comparative study made in 1972 38 per cent of Finns, but only 29 per cent of Danes and 20 per cent of Swedes belonged to the group 'No association memberships/I don't know' in the questionnaire (Allardt 1976). There are some more extensive comparative data on Nordic association activity from the 1980s. In 1986/7 Finnish participation in socio-political activities which demanded personal effort was less than the Nordic average. Membership in a political organization was rarer in Finland than in the other Nordic countries with the exception of Denmark (Vogel 1990). In 1984 in Sweden more than 90 per cent of the adult population belonged to at least one organization. In Finland a few years later, the corresponding percentage was 77 (Blomdahl 1990). Among juveniles (15 to 16 year olds) – the most problematic groups in the 1990s from the organizations' point of view – 80 per cent in Norway, 71 per cent in Sweden and 55 per cent in Finland belonged to at least one association (op. cit.). The differences have, however, diminished at the same pace at which Finnish participation has risen.

With some caution we can conclude that the share of non-members in Finnish associations has decreased steadily from 38 per cent in 1972 to 21 per cent in 1988 (see Table 6.2). Thus the trend has been contrary to the American one discussed by

Table 6.2 The number of memberships in voluntary associations among the Finnish adult population (percentage of all), 1972, 1975, 1981, 1986 and 1988

Number of memberships	1972[a]	1975[b]	1981[c]	1986[d]	1988[e]
None	38	27	28	25	21
One	37	34	39	36	35
Two	25	22	16	24	20
Three	–	9	8	10	11
Four	–	8	4	3	6
Five	–	–	2	1	3
Six	–	–	2	(0.2)	2
More	–	–	1	(0.1)	2
Total	100	100	100	100	100
N	994	1124	1436	2291	2008

Notes
a　Allardt 1976: 177, in which the alternatives to answer were: none/cannot say, 1, 2 or more memberships. Sample: 15–64 year olds (N = 994).
b　Pesonen and Sänkiaho 1979: 186. Sample: 16–74 year olds (N = 1224). The greatest alternative was at least four memberships.
c　Source: Data of the Finnish Luokkaprojekti (Class project) from 1981. Sample: 18–65 year olds (N = 1436) (see Luokkaprojekti 1984). The figure includes the no-answer category. If they are omitted, the share of those with no memberships goes down to 21.5 per cent.
d　Source: Tilastokesus 1986. Sample: over-15-year-old population.
e　Source: Luokkaprojekti 1988. Memberships in co-operative organizations (SOK and E-liike) are excluded.

Putnam (1995: 67–73). On the basis of the scanty data of the immediate post-war period, we can conclude that this rising trend has been going on since the end of World War II. In 1955, 46 per cent of juveniles (15–24 year olds) did not belong to any association, whereas in 1994 the percentage of non-members was 31 (cf. Allardt *et al.* 1958: 21).

Table 6.3 gives information about the present situation in comparison with the Baltic countries and two other Nordic countries. The table is based on the data collected by the research project 'Social changes in the Baltic and Nordic countries'. It shows that at the mid-1990s there are no differences in the membership figures between Norway and Finland. The average number of memberships is 1.9 in Norway and 2.0 in Finland. However, there are differences between Sweden and Finland. The average Swede has 2.7[4] which, most probably is among the highest number (if not the highest) in the world (see Table 6.3).

The most typical case (mode) in Finland and Norway is a person with one membership and in Sweden with two.[5] In Norway and Finland there is almost the same proportion of those with no memberships at all and association activists with three or more memberships. In Sweden there are about the same percentage of those with more than four memberships than persons with none. The proportion of those having multiple (more than two) memberships is 27 per cent in Finland, 26 in Norway and 43 in Sweden (including union membership). In the

Table 6.3 The number of memberships in voluntary associations in Finland, Norway, Sweden, Estonia, Latvia and Lithuania

Number of memberships	Finland %	Norway %	Sweden %	Estonia %	Latvia %	Lithuania %
None	23	25	9	54	70	67
One	30	29	23	29	22	25
Two	21	21	25	12	5	6
Three	12	12	17	4	2	2
Four	4	7	14	1	1	0
Five or more	8	7	14	1	1	0
Total	100	100	100	100	100	100
N	1788	1785	1607	1480	1617	1483

survey reported by Curtis *et al.* (1992), the highest proportion of multiple memberships in the early 1980s was in Sweden (25.5 per cent), followed by Norway (24.9 per cent). So it seems that the proportion of persons with multiple memberships has been stable in Norway and has increased in Sweden.

With regard to Finland, in comparison with the 1988 figures (see Table 6.2 above) the situation has not changed. The small increase in the share of non-members most probably could be explained by sampling differences. On the other hand, the proportion of those with more than four memberships has increased a little.

Even though the Swedes more often belong to associations than do the Finns and the Norwegians, there is no reason to exaggerate the differences. The situation is very different in comparison with the Baltic countries five years after the collapse of the Soviet system. The Baltic states are just starting to develop as integral states based on a functioning middle-class civil society. Currently, in Estonia more than half, and in Latvia and Lithuania about two-thirds of the adult population have no association memberships at all. This is due to a large extent to the collapse of membership of trade unions, sports associations, youth clubs and party organizations all of which were a central part of the Soviet ideological state apparatuses (see Ruutsoo and Siisiäinen 1996: 434–9).

In the mid-1990s the differences between the sexes were very small in Finland as well as in Norway and Sweden. The same holds true for Latvia whereas in the other Baltic countries women have less memberships than men.

Next, memberships of different subpopulations in Finland are examined. Greater differences than between the sexes can be found between different age categories: the most active association members are people 24 to 55 years of age. The youngest population (16 to 24 years) have fewer memberships than the others (31 per cent being non-members). As to differences between groups with more or less education, the results are as might be expected: only 5 per cent of people with an academic education have no memberships, whereas among the least educated the share of non-members varies from 17 per cent (senior primary school) to 28 per cent (primary school).

The average Finn (and Norwegian, not to speak of Swedes) has, in general, more memberships than his/her American counterpart and the same is true for different educational categories: among the American college-educated the average in 1993 was 2.0, in Finland among the secondary school-educated 2.2 and those with an academic degree 4.0. In the US, among those with fewer than 12 years of education, the mean was 1.1 memberships, in Finland among those with primary school education 1.8 memberships (Putnam 1995: 73).

Out of all occupational groups Finnish housewives, pensioners and the unemployed together with skilled agricultural workers/fishermen and entrepreneurs reported most often that they did not belong to any associations. The entrepreneurs category is most clearly polarized between those having none and those having more than four memberships. The proportion of those with five or more memberships is highest among professionals, farmers and entrepreneurs.

As could be expected, persons with many memberships are also elected more often to positions of trust in associations: 63 per cent of those with five or more memberships hold some position of trust as distinguished from 12 per cent among those with one membership only. It is also easy to see that memberships are a part of a cumulation of active hobbies. Those with five or more memberships go more often to the theatre, concerts and take part in self-education. The differences diminish – but still to the advantage of those with numerous memberships – when we take such hobbies as piano playing or reading books into consideration, and disappear altogether with hunting, fishing, berry picking, visiting friends or relatives, going to restaurants and cinema, doing needlework or gambling.[6]

We can get a more detailed picture (see Siisiäinen and Ylönen 1996) of association memberships by comparing different association types with each other and to an earlier situation (see Table 6.4). In the Nordic comparison Swedes lead, especially in the number of memberships in trade unions, sports clubs and co-operatives, whereas differences between Norway and Finland are small. Balts have less memberships in all kinds of associations. The most popular types of associations are trade unions, sports clubs and religious associations.

As to Finland, from 1988 to 1994 those organizations which lost members were trade unions (from 62 to 53 per cent) political organizations (from 10.4 to 7.7 per cent) and the so-called 'friendship societies' and international associations (see Table 6.5). The declining trend can also be seen in the membership figures of the four biggest parties: the Social Democrats (−30 per cent), the centre (−15 per cent), the National Coalition (Conservatives) (−39 per cent) and the People's Democratic League/the Left-Wing Alliance (−60 per cent)[7] have lost a large part of their membership from 1980 to 1995) (Sundberg 1996: 89). The loss of members in the friendship societies is connected with the changes in the political map of Europe. They are also a good example of associations that were tied to the political and ideological values of earlier decades (some of them were founded soon after World War II and some as part of effort to build a Finnish people's front).

But there are also associations which have increased their membership: the best example of this is the group of study and art associations (from 10.7 to 15.3 per cent), environmental groups, professional organisations and women's associations.[8]

Table 6.4 Adult memberships of various associations in Finland, Norway, Sweden, Estonia, Latvia and Lithuania

Type of association	Finland %	Norway %	Sweden %	Estonia %	Latvia %	Lithuania %
Sports	23.1	33.8	42.9	8.7	5.6	6.5
Youth	4.9	7.6	8.2	1.7	1.6	2.0
Charity	11.6	17.4	16.1	1.0	0.9	0.6
Religious	9.5	10.2	10.7	4.4	5.1	7.7
Study and art	15.3	15.9	16.5	5.0	3.9	1.8
Regional history	3.5	–	–	3.9	1.8	1.8
Cultural	4.4	5.7	14.1	3.3	4.1	1.9
Co-operational producer	22.8	–	–	3.9	1.8	1.8
co-operation consumer	–	4.2	3.2	–	–	–
co-operation	–	22.0	36.8	–	–	–
Environmental/ nature protection	5.9	5.6	13.2	0.7	0.8	0.5
Friendship/peace	3.7	5.9	7.0	2.8	0.6	0.5
Village/ community associations	11.1	8.0	21.8	–	–	–
Farmer	–	–	–	2.9	0.6	0.5
Party	7.7	14.5	12.5	1.3	1.2	1.3
Alternative social movements	1.1	3.0	1.6	–	–	–
Trade union	53	49.7	83.5	17.1	12.1	34.2
National	–	–	–	1.7	0.7	0.4
Women's	3.6	2.6	3.2	4.0	0.2	0.5
Handicapped	4.6	–	3.7	–	–	–
Professional	12.0	20.4	16.7	4.0	2.4	2.0
Other	21.1	–	23.5	1.6	1.4	0.9
Total	100	100	100	100	100	100
N	1788	1785	1607	1480	1617	1483

In the Baltic countries respondents in the survey (1994) were asked retrospectively if they belonged to the different types of associations five years earlier. In all three countries memberships in trade unions, parties and youth organizations – all essential parts in the official Soviet organizational culture – had collapsed. Only religious associations and farmers' unions had been able to win more members (see Ruutsoo and Siisiäinen 1996: 439; see Table 6.5).

The data presented concerning three Nordic countries supports Dekker's and Van den Broek's thesis that the Scandinavian countries and the Netherlands belong to the same type of civil society (see Dekker and de Hart in this volume). Membership figures and the development of voluntary action do not support the

Table 6.5 Membership in different types of organization and association in 1988 and 1995 (percentage of members)[a]

Type	Estonia 1988	1994	Latvia 1988	1994	Lithuania 1988	1994	Finland 1988	1994
Sports	17.3	8.7	13.6	5.6	14.6	6.5	19.8	21.1
Youth	7.1	1.7	5.6	1.6	6.0	2.0	3.3	4.9
Charity	0.8	1.0	0.9	0.9	0.2	0.6	11.3	11.6
Religious	1.9	4.4	3.7	5.1	7.1	7.7	7.9	9.5
Study and art	6.4	5.0	7.6	3.9	2.2	1.8	10.7	15.3
Regional history	1.9	0.9	1.0	0.4	1.2	0.5	3.4	3.5
Cultural	4.1	3.3	6.4	4.1	3.0	1.9	4.2	4.4
Co-operational	4.4	3.9	2.0	1.8	2.1	1.8	22.8	22.8
Environmental	0.9	0.7	2.8	0.8	0.7	0.5	3.1	5.9
Friendship	2.5	2.8	0.6	0.6	0.3	0.5	6.7	3.7
Farmer	0.6	2.9	0.4	0.6	0.3	0.5	6.7	3.7
Party	6.1	1.3	5.0	1.2	4.5	1.3	10.4	7.7
Trade union	46.0	17.1	34.5	12.1	34.2	6.8	62.0	53.0
National	1.2	1.7	1.2	0.7	0.8	0.4	–	–
Women's	1.2	4.0	3.1	2.4	2.0	2.0	–	3.6
Professional	3.4	4.0	3.1	2.4	2.0	2.0	–	12.0
Hobby	9.8	8.6	4.6	2.7	9.8	5.8	–	–
Other	1.9	1.6	1.7	1.4	0.9	0.9	29.3	21.1
N	1499	1499	1636	1636	1485	1485	771	1788

Note
a   The figures concerning Finland are based on two surveys (1988 and 1994). The Baltic figures are based on the 1994 survey which contained retrospective questions about the situation in 1988.

hypothesis of declining organizational capital or a general crisis of voluntary associations. Rather we are witnessing a process of inner differentiation and transformation of the totality of voluntary associations (*Vereinswesen*). Some fields of collective action are losing members (especially political organizations) whereas others are winning more activists (certain hobbies (e.g. sports), nature and environment). So I would prefer to speak about renovation of the voluntary sector instead of proclaiming the general crisis of associations.

There are also typical associations of certain social groups. It is typical of Finland with a high percentage of female labour that there is almost no difference between the sexes in belonging to trade unions. Men are more eager to joint sports clubs, whereas women are more often members of study/art associations. Traditional females also belong to religious associations (which in Finland do not include church membership), charity societies and co-operatives.

As expected, trade union membership is more common among 25 to 54 year olds, whereas belonging to sports clubs diminishes according to age. Sports clubs are the only type of association activity – together with some special hobby clubs – whose popularity among young people has been increasing. Co-operatives and political parties are associations of people in their middle ages (especially 40 to

54 years). With the exceptions of two new ones, Finnish political parties inherited their ideological frameworks from the 1950s and 1960s. No wonder their appeal to generations raised in the 1970s and 1980s is more limited. Charity organizations are characterized by numerous older members, whereas professional associations are most popular among 24 to 39 year olds.

In Finland education is among the most important factors in influencing the choice of association types. Those with academic degrees belong more often (73 per cent vs. 47 per cent among the whole population) to trade unions, professional organizations, religious and charity associations than persons with a lower educational level. The same holds true to a lesser degree for cultural and political organizations. Memberships in political organizations are, however, also quite frequent among people with no more than primary or senior primary education, which is due to the fact that three of the four big parties have traditionally had their main social bases in the less educated classes: left-wing parties among the working class and the Finnish Centre among the agricultural population.

Professionals and technicians together with crafts workers and operators/ assemblers are, not surprisingly, most often members of trade unions. Legislators/managers together with operators and students belong more often to sports clubs than to other professional groups. Farmers are active party and co-operative members, whereas legislators/professionals act frequently in charity organizations and co-operatives.

I have also checked if clusters of correlations between memberships in different types of associations can be found. The clearest clusters exist between memberships in alternative movements on the one hand, two co-operative movements (0.61; 0.46), nature protection associations (0.45), friendship societies and/or peace movements (0.51) on the other. Also the correlation between charity and nature protection (0.35), women's associations and more leftist co-operatives (0.39), political organizations with culture (0.37) and regional societies (0.36) rise over 0.30. The more leftist oriented co-operative movement correlates highly with the other co-operative movement (0.49), friendship and/or peace associations (0.56) and associations of the handicapped (0.43).

One way to evaluate the meaning of different kinds of associations is to see how often the members take part in the activities organized by associations. More than half of trade union members had not participated in the activities during the previous year (1994). When people were given three alternatives for being a union member, 77 per cent of the members thought that it was a duty to be a member. Of all Finns 18 per cent chose 'increase in wages', whereas 66 per cent selected the 'duty' alternative and 17 per cent thought that it is 'not worth' being a union member at all. It is interesting that the proportion of those that supported the 'wages' alternative correlated negatively with age. There are also differences between the sexes: women are more for the 'duty' alternative than men (71 vs. 59 per cent). Those having the lowest and highest education selected duty more often as the reason for their union membership. The fact that older persons stress duty more as the main reason for union membership, whereas younger generations more often choose increase in wages as the membership basis can be a sign of changing union alignment in general. Younger and better educated union members are more rationally and individualistically oriented than older members. However, they can still have a high union consciousness and stress the importance of the union membership (see Jokivuori *et al.* 1996).

The interpretation of the changing pattern of alignment gets support from the comparison between the data from 1981 and 1994. The proportion of those who regard trade union membership as a duty has declined from 81 to 66 per cent and the share of those who think that it is not worth being a member has risen from 3 to 17 per cent.

As to the activities of the members in other types of associations, 50 per cent of the members of international friendship societies and peace associations and almost 50 per cent of the members in nature protection associations never took part in any activities. Perhaps a little bit surprising is the high proportion of non-participants in charity associations, but this probably can be explained by the fact that the Red Cross is included in this category and it has a large number of mailbox members.

The most active members (participating at least six times a year) can be found in study and art circles (68 per cent), religious groups (52 per cent), youth associations (40 per cent) and sports clubs (39 per cent). Party members take the middle position: 25 per cent of members did not participate whereas 30 per cent participated six or more times.

ASSOCIATION MEMBERSHIPS AND TRUST

It has become almost a commonplace in Finland to see association activity as a cornerstone of democracy and the active members of associations as its attitudinal base. Therefore it is interesting to see what differences exist between those with many memberships as compared with those with few in trusting the institutions of Finnish society.

In 1994 the respondents were asked: 'How much do you trust the following institutions?' and given five possibilities from very much to not at all (see Table 6.6). It is easy to see that association activists still belong to the supporting pillars of Finnish society. Association activists are more trustful of political institutions than the average population. Differences to the advantage of the activists are greatest in their relationship to Parliament and the church, the two most important representatives of bourgeois democracy and civil society. The same holds true of other state institutions (including universities): government, tax and social service authorities, courts and police. Only newspapers, magazines and radio and TV are trusted less by activists than the rest of the population. Finns seem to have more trust in institutions that are state-based or semi-state-based. This is most probably connected with positive attitudes towards the Finnish welfare state. As mentioned earlier Finnish social movements have also traditionally been state-centred and oriented towards the state.

Table 6.6 The trust in different institutions among Finns in 1995 (percentage of those who answered very much or quite a lot)

Institution	All respondents	Those with five or more memberships
Parliament	21.2	40.0
Church	27.4	41.8
Government[a]	29.1	32.9
Universities	44.7	55.3
Tax authorities	28.7	39.1
Courts of justice	49.4	59.0
Social service authorities	23.3	32.0
Police	69.2	77.1
Trade unions	33.2	39.9
Health service system	61.4	66.8
Banks	23.5	28.5
Military forces	62.0	66.7
President	45.4	46.7
Women's magazines	3.2	2.5
Radio and television	39.9	33.8
Newspapers	49.1	45.0

Note

a   At the time of the survey there was a bourgeois coalition government led by Esko Aho, the leader of the Finnish Centre.

Persons with numerous memberships are also more likely actively to take part in collective action by trying to influence political affairs. They give financial or other support to voluntary associations or to presidential campaigns, sign political petitions, take part in demonstrations, or write their opinion in a newspaper more often. The only form of collective action where no differences were found is in relation to strike action. Thus all the results of the survey presented above give general support to the argument about association activists as being supportive pillars of political democracy.

In the Baltic countries the differences between those with two or more memberships and those with one or no membership are smaller and less consistent than in Finland reflecting the unstable situation of democracy in these states.

CONCLUSIONS

The number of memberships in voluntary associations has not been declining in Finland in the 1990s. The 1990s also saw the foundation of more than 2,000 new registered associations per year. So there is no general crisis of voluntary associations, or of social capital manifest in association memberships or activism involving the use of associations to further political goals.

It is more justifiable to conclude that Finnish society is going through some kind of transition period. Some of the traditional types of organizations are in trouble, and this holds true especially for political parties that are losing members. Other central organizations are also experiencing internal changes as the interests of members are turning from a collectivist towards a more instrumental and individualistic orientation, especially among the young members. This is the case, for example, with trade unions.

Voluntary association has preserved its position as a dominant form of collective action in Finland. All movements, including the new social movements, have accepted the form of registered association as their own. Voluntary associations are still the most central means of mediation between civil society and the political system. The borderline between state and civil society runs within voluntary associations. In this respect, the role of the state has been very strong since the development of the nationalist movement in the nineteenth century. As a matter of fact the state is built implicitly as a component of the Finnish model of 'bourgeois ideal association'.

Even though it can be said that civil society is functioning quite well, the state centredness of associations speaks also for the fact that there are certain weak points in civil society and civic culture. In addition to a quite weak trust in trade unions by the Finns, the trust in nature protection organizations, such as WWF and Greenpeace, is also low by international comparison. According to a recent Eurobarometer, 35 per cent of the citizens in the whole EU regard nature protection associations as the most reliable source of environmental information, whereas in Finland only 20 per cent think this. In Finland scientists are found to be the most trustworthy of all sources (*Helsingin Sanomat* 1996). A possible explanation for the low trust in movements/organizations like WWF and Greenpeace is that they are not actually understood as voluntary associations proper, in the Finnish meaning of the word. Rather, they can be associated – especially Greenpeace – with illegal and action-oriented activities that are not compatible with the Finnish model of registered association. On the other hand, the distrust in movements fits well with the closeness of Finnish associations to the state. International movements are, most probably, understood as unpredictable phenomena, not as islands of order in a chaotic and contingent world, like associations established through the Registry of Associations.

In any event, active association members are still more trustful of the institutions of the state and the political system and in this respect are a central supporting pillar of Finnish democracy.

Notes

1   It is, of course, disputable how well Finnish squatters' groups meet the criteria of a 'new social movement' (see e.g. Rammstedt 1978; Tarrow 1989; Siisiäinen 1992a). It may suffice here to say that squatters' groups are a central part of the new urban movement sector which is renewing the whole organization of collective action. They form a totality which, together with ecological and other movements, challenges the political system, albeit so far in a modest way. Thus, at least in their challenging function, they can be regarded as 'new social movements'.

2   Trust in the state is deep-rooted in the majority of Finnish social movements. For example, the new feminist movements have relied heavily on the Finnish welfare state, which explains some of the differences between Finnish and e.g. German movements, for example the greater degree of institutionalization of Finnish feminism (see Bergman 1991).

3   Unfortunately Finland was excluded from the analysis because of some missing control variables (Curtis *et al.* 1992: 142).

4   A part of the difference can be explained by the greater frequency of trade union memberships in Sweden.

5   The real number of memberships is greater because people tend to remember only certain kinds of associations when the questions are asked. Thus, it is easy to forget both very self-evident and distant and general types of memberships. Second, respondents were only asked about their membership in certain types of associations. Therefore multiple memberships in the same kinds of associations, for example in different sports associations, are counted only once in this survey. The same holds true for many other surveys like the one reported by Curtis *et al.* 1992.

6   Actually gambling is the only hobby among those that were asked which was more frequently pursued by those with no memberships than those with numerous memberships.

7   This decline is to a large extent explained by the problems of the strongest part in the Coalition, the Communists, after the collapse of state socialism in Eastern Europe: in one year the membership dropped from 37,804 (1992) to 17,031 (1993) (Sundberg 1996: 89).

8   These types of associations have progressed. However, there is no comparative material from the 1980s so it is impossible to evaluate the magnitude of the increase.

References

Alapuro, Risto (1989) 'The intelligentzia, the state and the nation' in David Kirby (ed.), *People, Nation, State*. London: Hurst, 147–65.

Allardt, Erik (1976) *Hyvinvoinnin ulottuvuuksia*. Porvoo: WSOY.

Allardt, Erik, Jartti, Pentti, Jyrkilä, Faina and Littunen, Yrjö (1958) *Nuorison harrastukset ja yhteisön rakenne*. Porvoo: WSOY.

Bergman, S. (1991) 'Researching the women's movement. Considerations arising out of a comparative study of the new women's movement in Finland and the Federal Republic of Germany' in Andreasen, T. *et al.* (eds), *Moving on. New Perspectives on the Women's Movement*. Aarhus: Aarhus University Press, 208–20.

Blomdahl, Ulf (1990) *Folkrörelserna och folket*. Helsingborg: Carlssons i samarbete med Institutet för Framtidsstudier.

Connerton, Paul (1989) *How Societies Remember*. Cambridge: Cambridge University Press.

Curtis, James E., Grabb, Edward G. and Baer, Douglas E. (1992) 'Voluntary association membership in fifteen countries: a comparative analysis'. *American Sociological Review*, Vol. 57 April, 139–52.

Eronen, A. (1991) *Talonvaltaus uutena kollektiivisen toiminnan muotana – Tutkimus Suomen talonvaltauksista 1979–1990*. University of Jyväskylän, unpublished master's thesis in sociology.

142 *Martti Siisiäinen*

Eronen, S. and Ristimäki, A. (1991) 'Oranssi r.y. Helsingissä', *Nuorisotutkimus* 9, 28–32.

Helsingin Sanomat (1996) 'Suomalainen uskoo tutkijoihin ympäristöjärjestöjen', 19 July.

Järvikoski, T. (1991) 'Ympäristöliike Suomessa' *Historian ja uhteiskuntaopin opettajien vuosikirja* XX. Jyväskylä HYOL ry, 150–65.

Jokivuori, Pertti, Kevätsalo, Kimmo and Ilmonen, Kaj (1996) 'Ay-jäsenen monet kasvot – Tutkimus SAK:n STTK:n ja AKAVAN jäsenistä'. Publications in Sociology, University of Jyväskylä 60.

Konttinen, E.sa (1991) 'Professionalism as status adoption: The nobility, the bureaucracy, and the modernization of the legal profession in Finland'. *Law & Social Inquiry* 16 3, 497–526.

Litmanen, Tapio (1990) *Kansalaisaloite ympäristökamppailuna. Sievin, Nivalan ja Reisjärven suojelijoiden tarkastelua 1980-luvun ympäristökappailuna ja kansalaistoimintana.* University of Jyväskylän, unpublished master's thesis in sociology.

Luhmann, Niklas (1978) 'Handlungstheorie und Systemtheorie'. *Kölner Zeitschrift für Soziologie und Sozialpsychologie* 30 2, 211–27.

Luhmann, Niklas (1987) *Soziale System.* Frankfurt am Main: Suhrkamp.

Luhmann, Niklas (1991) *Ecological Communication.* Cambridge: Polity.

Luokkaprojekti (1984) *Suomalaiset luokkakuvassa.* Jyväskylä: Vastapaino.

Luokkaprojekti (1988) *Suomalaiset iuokkakuvassa.* Jyväskylä: Vastapaino.

Maffesoli, Michel (1996) *The Time of New Tribes. The Decline of Individualism in Mass Society.* London: Sage.

Michels, R. (1996) *Political Parties.* New York: The Free Press.

Negt, O. and Kluge, A. (1976) *Öffentlichkeit und Erfahrung. Zur Organisationsanalyse von bürgerlicher und proletarischer Öffentlichkeit.* Frankfurt a.M.: Suhrkamp.

Pesonen, Pertti and Sänkiaho, Risto (1979) *Kansalaiset ja kansanvalta. Suomalaisten Käsityksiä poliittisesta toiminnasta.* Porvoo: WSOY.

Putman, Robert D. (1995) 'Bowling alone: America's declining social capital'. *Journal of Democracy* 6 1, 65–78.

Rammstedt, Otthein (1978) *Soziale Bewegung.* Frankfurt am Main: Suhrkamp.

Richter, Rudolf (1995) 'Soziokulturelle dimensionen freiwilliger Vereinigungen'. *Beiträge zur Kommunal-wissenschaft* 19. München.

Ruutsoo, Rein and Siisiäinen, Martti (1996) 'Restoring civil society in the Baltic States 1988–1994' in Máté Szabó (ed.), *The Challenge of the Europeanization in the Region: East Central Europe.* Budapest: Hungarian Political Science Association and the Institute for Political Sciences of the Hungarian Academy of Sciences. European Studies 2 (pp. 419–45).

Siisiäinen, Martti (1988) 'Järjestöllinen pääoma: käsite ja merkitys yhdistystutkimuksessa'. *Hallinnon tutkimus* 7 3 (s. 154–69).

Siisiäinen, Martti (1990a) *Suomalainen protesti ja yhdistykset. Tutkimuksia yhdistyslaitoksen kehityksen ja protestijaksojen suhteesta suurlakosta 1990-luvulle.* Jyväskylä: Tutkjaliitto.

Siisiäinen, Martti (1990b) 'The spirit of the 1960s and the formation of voluntary associations in Finland' in Marin, M., Pekonen, K. and Sissiäinen, M., *Ageing, Generations and Politics.* Publications of the Department of Sociology, University of Jyväskylä 46 (pp. 56–97).

Siisiäinen, Martti (1991) Associations. *Atlas of Finland*, Appendix 321. Helsinki.

Siisiäinen, Martti (1992a) 'Cultural and political traditions and the repertoires of collective action in new social movements in Finland'. Paper presented at the Workshop on Culture & Social Movements at the University of California, San Diego 18–20 June 1992 (19 p.).

Siisiäinen, Martti (1992b) 'Social movements, voluntary associations and cycles of protest in Finland 1905–1991'. *Scandinavian Political Studies* 1/1992 (pp. 21–40).

Siisiäinen, Martti (1995) 'Gamla sociala kitt i upplösning – föreningverksamhetens uppgång och fall' in Teoksessa Kurt Klaudi Klausen and Per Selle (eds) *Frivillig organisering i Norden*. Oslow: Tano og Jurist- & Økonomieforbundets Forlag, s. 96–114.

Siisiäinen, Martti & Ylönen, Marja (1996) 'Political and social participation'. Teoksessa: Pohjoismaat-Baltia-projekti: National reports. University of Tampere (mimeo).

Stenius, H. (1987) 'Frivilligt, jämlikt, samfällt. Föreningsväsendets utveckling i Finland fram till 1900-talets början med speciell hänsyn till mass-organisationsprincipens genombrott'. *Skrifter utgivna av Svenska Literatursällskapet i Finland*, No. 454. Ekenäs.

Sundberg, Jan (1996) *Partier och partisystem i Finland*. Jyväskylä: Schilds.

Tarrow, S. (1989) 'Struggle, politics, and reform: Collective action, social movements, and cycles of protest'. Western Societies Program, Occasional Paper No. 21. Center for International Studies, Cornell University.

Tilastokeskus (1986) *Elinolotutkimuksen aineisto vuodelta 1986*. Helsinki.

Tilly, C. (1988) 'Repertoires of contention in America and Britain, 1750–1830' in Teoksessa M.E. Zald and J.D. McCarthy (eds.), *The Dynamics of Social Movements: Resource Mobilization, Social Control, and Tactics*. Boston: University Press of America, 126–55.

Vogel, Joachim (1990) 'Leva i Norden. Levnadsnivå och ojämlikhet vid slutet av 80-talet'. *Nordisk statistisk skriftserie* 54. Copenhagen: Nordiska Statistiska Sekretariatet.

7 The transformation of the voluntary sector in Norway

A decline in social capital?[1]

Per Selle

INTRODUCTION: THE RELATIONSHIP BETWEEN VOLUNTARY ORGANIZATIONS AND SOCIAL CAPITAL

This chapter deals with the transformation of the Norwegian voluntary sector, which includes all types of voluntary organizations, from the largest sports and welfare associations to the smallest hobby clubs or self-help groups. It is primarily empirical in that the main objective is to give a view of the deep ongoing changes in the voluntary sector. However, these changes definitely relate to the renewed interest in the importance of civil society (e.g. Cohen and Arato 1992), to the new rise in communitarian thinking (e.g. Etzioni 1988), and not the least to empirical informed democratic theory, in the neo-Tocquevillian tradition.

To the extent that the findings are linked to theory, it is with the neo-Tocquevillian approach to the analysis of social capital and its importance for the workings of viable democracy. Here voluntary organizations are seen as crucial democratic agents, as intermediate structures between the individual and the social and political system at large (Putnam 1993, 1995a, 1995b). In Putnam's view social capital, refers to: 'features of social organizations, such as trust, norms and networks, that can improve efficiency of society by facilitating coordinated action' (Putnam *et al.* 1993: 167). His work has aroused great interest (e.g. Laiten 1995; LaPalombara 1993), but it has also prompted heavy criticism (e.g. Tarrow 1996; Lipset 1995; Jackman and Miller 1996.; Rueschemeyer 1992; Norris 1996, and several of the chapters in this volume). What is Putnam actually saying about voluntary organizations? We examine this next.

PUTNAM'S PERSPECTIVE: THE ROLE OF VOLUNTARY ORGANIZATIONS IN PRODUCING SOCIAL CAPITAL

Putnam gives two main reasons why voluntary organizations are so important for 'making democracy work': Civil associations contribute to the effectiveness and stability of democratic government, it is argued, both because of their 'internal' effects on individual members and because of their 'external' effects on the wider polity (Putnam *et al.* 1993: 89); The organizations' 'internal' effects are those that 'instil in their members habits of cooperation, solidarity, and public-spiritedness', while they have an important 'external' effect because ' "interest articulation" and "interest aggregation" are enhanced by a dense network of secondary associations' (Putnam *et al.* 1993: 89–90). A necessary condition for organizations to have such an educational and socializing effect is that there exists extensive face-to-face contacts between the members of the organization, while at the same time institutional links are required between citizens and the political system at large.

Putnam's understanding of democracy has a lot in common with participatory democratic theory (e.g. Pateman 1970, Held 1987). The important thing is that one learns democratic norms and values through meeting and working together with others, i.e. through extensive face-to-face contact. Underlying this interpretation is a fear of passivity which results in individual marginalization and poor political outcomes, and opens up the possibility for elite manipulation. In this respect Putnam's perspective is also connected to an older mass society literature (Kornhauser 1960).

However, even if Putnam seems to put the internal and the external functions or roles on an equal footing, i.e. as two equal parts of a whole, the core idea is that face-to-face contact produces social capital; without this contact there would be no democratic education or socialization. Without that, one cannot see oneself in relation to others, which Putnam believes is absolutely necessary for the development of trust.[2] Trust in others is a necessary condition for ending up as a good citizen, and it is a necessary, if not sufficient condition for sustaining a viable democracy. So, the theory has a very strong micro-orientation. Higher-level norms and behaviour are aggregated from this micro-level, and as such they have little or no autonomy or influence on their own.

Putnam argues that it is essential for voluntary organizations to be real, broad-based membership organizations. He goes a long way in connecting what he sees as an extensive decline in social capital in the US to the decline in such broad membership-based organizations, a decline that is not compensated for by the growth of new organizations such as small local groups with limited goals, tertiary groups such as cheque-book organizations, or non-profit, i.e. service organizations that are not based on active memberships. In the first type of organization extensive face-to-face contact exists and the emphasis is upon what is close and local, but few if any outside links exist. In contrast, among the tertiary and the non-profit organizations such institutional links do exist, but there is very limited face-to-face contact within the organizations. It seems reasonable to suggest that Putnam sees face-to-face contacts and institutional links as two independent dimensions, with the presence of one never compensating for the lack of the other.

PROBLEMS WITH PUTNAM'S ANALYSIS

There are important parts of Putnam's approach that are problematic. First of all, the pure micro-level orientation, which takes as its starting point spontaneous local interaction, gives the analysis a strong bottom-up perspective so that everything else is aggregated from the micro-level. In a state-friendly country like Norway this is very unrealistic. In Norway, the voluntary sector is, and always has been, deeply influenced by government. Local spontaneous processes cannot be understood by leaving national public policies out of the picture; moreover, governmental action cannot be reduced to being only an aggregation of spontaneous local processes. Top-down initiatives not only strongly influence local initiatives, but they facilitate the work of the voluntary sector, in opposition to what writers like Nisbet (1962), acknowledge. Governmental influence or top-down processes in general, are not synonymous with removing power and autonomy from the voluntary sector (e.g. Tarrow 1996; Kuhnle and Selle 1995b; Walzer 1994; Salamon and Anheier 1997). The extent and type of such influence depend on context and differ across time and space, and cannot be regarded as an a priori assumption.

Our second main criticism is related to the first, but is less general and methodological. It has to do with the relationship between the internal and the external role of voluntary organizations. Because of his micro-level orientation, Putnam strongly emphasizes face-to-face contacts and the socializing and educational effects of internal processes. In contrast, for a number of reasons we think the external role is more fundamental. First of all, most democratic socialization goes on outside of voluntary organizations. This is not least because most people devote very limited time to interactions within voluntary organizations in comparison with their family, friends, schools and their workplaces. Furthermore, over the last generation or so there has been a strong process of democratization going on within institutions like the family, schools and public and semi-public institutions (Gundelack and Torpe 1997).

In addition, it is hard to accept that all types of organizations, whether they are of a political nature or not, have the same positive effects, or in some cases any effect at all. The tradition of assigning importance to non-political organizations in creating democratic norms is long established (e.g. Almond and Verba 1963), but that does not remove the task of developing a typology of how different types of organizations contribute to social capital. Furthermore, civil society is not on the face of it filled with trusting and democratic voluntary organizations. Thus it is an empirical question, varying greatly across time and context, to what extent voluntary organizations built and sustain or even destroy social capital (Cohen and Arato 1992; Rueschemeyer 1992; Hadenius and Uggla 1996).[3]

We also see Putnam's understanding of norms and integration as somewhat old-fashioned, i.e. based on traditional social-psychology. New types of socialization, knowledge, and social integration, as aspects of the communication structure of societies in the information age are not really discussed. Thus it is possible to build trust and identities where face-to-face contact between individuals is not the primary mechanism.[4] For example, it is possible to build trust and commitment within new types of centralized organizations in which passive support is the norm. Passive supporters of, for example, the environmental movement are both connected to their organization through a very extensive information system even without being active, at the same time as these organizations have strong institutional links to the wider political system.

New ideas-based organizations that are not democratically structured or membership-based, and in which passive support and not face-to-face contact is the rule, may be important as producers of social capital (Selle and Strømsnes 1996, 1997; Maloney 1997; and in this volume). It should not be taken for granted that only traditional types of communication produce civic virtue and civic involvement.

However, while Putnam strongly overemphasizes the importance of the internal effect of organizational participation, his emphasis upon voluntary organizations as crucial intermediate structures, is a fundamental one. The romantic view of small-scale democracy, i.e. a retreat to the local level, leaving out the society at large, even if that should produce trust in others, would mean both decline in social capital and a decline in democracy.

In the next section we examine the most typical features of Norwegian voluntarism, features that have been dominant since the turn of the century right up to the present day. We then describe the new organizational society that gradually developed from the 1960s and was closely linked to the leisure society. By the beginning of the 1990s, the changes had become so comprehensive and fundamental that we now speak of a qualitatively new organizational society. We end this section by briefly relating these changes to the Putnam perspective, concluding that voluntary organizations to a lesser degree are real intermediate structures. However, we also examine new developments in the voluntary sector, which represent a decline of social capital from a Putnamian perspective, but which may foster social capital in important respects.

THE NORWEGIAN CASE

Historically, in Norway voluntary organizations have been very close to the public sector, while at the same time being largely autonomous associations. Thus changes in government policies significantly affect the voluntary sector and voluntary–government relationships. To understand this it is necessary to break with the Putnam perspective, assigning a decisive role to the public sector in defining the space within which the voluntary sector operates, and therefore in the production of social capital.

In that discussion we use the term 'professionalization' in its broadest sense, as a collective term or a common denominator for the changes in the organization's society which are evident. We look especially at how the changes in the voluntary sector are linked to the growth of a new type of contracting-out culture in the relationship between the public sector and voluntary organizations. The public sector increasingly makes use of the voluntary sector to implement government policy. At the same time there appears to be a significant transition from independent basic support, to a more hands-on controlling approach. This reorientation affects the public sector–voluntary relationship because tighter control leads to a different type of integration. It is a type of integration that may endanger the autonomy of organizations. In other words we see a development in which governmental policies are moving from having a positive effect on the voluntary sector towards a situation in which government in effect weakens the power and autonomy of the sector.

Looking to the future, we therefore ask if these tendencies, both internally in the voluntary sector and in the governmental–voluntary relationship, mean that voluntary organizations will play a more restricted role in civil society and therefore in democracy in the future, while simultaneously their service-providing role may paradoxically grow more important.

However, one should keep in mind that social capital within the Putnam tradition is something much broader than what is going on in voluntary organizations and we have no intention of giving a detailed picture of all types of trust (or lack of it), norms and networks to be found in Norway, not to speak of the relationships between them. This is an important point, because it means that we are in no position to decide whether there is a decline or an increase in social capital. What we shall do, is to concentrate on the changing role of voluntary organizations in Norwegian democracy, and see how that fits with the role given to such organizations within the social capital literature.

THE NORWEGIAN VOLUNTARY SECTOR

In the past, the typical features of Norwegian voluntarism have been that voluntary organizations of all types, such as political, social or cultural organizations have been democratically structured. The local branches have formed the core of the organization society; the local and the national levels being linked in a hierarchical organization. Even though there have always been local associations that have shown no interest in joining regional and/or national organizations, and there is the odd organization at national level which has not built up local associations at all, this is not typical. As a consequence, Norway (and Scandinavia) contrary to most other countries has not developed a dual organization society, i.e. a local and a national one (Seip 1981; Try 1985; Selle and Øymyr 1995). This has made Norwegian voluntary organizations crucial in the evolution of democracy, indeed, in nation building itself (Rokkan 1970). This is not just about a decentralized organization structure, but is also closely linked to the role of the individual member. In many ways it is the members who have owned the organizations, so that active members have been the foundation of the voluntary organizations.

Compared to other countries, Norwegian voluntary organizations have recruited members from an unusually wide range of social spheres.[5] That the organization society through such a hierarchical organizational model has reached most people means that the voluntary organizations have played a singular role in making ordinary people full citizens. They have drawn large and new groups into the political arena and incorporated them at the local and national levels at one and the same time. Local society has been represented externally by the integral institutional channels that the voluntary organizations have represented. This has prevented extensive political, social and cultural marginalization (Rokkan 1970; Lafferty 1981; Selle and Øymyr 1995).

These features have contributed to the character of both voluntarism and governance, i.e. to the quite unusual degree of citizen integration, the open access structure and the state-friendliness that is found in Norway (Hernes 1987; Lafferty 1986; Kuhnle and Selle 1990; Selle and Øymyr 1995). This makes voluntary organizations real empirical intermediate structures between citizens and society. The social movements, especially the differentiated and specialized throngs of organizations with their roots in the last century, were absolutely decisive in shaping the political system (Gundelack 1993, Selle 1996). The agricultural movement, the labour movement, the temperance movement, the lay movement, the Norwegian language and cultural movement, and the growth of the athletics movement are all examples of this.[6] At the same time Norway has a rich tradition of social and humanitarian associations which expanded greatly as early as the beginning of the century. Some of these have been linked to the other social movements, while others have been more independent. These associations have had important political functions through their close cooperation with the government. Historically they have been a driving force in publicizing social responsibility, and were a strong social and political force well into the 1960s (Kuhnle and Selle 1990, 1995b; Seip 1994).

As early as the turn of the century Norway was an organizational society with many of the features which are familiar; organizations were created by members who may not have had any previous connection beforehand; they were in principle independent of the public sector, built on voluntary membership, where a member could join or leave at will; they had their own written statutes which the individual members were bound by; they had more or less clearly formulated, but limited objectives, and were democratic; the organization principle extended beyond the locality to the regional and national levels (Try 1985; Selle and Øymyr 1995).

The wide recruiting base of this organizational society was connected to social movements seeking political power, and provided the basis of one of the most important characteristics of Norwegian social life and voluntarism; the principle that everything perceived as important must be formalized and organized, amounting to an organizational 'syndrome'.

The period from the turn of the century to World War II may be seen as a further differentiating and strengthening of the organization society, that was already apparent at the beginning of the period. Nevertheless, it was then that the organizations within the health and social field grew strong, and that children's and youth associations begin to develop noticeably (Selle and Øymyr 1995). Soon another typical feature of Norwegian voluntarism also appears; the closeness to, and integration with the public sector, and an openness in political processes, that we scarcely find in other countries (Kuhnle and Selle 1990, 1995b).[7] From the 1930s onwards, the emergence of cooperation between the public and voluntary sectors in developing social policy as well as in relation to planning and reconstruction after World War II, became quite crucial for such integrating functions (Rothstein 1994; Kuhnle and Selle 1990).

The early post-war years were a period of dynamic expansion for many types of association, not least for those within the health and social sector, and especially those at the local level (Selle and Øymyr 1995). There was a wish to rebuild after the war, and not least a wish to be responsible for new and highly visible and demanding tasks. This is the great expansion phase of the welfare state, and the public sector became much more actively engaged in the planning work, thus affecting the negotiating position of voluntary organizations. In this period welfare state growth and voluntary sector growth definitely went together.

However, it is not correct to say that the organization society of the 1960s is fundamentally different from that at the turn of the century. It is more valid to say that around 1960 the transition from an agricultural to an industrial society was complete and the organizational state was by that time mature (Selle and Øymyr 1995). The organization types that were central in the early phase are still dominant, but they have matured and often changed their character, being linked to the public sector in new ways. Some of them have already reached their zenith.

ORGANIZATIONAL CHANGE

It is from early in the 1960s that we really see the emergence of something qualitatively new: the mass organization of leisure (Selle and Øymyr 1995). The social movements, so historically important, gradually changed their character and to an increasing degree became professional, negotiating institutions closely linked to the public sector, where mass mobilization no longer played the same role as in former times. There was a strong decline in what for a time was the largest people's movement in Norway, the temperance movement. In addition the lay movement had its difficulties, even though the steep organizational decline did not really begin before the 1980s. But by then the influence of the lay movement on those other than its supporters had long since decreased.

The labour movement also gradually changed its character, and the expression cultural movement is by no means any longer appropriate. The historically important and intimate liaison between the cultural and more limited instrumental organizations was broken, so that the labour movement as a cultural movement had clearly lost its power. Nor are the large organizations within the health and social sector what they once were. The role of large organizations within this sector gradually became more limited with respect to health policy, and innovation in this field is now much less dependent on them than in the past (Kuhnle and Selle 1990). At the same time the rural districts have steadily become more differentiated than before.

Nevertheless, organization activities increase considerably in the period after 1960, because of the emergence of the leisure society, which became rapidly and strongly reflected in the organization society. There was a rapid growth of leisure organizations in the broadest sense, including everything from song and music and sports to different types of hobby clubs. It is in this period too that organized work for children and young people really gained momentum, so that the Norwegian Athletic Federation soon became the largest organization in the country.

The entrance of children, young people and women into the types of organization where they were previously largely invisible, is a distinctive feature of these developments. It is connected to the fundamental changes in the relationship between work and leisure, something which also affects the relationship between the sexes. There is a general shift away from the situation in which men and women have complementary roles in society towards one in which they have more equal roles, where the opportunities available to women have fundamentally changed.[8]

This growth of organizations is in part one result of the further specialization and differentiation that came from the social movements. New organizations most often have a great degree of autonomy and frequently rapidly become quite independent from one another. A new and important feature is that a large part of the emerging new leisure organizations has developed independently of the social movements. Thus important parts of the organizational society are more and more disconnected from the social movements, while at the same time several of them have passed their peak. Nevertheless, associations linked to the social movements still account for a large, though decreasing part of the organizational society during the whole period (Selle and Øymyr 1992, 1995).

We can perhaps say that by around 1980 the mature leisure society, strongly reflected in the organization society, had arrived. Compared to around 1960, the composition, structure and density of the organizational society has changed radically as have its political functions and interests. The changes are of such a dimension that we believe it is correct to say that a qualitatively distinctive organization society emerged in that period.

However, some things have not changed; the core of the organization society and most of the typical features of Norwegian voluntarism from the turn of the century onwards are present in these new organizations. The local association is still fundamental, as is membership in democratically structured organizations. The hierarchical organizational model is still predominant, i.e. we have not developed any dual organization society (Selle and Øymyr 1995). Nevertheless we see tendencies that indicate increasing professionalization, centralization, specialization and self-referential activities (i.e. activities directed primarily at the organization's own members), over time.

At the same time new ideas-based movements such as the modern women's movement and the environmental movement, influence government policies without having the weight of strong organizations that comes from a large membership.[9]

From the late 1980s a new structural feature that may strongly influence the organizational society is observed. The result may be a break with some of the most typical features of Norwegian voluntarism in the past. It is possible that we are now on the way to the greatest transformation ever, a period where we see severe pressure on the core of Norwegian voluntarism; the organization society which has the local branches as its basis, which is member-based and democratically structured, binding the individual to both the local community and the national society at one and the same time through a hierarchical organization model (Selle and Øymyr 1995).

From the 1980s the power of a number of older organizations has declined, not least those linked to the historically important social movements. Furthermore, organizational differentiation is flattening out. Gradually, not only the ideas-based but also the more activity-oriented associations begin to face adversity. Perhaps we are witnessing the emergence of a weakening of the organization syndrome, i.e. a saturation point or even a turning point regarding voluntary organizations (Selle and Øymyr 1995).

At the same time it may be that drawing the borderline between the voluntary and public sector is even more difficult than it was previously, if not completely impossible. New hybrid organizational forms have emerged, and there has also been vigorous growth in voluntarism arising from government and semi-government institutions such as schools, churches, sports installations, museums, community centres, etc. The base for voluntary work, and thus the meeting place, is increasingly more the building as an institution, rather than the voluntary organization itself. The result is an increased distinction between voluntary organizing and voluntary work, and thus a fundamental change in one of the most typical features of Norwegian voluntarism: that voluntary work and voluntary organizing for the most part have been two sides of the same coin (Kuhnle and Selle 1990; Lorentzen 1994; Selle and Øymyr 1995).

In Norway, traditionally, professions and trade unions have been afraid that extensive voluntarism would deprive people of work and have been especially sceptical about all types of voluntary work not undertaken under the auspices of organizations. Now, however, we see tendencies towards municipalities working to promote voluntary work. This applies not only within the organizational society, but also within public institutions, or at least to those disconnected from the typical voluntary organizations. The emergence of voluntarism centres, where the authorities pay for organizing local voluntary work (Lorentzen *et al.* 1995), and not least the full-day school where attempts are made to involve organizations as well as individuals, is particularly interesting (Selle and Øymyr 1995). These developments are expressions of a significant institutional change which not only affects public–voluntary sector relations, but changes the general conditions of voluntary work and voluntary organizing.[10]

The government increasingly wants to use voluntary organizations, preferably the professional ones, to help in the implementation of government policies. More and more organizations, especially within the welfare area, are to an increasing degree, specialized recipients of a government/voluntary contracting-out system (Smith and Lipsky 1993; Kramer *et al.* 1993; Kuhnle and Selle 1995b). This system has a professionalizing affect on organizational work, increases the need for paid staff and has led to the centralization of power.

Another significant change is in the relationship between the voluntary sector and the market. Large parts of the voluntary sector have become more closely associated with the market. This is so both in relation to ideology, which is linked to the increasing legitimacy of neo-liberal ideas, and also to changed tasks in the voluntary sector. Big companies increasingly develop their own policies on voluntarism, and are becoming an integrated part of voluntary activities in their environments. In the past the Norwegian voluntary sector had, in the main, very limited connections to the market, and market forces were very often deliberately disregarded for ideological reasons. Today the situation is very different. Now, even many of the organizations with no direct relationship to the market are, nevertheless, strongly influenced by market ideas. This has become apparent with the current interest in the leadership question and management theory (Heitmann and Selle 1993).

We also see tendencies, especially in the health and social fields, of an increasing number of professional voluntary organizations signing contracts with individuals to carry out concrete tasks. But these types of voluntary workers are not full members of the organizations and are outside the administrative work and democratic process of the organization. It is more a matter of undertaking a contract than supporting a particular organization which is important. It indicates that there is a concord between the wishes of the individual and the requirements of the organization. The changes are undoubtedly linked to the increasing pressure of time and the dilution of ideology in the organizational society. In the main, it is not something the organizations have tricked the individuals into, motivated by a desire to keep them outside of the daily work. It is more an organizational adjustment to changes in the environment. Although it is becoming more difficult to get people engaged in ordinary organization work, it is still possible to get them to carry out specific limited services.

More and more often we are faced with a semi-professional voluntarism, and especially in the health and welfare social fields we also see tendencies for professionals to encroach on amateur voluntarism and to exert pressure on it (Høgsbro 1992; Lorentzen 1994; Selle and Øymyr 1995). Professionalization and a preoccupation with efficiency are the chief reasons for the professionals to enter the field of self-help organizations. They want to use the ideas of self-help to treat clients, something that will significantly change the very content of the idea of self-help.[11]

The very broad and general processes of professionalizing, centralizing, specializing and self-referencing, which we now see very clearly in the organization society, influence ideology, forms of activity and organizational socialization to a significant degree. First, the typical ideas-oriented associations are becoming a relatively minor part of the organizational society. Many associations try to the best of their ability to conserve the older ideas, often without success, while at the same time new social movements, such as the women's movement and the environmental movement are by no means guaranteed to produce new strong membership-based organizations.

Simultaneously organization activity is becoming more inner-directed, concentrating on its own members within an increasingly limited field, if we disregard the struggle over shares of public funds. There appears to be a declining interest in what happens outside the organization, and therefore a decreasing interest in, and/or belief in, changing the outside community. The weakening of external links outside of the organizations is accompanied by a weakening of the ideas-based associations. Organizations spend less effort getting individual members to commit themselves to activity within the organization. Such integration has become more difficult, but also less relevant now when the basic philosophy is weakened and diffuse. The mass social movements, traditionally characterized by a strongly ideological, outward-looking approach, have not previously played such a limited role in the organizational society as they do now (Selle and Øymyr 1995).

All in all, we believe that with the transition to the information society, these developments are in the process of changing our organizational society fundamentally. Many voluntary organizations are no longer intermediate democratic structures between individuals and the government in the traditional sense. Of course many of them still represent powerful interest groups and influence government policy, but it has become more and more difficult to clarify just who they actually represent. It will not be any easier to find out now when we see tendencies pointing towards a dual organization society; one local and one central.

We thus see the weakening of the local organizational society's role in democracy, at least in large-scale democracy, i.e. a weakening of the broadly organized and politically important institutional links outside the local community. At the same time it indicates a possible weakening of something that is most typical of Norwegian voluntarism: the fact that so-called low-status groups have been visible to such a degree in government policy because of belonging to strong organizations with political influence (Selle and Øymyr 1995).[12]

The decline in prototypical voluntary organizations, which are membership-based, democratically run and with extensive internal membership participation, and a weakening of the institutional links from the local to the central level, means that voluntary organisations are declining as intermediate structures from the Putnam perspective. That is, there is a decline in civic connectedness, or social capital. A possible increase in locally based networks, different types of self-help groups, and very narrow neighbourhood groups without extensive external links, does not really compensate for these developments. In this respect Putnam is correct.[13]

However, there has been an increase in the centralized, non-membership-based organizations, whether they are of the tertiary or non-profit type (Selle and Øymyr 1995, Strømsnes and Selle 1996), and their potential contribution to the production of social capital is a question which has not been adequately researched (see Maloney 1997, and in this volume). Both types of organizations may have important democratic functions, being both producers of, or sustainers of social capital that has been produced elsewhere.

We really do not have enough information to decide if the decline of the traditional type of organization is compensated for by the increase in new types of organizations. However, our understanding would be that voluntary organizations are now less real intermediate structures than before, and play a more limited role in teaching people democracy and integrating them into the system at large.

CHANGES IN GOVERNMENT – VOLUNTARY SECTOR RELATIONS

It seems clear that we are seeing increased professionalizing at all levels in voluntary organizational life, while at the same time seeing an increase in more informal groups, such as self-help groups, on the margins of the traditional voluntary sector. In this context, professionalizing indicates two different features: the activity and organization. First, we see pressure on the amateur in the work of the organizations. The individual appears to place more value on time, and consequently voluntary activity is thus much more instrumental than previously, while at the same time organizations expect more of the active members (Smith and Lipsky 1993; Klausen and Selle 1995; Selle and Øymyr 1995).

There is also professionalization in how the organization is run. Similarly, organization bureaucracy has grown noticeably, as has the use, centrally and to some extent at the intermediate level, of paid volunteers (Selle and Øymyr 1995). This development strengthens the central level at the expense of the intermediate level, the intermediate level at the expense of the local level, and the leadership at the expense of the ordinary members. It is a significant shift away from what is historically typical. Furthermore, as voluntary organizations have to an increasing degree become the source of a livelihood for many people, this increases the distinction between voluntary work and voluntary organization (Smith and Lipsky 1993; Kramer *et al.* 1993; Lorentzen 1994).

The notion of professionalization increases not only the use of paid staff, but it also facilitates the use of contracts in the relationship between the government and voluntary sectors, making it easier to make the transition from member-based and democratically structured organizations to a more centralized non-profit organization without members in the usual sense (including foundations). The member's role itself is changing. The development indicates that more and more associations will have less use for large numbers of active members, perhaps even for members at all. They will choose other organization models, something that is clearly seen within the emerging and important fields of environmentalism and development aid. The newest and most modern organizations do not choose the membership-based and democratic organizational form, while many of the older and membership-based organizations are looking for new members/supporters without ever expecting them to become active[14] (Selle and Strømsnes 1997; see also Maloney in this volume).

A possible long-term consequence of the development would be a further strengthening of the gradual move towards a more dual-organization society, because it is impossible for each local association to adjust to the new professionalizing demands at the same time as many associations get less benefit from the local associations and their members. Perhaps we will get national organizations that are increasingly professional, whereas locally there will be increased professionalization with regard to fund raising, while simultaneously there is also a withdrawal to the closest local environment. However, such neighbourhood organizations, as well as non-organized and more informal networks, may be professional and instrumental in the sense of being efficiency and results-oriented. We see that quite clearly within important parts of the new neighbourhood movement. But more informal local networks emerge at the same time as meeting places in the true sense of the word, that is places where attempts are made to keep the professionalization pressure out. Nevertheless, to a large extent these, whether they are instrumental or more of the expressive type, will be dissociated from large-scale democracy, and will have limited outside connections.

It must be said that increasing professionalization of the voluntary sector is not just a result of government policy, but part of far more general processes. We would not have had anything like the extent of voluntarism we now have in Norwegian society without a strong growth in the public sector, and without the financial support and close cooperation between the voluntary and public sectors. For example, in the overseas development field, the organizations that receive support have established very close relations with the public sector, resulting in substantial professionalization. Some of these organizations have adjusted fully to this new niche or market but have little domestic support; however, in some cases organizations with extensive activity at home have been able to strengthen the overseas development department at the expense of other departments (Steen 1994; Tvedt 1993).

How far one wants to go in the direction of professionalization is dependent on the view one has of voluntary work. Is it valuable in itself? Are there qualities in the relationship between voluntary donors and recipients, i.e. in voluntary work in its traditional meaning, which cannot be replaced by other forms of togetherness and communication and which are partly spoiled when we put pressure on the unemployed to do voluntary work (for which some payment is received). The amateur–professional relationship is thus far more complex than the paid–unpaid work relationship, and is by no means two sides of the same coin (Lorentzen 1994; Habermann 1993; Høgsbro 1992). Professional unpaid or partly paid voluntarism is in other words qualitatively different from traditional voluntarism (Habermann 1993). Unpaid professional work, common in many countries, is probably on the increase also in Norway (e.g. Middleton 1987). Such a shift would mean a professionalizing of Norwegian voluntarism and could estrange groups which might otherwise intend to undertake voluntary work (Selle and Øymyr 1995).[15]

The increasing professionalization, and thus the increasing emphasis on paid work, undermines the moderate line in the voluntary sector. Even if historically there has been some diversification across the association types, the moderate line has permeated the ethos of large areas of the sector from the end of the last century up to the present. It has been regarded as more of a cultural manifestation. The development features we have pointed to have changed a great deal of that culture, and even been primarily responsible for many looking upon them as outdated. Not only is there less concern about how money is spent, but simultaneously there is less resistance to the use of paid staff (Klausen and Selle 1995; Selle and Øymyr 1995). To the extent that care is now being exercised in using money and paid staff, is more the result of circumstances, the lack of resources, rather than moral considerations.

Government policy thus affects the ideology, organization form, scope, and type of activity in the organizational society. At the same time organizations also influence government policy. This has been obvious in the growth of the field of developing countries as an important policy domain (Steen 1994; Tvedt 1993), just as it was within the fields of health and social welfare (Kuhnle and Selle 1990; Klausen 1995). In other words, the type of governmental support matters.

The type of support given by government has very different consequences for the voluntary sector. There is a distinction between basic support and project support; basic support leaves the recipient relatively free, while project support imposes much more of an obligation and controls activity to a greater degree.[16] Project support should not become overly dominant, if the objective is to have a pluralistic and ideas-based voluntary sector, i.e. if the main concern is with the democratic role of the voluntary sector. On the other hand, if the concern lies with improving outcomes, i.e. the production of services, such a transformation may lead to real voluntary growth in close cooperation with the public sector (Selle and Øymyr 1995). It probably also leads to diminishing distinctions between public and voluntary sector service production (Lorentzen 1994; Selle and Øymyr 1995; Smith and Lipsky 1993; Salamon 1987).

Where the borderline should be drawn between the two forms of support in a state-friendly society like Norway, in which there is no tradition of voluntary organizations operating completely independently of the state, is one of the most interesting policy challenges the voluntary sector now faces. Increased project support strengthens the central link, promotes in most cases more paid work and in general weakens the role of members and thus the internal organizational democracy. As project support may also influence what the organizations are engaged in and concentrate on, indeed even their overall philosophy, it may also weaken their external democratic role. In other words it affects the values manifested by the voluntary sector and this in turn influences the rest of society.

In effect, this debate is about efficiency, both within the organizational society itself, and also within government. The question is how much should efficiency considerations be allowed to dominate relationships between the state and voluntary sectors, and how much consideration should be given to democracy and participation (Rothstein 1994; March and Olsen 1995). This discussion is, furthermore, related to the debate about whether a large public sector and very extensive public responsibility take the vitality out of voluntarism, a topic in which Scandinavia has played a central role in international discussions.

Is there less voluntarism where a large public sector exists? Probably not.[17] We believe there would be much less voluntary organizing and work in Norway if the government had not arranged such favourable conditions. The closeness to and dependence on the government has so far not led to the organizational society losing its autonomy. This is not least because of its unusual openness and the accessibility of the public sector (Rothstein 1994; Klausen and Selle 1996; Selle and Øymyr 1995).

Public sector growth has been followed by growth of voluntarism, without this being at the expense of either.[18] The growth of voluntary organizations was greater during the expansion period of the welfare state from the early 1960s onwards than ever before. However, if the role of the government had been more limited, voluntarism would obviously have developed quite a different character.

In Norway, government control of, and at times scepticism towards, the voluntary sector has historically been much more widespread in the health and social welfare fields than in the cultural sector, including sports. That is, the control has been strongest where basic rights and life and death questions were at stake (Kuhnle and Selle 1995a). It applies not least to control of the philosophy of voluntary service in the health and personal social service sectors. But we have seen significant ideological reorientation here during the last ten years. It may be that financial control and legal control will gradually become as extensive as ideological control (Selle and Øymyr 1995).[19]

The government has a decisive influence on both the type of voluntarism, and its scope (Kuhnle and Selle 1995b; Klausen and Selle 1995; Anheier and Seibel 1990). A comprehensive transition to project support, which we now see in relation to most of the funding of the voluntary organizations,[20] will increase this influence and may affect one of the most typical features of Norwegian voluntarism, something which distinguishes it from countries outside Scandinavia – the fact that voluntary organizations have been very close to the government. At times this has been perceived as an integration between government and voluntary organizations, while the latter retain a high degree of autonomy. This may appear to be a paradox, but it is not (Kuhnle and Selle 1995b; Klausen and Selle 1996). It is, however, a systematic feature which may be undermined by a comprehensive transfer to project support. The effects will depend on how project support is organized, especially the extent to which public money will be available for innovation, and not least the forms of control introduced.

One should be prepared for the strong reactions that will be aroused in many organizations by increased financial and legal control by the government, because such procedures are unusual. A policy of no state interference in internal organization processes has been one of the main distinctive features of Norwegian voluntarism (Selle and Øymyr 1995). For many years the closeness and mutual trust that exists between the voluntary associations and the government precluded any queries about whether the organizations used public money to the greatest advantage, or at least to the best of their ability. Many would have regarded increased monitoring and control as a lack of such trust.[21] At the same time, the organizational society has changed so that it can neither be taken for granted that the organizations are the same as they used to be, nor that they are what they profess to be.[22] It is therefore of no surprise that government creates new types of demands that take less for granted. More of a paradox is the fact that as neo-liberal ideas get more important, the more comprehensive becomes the detailed control of the voluntary sector.

A concentrated transition towards project support and thus increasing professionalization will in addition lead to growth in what we may call voluntarism lawyers and voluntarism economists. In countries where voluntarism is of a different character than here, i.e. more influenced by market ideology, and where the contract culture is much more extensive, such professionals (who are expensive and influential) play an important role in the organizations, as well as in control bodies (Smith and Lipsky 1993; Kramer *et al.* 1993). There are definite tendencies in this direction in Norway at the present time. In other words, government policy and public finance influence the general guidelines for voluntary organizing to a decisive degree (Selle and Øymyr 1995).

This point applies also to basic support (Selle and Øymyr 1992). However, project support at the expense of basic support will strengthen the more general professionalizing, centralizing and specializing tendencies, at the same time as it will probably augment the tendency for groups to concentrate on their own members, rather than outside society.

A comprehensive transfer from basic to project support nevertheless denotes increasing influence and control from the government, and in time may lead to changes in the organizational society that are unintended (Smith and Lipsky 1993). The allocation principles for the two forms of support are radically different in assessment criteria and consequences. From a social capital perspective this means that even if one rejects the pure micro-orientation of Putnam, the fundamental changes now going on in government–voluntary relations, may take power and autonomy out of the voluntary sector instead of reinforcing it. This puts pressure on the membership-based and democratic-organizational model and strengthens a move towards a more dual organizational society which will weaken voluntary organizations as real intermediate structures. However, as mentioned, we do not yet understand the democratic importance of the tertiary and non-profit organizations, which Putnam rather took for granted, without really studying them. Are they an indicator of the decline in social capital? This is not clear.

CONCLUSION: TRANSFORMATION OR DECLINE?

Adapting Putnam's perspective there is no doubt whatsoever that the transformation of the voluntary sector puts pressure on the classic roles of voluntary organizations. The growth is in organizational types that Putnam explicitly argues do not compensate for the decrease in more traditional organizations (Putnam 1995a). However, if taking our perspective as the point of departure, it is still an open question as to whether voluntary organizations are in a process of acquiring a more limited role in democracy. Extensive studies of tertiary and non-profit organizations are needed, in order to assess their contribution to the creation of social capital. However, even within such a perspective, our feeling is that the ongoing transformation of the voluntary sector has so far most probably weakened the role of voluntary organizations as intermediate structures. The growth in these types of organizations is not extensive enough to compensate for the decline in the traditional organizational forms.

The developments in the voluntary sector now make it necessary to develop a clearer distinction between the internal and external democratic role of the voluntary organizations. If voluntary organizations, and especially new associations, do not choose the democratic organization form, it is useless to cling to the past. The new must be taken seriously. Such non-democratically structured associations may in fact play a decisive role in democracy if there is a real alternative choice, i.e., real pluralism (Hertz 1966), which is the fundamental characteristic of a dynamic democracy (Selle and Strømsnes 1997). They may have a just as important, or even a more important, democratic role than older democratically structured organizations which have passed their zenith and have a role that it is no longer easy to discern.

One vital question which arises is should traditional voluntary organizations and professional tertiary and non-profit organizations, which are not membership-based and democratically structured, be treated differently by government? Would it be preferable for the government to support all types of voluntary organizations, or first and foremost those that represent a particular ideology and organizational form. To what degree is it the responsibility of the government to ensure a truly pluralistic organization society? This is a very important question in a state-friendly society like Norway, where the voluntary organizations and the government have been so closely linked.

In other words, this deals with just how strongly notions of efficiency are to be allowed to rule at the cost of democracy, both internal and external democracy. If it is the results or the output that counts, then a much greater portion of the funds should go to such non-profit organizations, if it is shown that they are most efficient.

The development in the organizational society means that not all tertiary or non-profit organizations are of the same type. They can have clear and distinctive fundamental values without being voluntary organizations in the usual meaning of the term (Anheier and Seibel 990; Selle and Øymyr 1995). However, they often do not have deep roots, and come into existence just to adjust in a pragmatic and professional way to new niches in the market place, niches often opened up by changes in government policy. It is mainly, but not only, the value-based organizations of the tertiary and non-profit type, that have an important role in democracy without necessarily being democratically structured (Selle and Strømsnes 1997; Malone in this volume).

These developments in the voluntary sector indicate that it is more important than ever before to distinguish between voluntary organizing as an arena for promoting values and interests, and voluntary organizing as an arena for producing services and organizing activity (Selle and Øymyr 1995). Whereas the first role, which is so decisive for a dynamic civic society and a living pluralistic democracy, is under pressure, it may be that the second role is strengthened by the voluntary organizations becoming even more responsible for implementing government policy.

A new type of organizational society is emerging, an organizational society with characteristics basically different from those in the past. We do not yet quite know what the new typical features will be, but in the discussion about voluntarism in the broad sense, consideration must be given to the fundamental changes outlined here. One area where we definitely need to improve our understanding concerns the democratic role of the value-based but not democratically structured organizations that compose an increasing part of the voluntary sector. In sharp contrast to Putnam we think these organizations are of crucial and increasing importance in a modern democracy. The research question should not be whether they are important or not, but to what extent and how.

Notes

1   This chapter is a summary of the transformation of the voluntary sector in Norway. For a more comprehensive discussion and data showing these important structural changes, see Selle and Øymyr 1992, and especially Selle and Øymyr 1995.

2   Putnam's conceptualization of social capital is very broad. It includes much and the causal links between the different parts are not specified (e.g. Newton and Whiteley's chapters in this book). However, as I read Putnam, he sees no need for, or finds it impossible, to specify the causal links between trust, norms and networks.

3   Mouzelis (1995) has important things to say here: '(M)icro sociologists tend to forget that actors, because of their very unequal access to the economic, political and cultural means of production, contribute just as unequally to the construction of social reality' (p. 16), and furthermore: 'The relationship between micro, meso and macro games is not one of aggregation at all, but one of subsumption: decisions taken at the top tend to become the value premises that those in subordinate positions have to consider when they take their own, more limited decisions' (p. 21). Within this perspective face-to-face contact is definitely not only micro-behaviour.

4   Warren (1996) has a very interesting critique of Fukuyama's (1995) important work on trust, arguing that his understanding of trust (and norms) is old-fashioned. Fukuyama has as far as I can see an understanding that comes close to that of Putnam.

5   This is already underlined in an important article by Campbell and Rokkan (1960), comparing citizen involvement and participation in Norway and the US. They show quite clearly extensive differences in the role of education for political involvement and participation in the two countries.

6   Klausen and Selle (1996) and Selle and Øymyr (1995) present a much more comprehensive discussion of how important it is to understand the implications of the social movements in order to comprehend the typical features of Nordic voluntarism. Both works also discuss the degree to which the new international research into the third sector is applicable to Scandinavia and argue that we must be extremely careful as regards importing models and theories developed in quite different contexts. See also Kuhnle and Selle (eds) 1995.

7   This is a crucial point, in my opinion fundamentally misunderstood by many foreign (and native) students of Norwegian politics, and especially obscured by the so-called corporatist perspective. This is discussed in Selle 1996. For a recent study taken for granted that Norwegian politics is best described as exclusive and closed, see the otherwise important work of Dryzak 1996.

8   Karvonen and Selle (1995), Raaum (1995) and Nagel (1998) contain comprehensive information about the incomparable improvements in the position of women in politics and civic life since the early 1960s. For an analysis of women's role in Norwegian voluntarism, see Selle 1997.

9   This is a very important feature of modern Norwegian politics and a great change from earlier. This is not the place to go more deeply into causes and consequences, but this change partly explains, or at least gives meaning to, the strong centralizing and professionalizing tendencies we now see in the voluntary sector.

10   The introduction of the full-day school immediately changed the general conditions of voluntary work with children to a quite decisive degree. It is not easy for organizations to recruit children for evening activities when the full-day obligatory school provides similar or identical activities after school hours.

11   Three important Scandinavian books on self-help and voluntary work also discussing these matters are: Høgsbro (1992), Habermann (1993) and Amnå (1995).

12   I believe it is appropriate to use the term 'belong' even though it does not imply that one must be active, and nor perhaps does one always need to be a member. What is important is that there are organizations that one knows about and feels close to.

13   In this field one should not come up with any definite conclusion, since the data on informal networks are not that comprehensive. For a discussion of the data that exists and possible interpretation pointing in the direction of an increase in such groups, see Selle and Øymyr 1995: chs 10 and 11.

14   It is now more important than ever before to amplify what we mean by membership. From what is taking place it appears that the distinction between real, and probably active members, and so-called passive members, or supporting members of different types is becoming even sharper. The organizations are constantly finding new and less binding ways of collecting contributions (e.g. telephone donations/supportive membership), and even the member concept has been stretched or extended. Today therefore, it is necessary to evaluate what membership in each individual organization means, if information about the strength, and meaning of an organization is wanted. The aggregate membership figures say less and less about the strength of an organization in relation to the organization society. A high membership does not automatically mean either high activity or enthusiastic support for the work of the organization.

15   van Til (1988), among others, has pointed out that the development in the USA after 1980 not only has been towards a more elitist participation pattern in the

voluntary sector, but that also voluntary service production is to a lesser and lesser degree directed at the weakest groups; those who cannot afford to pay.

16   This is an important point since it seems that many, both within and on the outside of the organizations, take it for granted that it is the other way around, i.e. that an organization receiving grant support is 'dominated' while those receiving project support are 'free' (see Strømsnes and Selle 1996).

17   One of the main conclusions from the largest comparative project on the voluntary organizations and voluntarism ever, The Johns Hopkins Comparative Nonprofit Sector Project, is that each voluntary sector in general is strongly dependent on governmental money and legitimation, i.e. strongly related to government in all types of political systems (Salamon and Anheier 1996, 1997).

18   This is a large scholarly discussion heavily influenced by ideology (e.g. Nisbet 1962). For articles discussing this not only from a philosophical or normative perspective, but which are also empirically informed, see Walzer 1994, Kuhnle and Selle 1995b, Dryzak 1996, Salamon and Anheier 1997.

19   This is a fundamental change, but we cannot amplify it here. It deals with the moderation of the requirements to standardized service production that the government is carrying out. Life philosophy organizations thus gain greater acceptance in the use of their philosophy in service production. However, there is also a simultaneous reinforcing of neo-liberal ideas, which 'contracting out' is linked to, towards constantly greater pressure on efficiency (entailing more and more financial control). This also makes the meaning of the content of contracts, their precise meaning, more important than previously.

20   The report by Statskonsult (state consultant), 'Statlege overføringer til frivillige organisasjoner' (The transference of state funds to voluntary organizations) (Statskonsult 1995: 3) is an important document showing the strong growth in the transference of funds by the ministries to voluntary organizations in the period 1989–92. There is no doubt that project support has benefited at the expense of basic support, but the shift is not equally clear in all departments.

21   One of the conclusions from the extensive corporatist literature on Scandinavia was that the system was built on and developed a kind of organized trust (e.g. Schmitter 1983). For an interesting analysis of the decline of organized trust in Sweden written within the social capital perspective, see Rothstein (1998).

22   In recent years a number of examples of voluntary organizations misusing public money have been uncovered, and several committees have been appointed to evaluate the tranfer of funds to this sector. This applies to basic support, project support and support to institutions. One of these was the Fjeld Committee which looked into funds transferred to children's and youth organizations (NOU 1995: 19).

References

Almond, G.A. and S. Verba (1963) *The Civic Culture. Political Attitudes and Democracy in Five Nations.* Princeton: Princeton University Press.

Amnå, E. (ed.) (1995) *Medmännsklighet att hyra?* Ørebro: Libris.

Anheier, H.K. and W. Seibel (eds.) (1990) *The Third Sector. Comparative Studies of Nonprofit Organizations.* Berlin: Walter de Gruyter.

Campbell, A. and S. Rokkan (1960) 'Citizen Participation in Political Life: Norway and the United States of America', *International Social Science Journal*, 12 (1): 69–99.

Cohen, J.L. and S. Arato (1992) *Civil Society and Political Theory.* Cambridge, MA: The MIT Press.

Dryzek, J.S. (1996) 'Political Inclusion and the Dynamics of Democratization', *American Political Science Review,* no. 1: 475–87.

Etzioni, A. (1988) *The Moral Dimension. Toward a new Economics.* New York: Free Press.

Fukyama, F. (1995) *Trust: The Social Virtues and the Creation of Prosperity.* New York: Free Press.

Gundelach, P. (1993) 'New Social Movements in the Nordic Countries'. In T. Boye and S.E. Olsen Hart (eds.) *Scandinavia in a New Europe.* Oslo: Scandinavian University Press.

Gundelach, P. and L. Torpe (1997) 'Social Reflexivity, Democracy, and New Types of Citizen Involvement in Denmark'. In J.W. van Deth (ed.) *Social Involvement and Democratic Politics.* London: Routledge.

Habermann, U. (1993) *Folkelighet og frivilligt arbejde.* København: Akademisk Forlag.

Hadenius, A. and F. Uggla (1996) 'Making Civil Society Work. Promoting Democratic Development; What can States and Donors Do?' In E.O. Eriksen (ed.) *Det sivile samfunn og moderniseringens dialektikk.* Bergen: Norwegian Research Centre in Organization and Management, Report 9609.

Heitmann, J. and P. Selle (1993) 'Styrets rolle i frivillige organisasjonar'. In T. Reve and T. Grønlie (eds.) *Styrets rolle.* Oslo: Tano.

Held, D. (1987) *Models of Democracy.* Cambridge: Polity Press.

Hernes, H.M. (1987) *Welfare State and Woman Power: Essays in State Feminism.* Oslo: Norwegian University Press.

Hertz, K. (1966) 'The Nature of Voluntary Associations'. In D.B. Robertson (ed.) *Voluntary Associations.* Richmond, VA: John Knox Press.

Høgsbro, K. (1992) *Sociale problemer og selvorganiseret selvhjælp i Danmark.* Frederiksberg: Samfundslitteratur.

Jackman, R.W. and R.A. Miller (1996) 'A Renaissance of Political Culture', *American Journal of Political Science,* no. 3: 632–59.

Karvonen, and P. Selle (eds.) (1995) *Women in Nordic Politics: Closing the Gap.* Aldershot: Dartmouth.

Klausen, K.K. (1995) 'Et historisk rids over den tredje sektors utvikling i Danmark'. In K.K. Klausen and P. Selle (eds.) *Frivillig Organisering i Norden.* Oslo: Tano and Jurist- og Økonomiforbundets Forlag.

Klausen, K.K. and P. Selle (eds.) (1995) *Frivillig Organisering i Norden.* Oslo: Tano and Jurist- og Økonomiforbundets Forlag.

Klausen, K.K. and P. Selle (1996) 'The Third Sector in Scandinavia'. In K.K. Klausen and P. Selle (eds.) *The Third Sector in Scandinavia.* Special Issue of *Voluntas,* no. 2: 99–122.

Kornhauser, W. (1960) *The Politics of Mass Society.* London: Routledge and Kegan Paul.

Kramer, R. *et al.* (1993) *Privatization in Four European Countries.* London: M.E. Sharpe.

Kuhnle, S. and P. Selle (eds) (1990) *Frivillig organisert velferd. Alternativ til offentleg?* Bergen: Alma Mater.

Kuhnle, S. and P. Selle (1995a) 'Governmental Understanding of Voluntary Organizations: Policy Implications of Conceptual Change in Post-war Norway'. In S. Kuhnle and P. Selle (eds).: *Government and Voluntary Organizations. Relational Perspective.* Aldershot: Avebury.

Kuhnle, S. and P. Selle (eds) (1995b) *Government and Voluntary Organizations. A Relational Perspective.* Aldershot: Avebury.

Lafferty, W.M. (1981) *Participation and democracy in Norway.* Oslo: Universitetsforlaget.

Lafferty, W.M. (1986) 'Den sosialdemokratiske stat', *Nytt Norsk Tidsskrift,* no.3: 23–37.

Laiten, D.D. (1995) 'The Civic Culture at Thirty', *American Political Science Review,* no. 1: 168–73.

LaPalombara, J. (1993) 'Review of Making Democracy Work', *Political Science Quarterly*, no. 3: 549–50.

Lipset, S.M. (1995) 'Malaise and Resiliency in America', *Journal of Democracy*, no. 3: 2–16.

Lorentzen, H. (1994) *Frivillighetens integrasjon. Staten og de frivillige velferdsprodusentene*. Oslo: Universitetsforlaget.

Lorentzen, H. *et al.* (1995) *Ansvar for andre. Frivillighetssentralen i norsk velferdspolitikk*. Oslo: Universitetsforlaget.

Maloney, W.A. and J. Jordan (1997) 'The Rise of Protest Business in Britain'. In J.W. van Deth (ed.) *Social Involvement and Democratic Politics*. London: Routledge.

March, J.G. and J.P. Olsen (1995) *Democratic Governance*. New York: Free Press.

Middleton, M. (1987) 'Nonprofit Boards of Directors: Beyond the Governance Function'. In W.W. Powell (ed.) *The Nonprofit Sector*. New Haven, CN: Yale University Press.

Mouzelis, N. (1995) *Sociological Theory: What Went Wrong*. London: Routledge.

Nagel, A.H. (ed.) (1998) *Kjønn og velferdsstat*. Bergen: Alma Mater.

Nisbet, R. (1962) *Power and Community*. New York: Oxford University Press.

Norris, P. (1996) 'Does Television Erode Social Capital? A Reply to Putnam', *PS: Political Science and Politics*, no. 3: 474–80.

Norges Offentlige Utredninger (1995) *Statlige tilskuddsordninger til barne- og ungdoms-organisasjonene*, Oslo: Stateus Trykningskontor.

Pateman, C. (1970) *Participation and Democratic Theory*. Cambridge: Cambridge University Press.

Putnam, R.D. (1995a) 'Bowling Alone: America's Declining Social Capital', *Journal of Democracy*, vol. 6, 1: 65–78.

Putnam, R.D. (1995b) 'Turning In, Turning Out: The Strange Disappearance of Social Capital in America', *P.S.: Political Science and Politics*, December issue: 664–83.

Putnam, R.D. *et al.* (1993) *Making Democracy Work. Civic Traditions in Modern Italy*. Princeton: Princeton University Press.

Raaum, N.C. (ed.) (1995) *Kjønn og politikk*. Oslo: Tano.

Rokkan, S. (1970) *Citizens, Elections, Parties*. Oslo: Universitetsforlaget.

Rothstein, B. (1994) *Vad bør staten gøra?* Stockholm: SNS.

Rothstein, B. (1998) 'Social Capital in the Social Democratic State. The Swedish Model of Civic Society'. In Robert D. Putnam (ed.) *The Decline of Social Capital. Political Culture as a Condition for Democracy* (forthcoming).

Rueschemeyer, D. (1992) 'The Development of Civil Society after Authoritarian Rule'. Bergen: Norwegian Research Center in Organization and Management (Publication 9247).

Salamon, L.M. (1987) 'Of Market Failure, Voluntary Failure and Third-Party Government: Toward a Theory of Government-Nonprofit Relations in Modern Welfare State', *Journal of Voluntary Action Research*, vol. 16 (1), 29–49.

Salamon, L.M. and H.K. Anheier (1996) *The Emerging Nonprofit Sector*. Manchester: Manchester University Press.

Salamon, L.M. and H.K. Anheier (1997) 'The Civil Society Sector: A New Global Force', *Society*, vol. 34 (4), May 1997.

Schmitter, P.C. (1983) 'Interest Intermediation and Regime Governability in Contemporary Western Europe and North America'. In S.D. Berger (ed.) *Organized Interests in Western Europe*. Cambridge: Cambridge University Press.

Seip, A.L. (1994) *Veiene til velferdsstaten. Norsk sosialpolitikk 1920–1975*. Oslo: Gyldendal.

Seip, J.A. (1981) *Utsikt over Norges historie. Tidsrommet 1850–1884*. Oslo: Gyldendal.

Selle, P. (1996) 'Marginanlisering eller kvinnemakt'. In P. Selle *Frivillige organisasjonar i nye omgjevnader*. Bergen: Alma Mater.

Selle, P. (1997) 'Women and the Transformation of the Norwegian Voluntary Sector'. In Jan W. van Deth (ed.) *Social Involvement and Democratic Politics*. London: Routledge (in press).

Selle, P. and B. Øymyr (1992) 'Explaining Changes in the Population of Voluntary Organizations: Aggregate or Individual Level Data', *Nonprofit and Voluntary Sector Quarterly*, no. 2: 147–79.

Selle, P. and B. Øymyr (1995) *Frivillig organisering og demokrati. Det frivillige organisasjonssamfunnet endrar seg 1940–1990*. Oslo: Samlaget.

Selle, P. and K. Strømsnes (1996) 'Organised Environmentalism: Democracy as a Key Value', *Voluntas*, no.3.

Selle, P. and K. Strømsnes (1997) 'Medlemskap og demokrati: Må vi ta passivt medlemskap på alvor', *Politica*, no. 1: 31–48.

Smith, S.R and M. Lipsky (1993) *Nonprofits for Hire. The Welfare State in the Age of Contracting*. London: Harvard University Press.

Statskonsult (1995) Statlege overføringar til frivillige organisasjoner. Oslo: Rapport 1995: 3.

Steen, O.I. (1994) *Norske organisasjoner i bistand og humanitært hjelpearbeid. En analyse av norske private organisasjoners forhold til det offentlege*. Dr.gradsavhandling, Institutt for geografi, University of Bergen.

Strømsnes, K. and P. Selle (eds.) (1996) *Miljøvernorganisering og miljøvernpolitikk mot år 2000*. Oslo: Tano-Aschehoug.

Tarrow, S. (1996) 'Making Social Science Work Across Space and Time: A Critical Reflection on Robert Putnam's *Making Democracy Work*', *American Political Science Review*, no. 2: 389–97.

Try, H. (1985) *Assosiasjonsånd og foreningsvekst i Norge*. Øvre Ervik: Alvheim og Eide.

Tvedt, T. (ed.) (1993) *En studie av frivillige organisasjoner i norsk bistand*. Senter for utviklingsstudier, University of Bergen.

van Til, J. (1988) *Mapping the Third Sector. Voluntarism in a Changing Social Economy*. New York: The Foundation Center.

Walzer, M. (1994) 'Multiculturalism and Individualism', *Dissent*, no. 2: 185–91.

Warren, M.E. (1996) 'Democracy and Trust'. Paper to the 1996 Annual Meeting of the American Political Science Association, 29 August–1 September.

8 Facets of social capital in new democracies

The formation and consequences of social capital in Spain

Mariano Torcal and José Ramón Montero

INTRODUCTION

One of the most controversial issues about social capital is how it is formed. Many scholars agree that trust itself 'lubricates' cooperation and that cooperation, in turn, promotes trust (Putnam 1993: 171). This model of the origins of social capital derives from Coleman (1988 and 1990) and his rational-choice approach, according to which of the elements that form social capital are mutually self-reinforcing. This interactive process can only reach two equilibria, a low-intensity one (lack of social capital) and a high-intensity one (a community of civicness).

How, therefore, is it possible to pass from the low to the high equilibrium? This is not an easy question to answer. First, because the question hides a paradox commonly referred to as the 'bootstrap' problem: 'a minimal amount of social capital has to exist already, if it is to be created, since networks of obligations can be constructed and maintained only in a context in which a minimal level of trust between individuals already exists' (see Whiteley's chapter in this book). Second, because a problem of collective action also exists with respect to the creation of social capital since individuals have an incentive to free-ride on the efforts of others (Whiteley 1997: 127), which can be modelled by a prisoner's dilemma game with a stable non-cooperative equilibrium (Olson 1965; Hardin 1971). We believe that some of the most significant paradoxical problems surrounding the creation of social capital relates to the concept of social trust. From a rational-choice perspective, social trust is a relational and rational, although not always fully calculated, *action* (Coleman 1988: 102; Levi 1996a: 3). In contrast, we argue that social trust may be also considered as a *cultural attitude*, and that it is its majoritarian presence in a collectivity which facilitates the creation of social capital.

If this is indeed the case, the analysis of social capital in new democracies could be very enlightening. At the outset of these democracies there may often be virtually no social capital: their citizens have been exposed to long experiences of authoritarian rule during which associative life was, at best, discouraged or repressed, or both. Successful transitions imply the creation or restoration of a set of democratic institutions, rules, and practices, but to what extent does this new institutional framework give rise to social trust and social capital?

We maintain that institutional change and democratic politics may foster the creation of social capital, but that there still might not be enough to break a situation of low-intensity equilibrium. This outcome seems evident in the light of the persistently weak associative and political life found in some countries with stable democracies like Spain (Torcal 1995; van Deth 1996). The installation and development of new democratic institutions do not *per se* create social capital. Any increase in social capital in these new democracies is conditioned by the attitudinal presence of trust among citizens. Whereas democracy may create the roots of social capital, the rate at which this changes is determined, as we hope to show, by intergenerational differences in the extent to which citizens trust each other.

We also maintain that face-to-face interactions cannot be the driving force behind rising social capital in new democracies, above all because these interactions are rare and irregular outside small voluntary organizations. A pre-existing level of trust among individuals has to exist, and, as Whiteley argues in his chapter, socialization is instrumental in the creation of social trust, and hence, in any significant increase in the levels of social capital. In order to escape from situations of low-intensity equilibrium, therefore, there must be a major intergenerational change in levels of trust. But socializing citizens to trust each other is not as axiomatic as some authors claim: it is not an automatic by-product of either economic or social modernization or regime change. Rather, it is much more strongly influenced by citizens' pre-adult experiences with organizations and institutions, as well as by the majoritarian content inherent in the cultural transmission which takes place. Contrary to what Putnam (1993) assumes,[1] politics can play a significant role in forming social capital (Levi 1996b: 50–1), although it works through the mediation of processes of political socialization.

In this chapter we examine the formation of social capital in a new democracy and its consequences for levels of political involvement. Thus, we begin by assessing the current situation of social capital in Spain through an analysis of ecological and survey data, and compare a number of behavioural and attitudinal indicators related to membership in secondary organizations in Western European countries. This comparative analysis shows that despite an increase since the advent of democracy, social capital in Spain remains in a low-intensity equilibrium. In the next section we briefly consider the problem posed by the formation of social trust and use cohort analysis to show that the existing levels of social trust in Spain are explained by specific patterns of inter-generational transmission. Cohort analysis proves that whilst the strength of democratic legitimacy has changed remarkably across generations, low levels of interpersonal trust have been transmitted from generation to generation. This suggests that the evolution of the political attitudes and orientations in which social capital is grounded has scarcely been affected by the economic, social, and political transformations of the last three decades. Finally, we will analyse the most important consequences of this weak social trust for social capital and political involvement.[2]

SOCIAL CAPITAL IN SPAIN: SOME COMPARATIVE DATA

Organizational life was extremely weak in Spain at the end of Francoism (Linz 1971). By the beginning of the political transition to democracy two important developments should have increased Spanish associative life. On the one hand, economic growth, educational change, and social modernization that began in the 1960s should have fuelled the emergence of more associations. On the other, the political transition to democracy, which required the creation of parties and other political or ideological organizations, together with the new climate of freedom, should have fostered the creation of associations of all kinds. Indeed, this seems to have happened, as figures for the number of associations created each year since 1968 show (Figure 8.1).[3]

With the consolidation of Spanish democracy in the early 1980s, the number of new associations continued to grow at an apparently ever faster rate. At first glance, therefore, social capital seems to have been increasing in Spain since the outset of the democratic regime, and it also seems to have achieved a high-intensity equilibrium responding to the setting of new democratic institutions.

Nevertheless, the number of associations is certainly an unsatisfactory indicator of organizational strength: it tells us nothing about the membership of the different organizations, the intensity of their involvement, the frequency of

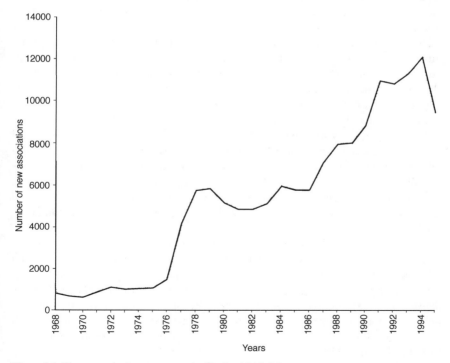

Figure 8.1 New associations per year in Spain, 1968–95.

their activities. Above all, it is impossible to know if and when an organization has effectively ceased to exist, surviving merely as an item in the official register. But Figure 8.1 is not without interest. First, it shows the impressive scale of organizational expansion during this period of almost thirty years. Between 1968, when only 5,650 associations were listed, and 1995, a cumulative total of no fewer than 156,019 new organizations were registered, that is, almost thirty times more than the original number. This increase is no less remarkable if we consider it in relation to the growth of the Spanish population in the same period. A simple associativity index reflecting the number of organizations per 100,000 inhabitants clearly shows the extraordinary leap in this period: from 18.4 in 1968 to 293.9 in 1995.[4]

Second, it is possible to identify the distinct waves in the rhythm of creation: this was slow during the final years of Francoism, intense during the period of the transition to democracy, steady during the 1980s, and relatively intense again after 1990. The crucial years were, naturally, those of political change: over 21,000 new associations were registered between 1977 and 1980 alone, that is, more than all those created in the preceding twelve years, or the equivalent of a 220 per cent increase with respect to 1976.

The third interesting aspect is the territorial scope of the organizations. At present, two out of three are local, and one out of four provincial; regional organizations account for only some 9 per cent of the total, whilst only 8 per cent operate nationwide. As was to be expected, the consolidation of the new decentralized state since 1980 has encouraged the formation of regional organizations through the federation of local and provincial ones. Although the number of national federations has increased more recently, the Spanish associative fabric is still characterized by its localism, the weak links between similar organizations, and the deficient communication between them all (Prieto-Lacaci 1994: 202–3).

Finally, the nature of their activities should be considered. According to the criteria employed by the Register of Associations, almost 40 per cent of the total are classified as cultural or ideological, 15 per cent educational, and a further 15 per cent sports or youth organizations. Economic and professional associations account for 6 per cent, family and consumer groups 5 per cent, and philanthropic organizations 4 per cent. It should be noted that whilst the number of cultural and ideological organizations has grown consistently as a proportion of the total over the past decade, the others have shrunk.

As has been stated above, this type of data casts no light on the levels of membership of the different associations, or the political attitudes connected with associative engagement. Nor do these data provide any information about the number of 'living' organizations, that is, those which in practice define the density of the associative fabric at any given moment. Some indication of this, however, may be gained by examining the affiliation rates of the Spanish political parties and trade unions. Those of the political parties are among the lowest in Europe (Montero 1981; Bartolini 1983). At the end of the 1980s, the ratio of members to electors was 10.5 in Western Europe as a whole; Spain, with a ratio of just 2.0, ranked last in the European league table (Katz *et al.* 1992: 333; Morlino 1995: 332). The ratio between the members and voters of the different parties is also extremely low. In the 1993 general elections, the Socialist Party (PSOE) and the Popular Party (PP) won more than 17 million votes; yet their combined memberships amounted to only some 800,000 (Gangas 1995). The very low levels of party affiliation in Spain accord with the Spaniards' even weaker propensity to play an active role in the parties, with the parties' scant organizational penetration of society, and with the weakness of party identification among the electorate.

Much the same is true of the unions. Spain and France share the lowest European indices of union density, calculated as the proportion of active and unemployed wage earners affiliated to unions (Price 1989). As was to be expected, the recognition of union liberty and the formation of numerous labour organizations in 1977 led to a spectacular, confusing, and short-lived increase in union membership. This immediately dropped sharply, but has slowly been increasing again since the end of the 1980s as a result of the economic cycle, closer collaboration between the different union federations, and their greater functional autonomy from the parties and economic actors. At present, the Spanish union affiliation rate lies somewhere between 15.5 per cent (van der Meer 1995) and 17.3 per cent (Jordana 1995).

Spanish workers' reluctance to join unions has created a paradoxical situation for the two main union federations, the *Unión General de Trabajadores* (UGT) and *Comisiones Obreras* (CC OO): whilst they enjoy both considerable institutional recognition in the political arena and hegemony in the large companies, their presence and influence are much weaker in the small- and medium-sized companies that are precisely the largest category of firms.

Survey data offer a more complete picture of the nature and dimensions of social capital in Spain. In general terms, these data show that levels of membership and participation in voluntary associations, intermediary organizations, and new social movements in Spain are relatively low as compared to most other Western democracies. As can be seen in Table 8.1, Spaniards are less likely to belong to, or work in, voluntary organizations than citizens in any of the other countries selected.[5] This is not only true of political parties and trade unions, but of all the many organizations of civil society that depend on the voluntary participation of citizens. Furthermore, even though the number of associations has risen in recent years, these data show that the levels of participation by Spaniards in these organizations has basically remained essentially stable since the early 1980s: 69 per cent did not belong to any organization in 1981, 66 per cent in 1990, and 68 per cent in 1994. According to a 1993 survey, fully 76 per cent of Spaniards did not belong to any organization, but more importantly, only 18 per cent declared that they belonged to one organization, 5 per cent to two, 2 per cent to three, and just 1 per cent to more than three (Gunther and Montero 1996, 28).

Of course, it may be argued that survey data do not reflect the real level of voluntary associationism. If this were the case, one would expect it to be a transnational phenomenon. Yet this does not alter the fact that significant

Table 8.1 Membership and voluntary work in voluntary organizations in Western democracies, 1981 and 1990 (percentages represent those who declare themselves to be members and do voluntary work in at least one organization)

Countries[a]	Membership		Voluntary work	
	1981	1990	1981	1990
Iceland	–	89	–	44
Netherlands	62	83	27	44
United States	–	69	–	44
W. Germany	50	65	73	29
Belgium	42	56	21	27
Austria	–	52	–	29
Great Britain	52	50	22	20
Ireland	66	48	22	26
Denmark	62	46	54	21
France	27	36	15	21
Italy	26	33	17	22
Portugal	–	32	–	18
Spain	31	20	23	7

Sources: 1981 European Values Survey and 1990 World Values Survey.

Note
a   Countries are listed in decreasing averages of both years.

differences are found in the data for the various Western European countries. Furthermore, the comparatively low level of participation in voluntary associations in Spain is not only confirmed by the ecological data discussed above, but also by other reliable survey items, for example, voluntary work or financial support for such organizations (Baumgartner and Walker 1988). The information given in Table 8.1 clearly shows that the gap between Spanish citizens and other Europeans is even greater with respect to the amount of voluntary work done for these associations (see also van Deth 1996).[6]

On the other hand, it has been argued (Pérez Díaz 1996: 40–1) that the strength of Spanish civil society lies in the rise of voluntary associations of a 'societal nature' (consumer, human rights, ecological, and tenants' organizations, etc.). Nevertheless, data from the 1990 World Values Survey reveal low levels of membership and involvement across the whole gamut of organizations – ecological, peace, human rights, youth, sport and recreational, cultural and artistic groups – as well as community associations. In fact, Spain ranks among the Western countries with the lowest levels of membership of societal organizations: in 1990 some 88 per cent of Spanish respondents declared that they did not belong to any organizations of this type.[7] Therefore, the lack of participation in traditional organizations such as parties and unions has not been compensated for by involvement in these new associations.

The evolution of membership by organizations since the early 1980s confirms this weakness. As can be seen in Table 8.2, the decrease in membership of unions and religious organizations has not been accompanied by any noticeable increase

Table 8.2 Membership in voluntary associations in Spain, 1981–96 (in percentages)

Organizations	1981	1990	1994	1996
Parties	3	1	2	2
Trade unions	11	5	6	5
Religious	15	6	7	6
Sports	–	5	9	10
Leisure	–	–	11	–
Charities	5	–	7	–
Cultural	5	4	7	8
Youth	3	1	2	4
Human rights	1	1	2	–
Ecological	–	1	2	–
Women	–	1	1	–
Peace	–	1	1	–
Voluntary work	–	–	–	5
Neighbours	–	–	–	11
None	69	66	68	64
(*N*)	(2,303)	(2,637)	(5,087)	(2,481)

Sources: For 1996, Centro de Investigaciones Sociológicas (CIS) Data Bank; for other years, Orizo (1996: 135–40).

in the societal associations, with the exception of those related with sporting or festive activities (Orizo 1996: 120–1).

The relatively low level of associative life in Spain accords with a series of attitudinal and behavioural characteristics which, as we will demonstrate below, are related to social capital. One of these characteristics is the relatively low level of interpersonal trust. The data shown in Table 8.3 suggest that Western democracies may be divided into two groups in terms of the strength or weakness of interpersonal mistrust: Spain lies on the border line which separates the countries in which distrusters formed a clear majority in 1990. In 1981, 61 per cent of Spaniards stated that they mistrusted their fellow citizens, a level similar to that found in Belgium and only surpassed in France and Italy. In 1990, the difference between these two groups of countries had widened; along with the French and Belgians, the Southern Europeans formed a distinctive group among the Western democracies. This point should be emphasized. Besides being low, the level of interpersonal trust in Spain has remained basically stable over time. This is even more striking if one considers the political, cultural, social, and economic changes of the last three decades. In the early 1970s only two out of ten Spaniards felt they could trust their fellow citizens (López Pintor 1982: 158). Twenty years later this figure had changed little: only one-third of the population affirms its trust in other people (Table 8.4).

Thus, social capital in Spain has increased since the return to democratic politics. As has been seen above, the number of associations has increased exponentially, just over one million Spaniards belong to political parties, and about two million workers are trade union members. This evolution has been

Table 8.3 Interpersonal mistrust in Western democracies, 1981 and 1990 (percentages of those who declare they do not trust other people)

Countries[a]	1981	1990
Portugal	–	76
France	71	72
Italy	72	62
Belgium	63	61
Spain	61	62
W. Germany	58	51
Ireland	56	52
Great Britain	54	55
Iceland	–	54
United States	–	47
Netherlands	49	44
Denmark	44	40

Sources: 1981 European Values Survey and 1990 World Values Survey.

Note

a   Countries are listed in decreasing averages of both years.

Table 8.4 Interpersonal trust in Spain, 1980–96 (in percentages)

	1980	1981	1987	1990	1994	1996
Trust	22	33	25	32	29	34
Not trust	74	61	73	62	67	61
DK, DA	4	6	2	6	4	5
(*N*)	(1,200)	(2,303)	(2,499)	(4,147)	(2,491)	(2,481)

Sources: For 1981 and 1990, European Values Survey and World Values Survey, respectively; for other years, CIS Data Bank.

accompanied by a small increase in the levels of interpersonal trust. However, new organizations are mostly local, fragmented, and probably enjoy only a short life. Parties and unions were virtually non-existent at the beginning of the democratic regime, and over the last twenty years only three out of ten Spaniards have belonged to any type of association. Furthermore, two out of three Spanish citizens consistently express distrust towards their fellow citizens. It is clear that after the natural upsurge in associative life provoked by the transition to democracy, social capital in Spain has failed to develop beyond a situation of low-intensity equilibrium.

THE FORMATION OF SOCIAL CAPITAL: POLITICS MATTER

We have already noted that the situation of low-intensity equilibrium that charaterizes social capital in Spain has persisted despite the major political, institutional and economic changes of the last two decades. Contrary to what is generally assumed (for instance by Levi 1996a), democratic regimes *per se* do not produce social capital. In fact the Spanish case shows that the full functioning of democratic politics does not result in an axiomatic increase in social capital. In order to explain this paradoxical outcome, we think that attitudinal factors should be taken into account. More particularly, the evolution of social capital in new democracies is conditioned by trust among citizens. Democracy may create social capital, but the rate of change is dependent on the extent to which different generations harbour different levels of interpersonal trust.

In order to substantiate this claim, we have analysed the evolution of trust through a longitudinal research design. Our basic tool is cohort analysis. It is well known that a longitudinal cohort design can detect three different effects that explain attitudinal change or stability. First, it can identify a cohort effect: some attitudes reflect consistent and enduring generational differences and are hardly changed by specific political events. The second is a period effect: some opinions or attitudes vary in all generations as a result of an event affecting all of them at the same time, without this necessarily giving rise to a lasting or consistent attitudinal shift. The third is the life cycle effect: some attitudes change as a cohort grows older. If the analysis of social capital by cohorts reveals life cycle effects, it would reinforce the argument that attitudes are acquired through a continuous learning process, lasting from adolescence into old age.[8] In this case, life cycle effects would mean that social trust increases as citizens age. The existence of period effects, in turn, would demonstrate that the level of social capital in Spain has varied as a result of political mobilization and the increasing numbers of associations created from the top: face-to-face interactions would thus have been the main source of at least temporary social trust. Finally, cohort effects would demonstrate the importance of pre-adult socialization for the creation of social trust.

For the purposes of this cohort analysis we have identified six generations of Spaniards, defined in accordance with the most significant historical events of this century (Torcal 1995).[9] As we will see in more detail below, the first notable finding is that social trust shows a dominant cohort effect, despite the presence of some small period effects. The next question is therefore to determine the extent to which these attitudes vary in the different generations: in other words, we must measure the size of these differences. If differences between generations are constant but quantitatively small, then we can conclude that there has been hardly any cultural change as a result of inter-generational replacement, and that these small differences reflect significant cultural continuity and hence inter-generational transmission. On the other hand, if the differences between generations are constant and also quantitatively important, then there will be good grounds to argue that these changes in political attitudes in the population as a whole are the result of a process of generational replacement.

Before examining social trust, a cohort analysis of education may perhaps be of some interest for illustrative purposes. Social modernization and public policies have fuelled an increase in educational levels in Spain in recent decades (Núñez 1992: 166–78). This tendency, however, has not affected all Spaniards equally, as

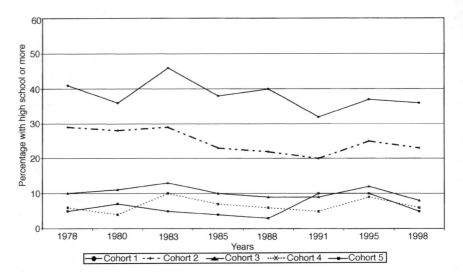

Figure 8.2 Education by cohorts, 1978–94 (percentage of those who have completed high school or more). Source: CIS Data Bank.

the younger generations have benefited most from rising education. Moreover, this is a phenomenon that should have a clear generational effect, since education is mainly acquired during the first two decades of an individual's life and tends to remain constant thereafter. Hence, educational level should display an extremely stable cohort effect, with major generational differences indicated by significant distances between the curves of the various cohorts. Figure 8.2, which presents data on the level of education for each cohort, reveals that the younger the cohort, the higher the proportion of individuals who have completed at least secondary education. This figure also shows that the qualitative change in educational levels occurred precisely between the fourth and third generations, that is, between the generation that experienced the economic take-off after the hard years of autarky and the generation that enjoyed the prosperity that followed the stabilization plans, the limited liberalization of the authoritarian regime, and, most importantly, the expansion of the university system. Thus, a cohort analysis of education clearly shows the relevance of inter-generational change in Spaniards' educational levels; at the same time, it confirms the reliability of this type of longitudinal research design. An examination of educational levels also shows that cohort analysis can detect whether or not inter-generational differences are significant. It is not enough merely to identify a cohort effect: this must be accompanied by an analysis of its magnitude, that is, of the quantitative differences between generations.

Generational effects can also be observed with regard to interpersonal trust. But in contrast to what was found with respect to education, there are very few differences between generations. Despite the dramatic changes that have taken

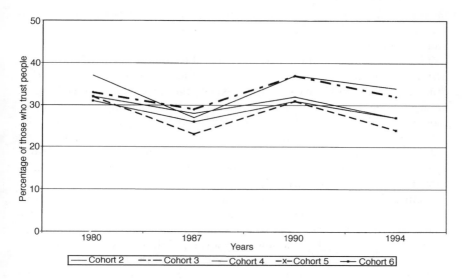

Figure 8.3 Interpersonal trust by cohorts, 1980–94 (percentage of those who trust people). Source: CIS Data Bank.

place in Spain over the last thirty years, the lack of social trust has been transmitted from one generation to another virtually intact. As can be seen clearly in Figure 8.3, the inter-generational variations in the proportion of Spaniards reporting that they trust other people are very small, and do not respond to the patterns of inter-generational change observed in the levels of education. It seems, therefore, that the political, social and economic transformations of the last few decades have not substantially altered the extent to which Spaniards trust their fellow citizens. Furthermore, social trust does not appear to evolve as a function of the life cycle. In other words, trust in others does not increase with ageing: note that in Figure 8.3 there is no progressive increase in all the curves. Finally, social trust hardly shows any period effects. The general pattern appears to have remained remarkably stable over time; and more importantly, the small period effect observed in 1990 neither coincided with a particular moment of political change and mobilization, nor led to any noticeable increase in the number of associations.

These results confirm the hypothesis that interpersonal trust is the result of a long-standing process of cultural accumulation, and that it tends to remain stable across generations.[10] As a result social capital is not disseminated in Spanish society. The mere proliferation of associations does not create social capital. It may be a necessary condition, but it is not a sufficient one. Participation in voluntary associations requires the widespread diffusion of social trust throughout a slow process of political socialization. Significantly, even the liberalization of the authoritarian regime and the return to democracy does not seem to have fostered a process of adult learning to trust others or to participate. The absence of interpersonal trust forms part of an entrenched cultural heritage transmitted from generation to generation. Furthermore, there are no signs of a positive change among the youngest cohorts.

This conclusion should not be interpreted as another type of cultural or historical determinism. We do not think it is necessary to go back to earlier centuries in Spanish history in order to explain the current lack of social capital among different generations of Spaniards. Rather our explanation is based on the more recent historical events that occurred before the transition to democracy. Moreover, these events are fundamentally political.[11] We argue, therefore, that politics also matter for the formation of social capital in the recent past (albeit mediated by the influence of political socialization), and that politics should be brought 'back in' to the model.

Political and social conditions in Spain over the last 150 years have scarcely favoured the development of voluntary associations. First, political life has been characterized by an extraordinary discontinuity. In the twentieth century alone, a liberal monarchy has been followed by a short military dictatorship, and a democratic republic ended in a bloody civil war and the establishment of the Francoist regime which, along with that of Salazar in Portugal, was the most protracted of the post-First World War European dictatorships.

During this period political instability obstructed the development of autonomous social organizations, traditions of cooperation between social and political elites, and relations based on mutual trust among citizens. Moreover, regime discontinuity was accompanied by fragility of political parties and the intense turnover among party elites. Economic backwardness also contributed to the weakness of Spanish social organizations, a deficient articulation of demands by many social groups, and a scant influence of modernizing social leaders as opposed to those of the powerful traditional oligarchies. The monarchical Restoration, which lasted from the end of the nineteenth century through the first third of the twentieth century, saw the consolidation of what Linz (1981: 367) has identified as the principal characteristic of interest politics in Spain: the primacy of politics over interests, of partisan cleavages over interest conflicts, of political alignments over economic interests.

This posed evident difficulties for the institutionalization of interest organizations and the consolidation of voluntary associations. These problems were only aggravated by systematic electoral fraud, the extensive functioning of *caciquismo*, and the increasingly widespread feeling of alienation from the political system. During the 1930s, the short democratic experience of the Second Republic was dominated by mass membership of social and political organizations as the result of intensive mobilization and by the extreme politicization of these organizations' strategies and interests, their alignment with the parties in the many conflicts which surfaced during these years, and by growing polarization in the articulation of their demands. Once again, therefore, the political climate prevented the institutionalization of interest group politics, as well as the diffusion of cooperative mechanisms beyond the ever more exclusive political identities.[12]

After the Civil War, the first fifteen years of the authoritarian regime saw the virtual elimination of most of the existing organizational traditions, the repression of opposition groups, and the imposition of a rigid interventionist framework for those voluntary associations that were able to emerge or survive. During this period, only those organizations linked to the Catholic Church or the governing party were able to operate with any degree of autonomy. In 1961, there were only 8,329 officially registered voluntary associations (Linz 1971), a figure which alone is sufficiently eloquent as to the weakness of the associative fabric in Spain. This historical background helps to explain the lack of social trust and participative attitudes among older Spaniards.

From the 1960s onwards, however, a number of significant changes began to take place that might have fostered the creation of social capital at least among the youngest generations. In 1964, the authoritarian regime introduced a Law of Associations which broke the virtual duopoly previously enjoyed by the single party and the Church. This enabled the regime to channel a limited development of social, *lato sensu*, organizations. Ten years later, the democratic transition necessarily required the creation of parties and political organizations, whilst the new climate of liberties fostered the creation of associations of all kinds. However, as we have seen in Figure 8.3, these two developments did not significantly foster attitudes of interpersonal trust either among the youngest Spaniards or among the older cohorts.

Two facts may account for this outcome. On the one hand, the previous authoritarian regime waged an intense and repetitive propaganda campaign against any kind of organizational life and political involvement beyond the hierarchical structures provided by the state. As a result, there was only a minority who were politically mobilized either against or in favour of the regime: the great majority of Spaniards only wanted progress and stability at the outset of the new political regime (Aguilar 1996). On the other hand, the Spanish transition was mainly achieved by elite settlements reached through negotiations among the most influential political figures (Linz 1993; Gunther 1992). At some points during transition there were important political mobilizations. But these tended to have short-term goals, and were discouraged as soon as the elites reached agreement, meaning that there was no time for participation to become institutionalized. These political events should have, therefore, facilitated the inter-generational transmission of attitudes favouring low levels of social trust and political involvement.[13]

If this is the case, how can we explain the majoritarian democratic support that Spaniards have consistently given to their new democracy? Contrary to what we have seen with respect to social trust, the preferences of each generation for a democratic regime have varied substantially. We argue that politics have an impact on this change too. A generation-by-generation comparison of preferences for the democratic regime reveals a clear cohort effect (Figure 8.4).[14] The differences between each generation are stable and considerable – even between the third cohort (born between 1950 and 1958, which came of age during the period just before the transition to democracy) and the fourth (born between 1933 and

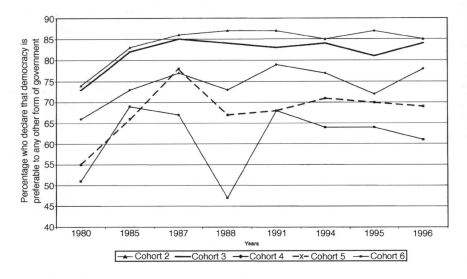

Figure 8.4 Legitimacy by cohorts, 1980–94 (percentage of those who declare that
democracy is preferable to any other form of government).
Source: CIS Data Bank.

1949, which experienced the most rapid period of economic growth and enjoyed
increasing educational levels during its formative years). The younger the cohort,
the greater the support given to the democratic regime, although those differences
tend to be smaller among the youngest cohorts. It should also be noted that this
inter-generational change in the levels of support for the new regime is found not
only between the third and fourth generations; changes are also evident between
the fourth and the fifth generations which preceded them.

These inter-generational variations reveal the distinct learning experiences
about democratic politics of the different cohorts, which were closely related to
different collective memories of the breakdown of the Second Republic and the
resulting civil war. As Aguilar (1996) has shown, these memories have had an
identifiable impact on different generations, conditioning their interpretation of
the Francoist regime and, more importantly, of the political changes that followed
it. In this respect, Spaniards were ready to support democracy once it was
achieved: their support was already considerable in 1980, reflecting the existence
of a range of attitudes favourable to democracy even before the start of the political
transition (Montero *et al*. 1997; Maravall 1995: 275). But not everybody was equally
disposed to accept the change. The oldest generations, those who had personally
experienced the collapse of the 1930s, expressed less support for democracy at the
time, and have lagged behind other generations in this respect ever since.

The roots of both the weakness of social trust and the majoritarian support for
democracy may be traced back to the recent past. But these two attitudes have
evolved very differently: although two decades of democratic life have reinforced

Table 8.5 Democratic legitimacy and interpersonal trust in Spain, 1996 (in percentages)

	Trust	
Preference towards	*Trusters*	*Non-trusters*
Democracy	89	82
Dictatorship	8	9
Indifference	3	9
(*N*)	(831)	(1,442)

Source: CIS Data Bank.

support for the regime, they do not appear to have substantially altered social trust. In contrast to what has been by said by some classic authors (Dahl 1971: 30–2; Converse 1969) and maintained more recently by some social capital theorists (Coleman 1990; Putnam 1993), the functioning of democratic institutions does not always generate *per se* political attitudes such as cooperation and trust. The Spanish case seems to demonstrate that the two set of attitudes – democratic legitimacy and interpersonal trust – can be independent. Table 8.5 clearly shows that there is no relationship between them. Whereas democratic legitimacy has evolved as a result of processes of political learning during the authoritarian regime and of adult resocialization during the early phases of the system, interpersonal trust has maintained similarly low levels across different generations as a consequence of processes of cultural accumulation which transmits images of political experiences crystallized under earlier regimes, and which periodically become revitalized through feelings of political cynicism, disaffection, and alienation (Montero *et al.* 1997; Maravall 1995: 290–1).

SOCIAL TRUST AND SOME OF ITS CONSEQUENCES

In this section we are going to analyse the extent to which this lack of trust affects social capital and political participation. In the case of the former, we should be able to examine the impact of social trust on the levels of membership of social and political organizations. The classic hypothesis suggests that the two are closely linked (Almond and Verba 1963: 212–27; Putnam 1993: 99–116). To what extent is this true in Spain? To test this hypothesis we have carried out a logistic regression analysis of survey data from 1996[15] in which the dependent variable is membership in any social or political organization.[16] The independent variables are social trust and four standard socio-demographic variables (age, gender, education, and occupation). The model obtained, shown in Table 8.6, is statistically significant, but the overall correct prediction of the categories of the dependent variable is only 64 per cent (the pseudo *R*-square is 0.03). Hence, it tells us very little about the explanation for membership of these organizations, though we can at least conclude that social trust is statistically significant (with a coefficient of 0.199 and an odds ratio of 1.22).

Table 8.6 Interpersonal trust and membership in voluntary associations in Spain, 1996 (logistic regression)

Variables	Coefficients	Odds Ratios
Social trust	0.199*	1.22
Age	−0.001	1.0
Gender	0.198	1.22
Education	0.273*	1.31
Occupation		
Housewife	Reference	
Retired	−0.328	0.719
Unemployed	0.102	1.1
Student	0.062	1.06
Work	−0.061	0.941
Intercept	−1.350	

Source: CIS Data Bank.

Notes
Overall prediction of the model 65 per cent; pseudo R-square 0.03; log likelihood −1452.2119.
a   Significant at $p < 0.05$

It seems clear, therefore, that the probability of becoming a member of one of these organizations increases with the existence of social trust. This relationship is found even when the standard socio-demographic variables are included in the model. Consequently, these results show that attitudes such as the lack of interpersonal trust also help to explain the relative scant presence of social and political organizations. Finally, we should emphasize the lack of statistical significance of age: this confirms once again that social capital, this time measured through membership of voluntary organizations, is equally absent in each and every generation of Spaniards.

Some of the comparative literature has also highlighted the effects of social capital on political participation and involvement in the more traditional democracies (Moyser and Parry 1996; van Deth 1996; Hooghe and Derks 1997). Putnam himself (1995: 68) has argued that the fall in social capital in the United States has resulted in a citizenship which is less psychologically engaged with politics. The effect of social capital on different levels of political involvement and participation could also have an impact on government responses and policy agenda setting. As Rosenstone and Hasen (1993) have demonstrated in the American case, the differential mobilization of the population has led to very particularistic demands. And according to Hardin (1993), those who trust are better off both economically and politically speaking. Is this also the case in Spain?

We believe that social capital (formed in part through social involvement) has a clear direct impact on political involvement, corroborating what van Deth (1997: 12) has called the *direct model* of the effects of social involvement on political involvement. We should begin to test this assertion by measuring the impact of social capital on political participation.

We start by recalling that the level of conventional participation is much lower in Spain than in other Western democracies. In terms of the well-known indicators of conventional participation used by Barnes *et al.* (1979), Spaniards participate less in those activities that require the least effort (for instance, 'reading the political section of the newspaper' or 'discussing politics'), although the gap shrinks and even disappears in terms of more demanding activities (Montero and Torcal 1990; Maravall 1984: 117). These differences have hardly changed during the 1980s and early 1990s (Torcal 1995), and are confirmed by the proportion of respondents who stated that they had participated in at least one of the conventional activities (besides voting) included in the 1990 World Values Survey (see Table 8.7).

Spain has the lowest levels of conventional participation in the whole of Western Europe. Moreover, these low levels of participation cannot be explained in terms of preferences for alternative forms of participation related to the so-called 'new politics' (Kaase and Barnes 1979; Dalton 1988). In any case, Spain also has one of the lowest levels of unconventional participation of all the Western European democracies: along with the Belgians, Spaniards are among the least likely to have participated in any of the four types of unconventional activities considered in the survey.[17]

Is this lack of participation related to low levels of social capital? To answer this question we have created indices of conventional and unconventional participation as dependent variables containing the frequency of participation in eight different political activities[18] (the data come from the same CIS 1996 survey

Table 8.7 Conventional and unconventional political participation in Western democracies, 1981 and 1990 (percentages of those who participate in at least one of the activities besides voting)

Countries[a]	Conventional		Unconventional	
	1981	1990	1981	1990
Norway	78	89	–	–
W. Germany	79	84	85	88
Denmark	80	78	78	81
Sweden	78	79	–	–
Iceland	76	79	–	93
Netherlands	74	76	80	86
United States	67	73	–	93
Great Britain	64	66	92	91
France	62	65	81	85
Spain	69	52	73	66
Ireland	5	59	77	83
Italy	5	58	80	87
Belgium	45	54	64	77

Sources: 1981 European Values Survey and 1990 World Values Survey.

Note

a   Countries are listed in decreasing averages of conventional participation.

Table 8.8 Social capital and conventional political participation in Spain, 1996 (OLS estimators)

Variables	Coefficients	Betas
Social trust	0.163^a	0.08
Membership in voluntary associations	0.487^a	0.238
Ideology	-0.002^b	-0.048
Age	0.001^b	0.057
Gender	0.289^a	0.145
Education	0.152^a	0.202
Intercept	-0.766^a	
R-squared	0.148	

Source: CIS Data Bank.

Notes
a   Significant at $p < 0.01$
b   Significant at $p < 0.05$.

which was already used in Table 8.6). A factor analysis of these data (not shown) produced two very different factors for the two types of participation, conventional and unconventional, and accordingly we have created the two dependent variables.[19] The set of independent variables included was similar in both models: social trust, membership of voluntary associations, self-placement on the left–right ideological scale, and the standard socio-demographic variables (with the exception of occupation, which consistently has been shown to have no effect).

Table 8.8 contains the results of a multiple regression analysis in which conventional participation is the dependent variable. The results reveal that the two items we have used to measure social capital (social trust and membership of voluntary associations) have a statistically significant relation with the index of conventional participation: that is, the greater the presence of social capital, the greater the probability of using any of the mechanisms of conventional participation. This relation holds even when we control for the effect of other variables, such as education, gender, and age. If the standardized coefficients of regression are compared, membership of voluntary organizations is found to be the best predictor. Of the socio-demographic variables included in the model, the relation with education (0.202) and gender (0.145) should be noted.

These coefficients reveal that less educated citizens and women are least likely to engage in conventional forms of participation, confirming that the distinct structure of opportunities for some specific social groups is an important differentiating factor in Spanish politics. In short, conventional participation may depend on a series of attitudes and socio-demographic variables, but it also depends on the level of social capital. It should be noticed that the R-square of the model is only 0.148, which is rather low. But if we include in the model other attitudinal variables related to social capital, such as interest in politics, the model improves to 0.31 without altering the relationships presented in Table 8.8. Social capital, therefore, has a clear direct impact on conventional political participation.

Table 8.9 Social capital and unconventional political participation in Spain, 1996 (OLS estimators)

Variables	Coefficients	Betas
Social trust	0.08[b]	0.039
Membership in voluntary associations	0.224[a]	0.108
Ideology	−0.09[a]	−0.198
Age	−0.095[a]	−0.272
Gender	0.132[a]	0.065
Education	0.08[a]	0.115
Intercept	0.689[a]	
R-squared	0.206	

Source: CIS Data Bank.

Notes
a   Significant at $p < 0.01$
b   Significant at $p < 0.05$

It might be thought that the weakness of social capital, contrary to what has been observed with respect to conventional mechanisms, would strengthen the predisposition for unconventional participation. The comparative literature has shown that the decrease in conventional participation in the advanced democracies over the last few decades has often been linked to a search for alternative forms of participation (Kaase and Barnes 1979: 532–3; Inglehart 1990: 369–70). Has this also been the case in Spain? The results presented in Table 8.9, in which unconventional political participation is the dependent variable, reject this hypothesis. Moreover, the signs of the coefficients for the social capital indicators are the same as those observed for conventional participation; that is, the higher the level of social capital, the higher the level of unconventional participation. The model presented in Table 8.9 fits even better, since the *R*-square in this case is 0.206 (and 0.26 when interest in politics is included).

Membership of voluntary associations is the best predictor of the dependent variable after ideology and education. Social trust is also statistically significant. These data are therefore relevant to our understanding of why Spaniards are comparatively unlikely to participate in politics regardless of the costs attributed to it, the different structure of opportunities for social sectors, the levels of education and the intensity of ideological polarization.

CONCLUDING REMARKS

This chapter has examined some of the distinctive patterns of the formation and evolution of social capital in the context of a new democracy. Despite the increase in social capital since the return to democracy, Spain constitutes an example of a low intensity equilibrium. We argue that this is a result of the low levels of interpersonal trust found among Spaniards. These levels have not changed across different generations, an attitudinal continuity which seems to be due to a certain cultural legacy transmitted from generation to generation and which has proved resistant to the major economic, social and political changes that have taken place over the last few decades. We also maintain that this transmission might be explained by political events which most Spaniards experienced and/or received from their elders during their processes of socialization. Politics matter in the creation of social capital, albeit through the filter of political socialization. The lack of trust has contributed to the low presence of social capital, and both factors have also a distinctive impact on democratic politics.

Political participation (both conventional and unconventional) in Spain is very low and highly non-equalitarian (Torcal 1997). While this could be the subject of a different chapter, we will end this one by asserting that the weakness of social capital is an important contributory factor to both the low levels of political participation and the political inequality related to them.

It is true that young people currently appear to be responsible for a certain revitalization of some associations, notably those related to sporting and social-charitable activities, as well as to human rights and ecological issues. Some increase in the level of acceptance of the new social movements has also been observed, although it seems to be rather less intense than in recent years (Orizo 1996: 120–3). Equally, it is also possible to detect increasing sentiments of solidarity, accompanied by more voluntary work in what is a growing network of non-governmental organizations (Casado 1992). But these trends, the evolution of which naturally remains to be seen, contrast with the irregularity of the day-to-day activities of many social movements, their relative isolation, and the limited response to their appeals. It is, as Álvarez Junco (1994: 439) has observed, a somewhat schizophrenic situation for social movements. They are incapable of winning sustained social support in the midst of the weak social fabric and generalized interpersonal mistrust that characterizes Spanish society. They can also emerge from periods of apathy as vehicles for political protest against governments held responsible for society's problems.

This chapter is more than just a study of social capital in Spain. It is a discussion of the formation of social capital in a new democracy. Many authors have sought an understanding of this problem in the rational-choice approach. In fact, the literature consists of yet another search for a solution to the non-cooperative equilibrium inherent in the problem of collective action that is also found in the formation of social capital (for instance, the argument of selective incentives, the appropriation of private goods, the prisoner's dilemma supergame, induced institutional equlibrium, and so on have all been used to this end). We maintain that the solution to the existence of free-riding in the formation of social capital may be found in the concept of social trust. We argue that social trust is an attitude, not a relational-rational action. This definition of social trust not only helps explain the rate of increase of social capital in new democracies, but also, when its presence is majoritarian, may change the marginal utility of the cooperative preference among actors, resolving the non-cooperative equilibrium to the prisoner's dilemma inherent in collective action.

Notes

* We would like to thank Carles Boix and Jacint Jordana for their invaluable comments, the Centro de Estudios Avanzados en Ciencias Sociales, Instituto Juan March, for the use of its excellent facilities, and the Comisión Interministerial de Ciencia y Tecnología (SEC95-1007) for its generous financial support.

1 However, in a recent article on the United States, Putnam (1995) discusses the positive role played by the government in the creation of social capital.

2 Before starting, we should emphasize that this chapter is eminently empirical in nature. It is largely based on survey data, most of which has been taken from the Data Bank of the Spanish Centro de Investigaciones Sociológicas (CIS [Centre for Sociological Research]). Other survey data come from the Centro de Estudios sobre la Realidad Social (CIRES [Center for Studies of Social Reality]), the 1980 European Values Survey, and the 1990 World Values Survey.

3 These figures have been taken from the Register of Associations; we would like to thank Mr Angel García del Valle for facilitating access to these data.

4 The index rose relatively steadily: 22.8 in 1970, 36.0 in 1975, 107.68 in 1981, 178.33 in 1986, 287.71 in 1991. See also Linz (1971).

5 The list of associations and organizations that respondents were asked if they belonged to comprised 10 items in 1981, 16 in 1990, and 12 in 1994. The percentages in Table 8.1 were calculated by recoding the variables measuring membership as 0 (do not belong) and 1 (belong), and then creating a new variable adding from the sum of them all. The percentages for voluntary work were computed in the same way.

6 We agree with Gundelach (1995) that grass-roots activity should be measured through more sophisticated instruments, especially in the case of the new type of associations in which membership is not so important. However, as we have seen in Table 8.1, the distribution of those people stating that they do some voluntary work is little different. Furthermore, as is discussed elsewhere in this volume (for instance, in Maloney's chapter), not all new forms of participation (for example, cheque-book membership) produce social capital. Moreover, we consider that assessments of social capital levels should include membership of more traditional organizations such as political parties and unions. As has often been noted, they could well produce more social capital than bowling clubs and sport clubs (Boix and Posner 1996; Tarrow 1996).

7 The order of the other countries was as follows: Portugal, 82 per cent; Italy, 80 per cent; France, 73 per cent; Austria and Great Britain, 72 per cent; Ireland, 66 per cent; Belgium, 61 per cent; United States, 60 per cent; West Germany and Iceland, 54 per cent; Denmark, 49 per cent; and The Netherlands, 33 per cent. This is the sum cumulative percentage of those who declare that they are not members of any educational-cultural, human rights, third world aid, ecological, peace, or youth organization, sports or leisure club, animal rights organization, or local voluntary association to fight poverty, unemployment, homelessness or race discrimination.

8 More specifically, it has been argued that whilst young people see politics as remote and irrelevant, these same individuals become more interested in politics as they mature and acquire greater social and economic responsibilities (Nie *et al.* 1974).

9   The six generations have been defined as follows. The oldest cohort comprises all those born before 1922, who reached adulthood at the end of the Monarchy, during the II Republic or the Civil War. The next cohort (cohort 5), which has been labelled the generation of autarky, consists of those people born between 1923 and 1937, who reached political maturity during the difficult years of the economic depression. The fourth generation (cohort 4) is that of the economic take-off, and includes those born between 1938 and 1952, who came of age when economic control passed from the Falangists to the technocrats, who went on to implement the Stabilization and Development Plans of the 1960s. The third generation (cohort 3) is that of the liberalization of the regime: those born between 1953 and 1962 acquired political consciousness during the liberalization and crisis of the dictatorship. The second generation (cohort 2) is that of the transition, and is made up of those born between 1963 and 1967, who reached political maturity during the political transition to, and consolidation of, the new democratic system. Finally, the youngest cohort consists of all those born since 1968 and who have only known a fully fledged democratic regime.

10   For the concept of cultural accumulation see Almond and Verba (1963: 213–21, 279) and Putnam (1993: 152–62).

11   We sustain that Putnam's argument about the origins of social capital in Italy may not only be historically inaccurate (Sabetti 1996), but, as Laitin (1995: 172–3) and Tarrow (1996: 393) point out, it also ignores many equally political and historical events that have taken place in Italy over the centuries (see also Boix and Posner 1996, 20–5).

12   For a clear theoretical argument about the risk of high levels of political organization in the context of a highly fragmented society, see Boix and Posner (1996).

13   For a similar argument, see Álvarez Junco (1994); and for detailed empirical evidence, Torcal (1997).

14   For the sake of clarity, Figure 8.4 does not show the pattern of the youngest cohort, which is almost identical to that of cohort 2.

15   This survey was carrried out by the Centro de Investigaciones Sociológicas (CIS) in June, 1996, covering a representative sample of adult Spaniards.

16   Originally, the dependent variable was a simple sum scale reflecting the number of organizations to which each respondent belonged in 1996. These organizations were neighbourhood associations, youth associations, mothers' groups, sports clubs, trade unions, voluntary work associations, political parties, cultural associations and religious organizations. This variable was in fact a count event variable that presented a Poisson distribution. However, we decided to convert it into a dummy variable with values of 1 ('member of at least one organization') and 0 ('no membership'). The results of the Poisson regression and of the logistic regression were very similar; for the sake of simplicity we only give those of the logistic regression. Since it has been argued that the strength of Spanish civil society lies in the growing number of voluntary associations of a 'societal nature' (Pérez Díaz 1995: 40–1), we decided to repeat the analysis with associations of that type. The results were also very similar.

17   Respondents were asked whether they had participated in any of the following four activities: 'signing a petition', 'joining a boycott', 'participating in demonstrations', and 'joining strikes'.

18   The activities were following political news; talking about politics; trying to

convince others; working to solve a problem that affects you or your community, town or city; and working for a party or a political candidate.

19   We have performed a factor analysis with varimax rotation, producing two clear factors that explain 58 and 26 per cent of the variance respectively. The first factor was formed from the following conventional participation activities: following political news, talking about politics, trying to convince others, working to solve a problem that affects you or your community, town or city, and working for a party or a political candidate. The second factor includes the following unconventional participation activities: attending political rallies, blocking the traffic, and occupying buildings, factories or other public spaces. Both dependent variables, conventional and unconventional participation, were created with the factor scores respectively resulting from two principal component analyses based on the previous results of the factor analysis.

References

Aguilar, Paloma. 1996. *Memoria y olvido de la guerra civil española*. Madrid: Alianza.

Almond, Gabriel A., and Sidney Verba. 1963. *The Civic Culture. Political Attitudes and Democracy in Five Nations*. Princeton: Princeton University Press.

Álvarez Junco, José. 1994. 'Movimientos sociales en España: del modelo tradicional a la modernidad postfranquista'. In *Los nuevos movimientos sociales. De la ideología a la identidad*, ed. Enrique Laraña and Jospeh Gusfield. Madrid: Centro de Investigaciones Sociológicas.

Barnes, Samuel H. *et al*. 1979. *Political Action. Mass Participation in Five Western Democracies*. Beverly Hills: Sage.

Bartolini, Stefano. 1983. 'The Membership of Mass Parties: The Social-Democratic Experience, 1889–1978'. In *Western European Party Systems*, ed. Hans Daalder and Peter Mair. London: Sage.

Baumgartner, Frank R., and Jack L. Walker. 1988. 'Survey Research and Membership in Voluntary Associations'. *American Journal of Political Science* 32: 908–28.

Boix, Carles, and Daniel N. Posner. 1996. 'Making Social Capital Work: A Review of Robert Putnam's Making Democracy Work: Civic Traditions in Modern Italy'. Cambridge: The Center for International Affairs, Harvard University, Paper 96–4.

Casado, Demetrio, ed. 1992. *Organizaciones voluntarias en España*. Barcelona: Editorial Hacer.

Coleman, James S. 1988. 'Social Capital in the Creation of Human Capital'. *American Journal of Sociology* 94: 95–119.

——— 1990. *Foundations of Social Theory*. Cambridge, MA: Harvard University Press.

Converse, Philip E. 1969. 'Of Time and Partisan Stability'. *Comparative Political Studies* 2: 139–71.

Dahl, Robert A. 1971. *Poliarchy. Participation and Opposition*. New Haven: Yale University Press.

Dalton, Russell J. 1988. *Citizen Politics in Western Democracies. Public Opinion and Political Parties in the United States, Great Britain, West Germany and France*. Chatham: Chatham House Publishers.

Gangas, Pilar. 1995. *El desarrollo organizativo de los partidos políticos españoles de implantación nacional*. Madrid: Instituto Juan March. PhD dissertation.

Gundelach, Peter. 1995. 'Grass-Roots Activities'. In *The Impact of Values*, ed. Jan W. van Deth and Elinor Scarbrough. Oxford: Oxford University Press.

Gunther, Richard. 1992. 'Spain: The Very Model of the Modern Elite Settlement'. *In Elites and Democratic Consolidation in Latin America and Southern Europe*, ed. John Higley and R. Gunther. Cambridge: Cambridge University Press.

Gunther, Richard and José Ramón Montero. 1996. 'Spain'. Paper presented at the Conference on Comparative National Election Project, Instituto Juan March, Madrid.

Hardin, Russell. 1971. 'Collective Action as an Agreable N-Prisoner's Dilemma'. *Behavioral Science* 16: 472–81.

—— 1993. 'The Street Level Epistemology of Trust'. *Politics and Society* 21: 505–29.

Hooghe, Mark, and Anton Derks. 1997. 'Voluntary Associations and the Creation of Social Capital'. Paper presented at the ECPR Joint Sessions, Bern.

Inglehart, Ronald. 1990. *Culture Shift in Advanced Industrial Society*. Princeton: Princeton University Press.

Jordana, Jacint. 1995. 'Trade Union Membership in Spain (1977–1994)'. Labour Studies Working Papers, Center for Comparative Studies, University of Warwick.

Kaase, Max and Samuel H. Barnes. 1979. 'In Conclusion. The Future of Political Protest in Western Democracies'. In *Political Action. Mass Participation in Five Western Democracies*, by S.H. Barnes *et al*. Beverly Hills: Sage.

Katz, Richard S. *et al*. 1992. 'The Membership of Political Parties in European Democracies, 1960–1990'. *European Journal of Political Research* 22: 329–45.

Laitin, David P. 1995. 'The Civic Culture at 30'. *American Political Science Review* 89: 173–86.

Levi, Margaret. 1996a. *A State of Trust*, EUI Working Paper, 96/23. San Domenico: European University Institute.

—— 1996b. 'Social and Unsocial Capital: A Review Essay of Robert Putnam's Making Democracy Work'. *Politics and Society* 24: 45–55.

Linz, Juan J. 1971. 'La realidad asociativa de los españoles'. In *Sociología española de los años 70*. Madrid: Confederación Española de Cajas de Ahorros.

—— 1981. 'A Century of Politics and Interests in Spain'. In *Organizing Interests in Western Europe: Pluralism, Corporativism and the Transformation of Politics*, ed. Suzanne D. Berger. Cambridge: Cambridge University Press.

—— 1993. 'Innovative Leadership in the Transition to Democracy and a New Democracy: The Case of Spain'. In *Innovative Leaders in International Politics*, ed. Gabriel Sheffer. Albany: State University of New York Press.

López Pintor, Rafael. 1982. *La opinión pública española del franquismo a la democracia*. Madrid: Centro de Investigaciones Sociológicas.

Maravall, José María. 1984. *La política de la transición*. Madrid: Taurus, 2nd edn.

—— 1995. *Los resultados de la democracia*. Madrid: Alianza.

Montero, José Ramón. 1981. 'Partidos y participación política: algunas notas sobre la afiliación política en la etapa inicial de la transición española'. *Revista de Estudios Políticos* 23: 33–72.

Montero, Jose Ramón, and Mariano Torcal. 1990. 'Voters and Citizens in a New Democracy: Some Trend Data on Political Attitudes in Spain'. *International Journal of Public Opinion Research* 2: 116–40.

Montero, José Ramón, Richard Gunther and Mariano Torcal. 1997. 'Democracy in Spain: Legitimacy, Discontent, and Disaffection'. Madrid: Instituto Juan March, Estudio/ Working Paper 100.

Morlino, Leonardo. 1995. 'Political Parties and Democratic Consolidation in Southern Europe'. In *The Politics of Democratic Consolidation. Southern Europe in Comparative*

Perspective, ed. Richard Gunther, P. Nikiforos Diamandouros and Hans-Jürgen Puhle. Baltimore: The Johns Hopkins University Press.

Moyser, George, and Geraint Parry. 1996. 'Voluntary Associations and Democratic Participation in Britain'. Paper presented at the ECPR Joint Sessions, Oslo.

Nie, Norman, Sidney Verba and Jae-On Kim. 1974. 'Participation and the Political Cycle'. *Comparative Politics* 6: 319–40.

Núñez, Clara Eugenia. 1992. *La fuente de la riqueza. Educación y desarrollo económico en la España contemporánea*. Madrid: Alianza.

Olson, Mancur. 1965. *The Logic of Collective Action. Public Goods and The Theory of Groups*. Cambridge, MA: Harvard University Press.

Orizo, Francisco A. 1996. *Sistemas de valores en la España de los 90*. Madrid: Centro de Investigaciones Sociológicas.

Pérez Díaz, Víctor. 1996. *España puesta a prueba, 1976–1996*. Madrid: Alianza.

Price, R. 1989. 'Trade Union Membership'. In *International Labour Statistics. A Handbook, Guide, and Recent Trends*, ed. R. Bean. London: Routledge.

Prieto-Lacaci, Rafael. 1994. 'Asociaciones voluntarias'. In *Tendencias sociales en España (1960–1990)*, ed. Salustiano del Campo, vol. I. Bilbao: Fundación BBV, 2nd edn.

Putnam, Robert D. 1993. *Making Democracy Work. Civic Traditions in Modern Italy*. Princeton: Princeton University Press.

—— 1995a. 'Bowling Alone: America's Declining Social Capital'. *Journal of Democracy* 6: 65–78.

Rosenstone, Steven J., and John Mark Hansen. 1993. *Mobilization, Participation, and Democracy in America*. New York: MacMillan.

Sabetti, Filipo. 1996. 'Path Dependency and Civic Culture: Some Lessons From Italy About Interpreting Social Experiments'. *Politics and Society* 24: 19–44.

Tarrow, Sidney. 1996. 'Making Social Science Work Across Space and Time. A Critical Reflection on Robert Putnam's *Making Democracy Work*'. *American Political Science Review* 90: 389–97.

Torcal, Mariano. 1995. *Actitudes políticas y participación política en España: pautas de cambio y continuidad*. Madrid: Universidad Autónoma de Madrid, PhD. Dissertation.

—— 1997. 'Southern Europeans between Legitimacy and Disaffection: Attitudinal Change and its Consequences in New Democracies'. Paper presented at the XX International Congress of the Latin American Studies Association. Guadalajara (Mexico).

van Deth, Jan W. 1996. 'Social and Political Involvement: An Overview and Reassessment of Empirical Findings'. Paper presented at the ECPR Joint Sessions, Oslo.

—— 1997. 'Introduction. Social Involvement and Democratic Politics'. In *Private Groups and Public Life. Social Participation, Voluntary Associations and Political Involvement in Representative Democracies*, ed. Jan W. van Deth. London: Routledge.

Van der Meer, Marc. 1995. 'Trade Union Membership in Spain'. Manuscript.

Whiteley, Paul F. 1997. 'Political Capital Formation Among British Party Members'. In *Private Groups and Public Life. Social Participation, Voluntary Associations and Political Involvement in Representative Democracies*, ed. Jan W. van Deth. London: Routledge.

9 The myth of American exceptionalism

A three-nation comparison of associational membership and social capital*

Dietlind Stolle and Thomas R. Rochon

The theory of social capital makes some remarkably general claims about the role of societal trust and networks in improving the quality of political, social and economic life. The existence and maintenance of social capital in certain communities or regions is believed to lower the amount of drug use, criminal activity, teenage pregnancy and delinquency, to increase the success of schools and their pupils, to enhance economic development, and to make government more effective (Putnam, 1993; Fukuyama, 1995; Hagan *et al.*, 1995; Jencks and Peterson, 1991; Case and Katz, 1991; Granovetter, 1985). In short, social capital links citizens to each other and enables them to pursue their common objectives more effectively.

Although the origins of social capital remain in some respects unclear, we do know that it is generated through different kinds of interactions between people that build trust, skills and habits of cooperation. The social capital school has therefore proposed that one of the mechanisms for the generation of social capital is participation in voluntary associations (Putnam, 1993; 1995a; 1995b). This claim is based on research that focuses on the external role of associations as important intermediaries between citizens and the government, as well as research on mobilization effects, democratic learning processes and socialization effects within voluntary associations.[1] The latter approaches find that membership in such associations is connected to members' higher political and societal engagement as well as more trust and higher civic orientations.

More specifically, Almond and Verba in *The Civic Culture*, and many other authors, found that members of associations are more politically active, more informed about politics, more sanguine about their ability to affect political life, and more supportive of democratic norms (Almond and Verba, 1963; Olsen, 1972; Billiet and Cambré, 1996). The authors also noticed that the number of associations to which people belong, and the extent of their activity within the organization, are related to political activity and involvement. In later research, Verba and his colleagues found that members of voluntary associations learn self-respect, group identity and public skills (Verba *et al.*, 1995; Moyser and Parry, 1997; Koopmans *et al.*, 1997).

To these findings, the social capital school adds that membership in associations also facilitates the learning of cooperative attitudes and behaviour, including reciprocity. In particular, membership in voluntary associations increases face-to-face interactions between people and creates a setting for the development of trust. This in-group trust can be utilized to achieve group purposes more efficiently and more easily. However, the social capital school says more than this. Through mechanisms that are not yet clearly understood, the development of interpersonal trust between members tends to be generalized to the society as a whole. In this way, the operation of voluntary groups and associations contributes to the building of a society in which cooperation between all people for all sorts of purposes – not just within the groups themselves – is facilitated.[2]

In the recent enthusiasm for the importance of voluntary associations in building social capital, differences between countries and institutional settings have tended to be lost. The literature on social capital has developed evidence for the importance of formal networks, such as voluntary associations, mainly in one-country settings.[3]

There is good reason to undertake comparative work on associations and social capital. Even though the theory of social capital is a general one, operationally its effects are mediated through networks of formal associations and informal contacts that are contextual. Social interactions are deeply embedded in institutional and cultural settings that are highly variable between countries and regions. Interactions between people are characterized by the culturally embedded patterns of inclusion and exclusion of social groups. Those patterns are created by the tracings of social cleavages that themselves result from historical conflicts and tensions. The severity of these cleavages, and the extent to which they affect patterns of associational life, vary over time and space. Moreover, the density and style of associational life vary between countries, and even between regions within a country. Some cultures are more prolific in the creation of associations than others. In some cultures, associations spring primarily from a grass-roots, voluntarist impulse, while in others associations may be primarily created by such central agencies as the state. We do not know how such differences in density, origins, and inclusiveness of associations might affect the creation of social capital. But there is reason to suspect that these traits matter, and hence that the connection between associational life and social capital will not be invariant across national settings.[4]

This chapter is an investigation of the link between associational membership and social capital in three countries: Germany, Sweden and the United States. We rely on data from the two waves of the World Value Survey to probe the areas of continuity and distinctiveness in associational membership and in the connection of membership to social capital. Of course, the United States has been considered a seedbed of voluntary associations and social capital at least since the time of Tocqueville, who has called the US a 'nation of joiners' (Tocqueville, 1961). Max Weber also joined the chorus, calling the United States 'association land *par excellence*'.[5] The multi-headed hydra of American exceptionalism thrives in no small part on belief in the prevalence and importance of associational life in the United States.

Table 9.1 Percentages of memberships in association types by country

	Germany	USA	Sweden
Political associations	12.7	20.1	21.0
Economic groups	23.1	23.4	54.6
Group rights	6.4	6.7	4.8
Community groups	29.7	22.9	24.9
Cultural associations	22.1	56.9	20.1
Private interest	21.5	19.8	21.3

Note
Average number of memberships: Germany 1.13; USA 1.74; Sweden: 1.59.

Table 9.1 verifies this American tradition of associational membership, particularly in the broad area of cultural associations, which includes groups devoted to education, arts, music, and cultural activities as well as church groups.[6] Overall, the average adult American belongs to one-and-three-quarters associations. However, both Germany and Sweden have their own vibrant traditions of associational membership. In Sweden that is reflected particularly in a high rate of membership in economic associations, including professional associations and, pre-eminently, labour unions. In Germany we also find a broad array of associational memberships, most conspicuously among community groups, which includes social welfare organizations for the handicapped, elderly and deprived people, as well as voluntary health care groups and local action groups on issues like poverty, employment, housing and race discrimination. In Germany, we find fewer memberships in political organizations. Germany is also the country with the most people who are associationally not affiliated (40 per cent, as opposed to 27.5 per cent in the US and 24.4 per cent in Sweden).

Our choice of the US, Sweden and Germany for comparison rests partly on the fact that average associational density in all three countries is greater than one membership per person. If the production of social capital relies on an associational density sufficiently great that people will assume that their 'average' fellow citizen also joins associations, then all three countries are above this threshold. In other words, we are able to hold the factor of associational density somewhat constant across our cases.

At the same time, differences in the distributions of associational memberships between the US, Germany and Sweden reflect the distinctive institutional and cultural legacies of these states and societies. We seek to capitalize on those differences to answer two questions about the connection between associational membership and social capital, using the logic of a most different systems design. First, do memberships in all kinds of voluntary associations matter equally in the three countries for political activity, trust and other social capital indicators just as much in Sweden and Germany as they do in the US? In other words, is the level of involvement in various kinds of associations more or less productive of social capital in strong state settings that subsidize associational life, as compared to weak state settings where associations are products of civil society? Second, can we expect different types of associations to have varied impacts in different societal and institutional settings? By attempting to answer these questions we will connect micro approaches concerned with the mobilizing effects associations have on individual members to macro considerations of the institutional context in which voluntary associations operate.[7] The most different systems design, which is based on the difference in institutional structures and associational cultures in these three countries, enables us to answer these questions.

There are several reasons why we would expect the impact of voluntary associations to depend on the institutional and cultural setting in which those associations operate. Some of these reasons have been identified in the literature on civil society and states, as well as in literature that examines political participation in a cross-national setting.

The primary issue in past research was to explain cross-national variance in the density of associational memberships (Almond and Verba, 1963; Curtis *et al.*, 1992). Lipset for example, traces differences in the density of associational networks to the structure of value systems in different societies (Lipset, 1985). According to Lipset, the American democratic value system, which grew out of the nation's revolutionary past, gives a comparatively high priority to individual participation in community organizations. In contrast, collectively oriented values coming from the counter-revolutionary past led to less emphasis on voluntary activity by individuals. In those cultures one finds more reliance on the state for solutions to community problems. Other proposed determinants of membership in voluntary associations include type of religion, levels of industrialization and urbanization.

None of these explanations can elucidate various cases consistently. The problem is that differences between societies in the pluralistic character of the voluntary sector were shaped in the period of Enlightenment, during bourgeois revolutions, and in the course of workers' and farmers' mobilizations. Societies that developed pluralistic traditions of competing religious organizations fostered an active voluntary religious sector in opposition to secular groups. In contrast, societies that developed close connections between an established church and other dominant political groups opened fewer opportunities for associations to blossom freely (Wuthnow, 1991). Such divergent historical patterns have had an impact not only on the density of voluntary associations, but also on their character and on their democratic and civic potential, i.e. their potential for creating social capital.

One of the fundamental assumptions about the connection between associations and social capital is that associational memberships are more productive of social capital in weak state settings and in a pluralist civil society. The United States, of course, epitomizes this profile. Associations may be less productive of social capital in a strong state setting with a more institutionalized and less competitive civil society, such as Germany and Sweden. Strong states subsidize associational life to a greater extent and in a more pro-active (visible) mode than weak states. Moreover, associational life in Germany and Sweden does not fully resemble the voluntary aspects that Tocqueville envisioned. There, organizations developed around upper- and middle-class interests, focusing particularly on the representation of these interests in the political arena through the development of peak organizations. Greater state involvement in support for associations in Sweden and Germany is also reflected in public subsidies and financial backing. Germany, for example, is known for a very high level of state subsidies for various kinds of voluntary associations (Anheier, 1991).[8] Associations in the US are more dependent on contributions and membership fees. While state support may produce an extensive associational network, participation in a state-fostered network may also diminish the impact of associations on social capital.

Tocqueville was already concerned in the nineteenth century about the possibility that states would take over the functions of voluntary associations. As a result, the public could become apathetic and susceptible to totalitarian tendencies. Similar concerns were expressed by Durkheim. In modern anti-state social thought, a common thesis shared by critics of the left and right is that the spirit of voluntarism is influenced by state extension (Habermas, 1984). This reduces the spirit of moral obligation and diminishes personal responsibility for the collective welfare. In nations where states have expanded their activity levels we would, therefore, expect more apathy, less involvement, and less impact of voluntary associations.

In the remainder of this chapter we will be examining several indicators of social capital. We will analyse how certain dimensions of social capital relate differently to membership in voluntary associations in the three countries under scrutiny, and we will consider whether different types of associations foster different dimensions of social capital.

MEASURING SOCIAL CAPITAL

In this section we provide a brief overview of the indicators of social capital we will be examining, their theoretical and logical foundations, as well as their relationship to associational membership. All the indicators were created on the basis of survey questions, the full wording of which is given in the appendix to this chapter.

The first set of indicators covers the theme of participation and engagement in politics. Studies of political participation have long demonstrated the stimulating and activating function of non-political organizations for political involvement and interest (Olsen, 1972; Verba and Nie, 1972; Erickson and Nosanchuck, 1990; and Verba *et al.*, 1995; Rogers *et al.*, 1975). Both formal and informal activities of the association impart an understanding of political and economic issues. Associations also open up possibilities for political participation by cultivating among their members the 'organizational and communications skills that are relevant for politics and thus can facilitate direct political activity'.[9] Organizing membership meetings at work, setting up a food pantry at church, and leading community charity drives are all activities that develop social skills transferable to politics. Those skills also increase the sense of political efficacy and political competence (Erickson and Nosanchuck, 1990). We will therefore examine the effect of associational membership on political action and interest in politics.

A second cluster of indicators includes a measure of generalized trust. Networks of civic engagement are said to foster norms of generalized reciprocity and to encourage the emergence of social trust (Putnam, 1995b). These norms of reciprocity are generalized when they go beyond specific personal settings in which the partner to be cooperated with is already known. Generalized norms of reciprocity are indicated by an abstract preparedness to trust others.[10]

It is not entirely clear how associational memberships build these generalized values which go beyond the immediate group of fellow members. Generalized trust involves a leap of faith that the trustworthiness of those you know can be broadened to include others whom you do not know. The social characteristics from representatives of the groups one knows may be extended to the social group in general, and therefore also to the people one does not know.[11] No matter how the process of generalization occurs, generalized trust and reciprocity are at the heart of the theory of social capital because they constitute the link between social capital and the quality of democracy. We will measure generalized trust with a single survey question on whether people can be trusted or whether one has to be careful with others.

The third block of indicators of social capital includes trust towards public institutions. Much of the scholarly and popular attention given to social capital in recent years has centred on its potential to redefine the partnership between public and private organizations in the provision of collective goods. For this reconstituted relationship to work, there must be a high degree of trust not only between citizens, but also between citizens and government. Hence, trust in public officials and institutions is part of the complex of attitudes and behaviour that makes up social capital.

In the United States, declining trust in government since the early 1970s involves not only institution-specific factors (scandal in the White House, partisan wrangling in Congress, controversial rulings by the Supreme Court), but also a more general loss of faith in government (Brehm and Rahn, 1996). The same point can be made in international comparisons of trust in public officials or institutions. Specific events may affect levels of trust throughout a society, but to the extent that associations add to social capital, their members will be relatively trusting of public institutions. We measure this type of trust with survey questions on the respondent's confidence in public institutions.

Our final set of social capital indicators represents an attitudinal trait that is also important to social capital: disapproval of free-riding. Social capital implies a willingness to do one's share in collective endeavours. In a setting rich in social capital, one is less likely to expect others to be free-riders and, partly in consequence, one is also less likely to be a free-rider. Associations are often depicted as productive of viewpoints broader than self-interest, even when the associations themselves pursue a more privately oriented interest. They broaden the members' sense of self, developing the 'I' into the 'We' (see Putnam, 1995a; Rochon, 1998). We hypothesize that members of associations will learn an ethic that considers it wrong to free-ride on governmental policies or public goods. Our measurements include questions on approval of free-riding in the use of public goods. The breadth of these indicators of social capital suggests the extent of the creative enthusiasm deployed in this literature.

RESULTS

The differences between our three country cases in state involvement and mobilization effects lead us to anticipate national differences in the impact of associational memberships on these social capital indicators. Some of these effects exist because of distinctive patterns of membership in different societies. Societies differ, for example in their degree of working class mobilization. State support for associations may exaggerate class differences (such as for example when state support is focused on high culture), or it may reduce such differences. One result that we can anticipate is that where there is no active agent of working class mobilization (whether governmental or private, such as through the union movement), there will be an upper class bias in associational membership.[12]

Table 9.2 shows that this class bias in associational membership exists in all three countries, but to varying degrees. The correlation between a person's social class and membership in any association is highest in the US ($r = 0.20$) and lowest in Germany ($r = 0.08$), with Sweden in between ($r = 0.14$). This overall degree of class bias is, however, a composite of widely differing experiences across associational sectors.

The greatest degree of class bias in all three countries can be found in economic and political associations, though the extensive organization of the Swedish Social Democratic Party (SAP) shows up in a relatively smaller class bias in party memberships. The extensive history of community organizing in working-class and poor neighbourhoods in Germany and in the US shows up in the relatively slight degrees of class bias there. The same factors account for the pattern of membership in group rights organizations. This is the only type of association in

Table 9.2 Class bias in associational membership

Correlation with SES	Germany	United States	Sweden
Number of memberships	0.06^b	0.22^b	0.19^b
Member/non-member	0.08^b	0.20^b	0.14^b
Community associations	-0.04^b	0.05^b	0.10^b
Cultural associations	0.03	0.13^b	0.04
Economic associations	0.13^b	0.29^b	0.17^b
Group rights associations	-0.09^a	-0.04^a	0.09^b
Political associations	0.15^b	0.20^b	0.09^b
Private interest associations	-0.02	0.11^b	0.11^b

Source: World Values Survey, pooled samples from 1982 and 1991.

Notes
Entries are Pearson correlations.
a $p < 0.05$.
b $p < 0.01$.

the US where lower social status is associated with a higher rate of membership, due to the decades of organizing in poor neighbourhoods that reached a peak during the civil rights movement.

If the history of social movements and grass-roots organizing is reflected in the degree of class bias in memberships, so is the extent of state activism and subsidy. German and Swedish governmental support for cultural associations has succeeded in extending their memberships further down the class scale than is the case in the US. State support also accounts for the extent of lower-class 'private interest' associations, which are comprised of sport clubs, youth groups, and the like.

National variations in the extent and distribution of class bias tell us that the upper-class accent of the associational choir is not always equally strong (Schattschneider, 1960). The generalization that people of higher social status are more likely to join associations is empirically valid, but the extent to which this is true varies between countries. Moreover, member accents are slightly more likely to be lower class in a few associational sectors.

The class composition of associations will almost certainly have an effect on the degree to which associational membership is associated with the attitudes indicative of social capital. People higher in social status are more likely to be trusting of others (Brehm and Rahn, 1996),[13] to be more politically active and engaged, and to have confidence in public institutions.[14] In order to compare the effects of associational memberships on social capital indicators across nations and across associational sectors, then we must remove the influence of socio-economic status and of other potentially confounding variables.

COUNTRY AND ASSOCIATION DIFFERENCES IN SOCIAL CAPITAL CREATION

In the following, we will test whether association memberships have a different impact on our social capital indicators in the three countries we have selected, controlling for differences in the socio-economic status of the memberships. Differences not due to social class must by default be attributed to a different mechanism inherent in the associations themselves and shaped by the national historical processes discussed above.

In Table 9.3 we examine the connection between associational membership and political engagement. Association membership is closely tied to political engagement (interest and information) and unconventional political participation (through demonstrations, petitions and boycotts).[15] This is particularly true for membership in a political organization, though membership in a group rights organization is also strongly associated with political involvement in the US. Membership in other organizations is associated with political involvement to a lesser but quite consistent degree. Though Swedish members of group rights associations or private interest groups are not significantly more politically engaged, the broader connection between associational membership and political involvement is so consistent that we

Table 9.3 Associational membership and political involvement

	Political engagement			Unconventional political participation		
	Germany	United States	Sweden	Germany	United States	Sweden
Number of memberships	0.26[a]	0.19[a]	0.19[a]	0.15[a]	0.13[a]	0.18[a]
Member/non-member	0.57[a]	0.46[a]	0.39[a]	0.33[a]	0.26[a]	0.32[a]
Community associations	0.37[a]	0.40[a]	0.19[a]	0.13[a]	0.27[a]	0.32[a]
Cultural associations	0.38[a]	0.34[a]	0.20[a]	0.21[a]	0.12[a]	0.18[a]
Economic associations	0.35[a]	0.37[a]	0.25[a]	0.23[a]	0.29[a]	0.25[a]
Groups rights associations	0.32[a]	0.66[a]	0.14	0.24[a]	0.56[a]	0.32[a]
Political associations	1.01[a]	0.88[a]	0.95[a]	0.59[a]	0.53[a]	0.64[a]
Private interest associations	0.41[a]	0.33[a]	0.01	0.19[a]	0.22[a]	0.21[a]

Notes
Entries are unstandardized regression coefficients, controlling for socio-economic status, community size, age and sex.
a $p < 0.01$.

would be reluctant to impute any cross-national differences in this area. This finding is strongly supported by theories of political participation and their empirical tests.

We turn now to an area where there are cross-national differences in the connection of associational membership to social capital, the phenomenon we label positive citizenship. In Table 9.4 we consider two aspects of positive citizenship: confidence in public institutions and rejection of the idea that it is sometimes right to cheat on one's taxes, wrongly claim eligibility for a governmental benefit, or avoid paying a fare on public transport. The publics of all three countries tended to condemn these actions. On a 30-point scale, where 30 is complete rejection of each behaviour, Germans averaged 25.9, while Swedes and Americans averaged 27.5 and 27.0 respectively. These means conceal significant variation, though, as 35 per cent of Germans, 51 per cent of Americans and 48 per cent of Swedes completely rejected all three types of behaviour. Of course, we cannot assume that people always articulate frankly their own morality in survey interview settings, but the questions do measure the extent to which it is deemed acceptable to free-ride at the expense of public welfare.

Are these attitudes dampened by membership in associations? Table 9.4 shows that they are, at least in Germany and the United States. Members of associations are more likely to reject free-riding behaviour, though not significantly so in Sweden.[16] When we break down the overall relationship between membership and public regardingness into the different associational sectors, however, intriguing differences appear between Germany and the US. In the US, most associational sectors are positively related to public regardingness, except for economic and community organizations (where the relationship is close to zero). In Germany, though, there is a sharper bifurcation between associational sectors that are positively related to public regardingness (such as community, culture and economic groups), and those that are negatively related (political and group rights associations). Inspection of the Swedish results shows that members of political and group rights associations are also less public regarding, though the differences are not significant.

The relatively negative attitude of political and group rights association members would seem to reflect the politicization of public services in Germany and Sweden. In Sweden, for example, conservatives are less likely to condemn cheating on one's taxes ($r = 0.16$), while liberals are less likely to condemn claiming a benefit to which one is not entitled ($r = 0.07$). In Germany, liberals are more accepting of all three forms of free-ridership ($r = 0.17$ for claiming benefits; $r = 0.24$ for avoiding a fare; and $r = 0.14$ for not paying taxes). The US does not know this extent of politicization of public services ($r = 0.02$ for claiming benefits; $r = 0.08$ for avoiding a fare; $r = 0.06$ for not paying taxes).

Something of the same polarization can be found with respect to the confidence of group rights association members in public institutions. Members of these associations, which in our study include women's groups and animal rights groups, express less confidence in parliaments, the civil service, the legal system and the police. In Sweden, the relationship is significant at the 0.05 level.

Table 9.4 Associational membership and positive citizenship

	Public regardingness			Public confidence		
	Germany	United States	Sweden	Germany	United States	Sweden
Number of memberships	−0.01	−0.01	−0.01	0.10[b]	0.00	0.00
Member/non-member	−0.38[a]	−0.39[a]	−0.12	0.32[b]	0.21[a]	0.10
Community associations	−0.31	0.10	0.01	0.37[b]	0.01	0.11
Culture associations	−0.73**	−0.57[b]	−0.30	0.37[b]	0.34[b]	0.27
Economic associations	−0.33	0.00	−0.22	0.01	−0.20	0.00
Groups rights associations	0.48	−0.21	0.33	−0.18	−0.20	−0.53[a]
Political associations	0.51*	−0.36	−0.26	0.00	−0.14	0.01
Private interest associations	0.21	0.25	−0.21	0.36[b]	0.00	0.22

Notes
Entries are unstandardized regression coefficients, controlling for socio-economic status, community size, age, and sex.

a $p < 0.05$.
b $p < 0.01$.

Overall though, membership in organizations is associated with a higher degree of confidence in public authorities. This is particularly true in Germany, it is somewhat true in the US (due chiefly to the influence of church memberships, which dominate the category 'cultural organizations'), and it is also true in Sweden, though not significantly so.

Finally, we put social capital theory to its hardest test. To what extent is it true that associations of all kinds and in different institutional contexts serve as the cradle of generalized trust creation? The results presented in Table 9.5 indicate a success for the social capital school in all three countries. It matters in all three countries whether citizens are members of any association, as opposed to being without any associational affiliation (significant at the 0.01 level). Similarly, the number of associations to which an individual belongs makes a difference in all three countries (at the 0.01 significance level). With a higher number of associational memberships, we also find a higher level of generalized trust.

The analysis of trust among associational members reveals that associations are most successful in creating trust among their memberships in the United States. Associational members score significantly higher on trust in all associational sectors in the United States. The magnitude of the factor for the change of odds[17] indicates that group rights associations and political associations in the US are particularly successful in producing trustful members. In Germany and Sweden, four out of six associational types have members significantly more trusting (at the 0.05 level) than non-members of each sector. In Germany, membership in economic associations and group rights associations does not seem to make a difference in trust. Membership in political associations in Sweden is strongly associated with trust. As we already observed with other indicators of social capital, cultural associations in Sweden are not influential for trust creation. Swedish group rights members are less trusting, though not significantly so.[18]

Since generalized trust constitutes the most important dimension of social capital theory, we want to conclude this analysis with one additional test. Social capital theory relies on the thesis that face-to-face contact is particularly important for the creation of trust. We would expect associational members who have volunteered time and effort for their particular association to be in face-to-face contact with their fellow members more frequently than others. Are activist members also more trusting in Sweden, Germany and the US?

We find that they are. In most associations and in all of our countries associational activists trust more than the rest of the population, and even more than other association members. That is particularly true for activists in community organizations in Sweden and Germany. In German economic associations activism is associated with a significant rise in trust. In a few associational sectors, including political associations in Sweden and the US, activists are less trusting than other members. Overall, however, activists are more trusting than inactive associational members, a finding consistent with the theory that face-to-face contact with others is the key ingredient to the development of generalized trust.

Table 9.5 Associations and generalized trust

	Germany		United States		Sweden	
	Members	Activists	Members	Activists	Members	Activists
Number of memberships	1.16[b]	1.29[b]	1.18[b]	1.19[b]	1.25[b]	1.32[b]
Member/non-member	1.46[b]	1.58[b]	1.35[b]	1.70[b]	1.39[b]	1.50[b]
Community associations	1.29[b]	1.57[b]	1.35[b]	1.37[b]	1.57[b]	1.96[b]
Cultural associations	1.42[b]	1.36[b]	1.36[b]	1.42[b]	1.24	1.17
Economic associations	1.11	1.68[b]	1.29[b]	1.62[b]	1.23[a]	1.48[a]
Group rights associations	1.26	1.52	1.92[b]	2.13[b]	0.80	0.66
Political associations	1.28[b]	1.61[b]	1.82[b]	1.31[a]	2.05[b]	1.54[a]
Private interest associations	1.33[b]	1.26	1.26[b]	1.33[b]	1.50[b]	1.60[b]

Notes
Entries are the changes in the odds of being trusted when the membership variable changes from 0 to 1. See also note 17. The analysis is based on logistic regression, including socio-economic status, age, sex and community size as control variables.

a $p < 0.05$.
b $p < 0.01$.

CONCLUSION

What does this investigation tell us about the relationship between organizational memberships and social capital? At the broadest level, we find a robust connection between membership in associations and the various indicators of social capital, controlling for socio-economic status, age, gender and size of home town. This connection is robust throughout the three countries. Within that broad canvass, however, there is a great deal of detailed variation by different social capital indicators, different associational sectors, and different countries.

Our primary findings can be summarized in two points. First, the most powerful effects of associational membership are on political involvement and trust. In all three countries, it mattered significantly for those two social capital indicators whether a person is a member of any association or not. This finding appears to be a bedrock continuity that marks the foundations of social capital theory. We find this relationship in strong states and weak states, societies dominated by church groups and societies dominated by unions. Participation in voluntary associations is associated with higher political activity and awareness, as well as with higher levels of generalized trust.

Second, there are national differences in the translation of associational memberships into social capital. But our expectation that associations in the US would be more successful in inculcating social capital traits was not confirmed. Although the findings vary depending on the specific component of social capital, we can say that associations in Germany are just as productive of social capital as are American associations with regard to political involvement and public regardingness. German associations are more widely productive of traits such as confidence in public institutions. Associational membership does not matter at all in Sweden for public regardingness or for confidence in public institutions. Members of Swedish associations are, however, particularly high in unconventional political participation – a significant finding in light of the state-sponsored or subsidized nature of many Swedish associations.

The core of the social capital theory is that associational membership creates generalized trust. We find this to be true in all three countries. The US stands out chiefly because its associations, no matter what their purpose, all help to create trust. But the trust-creation capacity of Swedish and German associations in most sectors is equal to or greater than that found in the US. American exceptionalism in the extent of associational life and its impact on social capital proves to be a myth.

The relationship between associational membership and social capital has been especially deeply probed in the United States, perhaps because Tocqueville commented upon it when he travelled around that country. Our findings, however, suggest that Tocqueville would have reached similar conclusions (on this topic at least) had his destination been late twentieth century Sweden or Germany. Although we can see the traces of distinctive national histories and patterns of mobilization into voluntary associations in Sweden, Germany and the US, our data confirm the generality of the link between associational membership and the traits connected to social capital.

Notes

* We should like to thank Nancy Bermeo, Vanya Krieckhaus and Paul Whiteley for comments on earlier versions of this chapter. In addition, Dietlind Stolle thanks Larry Bartels, Ezra Suleiman and Bo Rothstein for helpful conversations.

1   See Tocqueville as a proponent of both internal and external effects of voluntary associations.

2   Evidence for this relationship can be found in Stolle and Rochon (1998). See also Brehm and Rahn (1996). The relationship between membership in voluntary associations and democratic pay-offs in the wider society has been discussed and explored in Gundelach and Torpe (1997), Edwards and Foley (1996) and Boix and Posner (1996).

3   See Putnam (1993, 1995a). See also recent work by Hooghe and Derks (1997) on Belgium.

4   See Putnam (1993) on regional differences in associational life within Italy and on the effect of these differences on social capital.

5   As cited in Curtis *et al.* (1992: 139).

6   We categorized the 15 associational groups examined in the World Values Survey into six associational types. *Political associations* include political groups and political parties, peace, environmental and ecology organizations, as well as third world and human rights groups. *Economic associations* include unions and professional associations. *Group rights* associations include animal rights and women's groups. *Cultural associations* include church groups, and literary, music and arts societies. *Community groups* include local action groups, service and welfare organizations, and health care groups. *Private interest associations* are concerned with sport and youth.

7   For more on the distinction between microscopic and macroscopic approaches in the study of associations see Wuthnow (1991: 133ff.).

8   See more on the role of the state for the development and structure of civil society in Sweden in Rothstein (forthcoming), Wijkström (1997) and Micheletti (1995).

9   See Verba *et al.* (1995), also on the general connection between voluntary work and political activity.

10 See Yamagishi and Yamagishi (1994) on distinctions between general trust and knowledge-based trust.

11 For more on the distinction between public and personalized forms of social capital, see Stolle (forthcoming).

12 See Verba *et al.* (1976) on the impact of working-class organization on class bias in voting rates.

13 This relationship is mainly driven by education levels. According to Brehm and Rahn (1996) and others, education is more important than income as a driver of generalized trust.

14 Hooghe and Derks (1997) criticize the concept of social capital as describing a middle-class phenomenon.

15 See also Table 2 in Stolle and Rochon (1998).

16 As elsewhere in this chapter, we controlled for socio-economic status, age, sex and community size. In addition, we ran regressions which included level of religiosity and self-placement on the left–right political scale in our model. Even though both variables are related to aspects of positive citizenship, their inclusion did not change the main relationship of interest (between membership in

associations and positive citizenship). As a result, we did not include religiosity and left–right placement as control variables in our final model.

17 This factor is *e* raised to the power of B_i and indicates how the odds change when the *i*th independent variable increases by one unit. In our example, the factor indicates how the odds of trusting others changes based on one's status as an associational member. For membership in cultural associations in the US, for example, the odds of trusting are increased by 1.36.

18 This may have to do with the much higher share of animal rights organization members as opposed to women's associations in Sweden. Animal rights members may not trust people who are not interested in animals.

References

Almond, G. and Verba, S. (1963). *The Civic Culture*. Princeton: Princeton University Press.

Anheier, H. (1991). 'West Germany: The Ambiguities of Peak Organizations'. In Wuthnow, R. *Between States and Markets*. Princeton: Princeton University Press.

Billiet, J. and Cambré, B. (1996). 'Social Capital, Active Membership in Voluntary Associations and Some Aspects of Political Participation: A Case Study'. Paper presented at the *Conference on Social Capital and Democracy*. Milan, Italy.

Boix, C. and Posner, D. (1996). 'Making Social Capital Work: A Review of Putnam's Making Democracy Work' (Working Paper No. 96–4). Center for International Affairs, Harvard University. Boston, MA.

Brehm, J. and Rahn, W. (1996). 'Individual Level Evidence for the Causes and Consequences of Social Capital'. *American Journal of Political Science* 41 (3): 999–1023.

Case, A. and Katz, L. (1991). 'The Company You Keep: The Effects of Family and Neighborhood on Disadvantaged Youth'. NBER Working Paper No. 3705. National Bureau of Economic Research. Washington, D.C.

Coleman, J. (1990). *Foundations of Social Theory*. Cambridge, MA: Harvard University Press.

Curtis, J., Grabb, E. and Baer, D. (1992). 'Voluntary Association Membership in Fifteen Countries: A Comparative Analysis'. *American Sociological Review* 57 (April): 139–52.

Edwards, B. and Foley, M. (1996). 'The Paradox of Civil Society'. *Journal of Democracy* 7 (No. 3): 38–53.

Erickson, B. and Nosanchuck, T.A. (1990). 'How an Apolitical Association Politicizes'. *Canadian Review of Sociology and Anthropology* 27 (2): 206–19.

Fukuyama, F. (1995). *Trust: The Social Virtues and Creation of Prosperity*. London: Hamish Hamilton.

Granovetter, M. (1985). 'Economic Action and Social Structure'. *American Journal of Sociology* 91 (6): 481–510.

Gundelach, P. and Torpe, L. (1997). 'Social Capital and the Democratic Role of Voluntary Associations'. Paper presented at the *Workshop on Social Capital and Politico-Economic Performance, ECPR Joint Sessions*. Bern, Switzerland.

Habermas, J. (ed.) (1984). *Observations on 'The Spiritual Situation of the Age'*. Cambridge, MA: MIT Press.

Hagan, J., Merkens, H. and Boehnke, K. (1995). 'Delinquency and Disdain: Social Capital and the Control of Right-Wing Extremism Among East and West Berlin Youth'. *The American Journal of Sociology* 100: 1028–53.

Hooghe, M. and Derks, A. (1997). 'Voluntary Associations and the Creation of Social Capital'. Paper presented at the *Workshop on Social Capital and Politico-Economic Performance, ECPR Joint Sessions*. Bern, Switzerland.

Jencks, C. and Peterson, P. (1991). *The Urban Underclass*. Washington, DC: Brookings Institution.

Dekker, P., Koopmans, R. and van den Broek, A. (1997). 'Voluntary Associations, Social Movements and Individual Political Behaviour in Western Europe'. In van Deth, Jan (ed.) *Private Groups and Public Life: Social Participation, Voluntary Associations and Political Involvement in Representative Democracies*. London and New York: Routledge.

Lipset, S. M. (1985). 'Canada and the United States: The Cultural Dimension'. In Doran, C.F. and Sigler, J. (eds.) *Canada and the United States*. Englewood Cliffs: Prentice-Hall.

Micheletti, M. (1995). *Civil Society and State Relations in Sweden*. Brookfield: Avebury.

Moyser, G. and Parry, G. (1997). 'Voluntary Associations and Democratic Participation in Britain'. In van Deth, Jan (ed.) *Private Groups and Public Life: Social Participation, Voluntary Associations and Political Involvement in Representative Democracies*. London and New York: Routledge.

Olsen, M. (1972). 'Social participation and voting turnout'. *American Sociological Review* 37: 317–33.

Putnam, R. (1993). *Making Democracy Work*. Princeton: Princeton University Press.

Putnam, R. (1995a). 'Bowling Alone: Democracy in America at the End of the Twentieth Century'. Nobel Symposium Lecture. Uppsala, Sweden.

Putnam, R. (1995b). 'Tuning In, Tuning Out: The Strange Disappearance of Social Capital in America'. *PS: Political Science and Politics* 28 (December): 664–83.

Rogers, D., Barb, K., and Bultena, G. (1975). 'Voluntary Association Membership and Political Participation: An Exploration of the Mobilization Hypothesis'. *The Sociological Quarterly* 16: 305–18.

Rochon, T. R. (1998). *Culture Moves: Ideas, Activism and Changing Values*. Princeton: Princeton University Press.

Rothstein, B. (forthcoming). 'Social Capital in the Social Democratic State'. In Putnam, R. (ed.) *The Decline of Social Capital? Political Culture as a Condition for Democracy*.

Schattschneider, E.E. (1960). *The Semi-Sovereign People*. New York: Holt, Rinehart and Winston.

Stolle, D. and Rochon, T. (1998). 'Are All Associations Alike?' In Edwards, B. and Foley, M. (eds.) *Beyond Tocqueville: Civil Society and Social Capital in Comparative Perspective*. A thematic issue of the *American Behavioral Scientist* 41 (5).

Stolle, D. forthcoming. 'Public Life, Community and Social Capital: A Comparative Study of Sweden, Germany and the United States'. PhD dissertation, Princeton University.

Tocqueville, Alexis de. [1835] (1961). *Democracy in America*. New York: Schocken Books.

Uslaner, E. (1996). 'Morality Plays: Social Capital and Moral Behavior in Anglo-American Democracies'. Paper presented at the *Conference on Social Capital and Democracy*. Milan, Italy.

Verba, S., and Nie, N. (1972). *Participation in America: Political Democracy and Social Equality*. New York: Harper and Row.

Verba, S., Nie, N., and Kim J.-O. (1976). *Participation and Political Equality*. New York: Cambridge University Press.

Verba S., Schlozman, K., and Brady, H. (1995). *Voice and Equality: Civic Volunteerism in American Politics*. Cambridge, MA: Harvard University Press.

Wijkström, F. (1997). 'The Swedish Nonprofit Sector in International Comparison', *Annals of Public and Cooperative Economics* 68 (4): 625–63.

Wuthnow, R. (ed.). (1991). *Between States and Markets*. Princeton: Princeton University Press.

Yamagishi, T., and Yamagishi, M. (1994). 'Trust and Commitment in the United States and Japan'. *Motivation and Emotion* 18 (June): 129–66.

APPENDIX WORLD VALUES SURVEYS (1981–4 AND 1990–3)

Control variables: socio-economic status, age, sex and size of community.

Dependent variable list

1 Political involvement

The Political Engagement Scale consists of two items:

> Do you discuss political matters with your friends?
> How interested are you in politics?

The Political Participation Scale consists of three items:

> Signing a petition
> Joining a boycott
> Attending lawful demonstrations

2 Positive citizenship

The Public Regardingness Scale consists of three items:
  How justifiable are the following?

> Claiming governmental benefits to which you are not entitled
> Avoiding a fare on public transport
> Cheating on taxes if you have the chance

The Institutional Confidence Scale consists of four items:

> Confidence in:
> the parliament
> the judicial system
> the police
> the civil service

3 Generalized trust

Trust question

> Generally, can people be trusted, or does one have to be careful with others?

Part III
The political effects of social capital

10 Morality plays

Social capital and moral behaviour in Anglo-American democracies

Eric M. Uslaner

> Men, being naturally selfish, or endow'd only with a confin'd generosity, they are not easily induc'd to perform any action for the interest of strangers, except with a view to some reciprocal advantage, which they had no hope of obtaining but by such a performance. Now as it frequently happens, that these mutual performances cannot be finish'd at the same instant, 'tis necessary, that one party be contented to remain in uncertainty, and depend upon the gratitude of the other for a return of kindness. But so much corruption is there among men, that, generally speaking, this becomes a slender security; and as the benefactor is here suppos'd to bestow his favours with a view to self-interest, this both takes off from the obligation and sets an example of selfishness, which is the true mother of ingratitude. Were we, therefore, to follow the natural course of our passions and inclinations, we shou'd perform few actions for the advantage of others, from disinterested views; because we are naturally very limited in our kindness and affection.
>
> David Hume, *A Treatise on Human Nature* (1960 [1739]: 519)

A society such as Hume describes would be a harsh place. It would resemble the Italian village of Montegrano that Edward Banfield (1958: 110) described in the 1950s: 'any advantage that may be given to another is necessarily at the expense of one's own family. Therefore, one cannot afford the luxury of charity, which is giving others more than their due, or even justice, which is giving them their due.' Montegrano is a mean world, where daily life is 'brutal and senseless' (Banfield, 1958: 109), much like Hobbes's 'nasty, brutish, and short' existence. All who stand outside the immediate family are 'potential enemies,' battling for the meagre bounty that nature has provided. People seek to protect themselves from the 'threat of calamity' (Banfield, 1958: 110).

We aren't all Montegranans. Most people make promises and honour them. They don't lie consistently or steal at all. Few even cheat government (or admit to it). Why? We usually don't get burned when we trust each other. Our world doesn't look quite so bleak, so we can afford to take the risks that trusting others entails. But trusting others is more than a rational gamble. It is also a moral decision, stemming from deeply held values that go beyond direct experience.

I shall show how both expectations of reciprocity and values contribute to our intentions to behave morally, using data from the 1981 World Values Study (WVS) in the United States, the United Kingdom, and Canada. The WVS is a multi-nation survey that asks identical questions in each country. I focus on questions about moral behaviour: Is it ever acceptable to lie, to cheat on taxes, to claim benefits you are not entitled to, and the like? What shapes people's attitudes towards moral behaviour? I posit that trust in other people, together with personal moral codes, religious values, expectations of others' sense of morality, and ties to one's community all contribute to beliefs about morality. And I believe that your perceptions of how others behave are *not as critical* as your own moral code, your trust in others, and religious values.

But we should not expect the same patterns in each of the three Anglo-American democracies. Expectations of reciprocity should – and do – count most in individualistic political cultures, most notably the United States. Core values should – and do – matter everywhere. They take on particular importance in Britain and Canada, where reciprocity among individuals is not quite so central.

WHY WE TRUST

Montegrano behaviour is consistent with Hume's argument about our natural selfishness. Hume provided the basis for much of contemporary public choice. It is irrational to contribute to the provision of a public good. It is always more profitable to be a free-rider (Olson, 1965). More generally, it never makes sense for people to cooperate in any way wherever there are mixed motives. If you can gain at someone else's expense, as in prisoner's dilemma games, defection is always the dominant strategy.

Hume spelled out why: I can do little to prevent you from reneging on me later on. If we make binding agreements that would link my commitments to yours, we could resolve collective action problems. Without someone to enforce this contract, you cannot rest easy that I will fulfil my obligation. For a promise is just 'cheap talk' (Crawford and Sobel, 1982). It costs me nothing to make a promise. You will recognise that I have ventured little and discount the value of my commitment in your own estimation of the costs and benefits of cooperation.

If you have no incentive to contribute to a collective good, you have no reason to behave morally in other realms. Why should you keep your promises? Why, apart from any consequences of getting caught, would you refrain from stealing? You wouldn't. Moral behaviour is the same generic problem as contributing to a collective good. Someone who doesn't want to levy a tax to build a bridge would seek to find ways of cheating on taxes to pay for it. Both problems revolve around trust. If you trust someone, you will believe his/her 'cheap talk'. You could resolve collective action dilemmas; people who trust others are more likely to cooperate in prisoner's dilemma games (Deustch, 1960). People might contribute if they believe that others will pay their share. They use a similar guideline for moral behaviour, the Golden Rule: Do unto others as you would have them do unto you.

Public choice has taken multiple paths to account for how we get to co-operation. Two concern me here. One emphasises life experiences, the other values. I believe that both are essential to understanding why people choose to behave morally. Both explanations posit trust as the way we get around collective action problems, but differ on where confidence in others comes from.

The first stays closer to the traditional public choice model. Diego Gambetta (1988: 217) sets out the problem of cooperation:

> When we say we trust someone or that someone is trustworthy, we implicitly mean that the probability that he will perform an action that is beneficial or at least not detrimental to us is high enough for us to consider engaging in some form of cooperation with him.

We learn from experience. Each interaction with someone in our community leads us to re-estimate the costs and benefits of cooperation (Gauthier, 1986: 156; Hardin, 1992). Trust, on this view, is always contingent.

Hume (1960: 490) agreed that we learn by doing. We recognise that we are all better off if we fulfil our promises. From this experience we develop moral ideals about appropriate behaviour that shape our future interactions. But experience is not sufficient to *maintain* reciprocity: 'If we thought, that promises had no moral obligation, we never shou'd feel any inclination to observe them' (Hume, 1960 [1739]: 518). The second argument about cooperation agrees with Hume that experience alone will not account for moral behaviour. Without a cooperative disposition we would never make the first move toward cooperation (Bates, 1988; Frank, 1988).

The two accounts differ over the roots of trust. The first views trust as a set of expectations about others' behaviour based upon experience (Hardin, 1992). The second view considers confidence in others a form of 'social capital'. Social capital is a set of 'moral resources' that leads to increased cooperation. On my account, it refers to a society's core values. The more traditional sense of the word – ties to one's community (cf. Putnam, 1993) – I call 'social connectedness'. Trust depends upon both. But core values are fundamental. Newton and Whiteley make similar arguments in their contributions to this volume. *Such ideals lead people to trust each other even when our expectations tell us to be wary.* As Whiteley argues, 'individuals with a strong moral sense which promotes empathy with others and a desire for fairness are likely to be predisposed to trust other people in comparison with individuals who lack such a moral sense.' Ties to one's community are important too. They foster a sense of mutual obligation.

The social capital explanation does not denigrate the role of expectations of others' behaviour, but argues that it is insufficient to explain cooperation or moral behaviour. There must be something else that prompts people to make the first cooperative move. And this part of social capital is values (cf. Coleman, 1990: 320). As James Q. Wilson (1993: 231) argues: 'We are faithful both because we wish others to accept our word and because we consider dishonesty and infidelity to be signs of wickedness.' These values are the core elements of social capital and I use the term 'social connectedness' to emphasise the set of community ties that Coleman and Putnam consider essential to capital.

Our fundamental beliefs lead us to behave morally even when we might be better off looking out for ourselves. Core values are not contingent. The Ninth Commandment does not say, 'Thou shalt not bear false witness against thy neighbour unless (s)he defects first.' Our ideals provide guidance for how we should behave *especially in the face of contrary evidence in our environment.*[1]

What are the values that constitute social capital? How do they promote cooperation? And where do they come from? I see two values as fundamental: trust in others and religious ideals.[2] Trust helps us to look beyond our own self-interest and to longer-term stakes. De Tocqueville (1945: 122) referred to this 'enlightened regard' as 'self-interest rightly understood'. It leads people to 'willingly sacrifice a portion of their time and property to the welfare of the state'. Trust provides the glue that binds people together in the absence of enforceable contracts policed by external agents.

Trust as a value is different from trust as a strategic calculation. It is not a statement of unconditional commitment. Yet it reflects a fundamentally optimistic view of human nature. Trusters have great confidence that the future will be better than the past. This optimism makes it less risky to behave morally (Deutsch, 1958: 278). Optimism in the face of contrary evidence will tide trusters over to the next encounter, where they are likely to trust again because of long-term socialisation and a positive outlook on life. Trusters' moral decisions involve more than constant up-dating of information to determine what one's strategy should be for the next encounter (Hardin, 1992: 162, 170).

We can minimise our risks by cooperating only with our own kind or our close friends. People will burrow themselves into their own communities and trust only people they know. They will be suspicious of people unlike themselves. Their trust is 'particularised'. But it is generalised confidence that underlies the idea of social capital (Uslaner, 1996; Yamigichi and Yamigichi, 1994). The more dependent we are on our close associates and kin, the more we think of the world in terms of 'we' and 'they'. We won't trust 'most people'. Cultures that emphasise individual rights and especially consensus, such as the United States and the United Kingdom, depend heavily on generalised trust for a vibrant civic life and for moral behaviour. Countries that emphasise group rights, such as Canada, structure their civic lives around particularised trust. But this type of confidence excludes outsiders – and it is less likely to induce moral behaviour or active participation in civic life.

Trust is not the only core value that leads us to behave morally. Religion also matters mightily (cf. Newton, this volume). De Tocqueville (1945: 126–7) sees religion as the moral underpinning of self-interest rightly understood. Faith creates communal bonds that foster social connectedness, participation, and moral behaviour. Religious values and involvement with institutions of faith promote participation in other arenas: charitable contributions (Hodgkinson *et al.*, 1990: 107–9), voting (Rosenstone and Hansen, 1993: 273), and volunteering (Dynes and Quarantelli, 1980; Wuthnow, 1993: 199–200).

Many, perhaps most, of our moral standards come from religious guidance such as the Ten Commandments and other maxims from the Bible. The major religions offer great rewards or punishment for behaviour in the secular world. People with faith have 'something within', a spiritual commitment that religious values should shape behaviour in the secular world (Harris, 1994). And religious values, as de Tocqueville argues, abjure pure self-interest. Hillel asked, 'If I am for myself alone, what am I?' while Jesus argued that we should 'turn the other cheek' against transgressors. People who attend religious services regularly are less concerned with creature comforts and place a higher value on being helpful (Rokeach, 1973: 128). Experimental work in psychology shows that religious people place a high value on honesty: subjects who returned pencils they borrowed ranked salvation more highly than those who kept the pencils (Rokeach, 1973: 133).

Moral values help overcome collective action problems because they provide a sense of *shared* idealism. People don't develop value systems by themselves. Shared ties are the basis of a communal language of morals. If you are divorced from your community, you are less likely to share its values. Ideals and community ties both work to promote moral behaviour.

Trusting people are more likely to develop community ties and to work towards cooperative outcomes (Putnam, 1993: 170; Putnam, 1995; Uslaner, 1996). Something as simple as being married or belonging to a union helps connect people to their neighbourhoods and the broader communities. As Putnam (1993: 90) argues, 'a dense network of secondary associations both embodies and contributes to effective social collaboration'. And ties to one's community create moral obligations:

> Collective life [in regions in Italy where many people have social con-
> nections] is eased by the expectation that others will probably follow the
> rules. Knowing that others will, *you* are more likely to go along too, thus
> fulfilling *their* expectations. In the less civic regions nearly everyone expects
> everyone else to violate the rules. It seems foolish to obey the traffic laws or
> the tax code or the welfare laws, if you expect everyone else to cheat (Putnam,
> 1993: 111, emphasis in original).

Trust, religious values, and community ties all lead people to make the leap beyond self-interest towards moral behaviour. If you live in a world where most people are moral, you can make a reasoned calculation that obeying a society's maxim is a safe bet.

SOCIAL CAPITAL AND CULTURE

The three Anglo-American democracies are not mean worlds. Each ranks in the upper half of trusting nations, though hardly at the top. In 1981 50 per cent of Canadians, 45 per cent of Americans, and 44 per cent of the British agreed that 'most people can be trusted'. The three share a similar heritage: Canada and the

United States are former British colonies. But they have evolved into distinctive political cultures.

One common view sees the United States at the individualistic pole and Britain, with its monarchy and strong class divisions at the collectivist end. Canada lies in between (Hartz, 1964: 34; Kornberg, 1990: 713). Lipset (1996: 32–3) places Canada closer to the United States than to Great Britain;[3] Nevitte (1996) even speaks of a 'North American exceptionalism' that distinguishes Canada and the United States from the rest of the world. Canada resisted independence from Britain as America fought its revolution, and still has a strong Tory tradition. But it is also a creature of its southern neighbour. Canadians often joke (or lament): 'The United States is destined to be our best friend, whether we like it or not.' So Canada is a mixture of American individualism and British collectivism (Lipset, 1996: 92).

An alternative view, which I favour, focuses on the British tradition of support for individual rights, as encapsulated in the Magna Carta, dating from 1215 – long before European settlement in the New World. On this perspective, the British and American cultures both emphasise liberty (on Britain, see Russell, 1823, chs 12–13). American society emphasises individualism (Hartz, 1955). British culture puts greater emphasis on one's obligations to the larger society (Conover *et al.*, 1991: 822). Despite these differences, the two societies look a lot like each other. Americans and the British are strikingly similar in their support for – or opposition to – civil liberties (Barnum and Sullivan, 1990). Both recognise the need for reciprocity to achieve collective ends (Conover *et al.*, 1991: 818). American individualism is tempered by a sense of social responsibility (de Tocqueville, 1945: 122), while British collectivism is limited by belief in fundamental liberties.

Cultural similarities trump institutional differences (Barnum and Sullivan, 1990: 731–5). A Westminster system should provoke sharp differences in a society with strong class differences. But a strong commitment to national consensus among all classes tempers tendencies toward majoritarianism (Christoph, 1965; Russell, 1823: 17–18).

The British see their society as an organic whole bound together by national symbols such as the Crown (Conover *et al.*, 1991). Theirs is the least diverse society. Americans believe that they have – or can – transform heterogeneity into a common culture: *E pluribus unum*, one out of many, is the national motto. Canada has weaker social bonds. It has at least two 'founding nations' (the English and the French). While Britain sees itself as homogeneous and the United States views itself as a melting pot, Canadians have fewer national symbols. They consider their society a mosaic, where ethnic and religious communities are expected to maintain their own identities. Canadians define their culture more by what they are *not* than by what they are (Lipset, 1990: 53). They are not Americans, nor are they a single culture or 25 million people with inalienable rights. Former Prime Minister Joe Clark liked to call Canada a 'community of communities'. Yet each community largely trusts its own members far more than it does outsiders. Generalised interpersonal trust is not as important in Canada as it is in more individualistic societies such as the United States or more homogeneous societies such as the United Kingdom.

Britain has strong class cleavages and Canada has long been threatened with secession from Quebec Francophones. African-Americans constitute a significant fault line in the United States as well, but neither blacks nor the British working class are as numerous or concentrated geographically as French Canadians. Thus, *interpersonal* trust should be more important in shaping various forms of collective action (including moral behaviour) in the United States and Britain than in Canada. A key, though not the only, component of trust is reciprocity. So expectations of others' moral behaviour should be more central in the United States and Britain.

Where national identity is weak, as in Canada (or Montegrano), people rely more on particularised trust than generalised confidence.[4] But particularised trust doesn't go as far in producing collective action or, by extension, moral behaviour as generalised trust (cf. Uslaner, 1996). When you are primarily concerned with your own kind, you are less likely to be concerned with the welfare of people who are not part of your own group. Particularised trust has a different dynamic than generalised confidence. It reflects the exclusionary world of a Montegrano, where people fear for the future. Where people are primarily concerned with their own kind, they do not make the link between trust and optimism. So the nexus between optimism for the future and trust is weaker in Canada than in the United States or the United Kingdom.[5] Trust in people may not be so critical in Canada because it does not follow the same logic as it does in the United States and the United Kingdom.

Culture also shapes how – or whether – religion will promote collective action. I have argued that religion is an important form of social capital. Putnam disagrees (1993: 107). He argues that religion is an alternative to social capital in Italy. The Catholic Church there is hierarchical; it dissuades people from becoming involved in their communities. Who is correct? Both of us. Religion is not of one piece.

The Catholic Church in Italy is a state religion, governed hierarchically, with a strong authoritarian tradition. It discourages popular participation in civic life. Adherents often recede from civic life; the many who reject the church's pull cannot be influenced by its values. But religion has a different tradition in the United States. American churches and synagogues are governed more democratically; they have been at the forefront of many egalitarian social movements, spurred on by both Utopian and messianic undertones (Lipset, 1991: 19–23). There is no state church in the United States. The many denominations compete with each other for influence, thereby expanding their influence (Greeley, 1991). Churches in the United States play active roles in politics (Verba *et al.*, 1995). Britain has a state church, organised hierarchically (though not as much as Italy's). But the Church of England, like many Protestant denominations, has shied away from controversy. The church has a more limited role in civic life in Britain (Lipset, 1963: 71–2).

Promoting civic participation is not the same as inculcating values. Some churches prompt people to get involved, others shy away from getting their flocks involved. But all religions teach moral precepts. I suggest that a country's religious culture should play a key role in how values shape ideas about what is moral. A hierarchical state religion may not get its message across as well as a more pluralistic and democratic religious culture (Greeley, 1991). We should thus see stronger effects of religious values on moral values in the United States than in Britain. Canada should stand in the middle. Its Catholic Church is hierarchical and conservative (Lipset, 1990: 16; McRoberts, 1993: ch. 2). But it is concentrated in Quebec and has only modest influence elsewhere. In the rest of Canada, we see a religious diversity that resembles the United States more than Britain (Lipset, 1990: 83–7). Religion is not as potent a force in Canada as it is in the United States (Lipset, 1990: 84–5), but faith in North America should matter more than it does in Britain.

Regardless of the culture, personal moral codes should be the central force shaping our views of what is morally acceptable. These ideals could be more important in collectivist cultures, not because of anything inherent in these societies, but because we expect a smaller role for trust and expectations of others' behaviour. Personal morality might have a bigger role to carry in Britain and Canada than in the United States.

MEASUREMENT ISSUES

The data I shall analyse come from the 1981 World Values Study (WVS) for the United States, the United Kingdom, and Canada. The WVS has a good set of questions tapping our conceptions of morality. It asked whether a series of behaviours could ever be justified. The WVS did not inquire about whether people actually performed any of the acts. This problem is not severe, since people might be more truthful about evaluating prospective behaviour than in admitting any actual misdeeds. The acts, listed in order of their acceptability, are:

- keeping money that you have found
- failing to report damage you've accidentally done to a parked car
- lying in your own interest
- cheating on taxes 'if you have the chance'
- avoiding a fare on public transportation
- claiming government benefits you are not entitled to
- buying something you know was stolen
- joyriding

Respondents rated each item on a ten-point scale, with one indicating that the activity is never justified and ten always justified. I present the means and standard deviations for the three countries in Table 10.1, listed in order of acceptability in the United States. Morality reigns in all three cultures. In no nation are any of the eight items permissible. Only keeping money that you find is acceptable to many people. Americans and Canadians are most willing to pocket cash they find. The British are more reluctant to take the money and run. They see this as more objectionable than lying or cheating on taxes. For all three countries, joyriding is the least acceptable activity.[6]

Table 10.1 Means and standard deviations of moral behaviour measures

	United States		United Kingdom		Canada	
	Mean	Std deviation	Mean	Std deviation	Mean	Std deviation
Keep money found	3.907	2.817	2.665	2.265	3.831	2.979
Hit car/no report	2.541	2.551	2.618	2.309	2.111	1.976
Lie in own interest	2.467	2.049	2.957	2.324	2.686	2.250
Cheat on taxes	2.074	1.996	2.785	2.526	2.203	2.155
Avoid fare/public transportation	1.950	1.830	2.269	2.015	2.333	2.230
Claim government benefits unfairly	1.669	1.635	1.800	1.672	2.465	2.313
Buy stolen goods	1.665	1.496	2.048	1.947	1.901	1.824
Joyride	1.226	0.950	1.342	1.203	1.317	1.140

Americans are somewhat stricter than either the British or Canadians. Their mean score is 2.187, compared to 2.310 and 2.356. The US standard deviation is also smaller: 1.916 compared to 2.108 and 2.032. For all three countries, the strongest taboos occur for actions that appear the most dishonest: joyriding and buying stolen goods. Americans and Canadians have the most similar values, as predicted. The correlation of mean scores across the eight moral behaviours is 0.902. The British stand apart from both: the correlations are 0.692 with the United States and 0.593 with Canada.

What drives attitudes towards these moral behaviours? If our moral code (or collective action more generally) reflects our experience, then we should condition our conduct on our expectations of others. If values rather than experience form the core of our moral codes, how others behave will be less central to our standards for behaviour. Our ethical sense will reflect how we see ourselves as moral beings. If I believe that I generally do the right things, I will be loath to endorse behaviour that most people regard as unethical. The 1981 survey allows us to distinguish between people's own beliefs and their expectations of others. The WVS study asked respondents to indicate how well prescribed and proscribed behaviours in the Ten Commandments applied to themselves and to most people. The commandments relating to religious belief did not scale with those from everyday life. The behaviours I employ are: 1 honour thy father and mother; 2 thou shalt not kill; 3 thou shalt not commit adultery; 4 thou shalt not steal; 5 thou shalt not bear false witness against a neighbour; 6 thou shalt not covet a neighbour's wife; and 7 thou shalt not covet a neighbour's goods. Respondents rated themselves and others on a three-point scale, with one indicating that the commandment fully applies, two that it applies to a limited extent, and three that it doesn't apply at all.

The questions on the Ten Commandments are distinct from those on moral behaviour. The latter ask us which types of behaviour are acceptable: How wrong is it, for example, to lie? The former ask us to judge ourselves and others as ethical people: Do we lie (bear false witness)? It is difficult to separate the causal chain from moral behaviour to perceptions of one's own (and others') good deeds. But certainly the argument from experience places heavy emphasis on what people do rather than what they say. A smooth-talking con artist with a big smile can (and may be more likely) to cheat you than someone with a sneer on his face. And we often justify our own moral worth by how we perceive our own behaviour.

People rate themselves very highly. Almost everyone says that they obey all seven commandments. They are far less charitable to 'most people'. For every one of the commandments, we express only modest confidence in others: we believe that most people don't practise what we preach. The mean scores in the United States range from 1.557 for 'thou shalt not kill' – hardly an expectation of a peaceful society – to 1.726 for 'thou shalt not covet thy neighbour's goods'. In Britain, expectations of others range from 1.428 for killing to 1.893 for adultery. The Canadian scores mimic Britain's: 1.633 for murder to 1.993 for adultery. We think very highly of our own morality, but give our fellow citizens little credit for holding similar values.

I created factor scores for self and other observance of the commandments. If we condition our moral beliefs on how we expect others to behave, we should find stronger impacts for 'others obey commandments'. If we decide how to behave primarily on the basis of our own values, then 'self-obey commandments' should have much stronger effects on moral beliefs. In all three countries, both 'self-obey' and 'other-obey' are strongly unidimensional. It is easier to disentangle the self and the other than we might suppose. The simple correlations between the two measures are 0.255 for the United States, 0.307 for Canada, and 0.409 for the UK.[7] The modest correlations with 'self-obey commandments' – and its component parts – reflect the limited range of people's estimation of themselves. There isn't much variation to go around.

The WVS also includes the standard interpersonal trust question: 'Do you believe that most people can be trusted, or can't you be too careful in dealing with people?' Trust is not an estimate of how we expect others to behave. But neither is it a reflection of how we judge ourselves. Neither 'others-obey commandments' or our moral judgements about ourselves is strongly related to trust.[8] The weak connection between 'others-obey commandments' and trust shows that confidence in others reflects more than simple reciprocity. Trust is a broader world view that does not depend upon expectations of others' behaviour. I view trust as a core value partially based on experience, but also reflecting a more general sense of optimism that goes beyond what simple calculations might yield.

For religious values, I used two questions that tap distinct components of faith: Does the respondent believe that there are clear standards of good and evil and does (s)he believe in hell? The former is a simple expression of right and wrong that doesn't demand religious beliefs. But clear standards of good and evil are more important among religious people.[9] If you believe that there are straightforward criteria for moral behaviour, you don't need to look back at experience. Your values tell you what to do. Belief in hell indicates compliance with ethical standards out of fear for an afterlife. I chose these two measures because they represent different perspectives on religious values (positive versus negative incentives), because each is clearly connected to moral behaviour, and because (not surprisingly) they had among the highest correlations with the moral behaviour items of the multitude of items in the WVS.

The WVS has few good measures of social connectedness.[10] Two measures that I employ are being married and being a member of a union. Marriage gives you a greater stake in your community. Married people need to consider the needs of others – as well as the moral approbation for violating key norms of society. Unions also provide a sense of solidarity that should reinforce society's core values among members.[11] I explored other potential indicators of social connectedness such as having children, owning one's own home, and length of time in the community. But none was significant.

Beyond marriage, I employ a measure of how important people believe faithfulness is to a successful partnership. If our experience begins at home and spills over to more general behaviour, then attitudes about marital fidelity should have a strong impact on moral behaviour. The importance of marital faithfulness to ethical standards is a straightforward test of the linkage between personal experience and expectations for the larger society.

I employ three controls. Educational differences also point to fault lines in the society. Education is a surrogate for position in society; it is a key determinant of social trust (Putnam, 1995). The WVS measure is only a trichotomy (elementary school, high school, and college), so it does not pick up the nuances that extra years of education bring (Putnam, 1995; Uslaner, 1996). But there are key differences in education levels across the three countries. Forty-three per cent of British respondents only went to grade school, compared to 14 per cent of Americans and 18 per cent of Canadians. Only 13 per cent in the UK have gone to college, compared to 30 per cent in Canada and 37 per cent in the United States. I thus expect education levels to matter most in Great Britain, reflecting the class polarisation there.

If the primary conflict in Britain is along class lines, the key fault line in America is race. In Canada, the big struggle is linguistic. Quebec Francophones now seek to be *maitres chez nous*, to separate from the rest of Canada. There are also racial tensions in Canada and Britain. For Britain, I classify non-Europeans (blacks, Asians, and a lone Arab) as the out-group. For Canada, I consider both the French (who in this sample live exclusively in Quebec) and a category coded as 'other ethnics' (presumably dominated by blacks and Asians).

When there is a dominant race or class, people who endure discrimination may come to reject the values of the larger culture. They may reject attempts at socialisation into 'white' or 'upper class' values. Those at the very bottom, the 'underclass', have little to lose – and might even feel good – by flouting the standards set by the ruling culture. Because there are few non-Europeans in the British sample, I don't expect strong effects for ethnicity there. The non-Europeans in Britain may be less likely to sympathise with norm-busters for a different reason. Unlike African-Americans or Quebecois, they have a more tenuous status within the UK. Are they 'true Brits' or outsiders who maintain their own culture (cf. Conover *et al.*, 1991: 823)? You can't be alienated from a culture that you aren't part of. There are far sharper cleavages in social capital in the United States (where 17 per cent of blacks say that 'most people can be trusted' compared to 49 per cent of whites) and in Canada (where 32 per cent of Francophones are trusting compared to 54 per cent of Anglophones) than in Britain (where 36 per cent of non-Europeans are trusting compared to 43 per cent of Europeans).

People also become more concerned with morality as they get older. Young people with few stakes in the community feel less tied down by moral codes. Age also brings marriage and children. As we grow older, we are more concerned with passing traditional values, even ones that we might not have always accepted, to the next generation. Younger people will thus be less tied to standards of ethical behaviour.

MORALITY IN THREE CULTURES

How does the balance of forces stack up on the eight measures of moral behaviour? I estimate identical regression models for each in the United States, the United Kingdom, and Canada. Aside from the different ethnicities, the remaining variables are the same across the nations. Since the predictors are the same and the questions linked, it is hazardous to estimate each equation separately. Instead, I use the method of seemingly unrelated regressions (SUR) developed by Zellner (1963) to adjust for correlations among the residuals across equations. I present the results of the SUR regressions for the United States in Table 10.2, for the United Kingdom in Table 10.3, and for Canada in Table 10.4.

De Tocqueville got it right when he visited America a century and a half ago. Americans are moralists, motivated in part by trust in others but even more by a broad moral code that is based on religious values. *On all eight equations, self-obey commandments, clear standards of good and evil, and marital faithfulness are significant, often at p<0.0001 or better.* Expectations of reciprocity matter only for avoiding fares on public transportation and keeping money that you found (would others do the same?). But even here, the coefficients are smaller than those for self-obey commandments. For four behaviours – cheating on taxes, lying, avoiding fares, and joyriding – belief in hell is significant.

The most powerful effects for clear standards of good and evil (from the regression coefficients) come on lying in your own interests and keeping money you found. When you lie, you lie *to someone*. If you find money and a wallet, you also know who your victim is.[12] All of the other items involve cheating a government or some anonymous victim. Opportunities to lie more often arise with people we already know. We may worry that we will be punished in the hereafter for immoral behaviour (note the strong effect for belief in hell). But we are primarily motivated by our moral code: beliefs in our own morality and simple standards of right and wrong. Keeping money you found also calls forth moral values – but it is the most dramatic case of how experience matters as well. Here we find the most powerful impact for others-obey commandments and trust in other people, as well as a strong coefficient for belief in hell.

Trust has big effects on keeping money, buying stolen goods, claiming benefits you are not entitled to, and hitting a car without making a report. This list has two common elements. Three of the four items (with claiming benefits being the exception) involve *implicit contracts with strangers*. You are not likely to know whose car you hit, who was ripped off in the heist for your stolen goods, or how much the person who lost her/his wallet will miss it. Your commitment to do the right thing reflects a moral bond and an expectation of reciprocity with people you don't know. Lying, in contrast, involves an acquaintance. Cheating on taxes and avoiding fares (as well as claiming benefits, the exception) revolve around an impersonal government. Interpersonal trust in the United States is a deal among rugged individualists, not a contract with the American government.

Alienation from the larger society plays a big role in shaping moral behaviour. Blacks are less likely to endorse all eight societal norms. The effects are large across

Table 10.2 Regressions for moral behaviour indicators in the United States

Independent variable	Stolen goods	Claim benefits	Joyriding	Lying	Cheat on tax	Avoid fare	Keep money	Hit car
Trust in people	−0.195[c]	−0.181[b]	−0.035	−0.114	0.020	−0.065	−0.285[b]	−0.262[b]
	(0.074)	(0.083)	(0.049)	(0.102)	(0.100)	(0.091)	(0.141)	(0.134)
Self-obey commandments	−0.221[d]	−0.201[d]	−0.120[d]	−0.337[d]	−0.258[d]	−0.122[b]	−0.205[b]	−0.464[d]
	(0.045)	(0.051)	(0.030)	(0.062)	(0.061)	(0.056)	(0.086)	(0.097)
Others-obey commandments	−0.036	0.015	0.036	0.069	−0.058	−0.080[b]	−0.182[c]	−0.050
	(0.037)	(0.041)	(0.024)	(0.050)	(0.050)	(0.045)	(0.070)	(0.091)
Clear standards of good and evil	−0.112[c]	−0.070[b]	−0.038[a]	−0.242[d]	−0.167[c]	−0.138[c]	−0.236[c]	−0.130[b]
	(0.037)	(0.041)	(0.025)	(0.051)	(0.050)	(0.046)	(0.071)	(0.067)
Believe in hell	−0.022	−0.077	−0.087[a]	−0.198[b]	−0.312[c]	−0.180[b]	−0.165	−0.165
	(0.085)	(0.097)	(0.057)	(0.118)	(0.116)	(0.106)	(0.164)	(0.155)
Marital fidelity	−0.774[d]	−0.584[d]	−0.364[d]	−1.009[d]	−0.830[d]	−0.652[d]	−1.046[d]	−1.049[d]
	(0.136)	(0.153)	(0.090)	(0.187)	(0.184)	(0.167)	(0.259)	(0.245)
Married	−0.256[c]	−0.211[c]	−0.129[c]	−0.200[b]	−0.046	−0.482[d]	−0.301[b]	−0.130
	(0.073)	(0.082)	(0.049)	(0.100)	(0.099)	(0.090)	(0.139)	(0.132)
Union household	−0.054	−0.094[b]	0.008	−0.172[c]	−0.147[b]	−0.121[b]	−0.104	−0.246[c]
	(0.049)	(0.055)	(0.033)	(0.067)	(0.066)	(0.060)	(0.093)	(0.088)
Education	0.026	0.023	−0.026	0.041	0.164	0.044	−0.023	−0.026
	(0.057)	(0.064)	(0.038)	(0.078)	(0.077)	(0.070)	(0.108)	(0.102)
Race	0.319[d]	0.531[d]	0.091[a]	0.782[d]	0.518[d]	0.462[d]	0.887[d]	0.376[b]
	(0.087)	(0.099)	(0.058)	(0.120)	(0.118)	(0.108)	(0.167)	(0.158)
Age	−0.017[d]	−0.012[d]	−0.006[d]	−0.015[d]	−0.018[d]	−0.020[d]	−0.031[d]	−0.011[c]
	(0.002)	(0.002)	(0.001)	(0.003)	(0.003)	(0.003)	(0.004)	(0.004)
Constant	1.475[d]	1.744[d]	1.220[d]	1.580[c]	1.064[b]	1.923[d]	3.667[d]	2.190[c]
	(0.272)	(0.308)	(0.182)	(0.375)	(0.370)	(0.337)	(0.522)	(0.493)
R^2	0.151	0.092	0.059	0.140	0.120	0.132	0.120	0.042
Standard error of estimate	1.383	1.564	0.925	1.907	1.878	1.711	2.652	2.506

$N = 1599$

Notes

a $p < 0.10$.   b $p < 0.05$.   c $p < 0.01$.   d $p < 0.001$.

Table 10.3 Regressions for moral behaviour indicators in the United Kingdom

Independent variable	Stolen goods	Claim benefits	Joyriding	Lying	Cheat on tax	Avoid fare	Keep money	Hit car
Trust in people	-0.377[b]	-0.032	-0.173[b]	-0.201[a]	-0.177	-0.047	-0.244[a]	-0.182
	(0.132)	(0.116)	(0.087)	(0.156)	(0.177)	(0.140)	(0.152)	(0.158)
Self-obey commandments	-0.376[d]	-0.235[c]	-0.086[a]	-0.651[d]	-0.452[d]	-0.172[b]	-0.503[d]	-0.463[d]
	(0.081)	(0.071)	(0.054)	(0.096)	(0.109)	(0.086)	(0.093)	(0.097)
Others-obey commandments	-0.021	0.035	-0.037	-0.238[c]	-0.009	0.034	0.043	-0.050
	(0.075)	(0.066)	(0.050)	(0.089)	(0.101)	(0.080)	(0.087)	(0.091)
Clear standards of good and evil	-0.072	0.054	-0.018[a]	-0.234[c]	-0.191[b]	0.014	-0.120[a]	-0.141[a]
	(0.073)	(0.065)	(0.048)	(0.087)	(0.098)	(0.078)	(0.084)	(0.088)
Believe in hell	-0.083	0.025	-0.057	-0.142	0.158	0.141	-0.137	-0.090
	(0.144)	(0.127)	(0.095)	(0.170)	(0.194)	(0.153)	(0.166)	(0.173)
Marital fidelity	-0.387[b]	-0.107	-0.057	-0.389[b]	-0.444[b]	-0.181	-0.372[b]	-0.137
	(0.185)	(0.163)	(0.122)	(0.218)	(0.248)	(0.196)	(0.213)	(0.222)
Married	-0.387[c]	-0.525[d]	-0.289[c]	-0.321[b]	0.040	-0.367[c]	-0.228[a]	-0.461[c]
	(0.140)	(0.123)	(0.092)	(0.165)	(0.188)	(0.148)	(0.161)	(0.168)
Union household	-0.028	0.145[b]	0.062	-0.119[a]	0.107	0.097	-0.143[b]	0.061
	(0.074)	(0.065)	(0.049)	(0.088)	(0.010)	(0.079)	(0.086)	(0.089)
Education	-0.278[b]	-0.373[c]	-0.249[c]	-0.193[a]	-0.321[b]	-0.371[c]	0.157	-0.331[c]
	(0.113)	(0.010)	(0.074)	(0.134)	(0.152)	(0.120)	(0.130)	(0.136)
Non-European	-0.216	-0.130	-0.084	-0.069	0.012	0.052	-0.133	-0.961[a]
	(0.525)	(0.462)	(0.345)	(0.620)	(0.704)	(0.555)	(0.604)	(0.630)
Age	-0.028[d]	-0.023[d]	-0.011[d]	-0.029[d]	-0.032[d]	-0.036[d]	-0.030[d]	-0.033[d]
	(0.004)	(0.003)	(0.003)	(0.005)	(0.006)	(0.004)	(0.005)	(0.005)
Constant	3.385[d]	3.310[d]	2.362[d]	4.030[c]	3.411[d]	4.123[d]	3.493[d]	4.547[d]
	(0.448)	(0.395)	(0.295)	(0.529)	(0.602)	(0.474)	(0.516)	(0.538)
R^2	0.171	0.128	0.061	0.189	0.112	0.132	0.188	0.151
Standard error of estimate	1.785	1.572	1.174	2.108	2.397	1.890	2.056	2.143
$N = 791$								

Notes

a $p < 0.10$.   b $p < 0.05$.   c $p < 0.01$.   d $p < 0.001$.

Table 10.4 Regressions for moral behaviour indicators in Canada

Independent variable	Stolen goods	Claim benefits	Joyriding	Lying	Cheat on tax	Avoid fare	Keep money	Hit car
Trust in people	-0.039	-0.207[a]	-0.032	-0.040	-0.059	-0.051	0.179	0.042
	(0.117)	(0.147)	(0.079)	(0.150)	(0.148)	(0.140)	(0.195)	(0.133)
Self-obey commandments	-0.367[d]	-0.068	-0.095[b]	-0.300[d]	-0.271[c]	-0.163[b]	-0.325[c]	-0.233[c]
	(0.064)	(0.081)	(0.043)	(0.083)	(0.081)	(0.083)	(0.107)	(0.073)
Others-obey commandments	-0.001	-0.126[a]	0.044	-0.040	0.031	-0.084	-0.113	-0.106
	(0.062)	(0.078)	(0.042)	(0.079)	(0.078)	(0.079)	(0.102)	(0.070)
Clear standards of good and evil	-0.054	-0.135[b]	0.001	-0.112[a]	-0.071	0.106[a]	-0.016	-0.124[b]
	(0.064)	(0.081)	(0.043)	(0.082)	(0.881)	(0.082)	(0.106)	(0.073)
Believe in hell	0.087	-0.291[b]	-0.044	-0.511[c]	-0.206[a]	-0.285[b]	-0.398[c]	-0.092
	(0.120)	(0.151)	(0.081)	(0.154)	(0.152)	(0.154)	(0.200)	(0.137)
Marital fidelity	-0.341[b]	-0.470[b]	-0.248[b]	-0.174	-0.407[b]	-0.642[c]	-0.935[c]	-0.362[b]
	(0.171)	(0.156)	(0.115)	(0.220)	(0.216)	(0.219)	(0.284)	(0.195)
Married	-0.754[d]	-0.325[b]	-0.226[c]	-0.450[c]	-0.379[c]	-0.562[d]	-0.854[d]	-0.498[c]
	(0.124)	(0.156)	(0.083)	(0.159)	(0.156)	(0.159)	(0.206)	(0.141)
Union household	0.078	-0.116[a]	0.059	-0.004	0.170	0.064	-0.040	0.160
	(0.069)	(0.087)	(0.047)	(0.089)	(0.088)	(0.089)	(0.086)	(0.079)
Education	-0.278[b]	-0.227[b]	-0.007	0.089	-0.006	-0.078	-0.225[a]	-0.084
	(0.113)	(0.110)	(0.059)	(0.112)	(0.110)	(0.112)	(0.145)	(0.100)
French	-0.236[b]	-1.704[d]	-0.172[b]	-0.533[c]	-0.004	-0.680[d]	-0.567[c]	-0.146
	(0.141)	(0.178)	(0.095)	(0.181)	(0.179)	(0.181)	(0.235)	(0.161)
Other ethnic	-0.215[a]	-0.445[c]	-0.008	-0.337[d]	-0.218	-0.140	-0.753[c]	-0.143
	(0.141)	(0.178)	(0.095)	(0.181)	(0.179)	(0.181)	(0.235)	(0.161)
Age	-0.020[d]	-0.021[d]	-0.008[c]	-0.018[d]	-0.016[c]	-0.015[c]	-0.036[d]	-0.021[d]
	(0.004)	(0.005)	(0.002)	(0.005)	(0.005)	(0.005)	(0.006)	(0.004)
Constant	2.614[d]	2.455[d]	1.360[d]	3.028[d]	2.095[d]	2.216[d]	5.023[d]	2.262[d]
	(0.412)	(0.519)	(0.278)	(0.529)	(0.522)	(0.530)	(0.686)	(0.470)
R^2	0.200	0.211	0.066	0.133	0.081	0.118	0.167	0.112
Standard error of estimate	1.643	2.070	1.109	2.110	2.080	2.109	2.737	1.874

$N = 886$

Notes

a $p < 0.10$.   b $p < 0.05$.   c $p < 0.01$.   d $p < 0.001$.

most questions. Only joyriding has a modest impact. The effects are most pronounced for lying and keeping money you found, as we found for clear standards of good and evil. If, like the people of Montegrano, you believe that the system is fundamentally stacked against you, you won't expect reciprocity for any good deeds you do.

Social connectedness affects moral behaviour too. Being married makes one more likely to choose the right course in six of eight cases. Only hitting a car and making no report and cheating on taxes fail to reach significance. The biggest effects come on avoiding fares on public transit and buying stolen goods. In each case, marriage may change the social situation. If you are travelling with your spouse, cheating on fares might prove embarrassing. If you bring home something new, your spouse is likely to ask you where you got it. So marriage leads to social pressures. It may also bring forth a greater sense of responsibility to the larger society, so that we are not quite as tempted to engage in undesirable behaviour. Union members are also more likely to endorse moral behaviour, at least on five of the eight questions. The biggest impacts are for keeping money found, cheating on taxes, and lying.

Union membership does produce solidarity, but only in the United States. Union members are more likely to object to claiming benefits you aren't entitled to, to cheat on taxes, to avoid fares on public transportation, and to hit a car without making a report. Three of the four items involve government: unions tie people to larger institutions. On the other hand, we see no effect at all for education. At least part of the null effects come from the coding of education. A more refined measure would likely show greater effects among the college educated (cf. Putnam, 1995; Uslaner, 1996). But we shall see stronger effects for Canada and especially the UK. Finally, we see strong effects of age throughout.

THE BRITISH SECULAR MORALITY

Moral behaviour in the United States is driven mostly by personal morality, guided by religion. For the more collectivist British culture, expectations of reciprocity don't matter quite as much. The British are a moral people, but their ideals are more driven by secular values than religion. *Self-obey commandments is significant in all eight equations. The coefficients are almost uniformly higher in the UK than in the US.* The shared moral codes of British citizens picks up where religious values leave off. There are only sporadic significant relationships for clear standards of good and evil (for lying and cheating on taxes at $p < 0.05$ or better and for keeping money and hitting a car with no report at $p < 0.10$). Only joyriding gives a significant ($p < 0.10$) coefficient for belief in hell. And marital faithfulness is significant for only half of the measures of moral behaviour, all of which involve some element of deception (buying stolen goods, lying, cheating on taxes, and keeping money).

Expectations of reciprocity matter less in the more collectivist UK than in the United States. Others-obey commandments is significant only for lying. And trust is not so central. It counts most for buying stolen goods and for joyriding; it barely makes the grade for lying and keeping money. As in the United States, interpersonal trust counts most for relations among individuals, especially strangers. It matters less when you have to decide to whether to cheat the government, whether your target is tax money, fares on public transportation, or benefits.

As in America, connections count. Marriage makes one less likely to endorse amoral behaviour. So does growing older. But union membership in a more class-oriented society doesn't bring much solidarity. Union families are *more prone* to say that it is acceptable to claim benefits you aren't entitled to and to cheat on taxes. This probably reflects the greater class consciousness of the British in general and union members in particular. It could reflect class tensions – and a Robin Hood attitude: take from the government and redistribute to the lower classes. When you find someone else's money, you must return it. You could be taking money from a fellow worker.

There is no ethnic division. But, as we saw with union households, the British are polarised by education level. Even this crude measure produces powerful effects for most of the moral behaviour questions. Only keeping money you found fails to have a significant coefficient.

Attitudes toward morality depend less on reciprocity or religious values in Britain than in America. Ideals in the UK are driven more by a secular set of values that are not based on contingencies. How others respond is less critical in Britain than in the United States. While race polarises the acceptance of moral strictures in the United States, class divides the British population. While unions provide social capital binding people to one another in America, they sometimes lead people away from collective moral behaviour in Britain.

CANADA: A MIDDLE GROUND?

Canada should be a middle ground between Great Britain, the mother country, and the United States. On the surface, Canada does seem to be a mixture. Like Britain, moral behaviour in Canada is largely driven by self-obey commandments. Like the United States, religious values matter for six of the eight moral behaviours (though just barely for cheating on taxes). And marital faithfulness is important for all measures except lying (!) – where it has powerful effects in both the United States and Britain.

The British culture appears more individualistic than the Canadian. Canadians put *less* emphasis on interpersonal ties than the British do. People in both countries put little emphasis on whether others obey commandments. But trust in others matters some of the time in the United Kingdom. It affects only claiming benefits that you are not entitled to in Canada, and there at the generous $p < 0.10$ level. Both the British and Canadians depend heavily on personal moral codes.

But these value systems take different forms. The British constitutional tradition emphasises individual rights. The Canadian culture is more statist and collectivist, with an emphasis on group rights rather than individual liberties. So there are often sharp ethnic differences on moral behaviour. Other ethnics and especially Quebecois are less likely to endorse the standards of moral behaviour favoured by Anglophones. Francophones are more likely to accept cheating the government (claiming benefits and avoiding fares).[13] They are also less bothered by deceiving fellow citizens (buying stolen goods, lying, joyriding, and keeping money). Other ethnics, who are not well integrated into the Canadian mosaic, are also more tolerant of people who reject traditional moral values. If you believe that people outside your own group can't be trusted, you are less likely to sacrifice your own self-interest for the larger collectivity (Uslaner, 1996).[14]

In a more collectivist environment, encompassing institutions such as labour unions don't provide much social capital. But one's own personal life can be critical. Marriage has more powerful effects in Britain than in the United States and is more important yet in Canada. Canadians have similar education levels to Americans, and it is not surprising that they are less stratified by education. As elsewhere, age is consistently significant.

Canadians are like Americans (and unlike Britons) in a key way: religious values are critical for moral behaviour. The impacts are stronger for both clear standards of good and evil and belief in hell than we find in the United States. Putnam (1993) argued that religion was antithetical to social capital in heavily Catholic societies. But there is little support for his argument with respect to moral behaviour. Religious values are more potent in Canada, with a large Catholic population concentrated in a Francophone enclave, than they are in the more pluralist United States and the less devout United Kingdom. Nor is there evidence that religious values matter more for Catholics than Protestants. Religious values may serve as a guide to moral behaviour when we are less concerned with reciprocity. They may also reinforce group identity. If you trust your own kind much more than you trust all other people, the values you share with your group will be essential components of your personal moral code.

MAKING SENSE OF THE PATTERNS

Beyond summarising the tables, what can we learn about what underlies moral codes in each country? Even though we only have eight cases of moral behaviour, looking at patterns of coefficients across both moral measures and nations can be instructive.

First, we see that Canadians share a moral code with the United States more than either does with Britain. The mean scores in Table 10.1 for Canada and the United States correlate at 0.903. Canada and Britain are related at only 0.593, the US and the UK at 0.692. This surface similarity is deceiving. Canada *is* distinctive. It places far less emphasis on interpersonal trust than either Britain or the US. The correlations (not shown in Table 10.1) between the unstandardised betas for trust are 0.325 for the US and Britain. But both correlate *negatively* with the same measure in Canada (−0.433 and −0.482, respectively). There is a strong individualistic tradition in both Britain and its biggest colony, but it is lacking in Canada.

The correlation for trust coefficients is modest for the United States and Britain, but it is positive. Yet, there is even less commonality than we suspect. The correlation between the t ratios for trust in Britain and the United States is -0.797. In Canada, the t ratios are tiny compared to the United States (averaging -0.241 compared to -2.002), but they display a similar pattern ($r = 0.634$); Canada also differs from the UK ($r = -0.549$). In both Britain and the United States, trust matters more for interactions among people than dealings with government. But in dealings with others, trust helps Britons reject the temptation to deceive (buying stolen goods or joyriding). It is more central for Americans on more routine aspects of moral behaviour (as well as buying stolen goods): claiming benefits, keeping money, and hitting a car without making a report.

For Americans, trust matters most when the stakes are greatest. Confidence in others is less important where there are few costs. Joyriding may not impose any financial loss on the injured party. Avoiding fares on public transportation is a small ticket item. Buying stolen goods, keeping money you found, and getting benefits you are not entitled to may produce financial gains. Not making a report on a car you damage may save you increased insurance premiums. Lying does not always (generally?) bring a gain. These impacts show why trust is a key element of social capital in America. It delivers not only when we need it most, but when the stakes are highest. I constructed a measure of 'big effects'.[15] The correlation with the regression coefficients for trust is -0.916. In Britain, the correlation is far more modest (-0.343), while in Canada it is positive, though small (0.191). Americans chip in their social capital when it matters most. They are more tolerant for small ticket items.

Confidence in others also matters most for Americans when there is less agreement on the undesirability of an act. Trust is less important on joyriding than it is on keeping money you have found. This parallels my findings on social capital and collective action (Uslaner, 1996): trust has bigger effects on non-consensual forms of participation (where some people do them, others don't) than on consensual modes (where most people either participate or don't). The story is similar on the approbation of moral behaviour. When we are more divided over ethical standards, we look both to our values and to our expectations of what others will do.

In neither Britain nor Canada do big effects matter. In Britain, there is a very modest effect for consensus ($r = -0.170$). In Canada, trust has bigger impacts on *more* consensual actions ($r = 0.504$). What, then, shapes the impact of trust in these two nations? The relationship between citizens and each other is the key. I divided the moral behaviours into two targets: government (claiming benefits, cheating on taxes, and avoiding fares) and personal (the other five). This government index is correlated with the regression coefficients for trust at 0.713 for the UK and -0.612 for Canada.

The signs indicate that trust is more important for interpersonal dealings and less consequential for government in Britain. This makes sense: British culture is torn between majoritarianism and consensus. The Westminster system is the embodiment of the former, the unwritten Constitution (and the individualistic and consensual norms that underlie it) of the latter. Interpersonal trust induces moral behaviour for interactions among ordinary folk. Daily lives reflect social traditions, especially consensus and liberty. There is no impact for dealings with the government, which are more polarising and majoritarian. We see just the reverse pattern in Canada, though we should not make too much of it since trust matters little in Canada. (The only case where it counts at all is for claiming benefits.)

From one's personal moral assessment to clear standards of good and evil to marital faith, a pattern begins to emerge, though it is not consistent across the three nations. *In most cases, core values that don't depend on reciprocity have their greatest effects when they are most needed, when there is least consensus on what is acceptable moral behaviour.* We see this pattern for self-obey commandments in Britain ($r = -0.886$), for clear standards in two of the three countries ($r = -0.813$ in the United States and -0.742 in Britain), and for marital fidelity everywhere ($r = -0.811$ for the U.S., -0.703 for the U.K., and -0.741 in Canada). In the United States and Canada, there is even a moderately strong relationship with other-obey commandments ($r = -0.579$ and -0.656).

Social trust matters most in countries with strong traditions of individualism. Its impacts here are most powerful in the United States, followed by Great Britain. Canada, with its stronger group identifications and collectivist orientation, depends less on trust to achieve collective action. But even in individualistic societies, trust isn't equally as important in all arenas. Putnam (1993: 169) argues that social capital is a moral resource that expands as we use it. The American pattern best describes this idea of social capital. Confidence in others counts most when we need it most: when the stakes are highest and when there is less consensus within society on what is acceptable. Trust builds support for doing the right thing; it fills in the gaps that individual moral codes leave open. Trust helps out in societies with a mixture of collective and individual values, such as Britain. But it doesn't work in quite the same way. Confidence in others doesn't depend on either the stakes or the level of consensus in society. Instead, it helps us solve collective dilemmas, but only in the private realm. Where there is a stronger state, as in Britain and especially Canada, even interpersonal trust has a limited role. It has no impact on whether we should cheat the government; and where government is very strong, it doesn't have much impact on our daily lives either.

Trust is the only measure of reciprocity that matters. There are sporadic significant coefficients for others-obey commandments, but they are rare and display no coherent pattern. If trust were simply a summary of our experiences, it should be more highly correlated with our expectations of others. And others-obey commandments, which surely is an expression of our experience, should have more pronounced effects on what we consider to be acceptable moral behaviours.

Religious values also count most when there is least consensus on moral behaviours, providing support for the idea that faith is a form of social capital. But religion doesn't work everywhere. Its effects are strongest in the most religious society (the United States) and weakest in the most secular (Britain). What makes one society more religious than another? Greeley (1991) suggests that greater pluralism, where faiths have to compete for believers, can promote stronger religious beliefs. And the United States abjures the idea of a state church in favour of highly decentralised and often democratic religious communities. The more pluralistic the religious environment, the more faith is likely to serve as a form of social capital.

In all three countries, personal moral codes are the central key to the puzzle. Nowhere do we see big impacts for others-obey commandments. And everywhere self-obey commandments are central to moral attitudes. Only in Britain do we see a clear pattern for self-obey. In the United States and Canada, personal moral codes are important across the board.

MORAL CODES AND RECIPROCITY IN CONTEXT

The Anglo-American democracies, indeed most societies, are not Montegrano. There is plenty of morality to go around and not that much immorality to disrupt daily life. To a large extent, what we consider moral reflects our own moral codes, often embedded in religious values, *and* our expectations of others' behaviour.

But we should not press the distinction between ourselves and others too far. Our values depend upon expectations of reciprocity. If people were to cast aside values to behave as Hume suggested, our social fabric would wither. As Bok argues:

> The veneer of social trust is often thin. As lies spread – by imitation, or in retaliation, or to forestall suspected detection – trust is damaged. Yet trust is a social good to be protected just as much as the air we breathe or the water we drink. When it is damaged, the community as a whole suffers; and when it is destroyed, societies falter and collapse (1978: 26–7).

Values and expectations of reciprocity reinforce each other. As Hume argued, morality developed out of conventions. When Moses brought the Ten Commandments down from Mount Sinai, he did not address a population still in a state of nature. Warring parties would not accept moral codes based upon reciprocity. God, Jewish theology teaches, rewards people (including giving them the Commandments) when they show that they behave righteously. He punishes, as with Noah and the Ark and (some believe) the Holocaust, when they have lost their way.

In a mean world such as Montegrano, people won't reach the consensus necessary to impose clear standards of good and evil. In a nicer environment, we will face far less difficulty. There will always be some people who seek to get around society's strictures. And that is why experience matters too. But if we had to learn from experience without guidance from more general principles, our task would be far more difficult and less likely to succeed.

That is why trust reflects optimism. A world of pessimists, such as Montegranans, would not develop the values that lead people to adhere to moral behaviour. Only a world of optimists would. If someone takes advantage of you, you need to have a fundamentally positive view of human nature to keep up trust. If you were playing a game against rational egoists, optimism would give way to exploitation (Axelrod, 1984). Yet, most of us don't live in a Montegrano. Against their better instincts, optimists are likely to attribute a run of encounters with misanthropes as a stroke of bad luck.

Whatever the costs of deceiving yourself that the world is a better place than experience shows, believing that everyone wants to exploit you can be costlier in the longer run. Living in a world of pessimists leads to more destructive behaviour, while living among optimists makes people more likely to behave well (Frank, 1988). Values and experience may work in different ways. Sometimes one picks up the slack for the other. But, as *most* of the correlations with mean scores show, they largely reinforce each other. If you lack one, you probably can't get to the other.

These remarks apply equally to our three Anglo-American democracies and to other, more statist and hierarchical nations. Social trust is most critical where the collective action problem appears most severe, in more atomistic societies where people put their confidence in others they are not likely to know – or know much about. People who strongly identify with a socioeconomic class or an ethnic group, to the exclusion of others, will develop a truncated sense of social capital. They may help their own kind, but will take a less active role in their communities (Uslaner, 1996). Sharp cleavages in a society are a powder keg for social capital. Once we begin to think tribalistically, we no longer have enough goodwill for all of our fellow citizens. The more that American blacks, the French in Canada become pessimistic for their future, the less social trust they will have. And the less social capital the society will have to spread around.

Canada's problem is distinctive. It has an aggrieved ethnic group that is an overwhelming majority in its own enclave. This creates a dynamic of ethnic tension – and its consequent problems for social trust – that is different from the problems of its Southern neighbour. African-Americans aren't so geographically concentrated. This simple demographic fact makes it more difficult for blacks to seek redress of their grievances through a separate identity.

We see precisely the opposite dynamic for group identification in Canada and the United States. African-Americans may be less trusting than whites, but they *don't* distrust whites as much as whites distrust them. In the 1992 American National Election Study, blacks rated whites 71.5 on a feeling thermometer, compared to whites' own mean score of 71.3 ($p < 0.90$, two-tailed test). Whites were less positive (62.0) toward blacks than African-Americans were towards themselves (88.0). So the minority group feels positively towards the majority, but not vice-versa. In Canada, the minority distrusts the majority: a 1991 survey by the Canadian Broadcasting Company and the *Globe and Mail* shows that 78 per cent of Anglophones believe that English Canadians care about French Canadians, compared to only 48 per cent of Francophones. But there was virtually no difference on whether French Canadians care about Anglophones (60.3 per cent and 64.9 per cent respectively).[16] A minority that feels divorced from the larger society can detract from social capital. A minority that still identifies with the larger society may contribute less to generalised trust. Since it does not withhold fundamental loyalties, the smaller group may develop its own social institutions and norms without challenging those of the larger society.

There is an irony in these results for the study of social capital. We should be careful in making inferences about a country's set of values from aggregate figures. Recall that Canada ranks *slightly higher* (50 per cent) on interpersonal trust than either the United States or Britain. But stronger divisions within the society make generalised trust less potent as a source of social capital. The simple level of trust is not a fail-safe guide to its potency. Social capital depends on social context.

Social capital matters across a wide variety of behaviours. Most of the chapters in this volume (and elsewhere, as in Putnam, 1995 and Uslaner, 1996) point to the role of values and social ties in fostering membership in voluntary organisations and in other activities such as volunteering. In this chapter, I have shown that its reach extends to beliefs about moral behaviour. This is hardly surprising. Joining voluntary associations and behaving morally are both collective action problems. And the solutions to both collective action problems appear to rest in moral codes more than in expectations of others' behaviour, regardless of context or culture.

Notes

*   I gratefully acknowledge the support of the General Research Board of the University of Maryland, College Park and the Everett McKinley Dirksen Center for the Study of Congressional Leadership. The data I employ were obtained from the Inter-University Consortium for Political and Social Research, which is absolved from any responsibility for my claims. I have benefited from the comments (on earlier versions of this and other papers) of Sue E.S. Crawford, Keith Dougherty, Morris P. Fiorina, Mark Graber, Jennifer Hochschild, Virginia Hodgkinson, Ted Jelen, Margaret Levi, Robert Maranto, Kenneth Newton, Joe Oppenheimer, Anita Plotinsky, Edward Queen II, Robert Putnam, Wendy Rahn, Tom Rice, Tara Santmire, Kay Lehman Schlozman, Paul F. Whiteley, Raymond Wolfinger, Yael Yishai, and conversations with Karol Soltan, Jane Mansbridge, John Mueller, and Russell Hardin and from the clerical assistance of Anne Marie Clark and Yolanda Rich. Deborah D. Uslaner has been my most profound support system, both in things English and more generally. And the participants in the Conference on Democracy and Social Capital in Milan, Italy helped clarify my thinking and make this a better chapter.

1   Jewish law teaches that expressions of faith are based upon *exceptions to rationality.* Were moral commandments merely rational responses to our environment, there would be no need for values (much less religious commandments).

2   Elsewhere I deal with a third value, social egalitarianism (Uslaner, 1996). But the World Values Study has no good measures for this value, so I do not include it here.

3　On a hypothetical scale of 0 to 100 with the United States at zero and Britain at 100, Lipset (1996: 32–3) places Canada at 30. However, Inglehart's factor analysis of a wide range of cultural indicators places Canada closer to Britain than to the United States (see Figure 3-6 in Inglehart, 1997). All three countries, however, occupy the same cultural cluster.

4　The correlation between generalised and particularised trust is particularly low for Quebecois. Trust in others is related to confidence in fellow countrymen at only 0.049 and trust in Francophones at 0.093. For Anglophones, generalised trust is more strongly related to both types of particularised confidence (0.216 for all countrymen and 0.170 for Francophones).

5　The gammas between trust and hope for the future in the 1981 WVS are 0.334 for the United States, 0.402 for the United Kingdom, and just 0.184 for Canada. When the WVS in 1990 asked Canadians about trust in their fellow countrymen and trust in French Canadians, there was no identical question about expectations for the future. The closest I could come is whether hard work will likely lead to success. For Quebecois, the correlation between generalised trust and belief that hard work will pay off is −0.026 (the wrong direction), while the correlation with particularised trust (faith in fellow French Canadians) is 0.155. For Anglophones, the correlation between generalised trust and hard work is 0.054; for trust in fellow countrymen (presumably other Anglophones), it almost doubles to 0.098.

6　The 1990–3 World Values Surveys asked the same questions. Overall, there is much stability in responses, as the following table indicates:

	US	UK	Canada
Keep money	3.662*	2.544	3.974
Hit car/no report	1.961*	2.340*	2.042
Lie in own interest	2.332	2.771*	2.782
Cheat on taxes	1.929	2.518*	2.388
Avoid fare	2.140	2.048*	2.118
Government benefits	1.911**	1.812	1.877*
Buy stolen goods	1.598	1.748*	1.779
Joyriding	1.264	1.180	1.480

A single asterisk indicates what seems to be significantly greater disapproval in the later World Values Study; a double asterisk indicates a shift towards less disapproval. Overall the ratings seem quite consistent over time. In the United States and Canada, some measures move up while others move down. Only in the United Kingdom, where the means were higher in 1981 than in 1990–3, do we see consistent drops – towards convergence with the United States and (especially) Canada. Whiteley (this volume) uses several of these measures as factors shaping trust, whereas I use them as dependent variables. Yet our approaches are complementary, since we both see trust as based on morality.

7　The higher correlation for the UK may reflect its greater homogeneity. If people resemble you, their behaviour is more likely to be similar to your own.

8　The self-factor is correlated with social trust at just 0.047, the other factor at 0.107 in the United States. In Britain the correlations with trust are 0.015 and 0.067, respectively. For Canada, they are 0.081 and 0.143.

9   The gamma between the importance of God in daily life and clear standards of good and evil is about 0.35 for all three countries, about the same as we find for the importance of religion and whether one believes in a personal God. The correlation is within the bounds of other measures of religiosity.

10   There are questions on membership in organisations and volunteering, but I do not use them. It is doubtful that membership in organisations or volunteering *precedes* moral behaviour. More likely, people with high ethical standards are more likely to volunteer (Hodgkinson *et al.*, 1990). Second, even if we put aside theoretical doubts, neither membership nor volunteering had much effect on moral behaviour in estimations I made for the US.

11   Union membership is a trichotomous variable: respondent is a member, someone else in the household is a member, and no one is a member.

12   If you find money with no identification, the moral dilemma vanishes.

13   Ironically, Francophones are no more likely to cheat on taxes, which is a national pastime in their mother country.

14   The 1990 World Values Study asked whether Canadians trusted their fellow countrymen and whether they trusted French Canadians. Quebecois and Anglophones alike were generally more strongly motivated by group trust than by interpersonal confidence ('most people can be trusted').

15   I scored buying stolen goods, claiming benefits, keeping money, and hitting a car as 1, lying at an intermediate 0.5, and the other measures as zero.

16   I am indebted to Ken LeClerc of the CBC for providing me with these data. Neither the CBC nor the *Globe and Mail* is responsible for my interpretations. The 1990 World Values Study has a question (variable 350) on ethnic identity. More whites than blacks give their primary identification as 'American' (29.5 per cent compared to 18.3 per cent). But the difference in Canadian identity between Anglophones and Francophones is far greater (47.0 per cent to 10.4 per cent).

References

Axelrod, R. (1984), *The Evolution of Cooperation* (New York).

Banfield, E. (1958), *The Moral Basis of a Backward Society* (New York).

Barnum, D. G., and J. L. Sullivan (1990), 'The Elusive Foundations of Political Freedom in Britain and the United States', *Journal of Politics*, 52: 719–39.

Bates, R. H. (1988), 'Contra Contractarianism: Some Reflections on the New Institutionalism', *Politics and Society*, 16: 387-401.

Bok, C. (1978), *Lying* (New York).

Christoph, J. B. (1965), 'Consensus and Cleavage in British Political Ideology', *American Political Science Review*, 54: 629–42.

Coleman, J. S. (1990), *Foundations of Social Theory* (Cambridge, MA).

Conover, P. J., I. M. Crewe, and D. D. Searing (1991), 'The Nature of Citizenship in the United States and Great Britain', *Journal of Politics*, 53: 800–32.

Crawford, V., and J. Sobel (1982), 'Strategic Information Transmission', *Econometrica*, 50: 1431–51.

Deutsch, M. (1958), 'Trust and Suspicion', *Journal of Conflict Resolution*, 2: 265–79.

—— (1960), 'The Effect of Motivational Orientation upon Trust and Suspicion', *Human Relations*, 13: 123–39.

Dynes, R. R., and E.L. Quarantelli (1980), 'Helping Behavior in Large-Scale Disasters'. In D. H. Smith, J. Macauley, and Associates (eds), *Participation in Social and Political Activities* (San Francisco).

Frank, R. (1988), *Passions within Reason.* (New York).

Gambetta. D. (1988), 'Can We Trust Trust?' In D. Gambetta (ed.), *Trust* (Oxford).

Gauthier, D. (1986), *Morals by Agreement* (Oxford).

Greeley, A. (1991), In B. Shafer (ed.), *Is America Different?* (Oxford).

Hardin, R. (1992), 'The Street-Level Epistemology of Trust', *Analyse & Kritik*, 14: 152–76.

Harris, F.C. (1994), 'Something Within: Religion as a Mobilizer of African-American Political Activism', *Journal of Politics*, 56: 42–68.

Hartz, L. (1955), *The Liberal Tradition in America* (New York).

—— (1964), *The Founding of New Societies* (New York).

Hodgkinson, V. A., M. S. Weitzman, and A. D. Kirsch (1990), 'From Commitment to Action: How Religious Involvement Affects Giving and Volunteering'. In R. Wuthnow, V. Hodgkinson, and Associates, *Faith and Philanthropy in America.* (San Francisco).

Hume, D. (1960 [1739]), *A Treatise on Human Nature*, ed. L.A. Selby-Bigge (Oxford).

Inglehart, R. (1997), *Modernization and Postmodernization* (Princeton).

Kornberg, A. (1990), 'Political Support in Democratic Societies: The Case of Canada', *Journal of Politics*, 52: 709–16.

Lipset, S. M. (1963), *Political Man* (New York).

—— (1990), *Continental Divide* (New York).

—— (1991), 'American Exceptionalism Reaffirmed'. In B. Shafer (ed.)., *Is America Different?* (Oxford).

—— (1996), *American Exceptionalism* (New York).

McRoberts, K. (1993), *Quebec: Social Change and Political Crisis* (3rd edn; Toronto).

Nevitte, N. (1996), *The Decline of Deference* (Peterborough, Ontario).

Olsen, M. (1965), *The Logic of Collective Action* (Cambridge, MA).

Putnam, R. D. (1993), *Making Democracy Work* (Princeton).

—— (1995), 'Bowling Alone', *Journal of Democracy*, 6: 65–78.

Rokeach, M. (1973), *The Nature of Human Values* (New York).

Rosenstone, S. J. and J. M. Hansen (1993), *Mobilization, Participation, and Democracy in America* (New York).

Russell, J. (1823), *An Essay on the History of the English Government and Constitution* (London).

Tocqueville, Alexis de (1945 [1840]), *Democracy in America*, tr. H. Reeve (vol. 2; New York).

Uslaner, E. M. (1996), 'Faith, Hope, and Charity', Unpublished paper (College Park, Maryland).

Verba, S., K. L. Schlozman, and H. Brady (1995), *Voice and Equality* (Cambridge, Massachusetts).

Wilson, J. Q. (1993), *The Moral Sense* (New York).

Wuthnow, R. (1993), *Acts of Compassion.* (Princeton).

Yamigichi, T. and M. Yamigichi (1994), 'Trust and Commitment in the United States and Japan', *Motivation and Emotion*, 18: 129–66.

Zellner, A. (1963), 'Estimators of Seemingly Unrelated Regressions', *Journal of the American Statistical Association*, 58: 977–92.

11 Social capital, active membership in voluntary associations and some aspects of political participation

An empirical case study

Jaak B. Billiet and Bart Cambré

INTRODUCTION

This study analyses the relationship between the participation in different kinds of voluntary associations and three qualities of citizenship that are conceived advantageous for political participation. These qualities are trust in politics, interest in politics, and political knowledge. On both theoretical and empirical grounds, one may expect that trust, interest, and knowledge are positively related to each other, and that this cluster of qualities is affected by the level of education, occupational status, gender, and age of citizens (Wittebrood 1992; Maddens and Dewachter 1993), but why should membership of voluntary associations have an additional impact on these political variables? This expectation is derived from theoretical reflections and empirical findings in recent studies of social capital.

The recent[1] interest of scholars in sociology, political science, and economics in the development of 'social capital' is motivated by interest in the linkages between levels of social capital and collective outcomes. High levels of social capital appear to be crucial for such measures of collective well-being as economic development, effective political institutions, and a reduction of various social problems (Brehm and Rahn 1996). Conversely, phenomena such as family disintegration, educational failure, inner-city crime, juvenile delinquency, teenage pregnancy are partially explained by the erosion of certain kinds of social capital (see Fukuyama 1995; Hagan *et al.* 1995; Smith *et al.* 1995; MacMillan 1995). Political phenomena such as right-wing extremism (Hagan *et al.* 1995), policy failures (Wilson 1993), and the weakened performance of regional governments (Putman 1993) are also linked to a decline in 'social capital'.

Two aspects in the notion 'social capital' have our attention: first, it refers to a variety of phenomena, and second, it is an aggregate concept. According to Coleman (1988: 98; 1990: 302) 'social capital' is defined by its function. 'It is not a single entity but a variety of different entities, with two elements in common: they all consist of some aspect of social structures, and they facilitate certain action to actors – whether persons or corporate actions – within the structure'

(Coleman 1988: 598).[2] Aspects of social relations that can constitute useful capital resources for the individual are: obligations and expectations, information potential, norms and effective sanctions, authority relations, appropriate social organization, and intentional organization (Coleman 1988: 306–13). In *Making Democracy Work* Putnam refers to 'norms of reciprocity and civic engagement' (1993: 167) or to 'features of social organization such as networks, norms, and social trust that facilitate co-ordination and co-operation for mutual benefit' (see Putnam 1995: 67). In this sense, utilitarian individualism which emphasizes private interests at the expense of civic obligation (Bellah *et al.* 1985; Etzioni 1993; Wilson 1993) is conceived as one of the forces that inhibit or even destroy social capital (Coleman 1990: 321). Other factors that affect the creation and destruction of social capital are the closure and the stability of social networks (Coleman 1990: 319–20).

An inspection of recent empirical studies reveals that social capital can be measured by a range of indicators, such as participation in social networks and organizational affiliations (Putnam 1995); parental support, neighbourhood strength, and community interest (Coleman 1995); parents' occupational prestige, marital status, and presence of children (Dixon and Seron 1995); perceived access to time and money help from friends and family (Boisjoly *et al.* 1995); changes in the timing of significant life course events (MacMillan 1995). In short, all kinds of co-operative social relationships have the potential to function as 'social capital', but their importance needs to be established by careful empirical investigation.[3]

Social capital is an *aggregate concept* since it refers to features of social organization (Putnam 1995: 67). Theoretically, it provides a comprehensive explanation for why some communities or larger entities (municipalities, regions) are able to resolve collective problems co-operatively while others fail in bringing people together for common purposes. Consequently, a study which is focused on individual actors as research units (a micro-perspective) must argue in advance why inferences about the relationships between characteristics at the individual level can provide evidence about the consequences of social capital (Brehm and Rahn 1996). In order to achieve this, one should demonstrate that variations in social capital and its consequences can be measured at the level of the individual actor.

In our view, it is possible to measure *indirectly* the individual's contribution to social capital that is present in networks of voluntary associations, by measuring their active participation in voluntary associations. Voluntary associations are co-operative social networks as far as they are built on stable and repeated interaction among individuals. The processes of social control active in these organization networks, are likely to affect the conceptions and behaviour of the members. We may presume that trusting individuals are more likely to participate in organizations and to co-operate with each other. In turn, participation can support mutual trust and co-operation among the members (Putnam 1995: 67; Brehm and Rahn 1996). It is also reasonable to assume that the members share common values when they participate in voluntary associations belonging to social movements.

The voluntary associations under consideration develop all kinds of programmes which are directed to the cultural, social, and political development of their members. Those who actively participate are more likely to take part in the body of knowledge that is transmitted by the organizations' activities. The consequences in which we are interested (trust, interest, and knowledge) are clearly characteristics of individuals, but they may have repercussions for the political system as a whole. Political entities with high numbers of interested and informed citizens who trust the political leaders will certainly differ in performance from entities with substantially lower numbers of citizens sharing these characteristics.

We may conclude that from a 'social capital' perspective, it makes sense to study the relationships between participation in voluntary associations and the political consequences we mentioned relating to trust, interest, and knowledge at the micro level.

RESEARCHING SOCIAL CAPITAL

At the centre of research into the micro-level aspects of voluntary associations is the analysis of the function of these groups in mobilizing individual citizens. Membership in all kinds of voluntary associations is seen as a remedy against atomization and social disintegration which are conceived as characteristics of mass societies (van Deth 1997). These associations provide opportunities to meet other people and to co-operate with them. The works of the communitarians (cf. Etzioni 1993) as well as the studies of Putnam (1993, 1995) on social capital can be traced back to the view that voluntary associations can provide a protected environment for individuals to develop all kinds of skills and attitudes that are necessary to counter atomization and fragmentation. In that way, voluntary associations can contribute substantially to the integration of individuals in society, including into the political system. This optimistic view on the consequences of participation in voluntary associations for a democratic political system can be traced back to de Tocqueville (Stouthuysen 1992: 49–52).

The successful integration of citizens into extreme left revolutionary groups or into radical right-wing movements can create problems for political stability and democracy. However, these groups are excluded from this study because they do not promote social integration, and because they involve only a very limited number of individuals.

Active membership in voluntary associations can have an impact on several aspects of democratic political involvement, namely on actual participation such as voting and other political activities, on political orientations such as interest in politics, political efficacy, and on political knowledge. We will start with a short overview of the findings and explanations about the impact of voluntary associations on political participation, paying special attention to findings in Flanders. Most studies of the relationship between participation in voluntary associations and political participation report findings that suggest a positive relationship between the two. Empirical evidence collected by Almond and Verba (1963) in five countries showed that members of associations had higher levels of political sophistication, social trust, political participation, and subjective civic competence than people who were not involved. Verba and Nie (1972) found a positive relationship between involvement in social organizations and the development of decision-making skills. Moreover, such members were more likely to participate in decision-making processes.

Olsen explained the positive effect of participation in voluntary associations on political participation in terms of several kinds of activities within these associations. Participation in voluntary associations broadens one's sphere of interest and concerns; so that public affairs and issues become more salient. The individual develops contacts and relationships with many new and diverse people, and this draws him or her into political affairs and political activity. Participation increases one's information, trains a person in social and leadership skills, and provides other resources that are needed for effective political action (Olsen 1972: 318). In this view, the social activities within non-political voluntary associations have a direct impact on political involvement. Moyser and Parry (1996: 8) provide an analogous explanation. According to them, voluntary associations become relevant to political participation because they provide opportunities for individuals to engage in social activity in formal public settings. Moreover, they function as arenas in which explicitly political issues are raised and discussed, in which individuals can learn leadership skills, and in which lessons about democracy may be drawn. Moyser and Parry (1996: 24) state that the bulk of activity within associations is not 'political' in any obvious way, however such activity may be of considerable political importance.

With respect to voting behaviour, a clear and direct relationship is found between voluntary activity and voting in most studies, even when socio-economic status or political orientations are taken into account (Parry *et al.* 1992; van Deth 1992; Verba *et al.* 1995). Data from the 1991 General Election Survey in Flanders ($N = 2,970$) supports these findings indirectly. Since voting is compulsory in Belgium, we measured political orientation rather than voting behaviour, asking the respondents if they would 'always, most of the time, sometimes or never go to vote, when voting was no longer obligatory'. We estimated the net impact of active participation in voluntary associations using a logistic-regression model with a number of relevant explaining variables included (level of education, professional status, gender, generation, urbanization environment, and church involvement). The odds ratio (β) of 'always inclined to vote' versus 'never inclined to vote' was 1.46 ($p < 0.001$) for the active members, indicating that on the (geometric) average the ratio 'always/never' increased by 46 per cent when the respondent belonged to the category of active membership of a voluntary association, in comparison with a non-member. This is a strong indication of a relationship between the desire for democratic participation and active membership of voluntary associations, since this parameter is purged from the impact of all other relevant social-background variables.

There is a lot of empirical evidence about the impact of activities in voluntary associations on conventional modes of political participation like attending campaign meetings, or writing letters to politicians (see Parry *et al.* 1992; van Deth 1992; Verba *et al.* 1995), and party membership (Rokkan and Torsvik 1959; Berry 1970). In the Flemish population, on the average and again controlling for other factors mentioned earlier, the odds 'party member/no member' increases by 34 per cent if the respondent is an active member of voluntary associations instead of a non-active member, or no member at all ($\beta = 1.344$; $p < 0.001$). This is not surprising in a pillarized society with stable and exclusive links between traditional political families and large numbers of social organizations (Billiet 1996a).

Another aspect of democratic political activity, the so-called unconventional but legal modes of political participation like attending lawful demonstrations, signing petitions and the boycott of products for ethical reasons, are more likely to occur among active members of voluntary associations (Parry *et al.* 1992; van Deth 1992). Analogous results are obtained in the 1991 General Election Survey in Flanders in which attitudes towards the acceptability of these kind of activities and the readiness to participate in them were surveyed. Active membership in voluntary associations had a significant net impact on the acceptability of unconventional political actions. The odds expressing a positive attitude towards unconventional (but legal) actions versus a negative attitude increased with about 40 per cent among the active members compared with the others ($\beta = 1.397$, $p < 0.001$). However surprisingly, the active members were less likely to get involved in these kinds of activities. The odds of 'certain' involvement versus 'never' involvement decreased by 32 per cent among the active members ($\beta = 0.678$, $p < 0.001$). These seemingly contradictory results may indicate that among the Flemish who are not actively involved in voluntary associations, those who have a positive attitude towards unconventional political activities are more inclined to get involved in them. In contrast, actively involved citizens who are more likely to have a positive attitude towards these activities, are less inclined to actually do them. Is this an indication of a more socially integrated position of the members? This conclusion is somewhat premature and needs further investigation.

Active participation in voluntary associations is not mentioned among the determinants of interest in politics in van Deth's overview (1990). However, in the context of the preceding findings, we expect a positive relationship between participation and political interest. After controlling for the effects of age, gender, education, public/private employment, and occupation, Gundelach and Torpe (1996) found significant relations between political orientations like interest in politics, political efficacy, and political participation, and membership in different kinds of associations. However, with respect to the causal order of these variables they argue that individuals who are interested in politics are likely both to join more associations and to be more active in politics than those who are not interested in politics. The positive relationship between active membership of voluntary associations and these political orientations is also found in the 1991 National Election Survey in Flanders.

Interest in politics was measured by questions about reading political news, discussing social and political problems among friends, and convincing others

(Carton *et al.* 1993). A variable was constructed with the following categories: strong interest, moderate interest, no interest. In a logistic regression model with all other relevant factors included, on the average the odds 'strong interest/no interest' increased by 54 per cent for active members as compared with non-members ($\beta = 1.537$; $p < 0.001$). Using structural equation modelling, we did not find a significant impact of active membership on the lack of political efficacy (Billiet 1996b), however a significant effect was found with education, gender, generation, urbanization, and church involvement controlled in the model. The odds ratio of 'political inefficient/political efficient' decreased by 39 per cent when the respondent was actively involved in voluntary associations ($\beta = 0.697$; $p < 0.001$). Thus activism promoted political efficacy.

So far the empirical findings are about political participation and political orientations. What about political knowledge? The well-informed citizen has a central place in most normative models of democracy. 'In a democracy, the citizen is supposed to know what the issues are, what their history is, what the relevant facts are, what alternatives are proposed, what the party stands for, what the likely consequences are' (Berelson *et al.* 1954: 308). It is even suggested that every citizen should know about the structure, the principles and the functioning of the institutions in order to understand and to accomplish his or her democratic duties (see Wittebrood 1992: 135–6). This view however is in sharp contrast with the results of empirical studies showing that the model citizen has little knowledge of the workings of the political system (Maddens and Dewachter 1993: 131; Wittebrood 1992: 136; Cambré *et al.* 1995).

It has been shown that political knowledge is strongly associated with background variables such as education, gender, and age (Berelson *et al.* 1954; Bennett 1986; Wittebrood 1992) and with interest in politics, and media dependence (Bennett and Bennett 1993; Condra 1992; Wittebrood 1992). Wittebrood (1992: 143) proposed a complex theoretical model for the explanation of political knowledge in which interest in politics, perception of interests and media use are intermediary variables. In that model, the effect of both interest in politics and perception of interests occurred via media use which was assumed to have a direct effect on knowledge. She expected that political knowledge has in turn an effect on both political interest and the perception of interests. In this model, with the exception of education which was expected to have a direct effect on knowledge, gender, age, and political efficacy were not expected directly to affect political knowledge.

After several empirical tests and improvements of the model, age seemed not to play a significant role. Women were not as much interested in politics as men, and they were not as well informed as men, but they were somewhat more inclined to perceive their own interests than men. Political knowledge was most strongly and directly affected by education, gender, and political interest, and to a lesser degree by media use. Contrary to the expectations, political knowledge had no recursive effect on interest in politics and on the perception of interests (Wittebrood 1992: 153).

In the literature we did not find empirical evidence of a direct impact of active membership of voluntary associations on political knowledge. However, since active members of voluntary associations are assumed to be more likely to engage in conversations about politics, there may be an indirect effect. Kennamer (1988) found that, like exposure to the news media, political conversations with others leads to much learning, controlling for effects of education, gender, political interest, and media use.

Our own model of political knowledge is inspired by the model proposed by Wittebrood, but we are mainly interested in the effects of active participation in voluntary associations on interest in politics, media use, and trust in politics as an aspect of political efficacy. In the studies of political knowledge, it is suggested that the measurement of political knowledge must be differentiated and improved, suggesting a shift from measures of abstract knowledge toward measures of factual and practical knowledge (Luskin 1987; Maddens and Dewachter 1993; Wittebrood 1992). We consider this model and the methods used to estimate it next.

METHODOLOGICAL ASPECTS

The data of this study come from a survey carried out in 1995 in Flanders relating to a large number of issues about the new federal structures in Belgium.[4] Face-to-face interviews (N = 710) were conducted by trained interviewers of ISPO among the Flemish population. The sample[5] was constructed with an equal probability design and was representative of the Flemish population of 18–74 years of age.

Concepts and measurements

A global model including a measurement model for all concepts and the substantial relationships between the latent factors, was tested with LISREL8 (Jöreskog and Sörbom 1993). The measurement part of the model for the multiple indicator variables is reported in Table 11.1. The latent dependent variables are measured by several indicators. *Knowledge* of politics focuses on knowledge of the federal structures, the basic principles of the federal state, and about the typical policies of the Flemish government. These subjects were relevant since in 1995 the Belgian state arrived at a crucial stage in the reform process. For the first time direct election of representatives of the separate regional legislative chambers was planned for the 1995 national elections. In connection with this, citizens are supposed to be able to distinguish between three legislative bodies: the Chamber, the Senate and Council; between federal and regional policies and programmes; and between politicians functioning at different levels, in order to make adequate and conscious use of their democratic right to vote.

Knowledge of the federal structures (KNOW) consists of three sets of knowledge questions:

1   Nine 'true/false/do not know' questions about the basic principles of the federal structure (*structu*), including questions about the number of regions,

Table 11.1 Measurement model for the variables measured by multiple indicators (standardised factor loadings)

Observed indicators	Latent variables (completely standardized coefficients)					R^2
	KNOW	INTEREST	INFORM	AUTONOMY	DISTRUST	
authority	0.691	0	0	0	0	0.478
policy	0.622	0	0	0	0	0.386
structu	0.766	0	0	0	0	0.587
inter_2	0	0.649	0	0	0	0.421
inter_4	0	0.557	0	0	0	0.330
inter_5	0	0.513	0	0	0	0.263
news_1	0	0	0.903	0	0	0.816
news_2	0	0	0.921	0	0	0.848
autono_2	0	0	0	0.842	0	0.710
autono_3	0	0	0	0.862	0	0.743
ineff_2	0	0	0	0	0.704	0.496
ineff_3	0	0	0	0	0.733	0.537
ineff_5	0	0	0	0	0.542	0.294

inter-factor corre-lations	KNOW	INTEREST	INFORM	AUTONOMY	DISTRUST	corr. error inter_5
KNOW	1					inter_4	0.215
INTEREST	0.661	1					
INFORM	0.607	0.703	1			news_2	−0.134
AUTONOMY	0.280	0	0	1			
DISTRUST	−0.251	−0.235	−0.233	0	1		

Notes
Chi-square = 94.005; Df = 56; p = 0.001; RMSEA = 0.031; Adjusted GFI = 0.967 N = 710.

the authority of the federal and regional prime ministers, the composition of the Flemish council, the authority of the Flemish council, and the structure of the Flemish public administration.

2　A set of nine 'true/false/do not know'questions about typical Flemish policies (*policy*) on the domains of information, scientific research, education, environment protection, ethics, and state budgets.

3　A question in which the respondents must classify sixteen policy domains in the correct category of responsible authorities (*authority*) (Flemish authority, Federal authority, mixed, none, do not know).

For each set, the true answers were counted resulting in a score from zero to a maximum. The mean scores are 2.7 (*SD* = 2.17) for the 9 structure questions, 5.2 (*SD* = 2.1) for the 9 policy questions, and 8.1 (*SD* = 3.7) for the 16 authority questions. This was a hard part of the questionnaire, similar to an examination, however without any penalty. The most difficult set of items (*structu*) has the highest loading on the latent variable KNOW (see Table 11.1).

We tried to define a variable that measured *political interest* (van Deth 1990). Several objective questions were used concerning the frequency of reading domestic and international news about political, social, and economical affairs in daily newspapers (*news_1* and *news_2*), the frequency of listening to or watching political programs (*inter_4*), the frequency of taking political information at the occasion of the elections (*inter_5*), and the frequency of discussion about politics with family members, friends, or colleagues (*inter_2*). These five indicators were not explained by one underlying latent factor. The underlying structure consists of two different concepts which are strongly related ($r = 0.70$). The first concept (INTEREST) measured the interest in discussions and debates about politics (*inter_2, inter_4* and *inter_5*). These three indicators represent what has been labelled the 'positive saliency' of politics (Nie and Andersen 1974: 572). According to van Deth (1990: 285–6), the inclusion of these decreases the ambiguity in the empirical meaning of the concept 'interest in politics'. The second concept (INFORM) deals with the openness to information or media use in the broader field of political, social and economic affairs (*news_1* and *news_2*).

Another theoretical concept in which we are interested is the citizens' *trust in politics*. The selected items were part of a balanced scale that was intended to measure political efficacy. The negatively worded items with high loadings on one factor measured an underlying concept dealing with distrust in politics (DISTRUST). The three indicators express doubt about the promises of politicians (*ineff_2*), the disinterest of politicians in the opinions of ordinary people (*ineff_3*), and the unwillingness of politicians to listen to ordinary people (*ineff_5*).

Since our knowledge variable deals with aspects of federalism, the attitude of the respondents towards more autonomy for the Flemish 'state' is also included in this study. It is indeed reasonable to assume that the knowledge of the new structures of the state is not only affected by political interest but also by this particular ideological dimension of the respondents. The two indicators that measured this ideology (AUTONOMY) deal with the choice for complete federalization of two policy domains: the social security system (*autono_2*) and income taxes (*autono_3*).

The measurement part of the global model is reported in Table 11.1. According to several fit indices (Bollen and Long 1992), the fit of the measurement part of the model is reasonably good (bottom of Table 11.1). This model is proposed for theoretical reasons since each concept is only measured by the indicators that were selected, and there are no cross loadings. Only freeing some of the zero-loadings on DISTRUST leads to an improvement of the fit, but this is not advisable because it contaminates theoretically distinguished concepts. The high correlation of 0.70 between the two aspects of interest in politics (INTEREST and INFORM) may suggest reducing the model to only four latent variables, collapsing the two aspects into one single concept. However this leads to a considerable deterioration of the fit. Therefore we kept these two concepts as different aspects of political interest, one concerned with positive saliency of politics (INTEREST), the other dealing with a rather passive interest in actual affairs (INFORM). The high correlations between the objective knowledge variable (KNOW) and these two interest variables indicate expected substantive relationships between these variables. The validity of the measurements, evaluated by the factor loadings and the R^2s vary from acceptable to fairly good.

Each of the social-background variables, is measured by one observed indicator. The level of education is a four-level ordinal variable (EDUCAT) ranging from lower to higher education. The age of the respondents (AGE) is measured by the difference between time of the survey (1995) and the year of birth and ranges from 18 to 74. GENDER is a dichotomous variable with values 0 (man) and 1 (woman).

Four dichotomous variables for active membership in voluntary associations are constructed. They are the result of an exploratory factor analysis of the responses to yes/no questions about active membership of ten different associations. The *first* type of association (SOC_ORG) deals with organizations that operate in the social-cultural domain and in social organizations (trade unions, professional organizations) that are part of the so-called 'pillars'. These associations are not political, but they are indirectly related to the traditional political pillars (Christian democrats, socialists, liberals) by interlocking directorates (Billiet 1984; 1996a). A substantial part of the activities of these associations is devoted to the political education of the active members.

The *second* type (POL_ORG) grouped the memberships in organizations that are directly involved in political activity (milieu protection, the fight against poverty, the struggle for peace). Effects on the political variables are obvious for these organizations, however the knowledge transmitted in them has little affinity with knowledge of the federal system. So, effect on that kind of political knowledge is not so evident The *third* type consist of associations (CULT_REG) in the domain of culture (arts, music, theatre, etc.) or in the field of philosophy and religion. Impact of activities in these kinds of association is an open question. The *fourth* type deals with active membership in youth movements, sport clubs, and recreation clubs (SPORT_ORG), however we do not expect a relationship with the political variables. We are mainly interested in the main effects of the social, and the cultural-religious associations on the political variables.

ANALYSIS

The substantive model we will test is an adaptation of Wittebrood's (1992) model to our data. The crucial differences are the following: we have no such variable as 'perception of interests'; there are two variables for interest in politics; political attitudes towards more autonomy for Flanders is specific for the Flemish context and corresponds with the political values in the theoretical model of Wittebrood; and most important, our focus is on the active-membership variables which was not the case in Wittebrood's study. The theoretical expectations about the relationships that are discussed in the preceding section, are shown in Figure 11.1. For simplicity, the different kinds of variables are grouped.

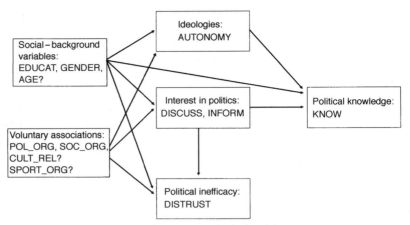

Figure 11.1 Schematic overview of the expected relationships.

In principle, a structural equation approach is the preferred strategy to test a model with observed and latent variables that are placed in causal order. In this approach a measurement model and a substantial model are evaluated at once (Bollen 1989). We used this approach, but not without reservations. The estimations of the standard errors are biased when the standard procedure is used (Pearson correlations or covariances, and maximum likelihood estimation), because the data do not meet the requirements for multivariate normality, and most of the variables are ordinal (education, and the attitudes). The consequences of these violations of the assumptions have been the subject of a large amount of research and many solutions have been proposed (see Babakus *et al.* 1987; Coenders 1996). Some scholars argue that the estimations are relatively robust when the normality requirements are not met and they claim that it does not matter too much what approach is used (Homer and O'Brien 1988), others propose transformations of the data and distribution-free estimation procedures (Jöreskog 1990). In a recent simulation study, Coenders found that none of the alternative strategies for testing performs uniformly better than the standard procedure (Coenders 1996: 133). We tried polychoric/polyserial correlations and the weighted least square (WLS) procedure as proposed by Jöreskog but this leads to theoretical unexpected results, possibly because of the small sample size ($N = 710$). The analysis of the covariance matrix using maximum likelihood (ML) estimation procedure leads to a theoretical meaningful model with an acceptable fit.[6] This too is a criterion to be taken into consideration (Bollen and Long 1992). The results of the ML estimations by means of LISREL8 are reported here.

Our main concern is that the conclusions about the impact of the membership variables are sound and stable. In the selected model, some of the direct and indirect effects are borderline significant (z-scores around 2). We cannot exclude the possibility that in the population some of the retained effects do not differ from zero, but that they appear significant because of underestimated standard errors. To be less uncertain, each of the effects of the membership variables on the political variables is tested with a supplementary logistic-regression procedure in which all the other variables (EDUCAT, AGE, GENDER, and AUTONOMY) are included. In this analysis, an additive scale for each political variable (DISTRUST, INTEREST, INFORM, KNOW) is constructed and subsequently categorised into three categories (two extremes and a neutral position). In logistic regression, the measurement levels and the distribution assumptions are adequate, and the standard errors may be more trusted (Agresti 1990: 303–13). The results section contains a brief overview of the relevant logistic-regression parameters (odds ratios) and a comparison of the two methods.

We start with an overview of the substantive part of the LISREL model (see Table 11.2). The fit of the global model, which includes the measurement part and substantive parts together, is acceptable.[7] The amount of explained variance (77 per cent) in the dependent variable political knowledge (KNOW) is remarkable, taking into account that this objective variable resulting from true/false answers, is not as subject to measurement error as attitudinal variables. Media use in the domain of social and political information (INFORM) is also explained very well (60 per cent), however, this is not so impressive because it is partly the result of our decision to distinguish between two closely related aspects of interest in politics. This decision was supported by the fit criteria of the measurement model.

The specification of a causal effect of one aspect (INTEREST) on the other (INFORM) suggests that the citizens are using the media for social and political information because of a positive saliency towards politics, that is they like to discuss and debate politics. In other words, in our model, interest in politics is an important motive for informative media use. Other solutions like a non-recursive relation between both aspects, or a causal effect in the opposite direction, lead to a serious deterioration of the fit. This finding is in line with Wittebrood's model (1992: 153).

As was expected, education has the strongest total effect on political knowledge (0.589). The direct effect of interest in politics (INTEREST) comes in second place with a large direct effect (0.573). This variable has a very strong effect (0.731) on the variable measuring media use for informative reasons (INFORM), and a moderate negative effect on distrust in politics (DISTRUST). Citizens who are interested in politics are less likely to distrust the politicians. Apart from a positive saliency of politics (INTEREST), a more general use of the media has no additional effect on the kind of political knowledge measured here. This is surprising since it means that, for example, well-educated and interested citizens' knowledge about the federal system does not depend on information in the daily newspapers. However, it is possible that other sources of information (weekly magazines, books, etc.) that are not included in the model have a direct impact on political knowledge.

The expected positive attitude towards more autonomy for the Flemish state has an independent moderate effect on knowledge about the federal system and structure (0.219). Gender has a negative direct effect on positive saliency of politics

Table 11.2 Substantive part of the model: standardized parameters (critical ratios[a] in brackets)

Explanatory factors	Explained variables (path coefficients)							
	AUTONOMY	INTEREST	INFORM direct	INFORM total	DISTRUST direct	DISTRUST total	KNOW direct	KNOW total
INTEREST			0.731 (11.579)	0.731	−0.228 (−3.710)	−0.228	0.573 (10.345)	0.573
AUTONOMY							0.219 (5.984)	0.219
INFORM							—	—
DISTRUST							—	—
EDUCAT	0.112 (2.741)	0.253 (4.746)	0.123 (3.229)	0.308 (7.722)	−0.228 (−4.053)	−0.286 (−4.975)	0.419 (10.749)	0.419 (13.458)
GENDER		−0.178 (−3.697)	−0.098 (−2.596)	−0.228 (−6.230)		0.40 (2.688)	−0.228 (−6.291)	−0.330 (−9.037)
AGE		0.252 (5.385)		0.184 (5.468)	0.210 (3.767)	0.152 (2.941)		0.144 (4.470)
POL_ORG		0.188 (2.331)		0.137 (4.500)		−0.043 (−2.651)		0.107 (3.605)

	EDUCAT	GENDER	AGE	POL_ORG	SOC_ORG	CULT_REL
SOC_ORG	0.120 (2.920)	0.094 (2.080)		0.069 (2.337)	−0.021 (−2.003)	0.080 (3.015)
CULT_REL		0.114 (2.536)	−0.096 (−2.278)	−0.12 (−0.337)	−0.026 (−2.728)	0.065 (3.278)
R^2 (%)	0.027	0.195		0.598	0.191	0.771

Correlations between the exogene variables

	EDUCAT	GENDER	AGE	POL_ORG	SOC_ORG	CULT_REL
EDUCAT	1					
GENDER	0	1				
AGE	−0.403 (−10.039)	0	1			
POL_ORG	0.137	0	0	1		
SOC_ORG		0	0	0	1	
CULT_REL	0.129 (3.413)	0	0.094 (2.517)	0.112 (2.976)	0	1

Note
a Parameter divided by its standard error.

(−0.178) and media use (−0.098), and a direct negative effect (−0.228) on political knowledge, resulting in a substantive negative total effect of gender (−0.330).

More important for this study, none of the four membership variables directly influences the kind of political knowledge that was measured here, but there are rather weak indirect effects in the expected direction. It is amazing that active membership in political organizations shows such a small total effect (0.107). The specialized political knowledge about the federal system and logic which falls behind the scope of most political-action groups may be responsible for that. The direct effect of active membership in political organizations on the positive saliency aspect of interest in politics (INTEREST) is not surprising, however it is rather low (0.188).

The weak direct and indirect impacts of active membership in social organizations are in the expected direction. Active membership has a direct effect on the attitude towards autonomy (0.12), moreover, the active members are more inclined to discuss politics and to use political news (0.094). The indirect negative effect on distrust in politics is only of borderline significance and much lower than was expected from the viewpoint of social capital. The effect of active membership in cultural and religious associations on positive saliency of politics (INTEREST) (0.114) was somewhat expected, the negative direct effect (−0.096) on media use was not. Active membership of youth movements, of sport clubs, or recreation clubs, had no effect at all.

Figure 11.2 provides a visual display of the direct effects on the endogenous variables and the correlations between the exogenous variables (see lower part of Table 11.2). How robust are the findings about the relationships between the membership variables and the political variables? Do we overestimate them with the structural equation approach using covariances and ML estimations or do we underestimate them? In order to answer that question, the logistic-regression parameters (odds ratios) of the relationship between each membership variable and each political (categorical) variable are evaluated, controlling for all other factors (education, age, gender, and the other membership variables). Table 11.3 contains the logistic regression parameters (odds ratios) of interest.

For several reasons, it is impossible to compare directly the parameters of the structural-equations analysis with the logistic-regression parameters. First of all, the construction of the dependent variables is different. The continuous scales are replaced by categorical variables. Second, the parameters have a distinct meaning. In the structural-equation model, the standardized parameters express the proportion increase in a dependent variable (in units standard deviation) resulting from a unit (standard deviation) change in an independent variable.

A parameter of the logistic regression model (odds ratio) expresses the factor by which the (geometric) average odds of the dependent variables is increased or decreased as a result of belonging to a category of an independent variable, and not to another category. Finally, the effects in the structural-equation model are decomposed into direct and indirect effects; the logistic-regression model only contains direct effects. For that reason, indirect effects can completely disappear in the logistic regression model.

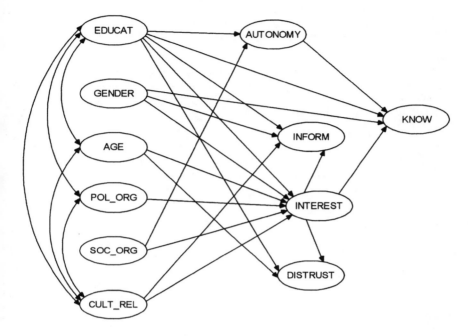

Figure 11.2 Visualization of the structural relationships between the variables.

Given all these differences, how to compare the models? In both cases the parameters express the net effect of one variable on another, controlled for all other factors in the model. It is possible to compare the critical ratios[8] of the parameters (total effects) in the structural-equation model with their counterparts in the logistic-regression model in order to control their stability. Do we find the largest effects between the same couples of variables, and do we find the same zero (non-significant) effects?

All parameters in the logistic-regression model are in the same direction (positive or > 1; negative or < 1), but not all are stable. We arrive at the same conclusions as in the structural-equation model with respect to the effects of active membership in political associations on interest in politics, media use, and distrust in politics. Most of the effects of active membership in social organizations are also stable. For example, the parameter expressing the relation between active membership in social organizations and interest in politics (2.274) indicates that on the average the odds 'strong/weak' interest is about 2.27 times higher for respondents belonging to the category of the active members than for respondents who are not active members of social organizations.

The relations between active membership in political associations and knowledge, and between active membership of cultural or religious associations with the political variables, disappeared after controlling for education and age. Taking all together, the logistic-regression analysis confirms that active

Table 11.3 Logistic regression parameters (odds ratios)[a] for the membership variables, controlled for the other factors (critical ratios[b] in brackets)

Active member-ship	INTEREST (strong/weak)	INFORM (often/never)	DISTRUST (strong/not)	KNOW (strong/weak)
POL_ORG (yes/no)	2.729 (2.899)	3.378 (3.080)	0.454 (−2.154)	1.073 (ns)
SOC_ORG (yes/no)	2.274 (3.379)	1.798 (2.359)	0.918 (ns)	1.938 (2.509)
CULT_REG (yes/no)	1.126 (ns)	0.990 (ns)	0.721 (ns)	1.714 (1.959)

Notes
a Only parameters for extreme categories of the response variables are reported.
b Parameter divided by its standard error.
ns: not significant (critical ratio < 1.96 or p < 0.05).

memberships in some kinds of associations have substantial effects on several aspects of political participation.

CONCLUSIONS AND DISCUSSION

This study analysed the relationship between active participation in different kinds of voluntary associations and several qualities of citizens that were conducive to their political participation. The qualities we intended to investigate were trust in politics, interest in politics, and political knowledge. However, in the measurement part of the study, we found that the indicators that were selected to measure 'interest' actually measured two different latent variables: positive saliency of politics and reading daily newspapers for information about political, social, and economic affairs. So, we ended with four 'conductors' for political participation.

Differences were found in the relationships between the membership variables and the four qualities. Active membership in sport organizations or youth movements had no impact on the four conductors. The impact of active membership associations in developing cultural or religious activities was ambiguous since it was not stable across the two analytic procedures that were used. The impact of active membership in political organizations was not surprising, but it was weaker than expected. We found an effect of active membership in social organizations on at least three of the conductors, after controlling for the other relevant variables in the model. In the following discussion we will focus on this finding.

Active membership in social organizations has a substantive impact on the 'positive saliency' aspect of interest in politics after controlling for education, gender, age, and the other memberships. This is stable across the two methods. However, about 20 per cent of the variance in interest in politics is explained by our model, and that is not impressive. Therefore, we cannot exclude the possibility that the relationships are spurious. The same argument holds for trust in politics. The explained variance of the other two political variables is much better, however, a large part of it relates to the effect of political interest, thus the question about spuriousness also arises here.

Which crucial explanatory variables for interest in politics that are related with active membership in social organizations, are not included in our model? In another unpublished study (Billiet 1996b), church involvement and professional status was included in an explanatory model for political interest. White-collar workers, leading professionals, regular churchgoers and non-religious humanists were more likely to be interested in politics. In such an extended model, active membership in voluntary associations still had a net impact on interest in politics. It is reasonable to accept this substantive but weak effect of active membership in social organizations on our indices of political participation.

Active membership in social organizations has an indirect effect on the kind of specific knowledge we have studied. The active members of these associations have thus more opportunities for a more strategic and conscious utilization of their votes in a complex situation in which three different lists of candidates are offered to them during the general elections. They are more likely to evaluate former policy decisions correctly, and they know better what kind of policies the political parties propose for the distinctive legislative bodies.

What qualities of active membership in social organizations encourage interest in politics, media use for informative reasons, and specific political knowledge? Many of the suggestions provided by Olsen (1972: 318), and by Moyser and Parry (1996: 8) apply to the social organizations in the Flemish pillarized context. Policy problems are explained in the weekly magazines of these organizations, active members participate in all kind of meetings in which political problems are discussed; they meet and discuss with other interested people more often. In short, apart from the power they have as privileged pressure groups in the pillarized system, these associations provide lots of opportunities for the social and political participation of their members. That is social capital.

This explanation brings us to a methodological critique of the measurements that were used. Active membership was measured by a single question: 'are you an active member of...?'. It would be better to measure more directly the activities we have mentioned if one wants to study the impact of active membership on political participation from the viewpoint of social capital. It may be that the effect we have found is underestimated because of the kind of measurement of active membership that was used. This, however, is a suggestion for further research.

APPENDIX: GLOSSARY OF THE THEORETICAL CONCEPTS AND THEIR INDICATORS

AUTONOMY   *Political ideology: more autonomy for Flanders.*

autono_2:   What is your opinion about the problem of federalization of the social security system, should it become completely Flemish or should it remain completely Belgian? (Card with 7 points: completely Flemish = 7 – completely Belgian = 1).

autono_3:   What is your opinion about the recovery and the management of the income taxes, should it become completely Flemish or should it remain completely Belgian? *Distrust in politics.*

DISTRUST   In the elections, one party promises more than the other,

ineff_2:   but in the end, nothing much happens (completely agree, agree, neither agree nor disagree, disagree, completely disagree).

The politicians are only interested in my vote, not in my opinion.

ineff_3:   The politicians have lost their ability to listen to ordinary people like me.

ineff_5:   *Openness to information or media news in the domain of social, political and economic affairs.*

INFORM   How often do you read the domestic news about political,

news_1:   social and economic affairs in the newspapers? (Nearly always, often, sometimes, seldom, never).

news_2:   How often do you read the international news about political, social and economic affairs in the newspapers? *Interest in politics.*

INTEREST   When you are among friends, does it happen that you

inter_2:   discuss social and political problems? (Nearly always, often, sometimes, seldom, never).

How often do you follow political programmes on television or on radio?

inter_4:   In the periods of elections, how often do you usually

inter_5:   follow the programmes about these elections on television or on radio? *Political knowledge.*

KNOW   Nine true/false statements about the basic logic of the

structu: federal structures in Belgium.

Nine true/false statements about the policy decisions

policy: taken by current Flemish government.

Classification of sixteen policy domains in the correct

authority   authority level (Flemish, Belgian, both, or none).

Social-background variables

AGE	*Age in number of years: 18–74*
EDUCAT	*Level of education.*
	Lower education (1), lower secondary education (2), higher secondary education (3), higher education (4).
GENDER	A dichotomous variable (woman =0; man = 1).
CULT_ORG	Active membership of cultural (arts, music, theatre) and religious or philosophical organizations (no = 0; yes = 1).
POL_ORG	Active membership of organizations that are directly involved in political activities (no = 0; yes = 1).
SOC_ORG	Active membership of social organizations that are linked with the traditional organizational networks ('pillars') related with the Christian Democratic, Socialist and Liberal political 'families' (no = 0; yes = 1).
SPORT_ORG	Active membership of sport organization.

Notes

1 A search in Sociological Abstracts in the period 1976–mid-1996 reveals 158 references to social capital of which 122 (77 per cent) appeared in the 1990s. There are 34 (21 per cent) references to publications that appeared in 1995.

2 In the work of Bourdieu (1979), 'social capital' refers to resources and to the opportunities to use effective power (1979: 128). It is necessary to make the economic and cultural capital work (1979: 389). It refers to social relationships and social networks which are related to the family background and with professions (1979: 133, 138).

3 The outcomes are not always in the expected direction. For example, the volume *The Economic Sociology of Immigration: Essays on Networks, Ethnicity, and Entrepreneurship* (Portes 1995) contained chapters in which rich social networks among immigrants are associated with second generation upward mobility (Portes 1995: 248–80), and in which they retard rather than facilitate mainstream economic success (Kelly and Fernandez 1995: 213–47).

4 The survey, a first stage in a two-wave panel, was promoted and supported by the Flemish government in order to study the impact of its information campaigns to the public. The knowledge of the Flemish citizens about the authorities, institutions, and policy of the Flemish federal state within the context of the Belgian federation, was the main subject of the study.

5 A two-stage sample with equal probabilities was used. In the first stage, the municipalities were selected at random. In the first stage, 77 clusters of sample units were selected at random with a probability proportional to the number of inhabitants in each municipality; 64 Flemish municipalities out of 316 were included in the sample. In the second stage, for each cluster a random sample of respondents was selected from the national population registers. The non-response rate was 38 per cent (refusals and non-contacts included).

6 The analysis of the same model using polychoric correlations and ML estimation provided nearly the same estimates but the fit of the model was much lower, and

the suggested improvements violated the theoretical measurement model too much.

7 Chi-square = 220.287 with 131 degrees of freedom; RMSEA = 0.031; Adjusted GFI = 0.953.

8 Critical ratio = parameter divided by its standard error.

References

Agresti, A. (1990), *Categorical Data Analysis* (New York).

Almond, G. A. and Verba, S. (1963), *The Civic Culture: Political attitudes and Democracy in Five Nations* (Newbury Park).

Babakus, E., Ferguson, C. E. and Jöreskog, K. G. (1987), 'The Sensitivity of Confirmatory Maximum Likelihood Factor Analysis to Violations of Measurement Scale and Distributional Assumptions', *Journal of Marketing Research*, 24: 222–9.

Bellah, R. N., Madsen, R., Sullivan, W. M., Swidler, A. and Tipton, S. (1985), *Habits of the Heart* (New York).

Bennett, S. E. (1986), *Apathy in America, 1960–1984: Causes & Consequences of Citizen Political Indifference* (New York).

Bennett, S. E. and Bennett, L. (1993), 'Out of Sight, Out of Mind: American's Knowledge of Party Control of the House of Representatives, 1960–1984', *Political Research Quarterly*, 46: 97–80.

Berelson, B., Lazarsfeld, P. F., and McPhee, W. N. (1954), *Voting: A Study of Opinion Formation in a Presidential Campaign* (Chicago).

Berry, D. (1970), *The Sociology of Grass Roots* (London).

Billiet, J. (1984), 'On Belgian Pillarization: Changing Perspectives'. In Van Schendelen, M. P. C. M. (Ed.), *Consociationalism, Pillarization and Conflict Management in the Low Countries*. *Acta Politica*, 19: 117–28.

Billiet, J. (1996a), *The Complex Relationship Between Political Parties and Social Organizations in Flanders (Belgium): Continuity and Change*. Paper prepared for delivery at The Joint Sessions of Workshops, European Consortium for Political Research, Oslo, 29 March–3 April, 17 pp.

Billiet, J. (1996b), *Sociaal kapitaal, kerkelijke betrokkenheid en maatschappelijke integratie in België*. Research Bulletin (ISPO/Department of Sociology, Leuven).

Boisjoly, J., Duncan, G. J. and Hofferth, S. (1995), 'Access to Social Capital', *Journal of Family Issues*, 16: 609–31.

Bollen, K. A. (1989), *Structural Equations with Latent Variables* (New York).

Bollen, K. A. and Long, J. S. (1992), 'Tests for Structural Equation Models'. *Sociological Methods and Research*, 21: 123–31.

Bourdieu, P. (1979), *La distinction. Critique sociale du jugement* (Paris).

Brehm, J. and Rahn, W. (1996), *Individual Level Evidence for the Causes and Consequences of Social Capital*, unpublished paper (Duke University, Durham).

Cambré, B., Billiet, J. and Swyngedouw, M. (1995), *De kennis van de Vlamingen en hun houding tegenover informatiecampagnes van de Vlaamse Overheid* (ISPO, Leuven).

Carton, A., Swyngedouw, M., Billiet, J. and Beerten, R. (1993), *Source book of the Voters' Study in Connection with the 1991 General Election* (ISPO, Leuven).

Coenders, G. (1996), *Structural Equation Modelling of Ordinally Measured Survey Data*. PhD dissertation (Esade, Universitat Ramon Llull, Barcelona).

Coleman, J. S. (1988), 'Social Capital in the Creation of Human Capital', *American Journal of Sociology*, 94: S95–S210.

Coleman, J. S. (1990), *The Foundations of Social Theory.* (Cambridge, MA).

Coleman, J. S. (1995), 'Families and Schools', *Zeitschrift für Sozialisationsforschung und Erziehungssoziologie*, 14: 326–74.

Condra, M. D. (1992), 'The Link between Need for Cognition and Political Interest, Involvement, and Media Usage', *Psychology*, 29: 13–18.

Dixon, J. and Seron, C. (1995), 'Stratification in the Legal Profession: Sex, Sector, and Salary', *Law and Society Review*, 29: 381–412.

Etzioni, A. (1993), *The Spirit of Community* (New York).

Fukuyama, F. (1995), *Trust: The Social Virtues and the Creation of Prosperity* (New York).

Gundelach, P. and Torpe, L. (1996), Voluntary Associations: New Types of Involvement and Democracy. Paper prepared for delivery at The Joint Sessions of Workshops, European Consortium for Political Research, Oslo, 29 March 29–3 April, 23 pp.

Hagan, J., Merkens, H. and Boehnke, K. (1995), 'Delinquency and Disdain: Social Capital and the Control of Right-Wing Extremism among East and West Berlin Youth', *American Journal of Sociology*, 100: 1028–52.

Homer, P. and O'Brien, R. M. (1998), 'Using LISREL Models with Crude Rank Category Measures', *Quality and Quantity*, 22: 191–201.

Jöreskog, K. (1990), 'New Developments in LISREL. Analysis of Ordinal Variables using Polychoric Correlations and Weighted Least Squares', *Quality and Quantity*, 24: 387–404.

Jöreskog, K. G. and Sörbom, D. (1993), *New Features in LISREL 8* (Scientific Software International).

Kelly, M. and Fernandez, P. (1995), 'Social and Cultural Capital in the Urban Ghetto: Implications for the Economic Sociology of Immigration'. In Portes, A., (Ed.), *The Economic Sociology of Immigration: Essays on Networks, Ethnicity, and Entrepreneurship* (New York), 213–47.

Kennamer, J. D. (1988), 'Political Discussion and Cognition in Richmond: A 1988 Look', *Journalism Quarterly*, 67: 348–52.

Luskin, R. C. (1987), 'Measuring Political Sophistication', *American Journal of Political Science*, 4: 356–99.

MacMillan, R. (1995), 'Changes in the Structure of Life Courses and the Decline of Social Capital in Canadian Society: A Time Series Analysis of Property Crime Rates', *Canadian Journal of Sociology*, 20: 51–79.

Maddens, B. and Dewachter, W. (1993), 'Politieke kennis'. In Swyngedouw, M., Billiet, J., Carton, A., and Beerten, R., (Eds.), *Kiezen is verliezen. Onderzoek naar de politieke opvattingen van de Vlamingen*, (Leuven), 131–46.

Moyser, G. and Parry, G. (1996), *Voluntary Associations and Democratic Participation in Britain.* Paper prepared for delivery at The Joint Sessions of Workshops, European Consortium for Political Research, Oslo, 29 March–3 April, 27 pp.

Nie, N. H. and Andersen, K. (1974), 'Mass Belief Systems Revisited: Political and Attitude Structure', *Journal of Politics*, 36: 540–91.

Olsen, M. E. (1972), 'Social Participation and Voting Turnout: a Multivariate Analysis', *American Sociological Review*, 37: 317–33.

Parry, G., Moyser, G. and Day, N. (1992), *Political Participation and Democracy in Britain* (Cambridge).

Portes, A. (1995), 'Childen of Immigrants: Segmented Assimilation and its Determinants'. In Portes, A. (Ed.), *The Economic Sociology of Immigration: Essays on Networks, Ethnicity, and Entrepreneurship*, (New York) 248–80.

Portes, A. (Ed.) (1995), *The Economic Sociology of Immigration: Essays on Networks, Ethnicity, and Entrepreneurship* (New York).

Putnam, R. (1993), *Making Democracy Work: Civil Traditions in Modern Italy* (Princeton).

Putnam, R. (1995), 'Bowling Alone: America's Declining Social Capital', *Journal of Democracy*, 6: 65–78

Rokkam, S. and Torsvik, P. (1959), 'The Voter, the Reader and the Party Press', *Fourth World Congress of Sociology*, Stresa.

Smith, M. H., Beaulieu, L. J. and Seraphine, A. (1995), 'Social Capital, Place of Residence, and College Attendance', *Rural Sociology*, 60 (3): 368–80.

Stouthuysen, P. (Ed.), (1992), *Alexis de Tocqueville: over de democratie in America, tweede boek*, (Leuven).

van Deth, J. (1990), 'Interest in Politics'. In Jennings *et al.* (Eds.), *Continuities in Political Action. A Longitudinal Study of Political Orientations in Three Western Democracies*, (New York) 275–312.

van Deth, J. (1992), 'De politieke betekenis van maatschappelijke participatie', *Acta Politica*, 27 (4): 425–44.

van Deth, J. (1997), 'Introduction: Social Involvement and Democratic Politics'. In van Deth, J., (Ed.), *Private Groups and Public Life*, (London).

Verba, S. and Nie, N. (1972), *Participation in America: Political Democracy and Social Equality*, (New York).

Verba, S., Schlozman, K. L. and Brady, H. E. (1997), *Voice and Equality: Civic Voluntarism in American Politics* (Cambridge, MA).

Wilson, J. Q. (1993), *The Moral Sense* (New York).

Wittebrood, K. (1992), 'Het politieke-kennisniveau van de Nederlandse burger', *Acta Politica*, 27: 135–59.

Index